Integrating Information & Communications Technologies into the Classroom

Lawrence Tomei
Robert Morris University, USA

Information Science Publishing

Hershey • London • Melbourne • Singapore

Acquisitions Editor:	Kristin Klinger
Development Editor:	Kristin Roth
Senior Managing Editor:	Jennifer Neidig
Managing Editor:	Sara Reed
Assistant Managing Editor:	Sharon Berger
Copy Editor:	Julie LaBlanc
Typesetter:	Sara Reed
Cover Design:	Lisa Tosheff
Printed at:	Yurchak Printing Inc.

Published in the United States of America by
Information Science Publishing (an imprint of Idea Group Inc.)
701 E. Chocolate Avenue
Hershey PA 17033
Tel: 717-533-8845
Fax: 717-533-8661
E-mail: cust@idea-group.com
Web site: http://www.idea-group.com

and in the United Kingdom by
Information Science Publishing (an imprint of Idea Group Inc.)
3 Henrietta Street
Covent Garden
London WC2E 8LU
Tel: 44 20 7240 0856
Fax: 44 20 7379 3313
Web site: http://www.eurospan.co.uk

Library of Congress Cataloging-in-Publication Data

Integrating information and communications technologies in the classroom / Lawrence Tomei, editor.
    p. cm.
 Summary: "This book promotes state-of-the-art application of classroom technology for teaching and learning. Teachers, educational researchers, and scholars are offered some twenty chapters filled with practical applications research, practice, and thought-provoking stances on many of the key issues associated with teaching and learning in today's classroom environment"--Provided by publisher.
 Includes bibliographical references and index.
 ISBN 1-59904-258-4 -- ISBN 1-59904-259-2 (softcover) -- ISBN 1-59904-260-6 (ebook)
 1. Educational technology. 2. Information technology. I. Tomei, Lawrence A.
 LB1028.3.I56538 2007
 371.33--dc22
                          2006027720
British Cataloguing in Publication Data
A Cataloguing in Publication record for this book is available from the British Library.

Integrating Information & Communications Technologies into the Classroom

Table of Contents

Preface

Integrating Information & Communications Technologies into the Classroom addresses the multiple perspectives of teaching and learning with technology and promoting research efforts, positions and practices advancing the state-of-the-art application of technology in formal education, corporate training, higher education, professional development and proprietary education. Further, this text focuses on contributions from all disciplines of information, educational and instructional technology.

Volume I offers educational researchers, scholars and practitioners with the most current investigations and best practices surrounding the uses of technology in the classroom. The text is divided into four sections. Section I includes eight chapters that examine business, computer science and information technology (IT) education and topics such as school improvement and reform, standards-based technology education programs, data-driven decision making and strategic technology education planning.

Chapter I, *Using Blended Learning to Develop Tertiary Students' Skills of Critique*, by Paul Lajbcyier and Christine Spratt, explores pedagogical strategies that engage students in ways that will assure development of their skills of critique and analysis. This chapter draws on data from a recent case-based evaluation study to argue that innovative assessment and the development of social presence in online learning environments contribute to developing skills in students. The chapter poses implications for further research in pedagogical practices; in particular, it presents a discussion of the potential of "blended learning" and "variation theory" for leading such research.

Chapter II presents Sherry Chen's research on the *Effects of Human Factors on the Use of Web-Based Instruction*. Chen examines the human factors that influence learner performance and perception in a Web-based instructional environment. Her study presents issues associated with instructional programs applied to instruction that teaches students how to use HTML. The master's degree students who participated produced a number of interesting findings. For example, student task achievements were affected by their levels of previous system experience, while post-test and gain scores were positively influenced by their perceptions and attitudes toward Web-based instruction. The implications of these and other findings will be of interest to both educators and scholars alike.

Chapter III, *Who's Talking Online II: Revisiting Gender and Online Communication*, by Taralynn Hartsell, investigates the association between gender and online communication. The study of two online graduate courses involved a descriptive model of "student involvement," recording the quantity and quality of student activity in targeted discussion threads. Readers will appreciate how quantity was recorded and quality examined. A difference was reported between the genders in both quantity and quality. Read the chapter to find out which gender excelled in online student participation.

Chapter IV presents a blended approach for delivering an online international master's program and comparing its results to the more traditional classroom format. In *Using a Blended Model to Improve Delivery of Teacher Education Curriculum in Global Settings*, Vivian Wright, Ronnie Stanford and Jon Beedle discuss the challenges, lessons learned and student reflections on the blended approach. A few of their more important contributions include a description of potential problems that must be addressed before online classes begin, including student enrollment and a single university-wide login username and password. Student-provided advantages to this approach are discussed, as students identify personal gains in subject matter content with simultaneous improvements in the additional skills and knowledge required to effectively use Web-based materials and interact with peers and instructors.

Chapter V by Andrew Targowski offers a historical perspective of the *Genesis, Political and Economic Sides of the Internet*. His chapter probes into the importance of the Cold War to the ultimate development and expansion of the Internet. As uncovered in this chapter, the research on the universality of information and communications technology was conducted on both sides of the Iron Curtain, divulging the similarities in thinking that occurred on both sides of the Cold War. The political significance of the Internet results not only from its roots in military command and control but also from its influence on the development of democracy and the ultimate eradication of dictatorships. The history of the Internet is also an example of the development of great engineering talents and research, and development centers and their impact on the emergence of a global civilization. This chapter is mandatory reading for all information technologists and educators.

Chapter VI, *Writing Across the IT/MIS Curriculum*, by Stephanie Etter and Jeff Merhout, substantiates the claim from popular literature that college graduates are entering the workforce without sufficient writing skills, and then moves the reader beyond the platitudes and offers an examination of writing across the curriculum based on the integration of writing into the MIS/IT curriculum. While traditional IT/MIS programs rely heavily on technology-based courses, the authors argue that these technology courses must also promote effective writing habits. It would be hard to reject the growing importance of preparing IT/MIS students to use their writing skills in their chosen career fields. This chapter illustrates how writing assignments can be used effectively in MIS/IT courses.

Chapter VII, *Learning IT: Where do Lectures Fit?*, revisits the established thinking on the effectiveness of the traditional method of classroom-based content delivery in undergraduate programs. Tanya McGill and Samantha Bax, both from Murdoch University in Australia, explore the factors that influence lecture attendance and student perceptions of the lecture format, while suggesting that students are recognizing the importance of active learning within the constraints of traditional learning settings. Their results suggest that students continue to acknowledge the contributions of the lecture format to their learning experience when coupled with the lecturer's expertise and experience in the content area.

Chapter VIII, *Training Sequences and Their Effects on Task Performance and User Outcomes*, by Anol Bhattacherjee and Clive Sanford, introduces the concept of IT training sequences and examines how sequencing impacts IT task performance, user satisfaction and users' self-efficacy. The authors present four hypotheses contrasting conceptual-procedural and procedural-conceptual training sequences in relation to performance of near-transfer and far-transfer IT tasks, satisfaction and self-efficacy. Read how these hypotheses were tested in a database design context using a quasi-experimental study involving student subjects and review the empirical results and implications for IT training.

Section II focuses on distance learning technology education and the impact of technology on adult learners. Four chapters provide the reader with unique perspectives on online group processes, models for online discussion, the cultural aspects of learning at a distance and collaborative learning in a virtual environment.

Chapter IV, *Group Process and Trust in Group Discussion*, kicks off our examination of distance learning technology education with a look at how successful group discussion is effected in online learning. Lorna Uden and Linda Wojnar share the results of their investigation into the benefits of group discussion for online learning. For group discussion to be effective in an online environment, the authors found it important to consider group process and the role of trust within groups. Matched with their considerable experience as online educators, the chapter combines experience and research to suggest practical implications to consider immediately as well as prudent recommendations for further study.

Chapter X introduces a new model for online discussion by Byron Havard, Jianxia Du and Anthony Olinzock. *Task-Oriented Online Discussion: A Practical Model for Student Learning* is based on three generally recognized learning processes: information, methods and cognition. Three modes of online discussion are prescribed: flexible peer, structured topic and collaborative task discussion, and are paired with tasks that encourage adoptive learning, adaptive learning and deep learning. The associated research examines two semesters of an online graduate-level course that investigated the robustness of the model and the strategies for dynamic task-oriented discussion in an online learning environment.

Chapter XI, *Addressing the Cultural Dimensions of E-Learning – Where to Begin?*, is a thoughtful exposition from Andrea Edmundson on the likely effects of culture on e-learning and e-learning on the lessening of cultural bias. The exploratory study included participants from two diverse cultures, the United States and India, who achieved equitable learning outcomes that the authors suggest results from the mitigation of cultural effects by the e-learning format. Also, cultural dimensions appeared to affect learners' preferences for and perceptions of e-learning while both were willing to try new approaches to learning. Particularly valuable to our readers is the amplification of the results to the cultural adaptation process (CAP) model, now presented as a general guideline for adapting e-learning courses for other cultures.

Chapter XII, *Project-Based Online Group Collaborative Learning Characteristics*, joins the efforts of four institutions; three in the United States and one in the Republic of China. Byron Havard, Jianxia Du, James Adams and Gang Ding present a framework for online group collaborative learning based on Jean Piaget's concepts of assimilation and accommodation and Lev Vygotsky's theory of social interaction. For the cognitive reader, the chapter is replete with ideas of how an online project-based learning approach affects students' cognitive skills development. It explores factors and identifies unique characteristics that lead to successful collaborative classroom projects, including: leadership style and individual role, goal setting and project management, accountability and commitment, peer supportive relationships, individual accomplishment and group accomplishments, and mixed gender and race group preference.

Section III considers communications technologies employed in the classroom and the effects of technology in society, equity issues, technology education and copyright laws, censorship, acceptable use and fair use laws, community education and public outreach using technology.

Chapter XIII, by Tanya McGill and Michael Dixon from Murdoch University in Australia, shares the latest investigation on *Information Technology Certification: A Student Perspective*. The chapter investigates student perceptions of both the benefits and risks of certification, its importance in obtaining employment, the impact on any associated financial benefits and the relationship of certification to 'real-world' experiences. Certification, it was found, has become a popular adjunct to traditional means of acquiring IT skills and employers increasingly specify a preference for those holding certifications.

Chapter XIV is an eloquent investigation into the *Management of Telecommunications Services: A Vital New Content Area and a Course Model for the College of Business,* by Faye Teer and Harold Teer and Young Choi from James Madison University. Their chapter argues for the importance of telecommunications services management as its own university discipline and describes a possible model for one particular undergraduate course, Management of Telecommunications Services. The chapter targets both university faculty and administration and corporate representatives for their inputs of potential course goals and objectives. If you have ever considered introducing a similar program of study, this chapter will provide a primer on the fundamentals of managing telecommunications services.

Section IV of this text concerns itself with the general topic of teaching and learning with technology. The constituent chapters examine the more specific applications of pedagogy and androgogy with respect to technology as a teaching strategy and learning style, and how technology can be made to work effectively to the benefit of students in the classroom.

Chapter XI, *Mind the Gap! New 'Literacies' Create New Divides*, by Madden, Baptista Nunes, McPherson, Ford and Miller, scrutinizes the rapid spread of ICT and its move from peripheral to integral status in the classroom. This chapter draws on the findings of a number of research projects to explore some of the 'generation gaps' that arise from differing perceptions of learning technologies. It presents an excellent primer for advanced courses in instructional technology along with distinctive insights into how technologies expand generation gaps that existed between and within students, teachers and parents; gaps that this research finds are exacerbated by as little as five years between groups. Results from a related project exploring Networked Information and Communication Literacy Skills (NICLS) are used to introduce a discussion on the nature of required technology skills and how they can be addressed in light of these recognized generation gaps.

Chapter XVI, authored by Nurul I. Sarkar, presents *An Interactive Tool for Teaching and Learning LAN Design*. This chapter is not for the faint of heart, as the author discusses his own creation – a software tool called LAN-Designer that provides an interactive learning experience to teach the technical side of designing local area networks. This chapter is a combination technical guide, textbook and instruction manual, and is required reading for anyone teaching about networking. The chapter describes the software application and measures its effectiveness as a teaching/learning tool. The author shares his investigation of the effectiveness of the package and presents an evaluation by both students and faculty colleagues on student learning and comprehension.

LeAnne Robinson provides Chapter XVII, *Diffusion of Educational Technology and Education Reform: Examining Perceptual Barriers to Technology Integration*. Her study examines educators' perceived barriers to technology integration and their relationship to education reform. Educators and administrators from four elementary schools in Washington State were interviewed during a 3-month period. The schools differed in size, location and social economic status, and reported variances in their state-wide assessment scores. All schools reported similar barriers to using educational technology, while differences were noted among schools who conducted long-range planning for technology and those that had not. Staff, curricula, performance standards and assessment tools where examined.

Chapter XVIII offers several *Perspectives on Twenty-First Century e-Learning in Higher Education*. Lalita Rajasingham explores a new higher education paradigm that considers events surrounding the advance of globalization and the rapid development of the Internet and its impact on the value of knowledge. The chapter makes an excellent primer for courses introducing structures, strategies, procedures and programs that deal with the processes of technology in general and globalization in particular. The international research presented in this chapter investigates a paradigm for re-constructing higher education in light of technological advances and as a potential platform to reframe future developments.

Chapter XIX examines the motivations of K-12 educators who participated in online professional development modules. *Guiding Our Way: Needs and Motivations of Teachers in Online Learning Modeling Responsive Course Design*, by King, Melia and Dunham, isolated four common themes pertaining to online teacher professional development. The themes reviewed include learner expectations, learner support and access, incentives and content. The study employed surveys and focus groups to identify critical factors in instructional design and implementation, and its large sample size (944 participants) makes the conclusions and recommendations appropriate for generalization across the gamut of teacher professional development. They will be of particular interest to readers with such responsibilities.

Chapter XX, the final offering in this first volume on Integrating ICT into the Classroom, is provided by Leping Liu. *Quality of Online Learning Applications: Impact on Student Enjoyment, Motivation, and Anxiety* explores the influence of quality-designed online learning applications on student enjoyment, motivation and anxiety level. As with the previous chapter, a considerable participant base (900 online K-12 applications) was evaluated to lay a foundation for generalizing the results across a wide population. Four design factors were examined: quality of information, design of information, quality of technology use and design of technology use, in relation to the three learning-related variables. Three prediction models were tested in this study that found an intermediate effect between the design of online application and resultant student learning. If you are a schoolteacher, designer or professional who uses online applications for education purposes, this is a must-read chapter.

This book provides a wealth of research, practice and thought-provoking stances on many key issues associated with teaching and learning in today's classroom environment. Teachers, educational researchers and scholars are well-advised to consider the practical applications of the many findings and recommendations contained in this text. These 20 chapters cover a wide range of instructional technology topics in specific educational areas of business, computer science and information systems; distance learning; and communications education, as well as the more general area of teaching and learning with technology.

Provocative topics are presented for review. They include topics such as the effects of human factors on Web-based instruction; the impact of gender, politics, culture and economics on instructional technology; the effects of technology on socialization and group processes; and the barriers, challenges and successes of technology integration in the classroom. The contributors to this first volume are justifiably proud of the scholarship that went into this text. They would be most pleased to know that the text has become a valuable tool in classrooms, training rooms and workshops.

Section I

Business, Computer Science, and Information Technology Education

Chapter I

Using "Blended Learning" to Develop Tertiary Students' Skills of Critique

Paul Lajbcyier, Monash University, Australia

Christine Spratt, Monash University, Australia

Abstract

Devising pedagogical strategies that will engage students in ways that will assure the development of their skills of critique and analysis presents a challenge to tertiary teachers. This chapter draws on data from a recent case-based evaluation study to argue that innovative assessment and the development of social presence in online learning environments can contribute to developing skills of critique and analysis in tertiary students. The chapter is underpinned by the belief that creative thinking about curriculum issues must continue to lead debates about tertiary pedagogy, the use of educational technologies and online learning. It concludes by posing implications for further research in pedagogical practices in tertiary settings; in particular, it presents a discussion of the potential of "blended learning" and "variation theory" for leading such research.

Introduction

Pedagogical approaches embedded in constructivism mean that tertiary teachers ought to offer students opportunities to be active learners. Such approaches should see students engaged in learning tasks that are relevant and directed towards mutually conceived learning outcomes and that such engagements ought to be reflect communities of learning (Marton & Trigwell, 2000). We believe this is imperative in undergraduate and postgraduate classrooms, particularly where such classrooms are becoming more diverse. Here we acknowledge the growth in full-fee paying international students; the imperatives of information and communication technologies to develop pedagogical models of flexibility; "creeping credentialism" – that is, the imperative for life-long learning and qualifications as one crucial step in assuring career progression; as well as the demands of increasingly sophisticated learners.

Therefore, tertiary education ought to exploit students' existing knowledge and experience. It ought to engage learners in meaningful, relevant and authentic learning experiences, including assessment tasks. Such a curriculum approach aims to promote opportunities for active learning and collaboration where students are engaged in deep learning experiences that develop their capacities to be self-reflective and critical. Deep learning is considered to be critical and transformative, where students develop the capability to:

relate ideas to previous knowledge and experience; check evidence and relate it to conclusions; examine the logic of argument cautiously and critically; become actively interested in the course content; and look for patterns and underlying principles. (Marton, Hounsell, & Entwhistle, 1998, p. 19)

This chapter uses a case-based evaluation study of a curriculum unit[1] to raise broader issues related to the design of online learning environments, the potential of social presence in such environments and innovative assessment to influence successful learning outcomes. As a case study, it provides "an evidentiary boundary around which to discuss educational problems" (Walker, 2001, p. 10). In this case, the educational problem concerned engaging students in forms of discourse in an online environment to develop their skills of critique, analysis and decision making.

The Study Focus

In previous years, students in this particular unit (a postgraduate unit concerned with financial computation and investment decision-making[2]) claimed that they enjoyed the unit and assessment tasks very much because they were aligned with their practical, applied interest in investments. While students appreciated the link between the assignments, the unit coordinator (the first author) was often dissatisfied and disheartened with what he considered was limited critical debate and discussion amongst the student cohort around substantive curriculum content.

To be a literate investor, it is essential that investment decisions be based on a prudent process, including: sound reasoning (considering all available resources), ongoing monitoring of investment performance and the incorporation of new information to modify risk exposure. A discourse among student peers, where they are given opportunities to reflect, debate and compare investment performance, is an ideal way to encourage this process. While the students in the unit are forced, weekly, to present their developing investment portfolios to their peers (and hence to monitor their investment performance), the unit coordinator believed that a potentially more valuable ongoing discourse of critique and analysis was not occurring both inter and intra group as much as he had hoped. In other words, a new strategy was needed, as it became apparent that students were not engaged in an ongoing discourse about their investment decisions as hoped in their large groups (of 10). Instead, only those students responsible for investment decisions on any one week were considering the issues involved in changing their portfolios.

Curriculum renewal is iterative and requires academic teachers to reflect critically on their practice and engage students and other stakeholders in the processes of pedagogical research and evaluation. While the evaluation in this case-based study broadly investigated the student experience in the unit, it focused on investigating the way in which the integrated assessment strategy especially achieved the desired outcomes and the way in which students engaged online to complete the assessment tasks and meet the unit's goals of developing skills of critique and analysis through debate and discourse. The study aimed to illuminate the following key questions:

- In what ways do electronic discussion fora promote the development of skills of critique and analysis through online debate and discourse?
- How does assessment as a learning strategy in online environments assist in developing the skills of critique and analysis?

Online Course Strategy

The unit is conducted in a flexible delivery mode and used WebCT to support this approach. Flexible delivery means an approach where the development of an online learning environment supports the on-campus experience in an integrated manner. In this case, the online environment was used to enhance learning and provide a degree of flexibility for students in where and how they studied. This is essentially one form of 'blended learning', and is discussed in more detail later.

The unit supported a well-designed and innovative assessment strategy that relied heavily on peer learning and group work. The unit coordinator wanted to create an assessment strategy that would create learning opportunities as well as measure learning outcomes. In doing so, the assessment strategy also created opportunities for students to be engaged in activities that were relevant and authentic to their employment settings.

The unit's pedagogical approach attempted to create a bridge between the pre-existing group assignment and an e-moderated online discussion group to encourage a discourse of critique and analysis that the unit coordinator suspected would ultimately contribute to the development of critical investment decision-making skills. He anticipated the potential challenges of e-moderation and chose to base his approach on the work of Salmon (2000, 2002), which he believed would provide a pragmatic structure and useful guiding principles.

Study Methodology

The study incorporated three principle data collection strategies. First, students' views of teaching in the unit were surveyed using the university-supported standard evaluation of teaching questionnaire (Monquest survey), which is part of its institutional quality improvement strategy. The Monquest survey was analyzed through the university's quality teaching unit.

Second, students' views of the online environment were surveyed. Students were asked to complete a questionnaire developed by the co-authors to gather more specific data about the unit assessment strategy. The unit coordinator devised the WebCT survey on the basis of the desired learning outcomes and his particular interest in ascertaining whether the student cohort believed they had met his intended pedagogical goals. Therefore, the WebCT survey was constructed to gather data about students' perceptions of the benefits of the online environment in promoting critical debate and discussion in the substantive content areas of the unit. The authors were particularly interested in investigating whether the students believed the unit developed their capacity to make investment decisions. Furthermore, the WebCT survey aimed to gather data about the perceived benefits of the online environment in promoting inter- and intra-group collaboration. The WebCT survey included 25 statements that students were asked to rate (the range was completely agree-completely disagree) on a 5-point Likert scale.

Third, students who had responsibility over the course of the unit as team leaders of designated peer learning groups agreed to participate in a focus group interview. Team leaders were interviewed, as it was believed they would bring a particular perspective to the study and would be able to comment particularly on the way the groups interacted in relation to the learning goals that were anticipated. Seven team leaders (three male, four female) agreed to participate in the focus group discussion. Team leaders appeared to be chosen by each group as a result of their own actions, such as organizing meetings (i.e., taking the initial step and showing some kind of leadership role, such as e-mailing others). As one student explained, "whoever spoke the most got to be leader!" The second author and a research assistant conducted the focus group interview using a semi-structured interview schedule. The qualitative data were transcribed, and the two interviewers analyzed the qualitative responses, isolated key themes and collaboratively annotated a summary of findings.

Study Results

Of the student cohort (n=94), 49 completed the Monquest survey and 49 completed the WebCT survey (a return rate of 52% for each survey). The students were first-time users of WebCT. Some experienced technical issues and were unable to use the synchronous online facility, chat, until mid semester. There were no major technical issues encountered. All students accessed the online environment from home as their primary access point.

The Monquest Survey

The Monquest survey data revealed that the students were highly satisfied with the unit, with 80% of students scoring very good or good responses for six of seven responses for the "Teaching Feedback" and four of five for "Subject Feedback" questionnaires.

The WebCT Survey

The WebCT survey data indicated that, with respect to the unit assessment strategy, the group work assignments were preferred over the individual assignment. Table 1 illustrates the WebCT survey responses. Students recognized that the unit coordinator aimed to develop an integrated assessment approach as a means of giving more coherence to the unit assessment as a learning strategy.

Further, with respect to the use of the online discussion forum to foster critical debate and discussion:

Table 1. Responses to WebCT survey

Panel 1

Survey Question#	1	2	3	4	5	6	7	8	9	10	11	12
Average	2.5	2.5	2.7	2.6	1.8	2.4	2.8	2.9	1.7	1.8	1.8	2.4
%	63%	66%	81%	75%	8%	56%	92%	100%	0%	3%	2%	59%

Panel 2

Survey Ques-tion#	13	14	15	16	17	18	19	20	21	22	23	24	25
Average	2.5	2.6	2.6	2.5	1.9	2.6	2.1	1.8	1.9	2.4	2.4	2.5	1.9
%	61%	69%	73%	61%	15%	71%	31%	7%	17%	56%	54%	61%	10%

Note: Average is the average response (between 1-5) and % is the normalized average response (normalized so that the highest response obtains 100% and the lowest 0%).

- Students felt that the online chat forum did not make the group assignment any easier.
- Students were neutral on value of the discussion forum (i.e., bulletin board).
- Students felt that the same amount of debate would have occurred without the online chat forum.
- Students liked to compare the performance of their group with the others using tools provided in the online site.

Focus Group Interview of Team Leaders

The focus group interview data suggested that students saw the online environment as a useful adjunct to the pedagogical structure of the unit. The focus group interview data identified that the online environment was highly valued as a single point of access to reference material, bringing resources together in one place; "the immediacy of it was great" and they liked the fact that "there was one point of reference for unit material." The following discussion expresses our analysis and interpretation of the focus group interview with the WebCT survey data.

Discussion

Creating an Online Learning Environment

Structured asynchronous online groups were established by the unit coordinator specifically to progress his aim to foster more discourse and debate as a precursor to skill development in investment decision-making. Interestingly, as noted earlier, the WebCT survey indicated that students were "neutral" on value of these discussion fora and felt that the same amount of debate would have occurred without the online chat forum.

However, this was neither reflected in the focus group interview nor in a very visible indicator; that is, the documentary evidence of the use of the online spaces. These spaces were used frequently and we believe relatively effectively by students. We acknowledge that the focus group interview was comprised of team leaders only; however, we argue that their insight into the groups' online engagement, coupled with the nature of the text evidence in the online discussion spaces (approximately 698 separate postings over the semester), demonstrates how the student cohort became adept at using the online discussion to meet their perceived needs.

Moreover, the synchronous chat facility was used by students in the absence of any intention in the pedagogical design from the unit coordinator. The synchronous chat facility came to be used by these strategic learners as a means of solving an immediate educational challenge: in this case, to assist them to prepare for the group presentations.

While the survey evidence of neutrality with regard to the discussion fora offers little of itself, the perceived value of the discussion fora and chat is highlighted beyond neutral in light of the focus group interview data. A substantial quantity of material in the form of discussion postings over the course of the semester was generated. This provided some evidence that students were engaging in discussion and debate in the way that the unit coordinator aimed to foster. However, the data generated from the discussion fora and the chat facility were not systematically analyzed as part of this study, and this is addressed subsequently.

In the focus group interview, students recognized that the success of any online discussion (synchronous or asynchronous) lies in their sense of its responsiveness. However, they were quick to point out that they felt, "it was not as good as face-to-face" and, importantly, that "its usefulness depends on the individual and their motivation." As one student explained, in chat, "you can't see how people are reacting, if they are arguing with you," and this can be a disadvantage in gauging the success of the discussion.

Social Presence in Online Learning Environments

Rourke, Anderson, Garrison and Archer (1999, p. 2) see social presence "as the ability of learners to project themselves socially and affectively into a community of inquiry." These authors draw on the work of Tinto (1987, cited in Rourke et al., 1999, p. 4) when they argue that social presence "supports cognitive objectives through its ability to instigate, sustain and support critical thinking in a community of learners." There is now an extensive literature that explores the way in which the discourses of text-based computer conferencing environments can develop critical thinking and other desirable cognitive skills in learners. Indeed, as Garrison, Anderson and Archer (2001, p. 1) argue, the acceptance of such environments and the way in which the higher education community has written about them, "has far outpaced our understanding of how this medium should best be used to promote higher-order learning."

Ostensibly, our intention for this case was the latter. In the context of this case study, the synchronous and asynchronous online groups served various purposes for students, and the signifiers of social presence that were evident (interaction, dialog, responsiveness of the teacher and student peers) may account for the way the students came to value the asynchronous online discussion and the synchronous chat. Furthermore, in this study, social aspects conducive to learning came into the use of chat, but the social elements were developed or formed *outside the online chat and discussion groups,* in the face-to-face environment that the unit already required of them (weekly lectures and tutorials).

However, the online chat and discussion groups were enhanced by those social bonds, which students claimed made it easier to work in online groups because of the pre-existing knowledge of personalities. One student also commented that working online "allowed us to talk more personally within the context of the large lecture class." Overall, online chat was seen to be useful as a collaborative tool to reach an educational goal (for example, preparing the presentation) and did contribute to maintaining the social relationships required for learning groups to function effectively.

Those who are researching in this field generally take one of two approaches, according to Garrison et al. (2001, pp. 5-7): those who look to investigate "absolute characteristics" of critical inquiry, such as logic, depth and completeness in discussion; and those who are interested in what they call a more "heuristic measure" of critique, where the effectiveness of the process of critical thinking is judged by participants. This supports the more recent and growing appreciation that measures of quality in online discussion are often difficult to gauge and time consuming to analyze (Gerbic & Stacey, 2003). Gerbic and Stacey (2003) review the changing emphasis from quantitative to qualitative research and evaluation approaches in the online learning environments of text-based computer mediated communication spaces. There is increasing evidence for this in the related literature (Agostinho, 2005). For example, in a recent study that explored the dynamics of networked e-learning groups, McConnell (2005) drew on both ethnography and grounded theory to explore the way in which e-learning groups reached their desired learning outcomes. He analyzed the transcripts of three e-learning groups as they collaborated to develop a defined product. The groups were undertaking a postgraduate professional qualification and the program was conducted entirely online.

We accept that the study reported here may well have benefited from a deeper, some might argue more rigorous discourse analysis of the text posted in the asynchronous discussion fora. However, we were more interested in the personal beliefs and perceptions that students had about the value of the fora in developing critical thinking skills and enhancing their experience of learning in the unit. In other words, we were interested in what students' perceptions of the unit were and the way it evolved for them as a learning experience, and this is more attuned to Garrison et al.'s (2001) 'heuristics' mentioned above.

While the focus group interview identified that the students saw the chat facility as a pragmatic solution to the educational need to meet to discuss their collaborative presentation, they did value the opportunity to talk, plan and debate online at a time convenient to them. The asynchronous discussion fora also played an important role in enabling the student groups to confer and discuss issues in ways that accommodated the unit's learning objectives and their personal lives. Yet, there was evidence that they did not see this as fundamental to their success in the unit or their personal perception of how they learned and developed their skills in critique for investment decision-making.

Online Learning and Assessment

In a recent paper with Eley (Eley, Labjcyier, & Spratt, 2005), we investigated some common assumptions about group learning and group assessment practices. The two key assumptions investigated were whether indeed assessment tasks or project outcomes reflect some aggregate of the individual group members' learning and that contribution to group functioning is sensitive to variation in that learning. In that study, we developed:

measures for individual students' contributions to group processes, for individual students' influence on the topic understanding of their group peers, and for the influence of the overall group experience on personal learning and understanding. (Eley, Lajbcyier, & Spratt, 2005, p. 1)

That study was positioned within the framework of the unit reported in this chapter but undertaken subsequently to the evaluation this chapter reports. We were interested in that study in exploring whether the group-directed project work was a valid measure of an individual's performance or learning. Typically, group work is encouraged in the tertiary environment. The same mark is given to all the group members, even if they have not all equally contributed to the group project. Eley, Lajbcygier and Spratt (2005) permitted groups to (anonymously) self assess and then tried to validate these marks by linking group performance with individual learning objective performance.

The "quality of group assignment outcome" seems *not* to relate to individual students' attainment of the objectives associated with that group work. That is, the a priori "hunch" was that group outcomes would relate to individual learning. However, we found that group outcomes do not relate terribly well to individual "learning from the group experience" performances. How might we imagine a group operating in such a way that good group cohesion results in higher group assignment quality, yet has minimal influence on the learning attained by the individual group members? Put another way, if you were a member of a group, and the aim was simply to maximize the mark that the group attained for the group product outcome, with no account needing to be given to the learning of the "lesser abled" members, then how might you most efficiently coordinate and organize who does what? These findings open questions a bit more fundamental about the structuring of group activities than just the "how do we make group marks more valid" issue that was our entry into the area reported here and in Eley, Lajbcygier and Spratt (2005).

In that paper, we concluded that:

... in the final analysis, individual learning should be assessed individually. We caution that the present study is just one within a particular instructional context. But if the findings here prove generalizable, then maybe we should re-define group projects to be not assessment opportunities, but a form of learning experience. (see Lejk, Wyvill, & Farrow, 1999)

Given the possible influence of contingencies discussed above, we might need to find ways to structure them to ensure that students commit and participate. This might mean not modeling group projects on workplace project teams, but rather deliberately designing them to encourage the student learning behaviors that we desire. But the simple conclusion here is that we cannot assume that individual assessments necessarily or directly derive from project outcomes. Perhaps this was an unfounded expectation in the first place. (Eley, Lajbcyier, & Spratt, 2005, p. 9)

The assessment strategy reported in this study was set in the pedagogical context of peer and group learning. Working in groups of about 10 students, all students were required to help decide on (virtual) investments across five market sectors, with the aim of maximizing their returns over the period of the project. The groups were constrained in their choice: They had to choose one company out of two for each of the five sectors (this was done to contrast the differing decisions made by different groups). Each group met at least once per week to review its portfolio and decide on any investment changes. The learning objectives associated with the project involved the use of various information sources in the making of investment decisions. These sources included company balance sheets, financial news media, technical price action reports and macroeconomic indices. The intent was for students to recognize that investment decisions are inherently ambiguous and are not uniquely determined by the range of information available.

The unit coordinator took pains to describe the assessment transparently and to make his expectations of the students unambiguous. The evaluation data revealed that students were very positive in their appreciation of the clarity and unambiguous nature of the assessment strategy. They felt they knew what was expected of them. They valued the way each lecture clearly outlined its aims and the relationship to assessment. They valued the way the lecturer was able to refer to the assessment tasks at various times in more detail over the course of the semester. They believed this assisted their understanding of what was expected of them. In the context of the assessment strategy, students generally felt that the "group work allowed members to see how they were faring compared to other members and other groups and their members." They believed this helped them learn and also contributed to developing their skills of analysis. The asynchronous discussion groups and the use of online chat enabled students to make their decisions about investments. They see these online strategies as complementing in a "supplementary way" the "negotiation that went on" in preparing investment decisions for the assessment tasks required. In conjunction with the assessment strategy, engaging in the online chat especially allowed them to be "task focused."

We feel confident that the students' perception of the success of the assessment strategy for them vindicates our attempts to be self-critical of our assessment practices. This critique reflects the recent growing interest in improving student learning through assessment and its place more strategically as a measure of institutional quality (Falchikov, 2001, 2005; James, McInnis, & Devlin, 2002; Knight, 2002). Given the mainstreaming of e-learning in higher education, then certainly assessment in e-learning environments will be similarly investigated (Gipps, 2005).

A cursory review of the assessment literature reveals that there is growing interest in using assessment to *lead* learning rather than simply *measure it* (James et al., 2002). We know that learners are 'strategic,' and our cohort in this study certainly presented themselves as such; they were generally employed in demanding professional positions in the field of financial computing and were studying to achieve their particular goals. The unit assessment, therefore, becomes an important (some world argue the primary) indicator of curriculum expectations for students. Associated with the interest in using assessment to lead learning is the role that assessment feedback plays in learning, and this is also becoming more prominent in the literature (Hounsell, Hounsell, Litjens, & McCune, 2005; Carless, 2006). Indeed, Carless (2006) puts forward a strong argument for the idea of 'feed forward' rather than feedback in the context of what he calls 'learning-oriented assessment' (LOA).

In LOA as he describes it, "learning comes first, both in the way the term is literally constructed and as a matter of principle which seeks to emphasize the learning aspects of assessment" (Carless 2006, p. 4). In other words, learning, not measurement, is emphasized and reconceptualizing feedback as 'feed forward' can assist students in taking what they have learned and how they have understood it to progress forward to future work. These ideas sit well with the deeper pedagogical approach of the unit reported here and with the research that we undertook into the assessment strategy specifically reported in Eley, Lajbcyier and Spratt (2005).

Blended Learning and Variation Theory

Intellectually, we were convinced of the potential of peer learning and peer assessment as effective and legitimate pedagogical strategies. However, we were attempting this in a relatively new learning environment. If we called this environment 'blended learning,' then most readers would anticipate that we were discussing some form of combination of traditional (that is face-to-face) pedagogies with an online component. While this was so for us in this case (mixing online learning with face-to-face experiences), we must acknowledge the controversy surrounding the use of the term 'blended learning' in current debates about e-learning in tertiary education.

In the contemporary e-learning literature in both higher education and corporate training settings, 'blended learning' has become 'amorphous' (Oliver & Trigwell, 2005) in that there is considerable debate about 'blended learning' as a unifying descriptor for particular forms of technologically supported teaching. Oliver and Trigwell (2005, p. 17) identified three common definitions of the term that they go on to critique; these are:

1.   The integrated combination of traditional with Web-based approaches
2.   The combination of media and tools employed in an e-learning environment
3.   The combination of a number of pedagogic approaches, irrespective of learning technology.

Oliver and Trigwell (2005) suggest that the first of these is the most common interpretation. They go on to present a comprehensive critical review of the literature and suggest that there are as many definitions of 'blended learning' as there have been of e-learning or online learning since the emergence of the Internet. They consider the array of definitions unhelpful and the remainder of their paper analyzes and critiques the three key definitions they identified. While we accept that clearly elucidated definitions are central to ensuring collective understandings among communities of scholars, be they teachers or researchers, we do concede that in the messy 'low lands of practice' (after Schön, 1995), clarity in definitions is often of less immediate interest to practitioners than scholars on the 'high hard ground of theory' (Schön, 1995). This is not meant to be flippant or to deny the importance of definition, per se, in research traditions. However, while Oliver and Trigwell's (2005) arguments for a reinterpretation of the term blended learning may be honorable, practitioners continue to confront definitional quagmires regarding anything to do with flexible, online or e-learning as they busy themselves trying to innovate and keep abreast of the rapidly changing learning environments created by advances in technology and research.

Martin and Oliver's (2005) critique highlights a number of other important issues; one is that the majority of the definitions of 'blended learning' are "teacher centered" in that they are "all described from the perspective of the teacher, the instructor or the course designer" (p. 18). This, of course, is the key to their critique and one that may be helpful for those of us who see teaching more as the 'context' for learning (after Green, 1998) rather than an end in itself. If blended learning is conceived less as a 'teaching methods approach,' face-to-face with online tasks or integrated multi-media for example, and more as a learning approach that develops 'variation' for students in learning engagements, then Oliver and Trigwell (2005, p. 22) believe that blended learning could be a defensible term, and therefore "redeemed."

The 'variation' they allude to here is a reference to variation theory, which suggests that for learning to occur, "variation must be experienced by the learner" (Oliver & Trigwell, 2005, p. 22). Variation theory has evolved from the early and highly influential work of Marton and Saljo (1976a, 1976b), which investigated qualitative differences in learning.

Variation theory is based on the idea that:

For learning to occur, variation must be experienced by the learner. Without variation there is no learning. Discernment is at the core of our ways of experiencing the world around us. (Oliver & Trigwell, 2005)

Where discernment is about the experience of 'difference,' variation becomes the context for discernment. The unit coordinator in our case was trying to find ways to create engaging learning opportunities so students would become active participants and collaborators on their own to develop their critical skills in investment decision making. If we liken the learning design of peer learning and peer assessment within our blended learning environment as an attempt to promote 'discernment' in students, then the strategy begins to be unpinned by Marton and Trigwell's (2000) variation theory.

The original impetus for the unit coordinator to reconsider and redevelop his pedagogical approach was his desire to promote particular cognitive skills; moreover, given his student cohort, he was also interested in progressing learning approaches that would be relevant for them and develop his students in their professional practice. Given the complex globalized world in which his students find themselves, this means that he was interested in preparing them to be able to function as professionals in settings of change. Marton and Trigwell (2000, p. 385) see variation theory as a means of explaining this; how "participation in one practice can prepare for participation in another practice."

While they argue that learning theories have traditionally seen this intellectually as a question of similarity, it is in their view a question of difference. In other words, as they explain:

The experience of similarity between two situations is a function of the pattern of variation between all other situations. (Marton & Trigwell, 2000, p. 386)

In the context of blended learning environments and in keeping with the ideological basis of constructivism in learning, we can see that variation theory might help explain how and why students engaged in learning environments have variable experiences and learn differently. It may also assist in framing pedagogical research that will investigate longitudinally, the influence of blended learning environments in tertiary settings on change in professional practice from the learners' perspective. In the context of the case discussed in this chapter, it may be that we now have grounds to reconsider the pedagogic of the unit in light of this more contemporary research in blended learning and variation theory.

Conclusion and Implications for Research and Practice

This chapter used a specific case report to illuminate the way in which assessment can be harnessed to foster deep learning of critical inquiry skills in tertiary students. It also provides evidence that students believe they benefit from use of an online learning environment constructed as a pedagogical support strategy, a form of blended learning.

There is an expansive and growing literature that explores many aspects of online learning environments in tertiary settings. It would be fair to say that in recent years this literature has begun to explore the importance of social presence and teaching presence as key determinants in improving the instructional effectiveness of online learning (Chih-Hsuig, 2001; Garrison, Anderson, & Archer, 2001; McConnell, 2005; Murphy, Smith, & Stacey, 2002; Stacey, 2002; Stacey & Rice, 2002). Social presence and teacher responsiveness, and the way in which sociality develops is important in developing the interaction that contributes to positive cognitive learning experiences. Indeed, it is these kinds of experiences that have been cited as predictors of successful e-learning groups generally and in cohorts similar to that reported in this case study, as the majority of the cohort was full-fee paying international students (Chih-Hsuig, 2001). The study results, despite some contradictions in conjunction with the experience teaching the unit, have led us to be confident that the social learning that can be engendered in peer learning groups online is potentially a powerful learning adjunct.

We have acknowledged that there was some contradiction between the survey findings and the focus group interview findings. Overall, students felt that the online environment in this unit, including the discussion forum and chat forum, were not fundamental to the deep learning that was trying to be instilled. Students believed that this kind of approach to learning could have been achieved without the online learning site. Despite this, however, we can suggest that online environments can be used effectively as successful pedagogical support. Students are well aware of the importance of motivation and social presence (what they have characterized as "responsiveness" in this study) to successful learning in synchronous and asynchronous discussion fora and integrating online teaching environments with assessment tasks that are relevant and practical to support successful learning outcomes.

Students recognized the online experience as providing a complimentary or supporting role in attaining the deep learning objectives of the unit: not essential but somewhat helpful. The students recognized that the unit instilled collaborative discourse, debate and decision making in investment decisions, and that they understood how investment decision processes can "incorporate debate and discussion and how that can lead to better investment decisions." However, they did not attribute the attainment of this knowledge purely to the online environment or the technology per se.

It is well recognized that "transforming a course by integrating new technologies is an increasingly common example of educational change and innovation" (Allen, Wedman, & Folk, 2001, p. 104). We acknowledge that assessing the efficacy of sustainable curriculum change brought about by technology innovation requires the application of longitudinal research approaches, such as that described by Allen, Wedman and Folk (2001). Moreover, our review of the more contemporary research in blended learning environments and learning theories—in particular, variation theory—as discussed by Marton and Trigwell (2000) and Oliver and Trigwell (2005) raises many new questions for research in the setting of e-learning environments.

Given this and based on the study reported here, as well as the issues raised by the literature in social and cognitive presence, blended learning, variation theory and peer assessment, new questions for research might include: If social presence and teaching presence are predictors of success in e-learning environments, how can they be modeled in academic practice? What kinds of research approaches in e-learning settings can help us explore the influence of social engagement on cognitive learning in groups? In what ways can synchronous and asynchronous e-learning environments be created to foster the development of skills of critique, analysis, debate and decision-making? How might variation theory support the development of blended learning environments? In what ways ought assessment to be structured to have a positive impact on students' attitudes to learning so that it is conceived as integral to the teaching context for learning? How do students perceive differences in a peer group assessment as a learning experience and the assessment of the learning attained because of it? How do we make group marks more valid?

References

Agostinho, S. (2005). Naturalistic inquiry in e-learning research. *International Journal of Qualitative Methods*, *4*(1), 1-13.

Allen, G., Wedman, J., & Folk, L. (2001). Looking beyond the valley: A five-year case study on course innovation. *Innovation in Higher Education, 26*(2), 103-119.

Biggs, J. (1999). *Teaching for quality learning at university*. Buckingham: The Society for Research into Higher Education.

Burbules, N., & Bruce, B. (2000). *Theory and research on teaching as dialogue*, 1-40. Retrieved January 15, 2006, from www.isrl.uiuc.edu/~chip/pubs/dialogue.html

Carless, D. (2006). Learning-oriented assessment: Conceptual basis and practical implications. *Innovations in Education and Teaching International, 43*(4), in press.

Cheng, C., & Warren, M. (2000). Making a difference: Using peers to assess individual student's contributions to a group project. *Teaching in Higher Education, 5*(2), 244-255.

Chih-Hsuig, T. (2001). How Chinese perceive social presence: An examination of interaction in an online learning environment. *Educational Media International, 38*(1), 45-60.

Eley, M., Lajbcygier, P. & Spratt, C. (2005). How valid are group marks as a proxy for the individual learning that comes from group assignment and project work? In C. Rust (Ed.), *Improving student learning: Diversity and inclusivity* (pp. 137-148). Oxford: Oxford Centre for Staff and Learning Development.

Falchikov, N. (2001). *Learning together: Peer tutoring in higher education.* London: Routledge Falmer.

Falchikov, N. (2005). *Improving assessment through students' involvement.* London: Routledge Falmer.

Garrison, R.D., Anderson, T., & Archer, W. (2001). Critical thinking. Cognitive presence and computer conferencing in distance education. *American Journal of Distance Education, 15*(1).

Gerbic, P., & Stacey, E. (2003, October 1-4). Evidence for sustainable e-learning in quality online learning communities: A purposive approach to content analysis. *The 16th ODLAA Biennial Forum Conference Proceedings,* Canberra.

Gipps, C. (2005). What is the role of ICT-based assessment in universities? *Studies in Higher Education, 30*(2), 171-180.

Green, B. (1998). Teaching for difference: learning theory and post-critical pedagogy, In D. Buckingham (Ed.), *Teaching popular culture: Beyond radical pedagogy* (pp. 176-197). London: UCL Press.

Hounsell, D., Hounsell, J., Litjens, J., & McCune, V. (2005, August 23-27). Enhancing guidance and feedback to students: Findings on the impact of evidence-informed initiatives. Paper presented to the *European Association for Research on Learning and Instruction, (EARLI) 11th Biennial Conference,* Nicosia, Cyprus.

James, R., McInnis, C., & Devlin, M. (2002). *Assessing learning in Australian universities.* Major report and electronic resource site from Centre for the Study of Higher Education, University of Melbourne. Retrieved January 15, 2006, from www.cshe.unimelb.edu.au/ assessinglearning/

Knight, P. (2002). The Achilles' heel of quality: The assessment of student learning, *Quality in Higher Education, 8*(1), 107-115.

Laurillard, D. (1995). *Rethinking university teaching: A framework for the effective use of educational technology.* London: Routledge.

Marton, F., Hounsell, D., & Entwhistle, N. (1997). *The experience of learning: Implications for teaching and studying in higher education.* Edinburgh: Scottish Academic Press.

Marton, F., & Saljo, R. (1976a). On qualitative differences in learning 1: Outcome and process. *British Journal of Educational Psychology, 46*, 4-11.

Marton, F., & Saljo, R. (1976b). On qualitative differences in learning 11: Outcome and process. *British Journal of Educational Psychology, 46*, 115-27.

Marton, F., & Trigwell, K. (2000). Variato est Mater Studiorum. *Higher Education Research & Development, 19*(3), 381-395.

McConnell, D. (2005). Examining the dynamics of networked e-learning groups and communities. *Studies in Higher Education, 30*(1), 25-32.

Murphy, K., Smith, P., & Stacey, E. (2002, December 3-6). Teaching presence in computer conferencing: Lessons from the United States and Australia. *Proceedings of the International Conference of Computers in Education (ICEE 2002).*

Oliver, M., & Trigwell, K (2005). Can 'blended learning' be redeemed? *E-Learning, 2*(1), 17-26. Retrieved January 15, 2006, from www.e-learningcentre. co.uk/eclipse/Resources/blended.htm

Rourke, L., Anderson, T., Garrison, D.R., & Archer, W. (1999). Assessing social presence in asynchronous text-based computer conferencing. *Journal of Distance Education, 14*(2), 2-18. Retrieved January 15, 2006, from www.cade. athabascau.ca/vol14.2/rourke_et_al.html

Salmon, G. (2000). *E-moderating: The key to online learning.* London: Routledge Falmer.

Salmon, G. (2002). *E-tivities: The key to active online learning.* London: Kogan Page.

Schön, D. (1995). Knowing-in-action: The new scholarship requires a new epistemology. *Change,* November/December, 27-34.

Stacey, E. (2002). Social presence online: Networking learners at a distance. *Education and Information Technologies, 7*(4), 287-294.

Stacey, E., & Rice, M. (2002). Evaluating an online learning environment. *Australian Journal of Educational Technology, 18*(3), 323-340.

Walker, R. (2001). *Case study, case records and multimedia.* Centre for Applied Research in Education, University of East Anglia. Retrieved January 15, 2006, from www.uea.ac.uk/care/ people/RW_recent_writing/ final_14_09.html

Endnotes

[1]   At Monash University, a 'unit' is equivalent to 13 weeks of full-time study. This unit was a postgraduate unit in Financial Computation.

[2]   The majority of the student cohort were full-fee paying international students working in professional fields related to financial computation and investments.

Chapter II

The Effects of Human Factors on the Use of Web-Based Instruction

Sherry Y. Chen, Brunel University, Middlesex, UK

Abstract

Web-based instruction is prevalent in educational settings. However, many issues still remain to be investigated. In particular, it is still open about how human factors influence learners' performance and perception in Web-based instruction. In this vein, the study presented in this chapter investigates this issue in a Web-based instructional program, which was applied to teach students how to use HyperText Markup Language (HTML) in a United Kingdom (UK) university. Sixty-one master's degree students participated in this study. There were a number of interesting findings. Students' task achievements were affected by the levels of their previous system experience. On the other hand, the Post-Test and Gain scores were positively influenced by their perceptions and attitudes toward the Web-based instructional program. The implications of these findings are discussed.

Introduction

Web-based instruction is prevalent in educational settings. The value of Web-based instruction lies in the capabilities of hypermedia, which permit significant flexibility in the delivery of non-linear course material (Khalifa & Lam, 2002). Students are allowed to learn in their own way—to determine their own path through the material available (Barua, 2001)—and to learn things at their own pace (Chen, 2002). However, the freedom offered by Web-based instructional programs may come with a problem, because flexibility increases complexity (Ellis & Kurniawan, 2000). Learners are forced to determine their own learning strategies and, therefore, will differ in their perceptions and approaches to learning. In particular, some learners who lack the skills of independent learning may find this difficult and become confused (Last, O'Donnell, & Kelly, 2001), so they may forget what they have already covered, and miss important information (McDonald, Stodel, Farres, Breithaupt, & Gabriel, 2001). This suggests that not all students will appreciate the flexibility and freedom offered by the Web and that human factors, therefore, are important issues to be considered in the development of Web-based instruction programs.

In this vein, the study reported in this chapter aims to investigate how human factors influence students' reactions to a Web-based instruction program. The chapter begins by building a theoretical framework to present the relationships between Web-based instructional programs and individual differences. It then describes an empirical study of students' learning experiences in a Web-based instructional program. Subsequently, the design implications are discussed based on the findings of this empirical study.

Theorectical Framework

Web-Based Instruction

Over recent years, the World Wide Web (Web) has been becoming a useful tool for information distribution (Sridharan, 2004). In particular, there is an increase in use of the Web for instruction (Evans, 2004). Web-based instruction provides a number of advantages, among which dynamic interaction and flexible schedule are two key items. In terms of dynamic interaction, Web-based instruction presents an enormous amount of information through various interconnections that offer students a rich exploration environment. The development of Web-based instruction provides learners with many opportunities to explore, discover and learn in theory according to their individual needs. Students can create individualized learning paths to reach the desired goals, move at their own speed and retrieve additional information as needed (Hui & Cheung, 1999). There is a shift away from didactic instruction to discovery of information (Smaldino, 1999). This approach is in line with the constructivist philosophy of learning, where the learner is encouraged to interact with the environment to construct individual knowledge structure (Mc-Donald et al., 2001).

With regard to flexible schedule, Web-based instruction allows learners to read course content through a computer network at any time and at different places (Chang, Henriquez, Honey, Light, Moeller, & Ross, 1998). Burton and Goldsmith (2002) found that such a flexible schedule makes Web-based instruction appealing to students, including the convenience of not having to be on campus during the week, to easily arrange personal commitments and to take courses around work schedules. This type of learning may be particularly beneficial to individuals who live in remote places (Daugherty, 1998). Individuals living in remote areas can have access to the same course content as those living in big cities. This is why many educators have tried to develop a distance learning program on the Web. As pointed out by Clark and Lyon (1999), Web-based instruction has been predicted to be the future of all types of distance learning programs.

However, these advantages may come with a price. Power and Roth (1999) reported that Web-based instruction is more dynamic and flexible than other learning material, but it creates new challenges related to the effect on learners' comprehension. Ng and Gunstrone (2002) indicated that although students had positive perceptions to self-based learning provided by Web-based instruction, the unstructured nature of the Web made some students need more time to search information. Quintana (1996) stated that while students gained the advantage of flexibility in time, pace and distance with Web-based instruction, many students, on the other hand, felt isolated, lack of motivation, or lack of support and feedback consequently to drop out of the course. Hedberg, Harper, and Corrent-Agostinho (1998) indicated that some students are still working to come to grips with a new and difficult way of learning. They exemplify the concern by asking for more incentive, more time, more structure and more guidance. These studies provide evidence that not all types of students appreciate being given freedom in their learning processes. In particular, students who need more guidance through the learning process may meet an increased number of problems in using Web-based instructional programs. To address this limitation, Web-based instruction should be developed to support the unique needs of each individual learner (Carter, 2002). Only when their needs are identified can developers of programs effectively enhance functionality and increase learners' satisfaction (Ke, Kwakkelaarb, Taic, & Chenc, 2002). Therefore, understanding of learners' individual differences arguably becomes an important consideration in the development of Web-based instruction programs.

Human Factors

Human factors play an important role in learning. Individuals differ in traits such as skills, aptitudes and preferences for processing information, constructing meaning from information and applying it to real-world situations (Jonassen & Grabowski, 1993). The effects of human factors on students' task performance in a computer-based learning environment have been a growing research area (Wang & Jonassen, 1993; Ke et al., 2002). Among all human factors, gender differences (Ford & Miller 1996), domain knowledge (Mitchell, Chen, & Macredie, 2005) and system experience (Reed &Oughton, 1997; Chen & Ford, 1998) have been recognized as especially relevant factors to users' interaction with the Web. In terms of gender differences, previous research indicates that gender differences influence users' navigation strategies in Web-based instruction. Schwarz (2001) found that females and males request different kinds of support when locating particular information. Male users need a larger frame of reference, while female users ask procedural directions. The other study by Roy and Chi (2003) indicated that males tended to navigate in a broader way than females. They also found that males tended to perform more page jumps per minute, which indicates that they navigate the information space in a nonlinear way.

In respect of domain knowledge, research suggested that less knowledgeable users experienced more disorientation problems in Web-based instruction (Last et al., 2001). This may be due to the fact that they are unfamiliar with the subject matter of the text, so they cannot rely on prior knowledge to help them structure it. On the other hand, more knowledgeable users may experience fewer navigation problems because their greater grasp of the conceptual structure of the subject matter can enable them to impose structure on the Web (McDonald et al., 2001). In regard to system experience, novices and experts demonstrate different attitudes toward the use of Web-based instruction. Liaw (2002) found students' experience using the Internet to be a good predictor of their computer and Web attitudes. Furthermore, Torkzadeh and Van Dyke (2002) found the transition from low experience to high experience could improve Internet self-efficacy.

Results from these studies suggest that human factors play an important role in the use of Web-based instruction programs. These studies also indicate that further empirical works are needed to identify the learners' different preferences, and their results may help to guide the development and evaluation of Web-based instructional programs. This chapter presents such a study, which aims to examine how human factors influence students' reactions to a Web-based instructional program.

Figure 1. Screen design of the HTML tutorial

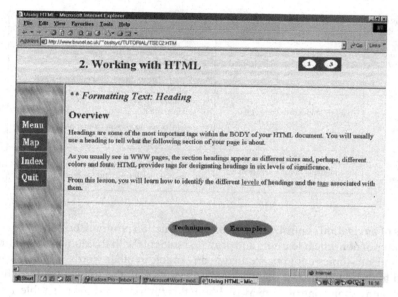

Research Design

Web-Based Instruction Program

The Web-based instructional program, which was used to give an HTML tutorial, began by giving an introduction to the learning objectives and explaining the available navigation approaches provided in the instructional program. The contents were divided into three sections: (1) What is HTML? (2) Working with HTML, and (3) Relations with Standard Generalized Markup Language (SGML) and the Web. Section 2 is the key element of the Web-based instructional program, which covers 12 sub-topics of HTML authoring. Each sub-topic was further split into five parts, comprising (a) overview, (b) detailed techniques, (c) examples, (d) related skills, and (e) references. Information was presented in 82 pages using texts, tables, an index and maps.

As shown in Figure 1, the screen was divided using frames. In the top frame was a title bar showing the section name being viewed and the other available section buttons. In the left frame were the Main Menu, Index, Map and Quit buttons. The right frame displayed the main content for each section, including topic buttons and text-based hypertext links.

Table 1. Three types of navigation control

Control	Purposes	Tools
Sequence Control	To allow students to decide the sequence of subjects to be learned	• *Subject Maps*: to show all topics and sub-topics in a hierarchical way • *Keyword Index*: to list keywords in an alphabetical way • *Back/Forward*: to see the page previously visited
Content Control	To allow students to control the selection of the contents they wish to learn	• *Section Buttons*: to choose three sections of the main content • *Main Menu:* to present main topics • *Hypertext Links*: to connect relevant concepts
Display Control	To allow students to choose one of several display options that cover the same concept	• *Display Options*: to include overview, examples and detailed techniques, and so forth

In terms of navigation control, the Web-based instruction program took advantage of the features of non-linear learning and provided students with freedom of navigation. Topics and sub-topics could be studied in any order. In other words, students were allowed to decide their own navigational routes through the subject matter. Three types of navigation control were available in this tutorial, as shown in Table 1.

Pre-Test and Post-Test

Examining students' learning outcome in theoretical knowledge was conducted by using a Pre-Test and Post-Test methodology. The students were evaluated with the Pre-Test to examine their levels of prior HTML knowledge, and with the Post-Test for assessing learning achievement. Both tests were presented in paper-based formats and included 20 multiple-choice questions. Only one correct answer was provided among the multiple choices provided in each question. The formats of the questions were similar, with only the specific subject of the question being modified. The questions covered all three sections of the Web-based instruction program, from basic concepts to advance topics.

Students were allotted 20 minutes to answer each test and were not allowed to examine the content presented in the program at the same time. Students' learning outcome was assessed by:

- **Post-Test score:** Each student's score on the Post-Test, ranging from 0 to 20 to identify general learning performance
- **Gain score:** Score difference between the Pre-Test and Post-Test, to measure improved learning performance by taking the HTML tutorial.

Task Sheet

Students were assigned to do a practical task, which involved constructing a Web page using Notepad to measure learning outcome on the real skills that they had learned. The practical task entailed 10 key areas (e.g., creating hypertext links, changing background colors, formatting text, etc.). A printed task sheet was given to the students that described the detailed features of the Web page to be completed. The students were allowed to decide the order in which they attempted to complete the task activities on the sheet, and could look at the content of the HTML tutorial simultaneously.

One and a half hours were allocated for each student to complete the task. The starting and end times for each student were recorded. Students' task achievement was evaluated by:

- **Task score:** A score consisting of summing items successfully completed, on a 0-10 scale
- **Task time:** The total time spent for completing the tasks.

Exit Questionnaire

The questionnaire was divided into two parts. The first part sought information regarding biographical data relating to the student and his or her experience of using computers, the Internet and HTML. The second, which was the main focus, consisted of three open-ended questions and 47 closed statements to collect students' responses to the Web-based instructional program. It took students approximately 20 minutes to respond to all questions.

The open-ended questions were related to students' opinions about the strengths and weaknesses of the HTML tutorial and the barriers that they met. Students were requested to express their opinions in their own words. Enough space was provided for them to write down their opinions. The closed statements were designed to collect information about students' comprehension, preferences, and satisfaction or dissatisfaction with the Web-based instructional program. It included five sections: (1) level of understanding; (2) content presentation; (3) interaction styles; (4) functionality and usability; and (5) difficulties and problems.

Each closed statement could be classed as either "in favor" or "not in favor" of the program. The number of 'favored' statements was almost equal to the 'not-favored' statements (20 favored statements and 27 not-favored statements), in an attempt to reduce bias in the questionnaire. All statements used a five-point Likert Scale consisting of: 'strongly agree'; 'agree'; 'neutral'; 'disagree'; and 'strongly disagree.'

Students were required to indicate agreement or disagreement with each statement by placing a check mark at the response alternative that most closely reflected their opinion. Their perceptions and attitudes were measured by:

- **Positive perceptions:** the total score for all favored statements of the Exit Questionnaire with the same Likert Scale
- **Negative attitudes:** The total score for all not-favored statements of the Exit Questionnaire with the same Likert Scale.

Procedure

All participants took part in the study in the same room at the same time, and they all interacted with the Web-based instructional program accessed using Microsoft's Internet Explorer. The participants were asked to do the following activities:

1.   Take the Pre-Test to ascertain levels of prior knowledge of HTML
2.   Interact with the Web-based instructional program (i.e., HTML Tutorial)
3.   Do a practical task, which involved constructing a Web page using HTML
4.   Complete the Post-Test to identify learning performance
5.   Fill out a paper-based exit questionnaire to describe their personal details and reflect on their opinions of the Web-based instructional program.

Data Analyses

To investigate how human factors influence student learning in the Web-based instructional program, the data obtained from Pre- and Post-Tests, practical tasks and the exit questionnaire were used to conduct statistical analyses to identify students' learning experience. T-test was applied to examine the gender differences, and ANOVA was used to identify the differences among different levels of prior knowledge. In addition, Pearson's correlation was employed to find the relationships between students' learning performance and their perceptions and attitude. A significance level of $P<.05$ was adopted for the study. In addition, the mean scores are employed to describe the learning outcome for each individual group.

Table 2. Distribution of participants

	Male (N=32)	Female (N=29)	Total (N=61)
Computer Experience			
None	0	0	0
Little	0	0	0
Average	9	11	20
Good	12	10	22
Excellent	10	9	19
Internet Experience			
None	0	0	0
Little	0	0	0
Average	12	10	22
Good	9	12	21
Excellent	10	8	18
HTML Authoring			
None	8	7	15
Little	9	11	20
Average	6	7	13
Good	8	5	13
Excellent	0	0	0

Discussion Results

The participants (N=61) consisted of master's students at Brunel University's Department of Information Systems and Computing. Despite the fact that the participants volunteered to take part in the experiment, the sample is evenly distributed in terms of gender and system experience. There were 32 males and 29 females. The computer experience and Internet experience reported by the participants ranged from average to excellent on a five-point scale. Their familiarity with the subject content, *HTML authoring*, ranged from none to good. As shown in Table 2, there is the similar proportion of computer and Internet experience and HTML authoring in both male and female groups.

Table 3 describes the students' overall learning performance. In terms of perceptions and attitudes, a majority of students (78%) felt that the Web-based instruction program was useful and they liked the Web treatment of the content.

Table 3. Overall learning outcomes

	Post Test	Gain Score	Task Score	Task Time
Mean	10.4	7.7	6.5	46.5
SD	1.8	0.9	1.6	6.8

Tasks vs. Tests

As indicated in Section 3, students needed to be assessed by both practical task and paper-based tests. It is important to note that both task and tests were markedly different. The distinctions between them are similar to those between open-book examination and closed-book examination. The practical task was completed in "open-book" examination style, with the students building their Web pages while being guided by the task sheet. The practical task could be completed successfully without recourse to memory by applying knowledge read from the screen at the particular time it was needed. On the other hand, the Post-Test looked like a closed-book examination, as it was a multiple-choice factual test that entailed recalling knowledge from memory and was completed after learning using the Web-based instructional program. These differences can also be associated with those between *procedural knowledge* and *declarative knowledge*. Derry (1990) distinguishes between these two, procedural being "knowledge how," and declarative being "knowledge that." Procedural refers to knowledge of how to do things, while declarative refers to knowledge about the world and its properties (McGilly, 1994). Practical tasks refer to procedure knowledge of how to use HTML, while paper-based tests refer to declarative knowledge about the properties of HTML.

Another interesting finding is that the students' task scores were affected by the levels of their previous Internet experience and HTML authoring (Table 4). On the

Table 4. Task score and prior knowledge

Internet Experience	Excellent	Good	Average	Little	None
Mean	8.2	6.9	4.3	N/A	N/A
SD	1.9	1.6	0.7	N/A	N/A
Significance					P<.01
HTML Authoring	Excellent	Good	Average	Little	None
Mean	N/A	8.4	7.2	6.0	4.2
SD	N/A	1.8	1.3	0.7	0.3
Significance					P<.05

other hand, there were positive relationships between the students' perceptions and attitudes and their Post-Test (P<.05) and Gain scores (P<.01). In other words, the students who had more positive perceptions toward the Web-based instructional program could obtain better Post-Test and Gain scores than those who had more negative attitudes toward the program.

This implied that performance on the practical task of applying procedural knowledge could be promoted by prior system experience in using the Internet and HTML authoring, but it would not be affected by the matching or mismatching of instruction with students' preferences. Conversely, the ability to recall declarative knowledge appears to have been facilitated mainly by matching instructional presentation with learners' preferences, but it is not influenced by prior system experience of using the Internet and HTML authoring.

Gender Differences

There were interesting correlations between the students' learning performance and their gender differences. Female students performed better than male students in the Post-Test. Conversely, the male students outperformed the female students in the practical task (Table 5). As indicated earlier, the differences between the Post-Test and practical task can be related with those between *declarative knowledge* and *procedural knowledge*. It implies that female students are better at acquiring declarative knowledge rather than procedural knowledge. Conversely, male students are skilled at gaining procedural knowledge instead of declarative knowledge.

For learning attitudes, the male students were patient in completing the task. On the other hand, the female students felt nervous doing the tasks, and some of them (N = 10) gave up doing the tasks within 15 minutes. In addition, the female students needed more guidance than the male students did. The female students tended to ask for instruction from the tutor, instead of trying to correct errors by themselves. These findings are in line with some previous studies, which found that males showed

Table 5. Gender differences in learning outcomes

	Post Test	Gain Score	Task Score	Task Time
Gender Differences				
Female				
Means	12.4	9.3	4.5	35.5
SD	1.9	1.1	0.6	3.8
Male				
Means	8.5	6.2	8.6	56.4
SD	0.8	0.7	1.8	7.8
Significance	**P<.01**	**P<.05**	**P<.01**	**P<.01**

more interest in using and learning about computers while females reported fear of using computers and feeling helpless around them (Shashaani, 1994; Koch, 1994). For this phenomenon, educators should help female students build their confidence in facing the challenge of using computers, instead of giving too detailed instructions. In addition, educational settings should ensure that instructional programs should not place any students at a disadvantage due to their gender differences (Owen & Liles, 1998).

Prior Knowledge

Through analyzing students' prior knowledge, one thing seems evident: For doing practical task, students who had greater experience of using the Internet or HTML authoring seemed able to look for relevant information in an efficient way. Conversely, students who were lacking prior knowledge of the subject content needed more time to decide the learning paths for completing the task (Table 6). It seemed that students' existing knowledge did influence their interaction with the Web-based instructional program. These findings arguably supported results from previous studies (Shih & Gamon, 1999; Gay, 1986), which found there was a positive relationship between learner control and prior knowledge.

Expert learners who had an adequate amount of prior knowledge on the subject felt familiar with the interface and the contents of the Web-based instructional program, so they were confident about being more active when navigating the Web-based instructional system. On the other hand, novice learners might not be aware of the best order to read the material or what the most important information was. Therefore, it is important to provide novice learners with an initial phase of orientation relating to both interface and domain contents (Linard & Zeillger, 1995). One way to do this is by providing visual paths, which can be displayed by means of cues to indicate how far students are along a path or by giving some conceptual description for the possible sequences. An alternative method is to provide good labels for the

Table 6. Prior knowledge and task time

Task Time					
Internet Experience	Excellent	Good	Average	Little	None
Mean	39.2	44.5	54.4	N/A	N/A
SD	5.5	6.1	8.1	N/A	N/A
Significance					P<.05
HTML Authoring	Excellent	Good	Average	Little	None
Mean	N/A	31.4	41.9	50.5	61.2
SD	N/A	3.2	4.3	5.9	7.3
Significance					P<.05

pages. Labels that clearly indicate the role of a particular page may help novices successfully tdecide the appropriate coherent path (Lewis & Polson, 1990).

Learning by Doing

In this Web-based instruction program, students were asked to do a practical task (i.e., designing a Web page with HTML). A significant number of students (44%) reported that doing the task was a useful way of helping them to set a focus in the Web-based instructional program. From this 44% of students, 52% of them obtained Post-Test scores above the average (=10.4) and 63% of them demonstrated more positive perceptions to the Web-based instructional program. These results implied that "learning by doing" could assist some students to set their effective learning strategies. As indicated by Smith and Parks (1997), tasks serve to simulate "goal directed" browsing in such a way that learning performance can be enhanced.

On the other hand, a few students (30%) reported that doing the task hindered their learning. They found that they lost other important information they needed to learn because they were concentrating on doing the task. From these 30% of students, 58% of them obtained Post-Test scores below the average and 54% of them showed more negative attitudes toward the Web-based instructional program. This raises some interesting questions for further studies: (a) whether task activities can facilitate promoting students' learning performance in a Web-based instructional program; and (b) what the relationships are between students' attitudes and their learning patterns as reflected in a Web-based instructional program with and/or without setting tasks.

Conclusion

The aforementioned findings provide evidence that Web-based instructional programs may not be suitable for all learners as an instructional methodology. Instructors must be aware of individual differences, such as gender and levels of prior knowledge possessed. Some learners—for example, novice learners—may need greater support and guidance from instructors, while others may be able to follow Web-based instructional programs relatively independently. Thus, instructors should not assume that every student would benefit equally from Web-based instructional programs in educational settings. There remains the need for guidance to ensure that all learners attain their learning potential.

Implementing Web-based instructional programs is a complex process composed of interactions among students, instructional content and the features of Web-based instructional programs. It is important for educational settings to have a good plan in advance. Instructors should remain cautious about making a sweeping decision to convert entire curricula onto Web-based instructional programs. The goals of such a process should be weighed against potential problems (e.g., alienating certain learners). To avoid alienating a certain group, instructors should continue to incorporate a number of different teaching strategies into their lectures. In addition, this transition requires time for the student and time in the classroom to acquaint students with Web-based instructional programs. This is especially the case for students who have difficulties in independent learning; there is a need to let them have a longer time for this shift. With this issue in mind, such innovation in teaching and learning will be more meaningful and valuable.

This study has shown the importance of understanding individual differences in the development of Web-based instructional programs, but it was only a small-scale study. Further studies need to be undertaken with a larger sample to provide additional evidence. The other limitation is that this study adopted self-developed Pre- and Post-Tests, so the reliability and validity of these tests are questionable. Therefore, testing and modification of the tests are needed in the future. There is a need to conduct future research that would examine the impact of other individual differences, such as cognitive styles, cultural background or domain knowledge. Such research should also be conducted within a more sophisticated multimedia Web-based instructional program, including the presentation of animation and video. It would be interesting to see how individual differences influence student learning in multimedia Web-based instructional programs. The findings of such studies could be integrated to build robust user models for the development of personalized Web-based instructional programs that can accommodate individual differences.

References

Barua, S. (2001). An interactive multimedia system on "Computer Architecture, Organization, and Design." *IEEE Transactions on Education, 44,* 41-46.

Burton, L., & Goldsmith, D. (2002). *Students' experience in online course: A study using asychronous online focus groups.* Newington: Connecticut Distance Learning Consortium.

Carter, E. W. (2002). Doing the best you can with what you have: Lessons learned from outcomes assessment. *Journal of Academic Librarianship 28,* 36-41.

Chang, H.H., Henriquez, A., Honey, M., Light, D., Moeller, B., & Ross, N. (1998). *The Union City story: Education reform and technology students' performance on standardized tests.* New York: Center for Children and Technology.

Chen, S.Y. (2002). A cognitive model for non-linear learning in hypermedia programmes. *British Journal of Educational Technology, 33,* 449-460.

Chen, S.Y., & Ford, N.J. (1998). Modelling user navigation behaviours in a hyper-media-based learning system: An individual differences approach. *International Journal of Knowledge Organization, 25*(3), 67-78.

Clark, R., & Lyons, C. (1999). Using Web-based training wisely. *Training, 36*(7), 51-61.

Daugherty, M., & Funke, B.L. (1998). University faculty and student perceptions of Web-based instruction. *Journal of Distance Education, 13*(1), 21-39.

Derry, S. J. (1990). Learning strategies for acquiring useful knowledge. In B.F. Jones & L. Idol (Eds.), *Dimensions of thinking and cognitive instruction* (pp. 347-379). Hillsdale: Lawrence Erlbaum Associates.

Ellis, R. D., & Kurniawan, S.H. (2000). Increasing the usability of online information for older users. A case study in participatory design. *International Journal of Human-Computer Interaction, 12*(2), 263-276.

Evans, C., Gibbons, N.J., Shah, K., & Griffin, D.K. (2004). Virtual learning in the biological sciences: Pitfalls of simply putting notes on the Web. *Computers and Education, 43*, 49-61.

Ford, N., & Miller, D. (1996). Gender differences in Internet perceptions and use. *Aslib Proceedings, 48*, 183-192.

Gay, G. (1986). Interaction of learner control and prior understanding in computer-assisted video instruction. *Journal of Educational Psychology, 78*(3), 225-227.

Hedberg, J.G., & Corrent-Agostinho, S. (2000). Creating a postgraduate virtual community: Assessment drives learning. *Educational Media International, 37*(2), 83-90.

Hui, S., & Cheung, K.P. (1999). Developing a Web-based learning environment for building energy efficiency and solar design in Hong Kong. *Solar Energy, 67*(1-3), 151-159.

Jonassen, D.H., & Grabowski, B.L. (1993). *Handbook of individual differences, learning, and instruction*. Hillsdale: Lawrence Erlbaum Associates.

Ke, H., Kwakkelaarb, R., Taic, Y., & Chenc, L. (2002) Exploring behavior of e-journal users in science and technology: Transaction log analysis of Elsevier's ScienceDirect OnSite in Taiwan. *Library & Information Science Research, 24*(3), 265-291.

Khalifa, M., & Lam R. (2002). Web-based learning: Effects on learning process and outcome. *IEEE Transactions on Education, 45*, 350-356.

Koch, M. (1994). No girls allowed! *Technos, 3,* 14-19.

Last, D.A., O'Donnell, A.M., & Kelly, A.E. (2001). The effects of prior knowledge and goal strength on the use of hypermedia. *Journal of Educational Multimedia and Hypermedia, 10*(1), 3-25.

Lewis, C., & Polson, P.G. (1990). Theory-based design for easily learned interfaces. *HCI, 5*, 191-220.

Liaw, S.-S. (2002). An Internet survey for perceptions of computers and the World Wide Web: Relationship, prediction, and difference. *Computers in Human Behavior, 18,* 17-35.

Linard, M., & Zeillger, G. (1995). Designing navigational support for educational software. *Proceedings of Human Computer Interactions* (pp. 63-78).

McDonald, C. J., Stodel, E. J., Farres, L. G., Breithaupt, K., & Gabriel, M. A. (2001). The demand-driven learning model: A framework for Web-based learning, the Internet and higher education, *4*(1), 9-30.

McGilly, K. (1994). *Classroom lesson: Integrating cognitive theory and classroom practice.* Cambridge: MIT.

Mitchell, T. J. F., Chen, S. Y., & Macredie, R. D. (2005). Hypermedia learning and prior knowledge: Domain expertise vs. system expertise. *Journal of Computer Assisted Learning, 21*, 53-64.

Ng, W., & Gunstone, R. (2002). Students' perceptions of the effectiveness of the World Wide Web as a research and teaching tool in science learning. *Research in Science Education, 32*(4), 489-510.

Owen, M. B., & Liles, R. (1998). *Factors contributing to the use of Internet by educators.* Retrieved from http://outreach.missouri.edu/netc98/manuscripts/owen-liles.html

Power, D. J., & Roth, R. M. (1999). Issues in designing and using Web-based teaching cases. *Proceedings of the Fifth Americas Conference on Information System (AMCIS 1999)* (pp. 936-938).

Quintana, Y. (1996). *Evaluating the value and effectiveness of Internet-based learning.* Retrieved from www.crim.ca/inet96/pa pers/c1/c1_4.htm

Reed, W. M., & Oughton, J. M. (1997). Computer experience and interval-based hypermedia navigation. *Journal of Research on Computing in Education, 30*, 38-52.

Roy, M., & Chi, M. T. C. (2003). Gender differences in patterns of searching the Web. *Journal of Educational Computing Research, 29*, 335-348.

Schwarz, J. (2001). *Lost in virtual space: Gender differences are magnified.* Retrieved October 15, 2002, from www.washington.edu/newsroom/news/2001archive/06-01archive/k061301.html

Shashaani, L. (1994). Gender differences in computer experience and its influence on computer attitudes. *Journal of Educational Computing Research, 11*(4), 347-367.

Shih, C., & Gamon, J. (1999). *Student learning styles, motivation, learning strategies, and achievement in Web-based courses.* Retrieved from http://iccel.wfu.edu/publications/journals/jcel/jcel990305/ccshih.htm

Smaldino, S. (1999). Instructional design for distance education. *Techtrends, 43*(5), 9-13.

Smith, & Parks. (1997). *Virtual hierarchies and virtual networks: Some lessons from hypermedia usability research applied to the World Wide Web.* Retrieved December 4, 1998, from http://ijhcs.open.ac.uk/smith/smith-nf.html

Sridharan, K. (2004). A course on Web languages and Web-based applications. *IEEE Transactions on Education, 47*(2), 254-260.

Torkzadeh, G., & Van Dyke, T.P. (2002). Effects of training on Internet self-efficacy and computer user attitudes. *Computers in Human Behavior, 18,* 479-494.

Wang, S. R., & Jonassen, D. H. (1993, April). *Investigating the effects of individual differences on performance in cognitive flexibility hypertexts.* Annual Meeting of the American Educational Research Association. Atlanta, GA.

Chapter III

Who's Talking Online II:
Revisiting Gender and Online Communications

Taralynn Hartsell, University of Southern Mississippi, USA

Abstract

This descriptive study investigated the association between gender and online com-munication that involved participants from two online graduate courses. The study implemented a descriptive model in that "student involvement" was assessed by tabulating and recording the quantity and quality of student activity in the discussion threads. Quantity was recorded by the amount of times students posted online com-ments and the number of words that women and men used to make their responses. In addition, quality was examined by reviewing the content that women and men made concerning topics under discussion. A difference between the genders was found in that the quantity women contributed to the discussions exceeded the men. Women were also more inclined to give supportive or encouraging remarks than men, and addressed their classmates by name to promote a sense of online com-munity, all of which support previous studies.

Introduction

Delivering courses through the World Wide Web in higher education is a growing trend that has taken precedence at many colleges and universities. As the population of non-traditional students increase and the pervasiveness of computer technology reaches an all-time high in education, delivering online courses has become an alternative medium to offering coursework and degree programs to remote students who are not physically present on campus (Simonson, Smaldino, Albright, & Zvacek, 2003). The push for educators to offer more online courses or adapt existing courses to an online medium will not disappear. In fact, more online courses will be offered to students as an alternative mode for completing educational degree programs, an occurrence that was inconceivable 15 years ago (Picciano, 2001).

This trend for promoting online courses in higher education also creates concerns for both the teacher and student. Some of these concerns include factors such as management, communication, interaction, discipline and retention (Moore & Kearsley, 1996). Communication is one of these key factors for student success. Studies have looked at student isolation and disillusionment as contributory factors toward impairing student retention and effective learning. Communication between student-teacher and student-student is important toward alleviating feelings of isolation. Another aspect of communication is participation. There is an assumption that the more a student participates in an online course, the better success that student will find in acquiring and learning the material related to the course (Picciano, 2001b).

One question that arises concerning online communication is whether gender of the student is a contributing factor toward learning success. Although research has shown that females and males differ in terms of their attitudes toward computer use and computer aptitude, women and men are still both users of computer technology—a direct opposite to the notion that females are not as technologically inclined as males (Whitley, 1996). In addition, many have voiced that the Internet is a more neutral playing field for both men and women to enjoy. In a sense, the Internet has been claimed to lead toward greater gender equity because of its communication interface (Herring, 2001; Gorriz & Medina, 2000). Furthermore, scholars say that the Internet should be taken seriously to help create opportunities for less powerful individuals to participate with members who are more vocal, especially in asynchronous environments (Balka, 1993; Selfe & Meyer, 1991; We, 1993).

Because research on Web-based instruction is relatively new, particularly in the aspect of communication effectiveness in relation to gender, there is a paucity of research that investigates how women and men communicate online. Few studies investigate the use and integration of online communication in reference to gender, but more research needs to be performed that examines the amount of communication that occurs between men and women (Arbaugh, 2000; Shaw & Gant, 2002; Sullivan, 2001). The old assumption that women are more verbal and, thus, more inclined to communicate in online discussions and e-mail needs to be analyzed more closely (Shaw & Gant, 2002; Waldeck, Kearney, & Plax, 2001).

This report describes a study that investigated gender differences in two distance learning courses on the use of online communication tools. The chapter is divided into three sections. First, an overview of the study is discussed in addition to providing a summary of the literature. The literature is primarily based on the area of technology and gender differences in education to help build a theoretical base toward analyzing the influence of gender in online communication activities. Second, the report explains the results of the study, with the gender perspective in mind. The third section discusses the implications and recommendations for online instructors who are teaching diversified student populations, particularly those courses that have an even or odd distribution of women and men.

Overview of the Literature

Many factors influence how women and men use computer technology. It has been assumed that women and men differ in their attitudes toward, comfort with and anxiety levels concerning computer technology (Weiser, 2000). Research has suggested that women and men like to use computers to gain information and complete tasks. The disparities, if any, exist in their interactions toward computer technology and how women and men use the tool (McCoy, Heafner, Burdick, & Nagle, 2001).

Level of anxiety may contribute toward the use of and attitude towards computer technology. According to Whitley (1996), college women exhibited low levels of anxiety when it came to computers, but not as low as men. Among these subjects, Whitley found that less anxious men and women were more likely to take computer courses and spend more time on a computer. Namlu (2003) examined whether learning strategies (LS) were factors in controlling the levels of computer anxiety (CA). She concluded that LS, categorized into simple, advanced and derived, seemed to play an important role in handling CA in that those who had a solid foundation in monitoring their learning progress had lower CA. Hence, anxiety toward computers in association with learning styles can be contributing factors toward how women and men view computers and how they handle technical troubleshooting.

Differences in how the genders perceive technology also contribute toward varying computer usage. Women tend to view the computer as a tool to achieve and complete tasks (Fiore, 1999). They tend to see computer technology, particularly the Internet, as a way to gather information and communicate with others or to promote human interaction. In other words, females see the computer as a "tool" to be used for what it can perform. Males, on the other hand, have viewed the computer more as a recreational toy (Shashaani, 1994). According to the Commission on Technology, Gender, and Teacher Education (2000), males tend to view the computer as a "toy" or an extension of the self. For males, computer technology has been predominantly used for entertainment. In a study conducted by McCoy, Heafner, Burdick and Nagle (2001) that looked at the assimilation of IBM ThinkPads on a university campus, individual computer use was examined through the following categories: tool, communication, resources, entertainment and total use. These categories were compared between the genders using independent t-tests. The researchers discovered that males were more frequent users in the categories of resources, entertainment and total use. There was no significant difference for tool use or communication, meaning that women used the technology for these purposes more than for entertainment. This supports the previous finding that women, more than men, tend to use computer technology as a way to reach out and complete tasks than just "playing" with the technology to see what it can do and retrieve information/programs for personal use.

In regard to distance learning technology and Internet access, any gap that may have been in place between the genders seems to have narrowed (Novak & Hoffman, 1998). In fact, recent research has indicated that more females are enrolling in Web-based online courses and programs with comparable success to males (Ory, Bullock, & Burnaska, 1997). In a study investigating the use and attitudes toward asynchronous learning networks (ALN) in a university setting, Ory, Bullock and Burnaska (1997) discovered that both males and females made equivalent use of ALN and had similar positive attitudes about their experiences. Women also shared a common desire to take more courses that used computers as a result of their experiences with ALN in this situation.

The Internet has been said to be inherently democratic and, thus, leveling traditional distinctions of social status. This, in turn, would create opportunities for those who are often silent to speak out and participate with members of the more powerful group. It has been said that text-based computer-mediated communication allows men and women to participate equally in contrast to traditional patterns of face-to-face conversations. With the absence of physical and auditory cues, the gender of online communicators is irrelevant or invisible (Danet, 1998). This situation could help facilitate free communication between women and men in that gender roles have somewhat been removed.

With the rise of the Internet, researchers have begun to investigate whether gender disparities exist with Internet technology (Shaw & Gant, 2002). Researchers have predicted that males and females will differ in the ways they view and interact with the Internet, hypothesizing that males will be less anxious and more comfortable using the medium compared to females. This proposition supports the idea that women are more "technophobic" than men in that women are more afraid of technology and, therefore, slower to adapt technological advances (Shaw & Gant, 2002). Although studies have found that males report more experience using the Internet and score higher in areas of comfort, innovativeness and Internet self-efficacy, this does not explain the growing numbers of women accessing the Internet (Shaw & Gant, 2002). Women are accessing the Internet just as much as men. The explanation could be attributed to how the women may be using the Internet as compared to males. Communication is a motivating factor for women to seek out social interaction online. Men tend to seek information and entertainment through the Internet, which supports earlier studies on gender and computer usage (Hamburger & Ben-Artzi, 2000).

Based on studies of gender differences in communication and technology usage, the encouragement of collaboration in online courses can be quite favorable toward women. Because previous studies in communication patterns have revealed that men tend to communicate on the basis of social hierarchy, and women are more network-oriented and collaborative, a collaborative Web-based environment may help reverse this process (Kilbourne & Weeks, 1997). Thus, in a setting absent of competition, the playing field can be leveled between the genders.

There have been studies that look at the way men and women communicate in terms of online communication. The use of language and tone are primary areas of difference in that men tend to use more aggressive language to assert their point in the discussion as opposed to women (Herring, 1993; Rossetti, 1998). In addition, women tend to contribute more overt expressions of agreement, appreciation and support. They also present their assertions indirectly as suggestions (Kuntjara, 2002). Gender differences in online communication suggest that women prefer a "rapport" style while men generally speak in the tone of a "report" in that their postings sound as if they are simply providing information (Kuntjara, 2002). Susan Herring (1993) has been investigating gender rhetoric in online communications for quite some time and discovered that the topics of discussion influence the amount and type of participation that women and men contribute. Women tend to participate in discussions that are more associated to the real world than on the abstract and theoretical. Men, on the other hand, tend to be more concerned with receiving information from others and less interested in personal discussion.

Nonetheless, some studies do show the opposite in terms of gender differences in online communication. Kirsteen Monteith (2002) found in her study that women did not hesitate to take control over discussions and were participating equally among themselves. In addition, the women, at times, were dominating the discussions while retaining a collaborative environment. In fact, Monteith discovered that male participants were not the more formal, antisocial and controlling participants. Instead, the men tended to shift toward the collaborative approach by sharing information with others, responding to their female counterparts, and keeping a polite and courteous manner (traditionally a female characteristic). With this gender shift in mind, the Web-based medium does have implications for leveling the ground for all users.

In short, the literature supports the notion that women and men are almost equally equivalent in terms of computer and Internet usage, even though a difference exists in terms of the motives behind the use. Because the literature tends to sustain that communication is the main motive for women to use the Internet, this is an area that needs to be investigated further. The primary question is whether women participate more in online communication than men. In addition, do women's participation exceed men's in terms of quality, in that women explain their perspectives/ideas more thoroughly than men? It has been found that the tone and presence of women and men in their conversation styles differ and, thus, should be looked at more closely.

Purpose of the Study

The goal of this study was to examine whether online communication differed between the women and men enrolled in two distance learning courses. This particular study has been augmented from an earlier preliminary study published by the researcher (Hartsell, 2005). Discussion threads were the primary communication tool used between student-student in this study as opposed to e-mail, and thus, became the instrument of data collection. Discussion threads allow students and teachers to see the "trail of thought" among individuals, as postings to the discussion threads are made in response to previous postings. The research questions investigated in this descriptive study included whether women more than men: (a) participated or made postings to discussion threads, (b) supplied more explanation in their responses to support the topic under discussion, (c) provided more informal responses than formal, and (d) tended to provide more supportive/encouraging comments.

Methodology

Participants

The courses under study were graduate-level instructional technology courses in which 25 students were involved. Twelve females and 13 males participated in this study as participants. Of these 25 participants, 12 were doctoral-level students majoring in educational leadership, communications or mathematics; 10 were master's-level students majoring in instructional technology, and one was majoring in nursing, foreign languages and technology education. Other than for the 10 students majoring in instructional technology, one course used for this study was considered as an elective and/or for fulfilling minor requirements. The other course in this study was an elective for all participants involved. All students were required to interact in discussion threads over a 10-week period that involved topics stemming from course readings. Participants were expected to contribute at least four postings each week in response to the course material. However, a number of participants posted more than what was required.

Design and Measures

The research design was primarily descriptive in nature and the instrument for data collection was the documentation of the actual discussions that took place across the semester between the men and women. The study implemented a descriptive model in that "student involvement" was assessed by tabulating and recording the quantity and quality of student interactivity in the discussion threads. Raw data collected from the transcriptions of discussion threads were examined using a method of calculation rather than employing thick descriptions to explain the setting as in qualitative research.

The research design was not qualitative in that it did not go in-depth or describe the meaning of the findings from the perspective of the research participants. Instead, the data was analyzed by simply counting the words or the number of times a participant posted a response. Quantity was recorded by the amount of times students posted responses to the threads as well as the number of words that women and men used to make their responses. Quality was examined by reviewing the content that women and men made concerning topics under discussion. Tone was also studied, because the literature review indicated that this was a contributing factor in terms of how men used online communication tools as opposed to women. In short, quality of the postings were studied further in detail by looking at who responded to whom, the tone of the posting and whether the response contributed toward the discussion and not just a simple, informal comment made to someone.

Procedures

Data collection occurred during two different semesters. The discussion thread requirement for each course occurred over a 10-week period. Students in the online courses were required to make at least four postings to the weekly discussions, although the opportunity to contribute more was available and optional. The weekly discussion covered topics stemming from the course's reading materials.

The discussions progressed in an organized manner and occurred through WebCT's discussion tool feature. Each week, the students had to read two to three chapters within the textbook or from online articles. Either a facilitator or the instructor posted questions to the discussion threads each week. The weekly discussions began each Monday and concluded the following Monday, in which the instructor closed or locked the discussion thread to prevent miscellaneous postings made to the thread.

The discussion threads that occurred each week were then compiled into a text file that displayed who said what and to whom. With these text files, the postings were broken down by individual participants to help in the calculation of how many times males, as opposed to females, made postings and the number of words made in each posting. The text file was also used to determine whether the postings were in response to someone else's reactions or if a new topic/concern was initiated by the participant. Furthermore, the discussion threads were examined to assess the "quality" aspect of the postings that focused upon two areas: (1) tone of the posting and (2) the value of information given. Discussions were coded for ascertaining the quality aspect. The coding scheme used the following classifications: (a) *I* being informal in tone, more like a discussion or rapport style, (b) *F* being formal in tone, somewhat like a report of the facts, (c) *S* including supportive/encouraging comments and reacting to personal matters, (d) *B* including short replies of one to three sentences long or not really addressing content material, and (e) *R* for postings that directly made reference to course materials. Each discussion posting was coded; some postings had two or more codes ascribed to them because they crossed classifications.

Results

Results of the study are summarized and organized in terms of the original research questions. First, participation patterns for the genders are presented by the aggregate of individual weeks in Table 1. Table 2 shows the minimum, maximum, mean and standard deviation scores separated by gender for all 10 weeks of discussion. As predicted, the women participated more in the discussion threads, as can be seen by the number of postings. Overall, the women posted 91 more responses than their male counterparts. In addition, when one examines the minimum, maximum and mean scores, the women again surpassed their male counterparts in the collective 10-week period. Even for the week that the women did not contribute much toward the discussion, they still made 6 more responses than the men (MIN). These numbers are interesting in that the women comprised the minority group in this study, with 12 individuals as opposed to 13 men. One would expect to see more postings

Table 1. Class participation patterns by gender

Gender	Class postings per week										
	1	2	3	4	5	6	7	8	9	10	Total
Women (*n* = 12)	69	73	88	84	62	81	116	56	68	79	776
Men (*n* = 13)	54	77	84	77	63	63	81	61	50	75	685

Table 2. Frequency of postings by gender for all 10 weeks

Gender	Frequency of postings			
	Min	Max	Mean	SD
Women ($n = 12$)	56	116	77.6	16.78
Men ($n = 13$)	50	84	68.5	11.79

from the majority group of men because they have an additional member. However, this was not the case.

An independent-samples t-test using the total number of postings as the test variable was conducted to evaluate whether gender played a role. The test was not significant, $t(18) = 1.403$, p = .05, and most likely represented a chance occurrence. However, on average, the women did produce more postings to the discussion threads than men. A reason to account for this lack of significance could be due to the small sample size; thus, more participants are required to be included in future studies to help validate the t-tests.

A factorial ANOVA was also conducted to evaluate the effects of class (the two courses) and gender on the number of postings made to the discussion threads. The factorial ANOVA indicated no significant interaction between class and gender, F $(1, 21) = .182$, p = .674, $n^2 = .009$, nor was there a significant effect for gender, F $(1, 21) = 1.585$, p = .222, $n^2 = .070$. However, there was a significant effect for class, F $(1, 21) = 9.279$, p = .006, $n^2 = .306$. The difference between the classes could be attributed to the uneven number of participants in each course and that one course had less discussion activity than the other. Because there were fewer than three groups for the fixed factors, post hoc tests were not conducted in this ANOVA.

Findings from the data also demonstrated that women incorporated more explanation into their postings to support their ideas and opinions. Men tended to get "straight to the point" in their responses, while women wanted to expand and augment what they said through illustrations, experiences and examples. Table 3 presents the number of words used by the women and men in their postings. The results show that women used more words to explain their responses or defend their ideas as opposed to their male counterparts. In all, the women surpassed the men by more than 8,000 words during the 10-week period. Curiously, the men exceeded the women in weeks 1 and 3, but not by a great deal in terms of numbers.

For examining the quality of the responses, the discussion postings were coded into five classifications, as addressed in the procedures section. The distribution of responses according to the codes across the entire 10 weeks can be found in Table 4. The results indicated that women were more outspoken, whether formally or informally. This contradicts previous findings in that women tend to be more informal

Table 3. Number of words used in postings by gender

Gender	Number of words per week										
	1	2	3	4	5	6	7	8	9	10	Total
Women (n = 12)	5,662	10,920	9,342	10,274	8,471	8,119	8,688	8,765	8,509	7,810	86,560
Men (n = 13)	6,142	10,089	9,396	8,688	6,884	7,398	8,339	7,276	6,326	7,679	78,217

Table 4. Coding of discussion postings by gender

Gender	Codes				
	Informal	Formal	Support	Brief	Report
Women (n = 12)	576	97	305	223	90
Men (n = 13)	471	90	162	223	51

in their responses, because in this sample the women also made more formal comments as opposed to their male colleagues. In addition, women tend to give more supportive comments, which are broken down in Table 5. Both women and men were equal in terms of posting brief comments.

When the discussion postings were coded, the S code was broken down into several other classifications. Table 5 depicts the results in terms of the number of responses that have been coded with an S. The S code had been separated into different categories as (a) E for offering support or encouragement; (b) N for referring to people directly by name; (c) A as making a personal apology; (d) P as reacting to personal matters or responding to incidences not really related to class; and (e) D to indicate disagreement. This stratification helped determine what type of support was made by the participants. The results show that women offered more comments that were encouraging and thoughtful. They also directed their comments toward other colleagues by name. Males, on the other hand, exceeded in the area of disagreement, although this was not by a considerable number.

Results for the study show that women, more than men, participated in the discussions. In this case, women made more postings to the discussion threads than males and with greater explanation. In the area of quality, the women also excelled in their responses in terms of content matter and tone. Women also gave more encouraging remarks to others' comments and addressed individuals by name, indicating a sense of intimacy and amiability. In this area, external variables such as students' majors could have influenced the results in that majors in instructional technology would offer more comments in response to the issues addressed. However, this was not the case, because more males than females happened to be majors in instructional

Table 5. Number of postings classified as "S"

Gender	Support Classifications				
	E	N	A	P	D
Women (n = 12)	145	290	12	57	4
Men (n = 13)	78	134	7	19	8

technology. The women were diverse in their concentration fields, which included instructional technology majors (6), educational leadership majors (3) and a foreign languages major (1), nursing major (1) and communications major (1). Thus, the assumption that instructional technology majors would have contributed more because of their familiarity with the subject matter was non-existent in this sample.

Conclusion and Implications

Before addressing the conclusions to this initial study, limitations need to be discussed. First, the study is not generalizable because of the small sample size. In addition, the participants were part of a convenience sampling and not a true random sample. However, this sample could lead to larger studies, because it provided the preliminary basis for identifying exclusive variables to be studied further. Second, this study did not collect the perspectives and reactions from the participants themselves concerning the effectiveness of online communication. A more qualitative approach could be used to obtain such in-depth information as participants' perceptions toward online communication, behavior and learning. Coding of the discussion threads was also a limitation in that an inter-rater reliability test was not performed. Thus, coding conducted by the researcher could be biased. Finally, because the participants were required to make four or more postings a week, this could affect the number of postings made across the 10 weeks in that participation was not always voluntary. If students were concerned about their grades, they would have opted to make more postings than normal. Although limitations existed in this study, this should not discount the findings but be used as questions for further analysis.

This descriptive study investigated whether online communication differed between the women and men enrolled in two distance learning courses through the use of discussion threads. Four research questions were introduced and answered in this study. The first question asked whether women more than men made postings to the discussion threads. As a result, the female participants made more than 90 more postings during the 10-week period than males. Although the independent samples t-test and ANOVA did not indicate this direction, the raw data implied that women in these courses preferred and enjoyed to communicate online. For online courses, instructors should seriously consider integrating online communication tools to help women and men share their ideas with others. This may prevent social isolation that commonly occurs in distance learning courses.

The second question examined whether women supplied more explanation in their responses to support the topic under discussion. The women did surpass the men by more than 8,000 words. This implies that women in the course valued the opportunity to elaborate on their ideas, opinions and experiences without the restraint on length. The finding may also suggest that women enjoy the impartial environment of online communication because they are not obligated to remain within social norms of face-to-face interactions. In short, women can "speak" all they desire because they have a closed audience who will not silence them. For online course instructors, communication tools should be used to promote interaction among students from diverse backgrounds. Without the traditional physical and auditory cues, women may feel more inclined to participate. Thus, online participation should be encouraged by the instructor to offer individuals from non-dominant groups to discuss freely their ideas and opinions without fear of repercussions.

The third question investigated whether women, more than men, used more informal expressions in their responses. When viewing the findings, this was not the case. Women made as many informal responses as they did formal compared to the men. Women did use the "reporting" format that had been normally reserved for men (Kuntjara, 2002). This implies that the women in the courses were not afraid to use the more formal tone to prove their point. They were also adaptable in switching between tones depending on the topic under discussion. Online instructors should take this into account. Incorporating online debates should not be shied away from if course enrollment has more females than males. If these courses have online students who are similar to the participants in this study, women will not have any difficulty taking a more formal approach in defending their ideas.

The last question examined whether women provided more supportive/encouraging comments than their male counterparts. This was true in that the women contributed more encouraging comments than men. The women also addressed their colleagues by name that promoted a sense of familiarity and collaboration, something discovered in previous studies (Kilbourne & Weeks, 1997). This implies that the women searched for collaboration and friendship online, and needed the sense of community more than the men (Shaw & Gant, 2002). For online course instructors, communication tools should be used to promote collaboration, such as assigning group activities, discussing reading materials, deliberating over case studies and so forth. If women feel that they are part of the online community, their learning will be enhanced.

This study only provided the foundation of investigating gender differences in online communication. Some findings discovered in this study supported previous literature/studies, while others did not. Future studies should look into these areas that countered previous research because they could clarify the external variables that may have caused these effects to occur. Further studies should also be conducted to validate and support the findings of this initial study. Investigating a larger sample; using courses that have both undergraduate and graduate students; studying students from various disciplines; and performing more in-depth, qualitative studies should be performed to help support the findings addressed. This study is only the beginning, and many more should be performed to investigate the variables in question. With additional support from other investigations, the relationship between gender and online communication could be exposed and integrated effectively into distance learning activities.

References

American Association of University Women Educational Foundation Commission on Technology, Gender, and Teacher Education. (2000). *Tech-savvy: Educating girls in the new computer age.* Washington, DC: American Association of University Women Educational Foundation. Available at: www.aauw.org/research/girls_education/techsavvy.cfm

Arbaugh, J. B. (2000). An exploratory study of the effects of gender on student learning and class participation in an Internet-based MBA course. *Management Learning, 31*(4), 503-519.

Danet, B. (1998). Text as mask: Gender and identity on the Internet. In S. Jones (Ed.), *Cybersociety 2.0* (pp. 129-158). Thousand Oaks: Sage.

Gorriz, C., & Medina, C. (2000). Engaging girls with computers through software games. *Communications of the ACM, 43*(1), 42-49.

Hamburger, Y.A., & Ben-Artzi, E. (2000). The relationship between extraversion and neuroticism and the different uses of the Internet. *Computers in Human Behavior, 16*, 441-449.

Hartsell, T. (2005). Who's talking online: A descriptive analysis of gender & online communication. *International Journal of Information and Communication Technology Education, 1*(1), 42-54.5.

Herring, S. (1993). Gender and democracy in computer mediated communication. *Electronic Journal of Communication, 3*, 1-16.

Herring, S. (2001). *Gender and power in online communication (CSI working paper)*. Retrieved November 28, 2005, from http://rkcsi.indiana.edu/archive/CSI/WP/WP01-05B.html

Kilbourne, W., & Weeks, S. (1997). A socio-economic perspective on gender bias in technology. *Journal of Socio-Economics, 26*(1), 243-260.

Kuntjara, E. (2002). Gender issues in information technology communication. *Women in Action*, 2. Retrieved March 28, 2004, from www.isiswomen.org/pub/wia/wia202/genderissues.htm

McCoy, L.P., Heafner, T.L., Burdick, M.G., & Nagle, L.M. (2001, April 10-14). Gender differences in computer use and attitudes on a ubiquitous computing campus. *Proceedings of the Annual Meeting of the American Educational Research Association*, Seattle, WA.

Monteith, K. (2002). *Gendered learning and learning about gender online*. Open and Distance Education and Learning at the University of Sterling. Retrieved November 28, 2005, from www.odeluce.stir.ac.uk/docs/Gendered%20Learning.pdf

Moore, M. G., & Kearsley, G. (1996). Fundamentals of distance education. In M.G. Moore & G. Kearsley (Eds.), *Distance education: A systems view* (1st ed., pp. 1-18). Belmont: Wadsworth Publishing.

Namlu, A. G. (2003). The effect of learning strategy on computer anxiety. *Computers in Human Behavior, 19*, 565-578.

Novak, T.P., & Hoffman, D.L. (1998). *Bridging the digital divide: The impact of race on computer access and Internet use*. Project 2000, Vanderbilt University. Retrieved from www.2000.ogsm.vanderbilt.edu/papers/race/science.html

Ory, J. C., Bullock, C., & Burnaska, K. (1997). Gender similarity in the use of and attitudes about ALN in a university setting. *Journal of Asynchronous Learning Networks, 1*(1), 39-51.

Picciano, A.G. (2001). Introduction. In A.G. Picciano (Ed.), *Distance learning: Making connections across virtual space and time* (1st ed., pp. 1-20). Upper Saddle River: Merrill-Prentice Hall.

Picciano, A. G. (2001b). The student perspective. In A.G. Picciano (Ed.), *Distance learning: Making connections across virtual space and time* (1st ed., pp. 89-108). Upper Saddle River: Merrill-Prentice Hall.

Rossetti, P. (1998). Gender differences in e-mail communication. *The Internet TESL Journal, 4*(7). Retrieved November 28, 2005, from http://iteslj.org/Articles/Rossetti-GenderDif.html

Selfe, C., & Meyer, P.R. (1991). Testing claims for on-line conferences. *Written Communication, 8*(2), 162-192.

Shaw, L.H., & Gant, L.M. (2002). Users divided: Exploring the gender gap in Internet use. *CyberPsychology & Behavior, 5*(6), 517-527.

Simonson, M., Smaldino, S., Albright, M., & Zvacek, S. (2003). Foundations of distance education. In M. Simonson, S. Smaldino, M. Albright, & S. Zvacek

(Eds.), *Teaching and learning at a distance: Foundations of distance education* (2nd ed., pp. 4-25). Upper Saddle River: Merrill-Prentice Hall.

Sullivan, P. (2001). Gender differences and the online classroom: Male and female college students evaluate their experiences. *Community College Journal of Research and Practice, 25*, 805-818.

Waldeck, J.H., Kearney, P., & Plax, G. (2001). Teacher e-mail message strategies and students' willingness to communicate online. *Journal of Applied Communication Research, 29*(1), 54-70.

We, G. (1993). *Cross-gender communication in cyberspace* (paper for CMNS 855). Retrieved November 28, 2005, from http://feminism.eserver.org/cross-gender-comm.txt

Weiser, E. B. (2000). Gender differences in Internet use patterns and Internet application preferences: A two-sample comparison. *CyberPsychology & Behavior, 3*, 167-178.

Whitley, B. E. (1996). Gender differences in computer-related attitudes: It depends on what you ask. *Computers in Human Behavior, 12*, 275-289.

Chapter IV

Using a Blended Model to Improve Delivery of Teacher Education Curriculum in Global Settings

Vivian H. Wright, University of Alabama, USA

Ronnie Stanford, University of Alabama, USA

Jon Beedle, University of Southern Mississippi, USA

Abstract

This chapter describes how teacher educators have used a blended approach, online and traditional delivery, to structure course content for its international master's program. The authors discuss challenges they had to overcome, lessons learned, and students' reflections on the blended approach.

Introduction

The delivery of teacher education courses and/or total programs at overseas sites is often complicated and plagued with problems because of the distance between the home university and the location of the students. The Office of International Programs in the College of Education at The University of Alabama offers Master of Arts degree programs in elementary education and secondary education in five locations in Latin America: Asuncion, Paraguay; Bogota, Colombia; Lima, Peru; Mexico City, Mexico; and Quito, Ecuador. The students in these degree programs are teachers in private, United States (U.S.)-type, pre-K-12 schools. The delivery method used in the past has involved sending a professor to the foreign location for about 2 weeks to teach a 3-semester-hour graduate course. The course schedule consists of approximately 3 hours of class Monday through Friday, and 3 to 6 hours of class on Saturday. Two weeks of this daily schedule creates a considerable amount of pressure and strain for the professor in attempting to deliver a quality course in a short period of time, and a large burden on the students who, while taking the course, are also engaged in full-time pre-K-12 classroom teaching. In addition, access to library research materials and other course materials has been complicated because of problems associated with transporting these materials to the country where the course was taught.

Educational technology allows organizations the ability to modify courses and curriculums and, at the same time, become more flexible in their delivery (Kvavik, 2002). Graves (2001) predicted that higher education is moving toward a more student-centric approach and away from the traditional instructor-focused environment. Electronic access to information allows students the opportunity to explore, discover, create and communicate more efficiently than in the past. Virtual classrooms can allow for more creative ways to collaborate and communicate without "the constraint of a physical classroom" (Lao & Gonzales, 2005, p. 471). With these new opportunities come new challenges to serve students at all levels and from locations around the world. The challenges include how to create a system that both works and is user-friendly. Creating an online component through a Web-enabled course has the potential to give instructors and students a greater opportunity for interaction and learning (Dabbagh & Schmitt, 1998) and can possibly provide opportunities for the students to become acquainted with the course assignments/materials and their peers in advance of the beginning of the course. In this chapter, we will describe how we have used computer-based instruction via the Internet and a course management system (WebCT) to create a blended model of course delivery for students that provides a good mixture of technology-based instruction and traditional professor-led classes.

The Challenge

Electronic access of information allows students the opportunity to explore, discover, create and communicate more efficiently than in the past. With these new opportunities come new challenges to serve students at all levels and from locations around the world. Challenges include creating a system that works efficiently; is reasonably user-friendly; and offers opportunities for the students to become acquainted with the course materials, the instructor and their peers in advance of the instructor's on-site arrival. An additional challenge is creating ways technology can extend the learning timeline of the course through activities, assignments and/or assessments that occur after the instructor has departed the overseas location. Lao and Gonzales (2005) noted that instructors who teach online should consider how to "capitalize on the different technological components to make learning meaningful for students" (p. 472).

Our format begins with about 2 weeks of technology-based learning activities prior to the arrival of the professor at the overseas site. The course design includes communication tools, such as e-mail, discussion boards and online chats. Educational hyperlinks are located on the home page so students can access additional course-related references and materials before the instructor arrives. Course content sections are posted on the course WebCT home page, listing assignments to be completed prior to the instructor arriving. These sections also include the syllabus, assignment summary, reading list, course links, course topics, library use instructions, examples of student work, glossary, calendar, and instructions for after the instructor leaves. Such a design provides students with extensive learning activities that the professor extends and amplifies during the 2 weeks he or she is teaching the students in a "normal" face-to-face teaching format. When the professor returns to the U.S., WebCT technology and other online technologies make it possible for students to continue to complete assignments, receive feedback on those assignments and communicate with the instructor regarding questions, readings or discussions of course content. Thus, the technology has allowed us to extend the time frame of the course from the traditional 2 weeks of intensive professor-led instruction to a more relaxed blend of technology and traditional course delivery that lasts 6 weeks or beyond. Our pilot research with several courses and instructors has convinced us that this blend of technology and face-to-face teaching has many advantages for delivery of a teacher education curriculum overseas.

In the past few years, major universities have supplemented traditional library holdings with electronic databases of information that may be searched in a variety of ways. Given the correct set of circumstances (i.e., all of the technology works!), this information can be accessed from any location on the planet. It is now possible to locate, access, read, download and print articles from professional journals that are electronically housed in university library databases. In addition, computer technology and the Internet have made creating, editing and sending course information fast and inexpensive. The technology can include textual information and multimedia content. Similarly, computer technology has made it possible for students to create responses to class assignments and send these to the professor via e-mail or other electronic portals.

In our discussion, we describe how we have used technology to structure courses and course content. In addition, we discuss a variety of problems that had to be overcome to use the technology to maximum effect. We also present results of student evaluation and feedback. Although we describe how we have used technology to assist with course delivery in Latin American, a point to be made is that the technology can be used anywhere the course instructor and the students are separated by distance and/or where limited instructor-student time together is a factor in student learning. We feel that this concept has important implications for how teacher education professors interact with students in all learning environments.

Initial Blended Delivery Experiences

The first course in which we used WebCT was *Modern Elementary/Secondary School Programs,* which was taught in Lima, Peru. The course is an examination of the K-12 school in terms of its overall programs and the trends, issues and problems that impact the school and student learning. In this course, WebCT was used to present a variety of course information to the students. Access to WebCT and the University's computer system was made available to students 2 weeks prior to the professor's arrival in Lima. The materials posted on the WebCT site included the course syllabus, directions for use of University of Alabama online library journal databases, pre-course reading assignments and the specific requirements of writing assignments, including grading rubrics and "good" examples of those assignments. Providing such guidelines and examples helps guide the students through an online experience and online discussions, providing advance organization and structure (Lim, 2004). The pre-course readings were accessed by students via the Internet through the use of electronic databases in the University of Alabama College of Education Library. The result was that students had accomplished significant work prior to the first day of class. Students had prior information and experiences in the course, which allowed the instructor to "hit the ground running" on the first day of the class.

The second pilot course using WebCT was an elective course entitled *Computer-Based Instructional Technology* at the Quito, Ecuador site. The instructor began the class online via WebCT 2 weeks prior to arrival in Quito. Assignments and postings were due up to 2 weeks after the instructor's departure.

The course had 12 main links from the home page. These included sections for before the instructor arrives, syllabus, assignment summary, reading list, course links, course topics, library use instructions, examples of student work, glossary, calendar, discussion board, and instructions for after the instructor leaves. As Deubel (2003) suggested, we used various media throughout the Web site and included colorful graphics and animation useful in directing and keeping the students' attention and focus. Careful guidance by the instructor attempted to provide students with the necessary skills and tools to access the vast relevant resources on the Internet. Prior experience has indicated the necessity to consistently update and enhance the on-line courses, not only from semester to semester, but within the current semester as well. Palloff and Pratt (2001) suggested instructors typically will have a much more positive outlook on using Web-enhanced courses if they are given the freedom to make adjustments each time the course is taught. Additionally, it is essential that instructors understand how to upload content and other information to the Web site to make changes or add more materials. As in the research of others working with boundaries of locations (Ho & Burniske, 2005), we found that employing a teaching assistant and, in our case, an instructional technology graduate student, is helpful in working with faculty and students in troubleshooting problems that may occur in relation to technology.

For students, online discourse may be one of the most important characteristics of pedagogy used to benefit and facilitate effective communicative practice (Pittinsky, 2003). Some of the guidelines we followed are given by Palloff and Pratt (2001) and included collaborative assignments, posting of assignments so that peers can provide feedback, online areas to communicate (discussion boards and e-mail) and requesting a certain number of posts per week to the course Web site.

Following the two initial courses with the blended delivery model, we have had experience with several other courses taught in the overseas sites. One use of technology that was explored was providing overseas students with sample papers written by previous students in the course being taught. In a prior semester, the course professor assigned research papers on a variety of topics. The student's task was to provide a definition of the topic and discussion of how the topic related to elementary and/or secondary school issues. Students were limited to a final product of three pages maximum, including a brief references list. When these papers were graded by the professor, the students made the suggested corrections and gave the professor the edited copy via e-mail attachment. Thus, a mini-library consisting of about 55 edited, electronic papers existed. The professor created a number of CDs that contained the full set of papers and took these to the Latin American location for distribution to students. In teaching a course with a relatively short timeline, the students were given "good" examples of student work, which was used as the basis to begin their assignment. Their assignment was to use the on-campus electronic journal databases to update each paper with the latest references from the literature. In addition, for each topic, class discussion was used to identify new ideas, concepts, points of significance and relationships to other topics.

Another technology-based technique that extended the learning timeline of the course was delaying the final examination until a week or more after the professor had completed the on-site teaching and had departed for the U.S. This simply involved securing a computer lab at the local school at the Latin America site, getting one of the local school administrators to give and proctor the examination, and having the students send their examination answers to the professor via e-mail.

Delaying the final examination created multiple advantages. After 2 weeks of classes, the students were tired and in no mood to write a 2-plus hour discussion examination. The delay in the exam gave students additional time to read and study. The students were in favor of the delay and reported they felt much better prepared for the examination. The instructor graded the exams and sent each student an e-mail regarding the exam evaluation and final course grade.

Student Evaluations

There were 20 students in the Lima class. In this class, the majority of the use of technology was dealing with front loading of assignments. These included specific reading assignments, a first draft of one short research paper and initial research for a second short research paper. Thus, WebCT was used to make assignments, teach students how to use the library databases, show students examples of "good" work and present specific criteria for grading some assignments. Typical of student comments and feedback are the following items from the end of course assessment:

This was AWESOME!! It makes so much more sense to give the assignments (or readings) ahead of time so students can do thorough research and actually take in what is being read instead of rushing around once the course started. I would hope MORE instructors would use this method. Teacher and student satisfaction as well as student learning would increase!

It is very useful to have the info prior to the course. It allows for some preliminary work to be done, which is then reflected upon during the course. Additionally, the work is spread out over a longer period than the 2 weeks of class time.

Other students commented: "I loved this! I appreciated the info ahead of time." and, "I liked it. I felt prepared for the 1st class—it used my time better—I love having access to the database."

Fourteen Quito students were enrolled in the Computer Applications course. The students received e-mail instructions on how to enroll in the WebCT course and how to locate and complete the first assignment. Once this first assignment was completed, students were then directed fully from the WebCT instructions for each topic associated with the class. Tutorials on how to complete the assignments and links to helpful Internet sites were all part of the WebCT course. Additionally, students were required to use the WebCT e-mail tool to communicate with the instructor and others enrolled in the class. Students also completed several assignments via the discussion board. After the instructor's on-site teaching, and, on her return to campus, the instructor queried the students via the discussion board on their blended course delivery experience. Overall, the comments were positive and students enjoyed and appreciated the interactivity of the course. One student noted: "This is a good way to keep in touch with the teacher and also with the rest of the students. With this page we can read what the other classmates think about a certain topic, which is good." Another student wrote: "Overall, the WebCT experience for me has been technologically enriching and challenging, but not beyond comprehension with some effort."

Of the problems students noted in this discussion posting, most were associated with logging onto the course Web site with the first assignment, presented online in portable document files (PDFs) format. One student commented, "I don't feel confident and sure about if I'm doing the correct job. I had problems with topic one, because my computer couldn't open it." Another wrote:

It took me a while to find the 'Log in to WebCT' button because it seems to be only "a title." When I opened the page, all my attention was drawn to the different options listed for students, faculty/staff and other. I just didn't realize that the button was in front of me, so I think that it could help others if you add a 'click here to ...' next to the login button.

A couple of the students noted that the calendar tool had not been updated promptly as assignment due dates were adjusted, with one student writing, "Another recommendation would be to allow students to have the original tentative calendar with the teacher's entries and to create a new one with the modifications that the teacher sends afterwards."

In addition to articulating the problems they experienced, several students noted positive attributes regarding the feedback, instructions and interactivity with other students. For example, one student wrote, "In terms of logging in to the program, I did not have any problems ... instructions sent via e-mail were clear." Another commented, "The system is user friendly, I have found clear instructions and tutorials. There are many helpful links, too." Another student wrote that he was surprised more instructors do not use an online component, writing, "I have been really surprised how little and how rarely this technology has been taken advantage of." Finally, a student noted, "It has the possibility to unite people over vast distances."

What We Learned

Potential problems that must be addressed before the class begins deal with issues relating to student enrollment in the WebCT course and the necessity of each student acquiring a university-wide login and password for use with all university-related technology systems. It was imperative that students be "officially" enrolled early to ensure they received their university-wide account information in order to access the Web site and the university's online library databases. A registration problem sometimes occurs with short-term courses offered during the middle of a semester. Most university registration systems are set up to enter student enrollment data at the beginning of the semester. Adding student registration information into the university's student database at an odd time (i.e., other than the beginning of the term) can be a major challenge. Student information services can vary, and traditional identifiers, such as a social security numbers, student numbers or other "passwords" may not always apply. These details were addressed with the University's administrative structure prior to "registering" the class and with sufficient lead time to get all contact procedures working before students were informed that they could access the University's technology infrastructure. Additionally, a library tutorial was created and posted on the WebCT course home page in both PDF and Hyper Text Markup Files (HTML) formats. From past instructor experiences with online supplements, we were aware that some students' network connections at home, work or school were of limited bandwidth and the use of PDF files would result in longer download times, therefore requiring our use of html files in addition to PDF files. Network security, preferences and connectivity vary at each Latin American site. It is helpful to create a list of programs being used and any specific technological needs and questions prior to the course starting. Typically, each school has designated technical support personnel who can help troubleshoot and anticipate potential problems.

It was our goal to not give students too much technology in the beginning but to scaffold the technology into the course by allowing the students to become familiar with WebCT through the "Before Instructor Arrives" assignment on the home page. This process worked well with the pilot courses, with the exception of some students who did not have an Adobe Reader loaded on their machines and therefore could not read the PDF file. This problem created additional e-mails between the instructor and students prior to the instructor's arrival on-site. We noted this for future revisions to the Web site. It is important to constantly note and work toward eliminating any problems that might occur with the technology. With the International Programs office located in one country and the students located in another, it is sometimes difficult to understand some of the problems students might encounter. The instructors for the pilot courses maintained field notes of all problems encountered throughout the weeks of instruction in an effort to better inform future instructors using the WebCT model. For example, some students had problems learning to access and manipulate the library databases, and other students had problems properly posting to the threaded discussions.

The Murphy's Law dictum "Anything that can go wrong will!" certainly applies to using technology through a platform such as WebCT, especially when it is accessed through the security maze of a university-based computer system. The debugging process can be lengthy and trying. Students get easily frustrated and short tempered when things don't work "as advertised." Professors need to be prepared to devote a large amount of time to trouble shooting and assisting students with a variety of problems. There are also networking issues related to accessing the university's WebCT server and the library's database server from Latin American countries. These issues of access and connection speed continue to present challenges.

Conclusion

The students involved in our blended delivery courses believed there were many advantages to using this approach. Our philosophy is that the blended teaching approach offers a number of advantages. Students gained supplementary content through the online instruction, while gaining additional skills and knowledge using Web-based materials and interacting with their peers and instructor. Student access to educational research through library electronic databases is a major asset in increasing the quality of teacher education via distance education. The students must be able to e-mail the instructor with any problems or questions about the course before the instructor's arrival at the course site. Another important issue is the ability of the instructor to respond to student inquiries in a timely manner.

Planning is a key component in making the blended delivery methodology model work to its maximum potential. The instructor must carefully think through the entire course and plan the total learning experience well in advance of the first class. It has been helpful for the authors to think of the course in three components: (1) prior to the instructor's arrival; (2) while the instructor is on site; and (3) after the instructor departs. Each of these components may be elaborated as follows:

Prior to the instructor's arrival:

- Selection of the course delivery software and learning the limits of its use are essential. Many educational institutions are making a commitment to a course management system. Potential technology-based instructors are advised to determine if a particular platform is supported by their institution and to secure in-house staff development regarding its use.

- Planning the course should entail creation of assignments that the students will be asked to complete prior to, during and after the professor's time of face-to-face instruction. In addition to the assignments, methods of providing students with instructor feedback must be created.

- Instructions to students for using various aspects of the technology must be created and tested. Everything that students will be asked to do should be tested using technology infrastructure equivalent to what students will be able to access in their home location.

While the instructor is on-site:

- Instruction should include follow-up and feedback to students regarding assignments made prior to the instructor's arrival on-site.

- Instruction should be designed to take maximum advantage of student learning achieved prior to the instructor's arrival.

- Instruction can be slanted toward creating conditions and situations that will most effectively support learning assignments to be completed after the instructor departs.

- Student evaluation of the use of technology prior to and during the instructor's time on site should be secured. It is recommended that both formal and informal student feedback be solicited.

After the instructor departs:

- Methods of completing final course assignments and communicating these to the instructor must be in place.

- Opportunities for students to communicate with each other regarding assignments and learning activities should be considered. It is important for students to communicate with the instructor, but it is equally important for students to communicate with each other.

- Evaluation of student learning should be considered, especially how to effectively structure any examinations that may be needed.

- Methods should be created through which the instructor can provide students with feedback regarding their individual learning and the major elements of learning experienced by the entire class. Too often, students do "end of course" work and have no idea of its value or validity. The use of technology after instruction is formally concluded makes such feedback possible.

Success in implementing our past courses and future courses for the International Programs office will continue to rely on continuous evaluation and instructor/student reflections. Instructors should be trained on the use of WebCT tools (or the course management system of choice). Students should also receive advance instruction through the development of tutorials or extensive e-mail instruction prior to first use. Students in the pilot courses appreciated clear instructions in addition to the immediate feedback of the instructor and the interaction WebCT tools afforded them with the other students enrolled. Overall, our experience with the blended delivery approach of Web-based instruction coupled with traditional professor-led classes has encouraged us to continue to experiment with and refine the process.

References

Dabbagh, N., & Schmitt, J. (1998). Redesigning instruction through Web-based course authoring tools. *Educational Media International, 35*(2), 106-110.

Deubel, P. (2003). An investigation of behaviorist and cognitive approaches to instructional multimedia design. *Journal of Multimedia and Hypermedia, 12*(1), 63-90.

Graves, W. H. (2001). Transforming traditional faculty roles. In C.A. Barone & P.R. Hagner (Eds.), *Technology-enhanced teaching and learning: Leading and supporting the transformation on your campus* (pp. 35-44). San-Francisco: Jossey-Bass.

Ho, C., & Burniske, R.W. (2005). The evolution of a hybrid classroom: Introducing online learning to educators in American Samoa. *TechTrends, 49*(1), 24-29.

Kvavik, R. B. (2002). E-business in higher education. In R.N. Katz & Associates (Eds.), *Web portals & higher education: Technologies to make IT personal* (pp. 41-68). San-Francisco: Jossey-Bass.

Lao, T., & Gonzales, C. (2005). Understanding online learning through a qualitative description of professors and students' experiences. *Journal of Technology and Teacher Education, 13*(3), 459-474.

Lim, C. P. (2004). Engaging learners in online learning environments. *TechTrends: Linking Research & Practice to Improve Learning, 48*(4), 16-21.

Palloff, R. M., & Pratt, K. (2001). *Lessons from the Cyberspace classroom: The realities of online teaching*. San Francisco: Jossey-Bass.

Pittinsky, M. S. (2003). Transformation through evolution. In M.S. Pittinsky (Ed.), *The wired tower: Perspectives on the impact of the Internet on higher education* (pp. 1-11). Upper Saddle River: Pearson Education.

Chapter V

The Genesis, Political, and Economic Sides of the Internet

Andrew Targowski, Western Michigan University, USA

Abstract

The purpose of this chapter is to show that the Cold War is behind the invention of the Internet. This is one of very few positive results of this war, which had tremendous influence on the further development of civilization. The research on the universality of info-communication processes was conducted on both sides of the Iron Curtain, which indicates the similarities in engineering thinking, regardless of geographic locations. The political meaning of the Internet does not only result from its history but also stands for the support of democratic development and the obstruction of dictatorships. The history of the Internet is also an example of the development of great engineering talents and research and development centers, which rise to the occasion on such ambitious projects. All of these aspects of the Internet will be investigated in this chapter, as well as its impact on the emergence of the global civilization.

Introduction

The purpose of this chapter is to show that the Cold War is behind the invention of the Internet. This is one of very few positive results of this war, which had tremendous influence on the further development of civilization. Research on the universality of info-communication processes was conducted on both sides of the Iron Curtain, which indicates the similarities in engineering thinking, regardless of the geographic locations.

The political meaning of the Internet does not only result from its history but also stands for the support of democratic development and the obstruction of dictatorships. The history of the Internet is also an example of the development of great engineering talents and research and development centers, which rise to the occasion on such ambitious projects. All of these aspects of the Internet will be investigated in this chapter, as well as its impact on the emergence of the Global Civilization.

Challenges of the Cold War

The Cold War began to take shape just before the end of the World War II in April 1945 when President Harry Truman reprimanded Vyacheslav Molotow, the Soviet Foreign Minister and Stalin's confidant for sabotaging the Yalta Agreement in Poland, where a free election was postponed. Formally speaking, the Cold War began after Winston Churchill's speech on the Iron Curtain in Fulton, Missouri, on March 5, 1946. He said that an "Iron Curtain had fallen from Stettin in the Baltic to Triest in the Adriatic. The Soviets had installed pro-communist governments in every country which had been occupied by the Red Army as well in the Soviet zone of Germany" (Kissinger, 1994).

The Cold War lasted 46 years, from 1946 to 1991, when the Soviet Union collapsed. This war relied on the symmetry of military power between the United States (U.S.) and the USSR, who both kept their respective military forces in balance to avoid unwanted military confrontations. The U.S. treated this war as a means of promoting democracy and containing communism (Kennan, 1947), while the USSR used the war to conduct the double standard, officially promoting world peace and unofficially looking for the opportunity to defeat capitalism (Targowski, 2000).

The politics of communist containment was implemented by the strategy of circling the USSR by friendly states, which hosted American bases (Spykman, 1942, 1944). In Europe, NATO was organized to counter the Warsaw Pact armies (Moczulski, 1999). The architecture of the Cold War is shown in Figure 1.

Figure 1. The architecture of the Cold War and its major weapons

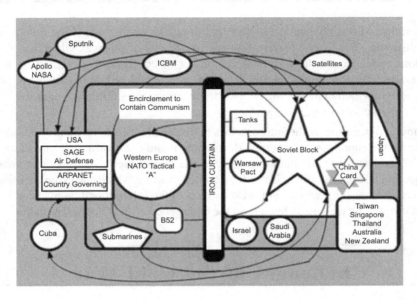

The Cold War was a good pretext for the development of different kinds of weapons, which pushed scientific and technological progress forward both in military and civilian areas. In this respect, the Soviets surprised the Americans when they sent Sputnik 1 into space in 1957. This was a message that the Soviets were transforming from the aircraft to the rocket-oriented strategy to reach the American homeland. In the U.S., there took place a short-lived consternation, which led towards the growth of funding for universities and research.

The development of American weaponry in the period of the Cold War was oriented around systems of communications, information, transportation and efficient destruction armaments as follows:

1. Offensive systems:

    1.1. Fusion bombs to enhance the striking power of the Air Force

    1.2. Long-range bombers, such as the B29 and B52

    1.3. "Polaris" atomic submarines

    1.4. Project Atlas: the development of Intercontinental Ballistic Missiles (ICBMs) during the 1950s

    1.5. Satellite technology for gathering intelligence in the 1950s

     1.6. Space technology for ruling space – the Apollo Project in the 1960s

     1.7. Other

2. Defensive systems:

     2.1. Semiautomatic Ground Environment Project (SAGE) – a real-time computer-and-radar-based air defense system, created in the 1950s under the Atlas project, to collect and process information for commanding the Air Force in defending the country

     2.2. A reliable telecommunication network ARPANET, later transformed into the Internet to assure governing the country "the day after" an atomic assault

     2.3. Other

3. Management and problem-solving systems:

     3.1. System analysis in the 1950s

     3.2. PERT in the 1960s

     3.3. Intelligence, Command, Control and Communication (I/C^3) in the 1960s

     3.4. Other

In the 1950s-70s, military-funded projects dominated the technological and management landscape. These projects were developed in the so-called military-industrial-university complex. Many young engineers and scientists had chosen to work in this complex, since they believed that they were responding to the threats of the Soviet Union. The commitment of these professionals, however, began to erode in the 1960s during the Vietnam War, and with the rise of counterculture values, were strongly present in the San Francisco Bay area.

Among the then-leading research centers was the RAND Corporation, created in 1948 in Santa Monica, Calif., and later transformed into the Air Force's Think Tank. Other leading centers were the MITRE Corporation, Western Development Division (WDD) of the Air Force Research and Development Command, the Ramo-Wooldridge Corporation, the Advanced Research Project Agency (ARPA), Betchel/Persons Brinckerhoff and the National Aeronautic and Space Administration (NASA).

At the beginning of its existence, RAND was involved in the development of the U.S. atomic strategy and later undertook projects on research operations and system analysis to optimize the complexity of large-scale weapons. For RAND, it was just one step in moving from system analysis to systems of info-communications in the military.

The Political Genesis of the Internet

In 1959-60s, the Cold War was dominated by the strong personalities of Soviet Premier Nikita Khrushchev and the American President John F. Kennedy. After sending Sputnik to space in October 1957, on November 10, 1958, Khrushchev delivered a speech demanding an end to Berlin's four-power status and warning that the Soviet Union intended to turn control of its access over to its German satellite. In May, 1960 an American U-2 spy plane was shot down over the Soviet Union. The summit in Paris was cancelled by the Russian Prime Minister. By the time John F. Kennedy entered office, one of his first projects was the attempt to send Cuban exiles to overthrow Fidel Castro at the Bay of Pigs in April 1961.

In the summer of 1961, the U.S. confronted the Soviet Union over the divided city of Berlin. Opposing Khrushchev's effort to break the long-standing impasse over Berlin on Soviet terms, Kennedy announced a new military buildup and employed martial rhetoric to summon U.S. citizens to a new test of their resolve. In response, the Soviets constructed the Berlin Wall in 1961, the hardware of the Iron Curtain. The following year, in 1962, the Soviet Union began building missile bases in Cuba, which threatened the U.S.. President Kennedy ordered a naval blockade of Cuba and demanded that the Russians remove the missiles. Faced with the threat of war, Khrushchev agreed to dismantle the bases if the U.S. secretly agreed to withdraw nuclear-tipped missiles from nearby Turkey.

The Technical Genesis of the Internet

After the Cuban crisis, the Americans became aware of how close to catastrophe they were if Soviet rockets could be launched from Cuba, just about 90 miles away from American soil. In such a political climate, the U.S. government initiated work on communication systems that could function the "day after." These systems brought the Internet to our civilization practice.

The official birth of the Internet is associated with the development of ARPANET in 1969-'72 by ARPA (located at the DoD (DoD) since 1958). At the beginning of its existence, ARPA was involved in researching how to detect attacking rockets and the enemy's atomic tests. In 1959, ARPA began sponsoring a research project on interactions between an operator and computer within a system of control-command. This project was done by the System Development Corporation (SDC), which trained hundreds of future computer programmers. It is worth mentioning that at that time, the education of computer specialists was in its infancy.

Prior to ARPA's involvement in the development of ARPANET, one must take into account RAND's work on telecommunication systems in the late 1950s. This was the post-Sputnik period, when both sides of the Cold War were developing intercontinental ballistic missiles targeted at the enemy's communication systems to stop the country's activities. Without an efficient communication system, the U.S. could not function. In 1959, Paul Baran began to work at RAND, and his first major project was to define the feasibility of a survivable communication system.

At RAND, Baran spent 2 years creating a workable design and another 3 years trying to prove it could work. In other words, his initial research lasted 5 years (1959-1964) until he could write an 11-volume outline of a decentralized network where the nodes have a redundancy level of three, thus making it extremely resistant to destruction. His ideas were published in open literature in 1964. "We felt," Baran said, "that it properly belonged in the public domain." Not only did RAND create it, they sent it to laboratories around the world. Therefore, RAND did not apply for a patent. These ideas have become the basis for the modern Internet.

In 1959-1964, years of the Berlin and Cuban crises, Baran was asking the question, "What is the minimum requirement for a survivable communication system?" He calculated that the U.S. network of AM radio stations could be used to relay messages by attaching a little digital logic at each of the broadcast "nodes." With this design, it would be possible to send a message under almost any circumstance, because once a message was sent, it would continue transmitting itself until copies of it bounced back. However, the idea was scoffed at by military leaders for lack of enough bandwidth.

To develop more communication capacity and efficiency, Baran devised five guidelines:

1. The network cannot be centralized
2. The network of nodes must have distribution, each node connected to more than one neighbor (Figure 2)
3. The network must have redundancy, which is where each node must be connected to more nodes than necessary for normal communications
4. Messages should be divided into small blocks, called "packets"
5. Message blocks should be digital rather than analog

Baran's inspiration for a non-centralized system is based on human brain functioning. He knew that the most reliable network is the human brain. His question was: How does the brain work? Does it have any centralized points? With such questions, Baran contacted a brain surgeon, Warren McCullough of the Massachusetts Institute of Technology. He said that if "you cut a piece of the brain or damaged a part, its functions will move over to the undamaged part." "So that is a distributed network—neurons connected to one another" (Baran, 2003).

Figure 2. Three topologies of a network

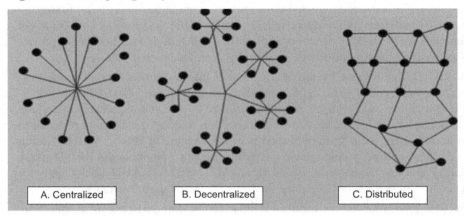

| A. Centralized | B. Decentralized | C. Distributed |

A distributed network was only a part of the plan. Baran's "decisive invention" was packet switching. This invention has changed the world. Baran's solution breaks a message into small blocks; hence, its transmission is more efficient. These small blocks can take a variety of routes and be rebuilt at the destination's node. It is how data travels online today.

To achieve the best transmission quality, message blocks must be digital, not analog, according to Baran's solution. Digital signals, unlike analog ones, do not degrade every time they are transmitted. Furthermore, if the signal is damaged, several error-correcting procedures can be used to correct distortions.

Moreover, Baran divided the signal into what he calls "message blocks." The message is broken into several data streams, and each is independently routed, using packet switching, for a destination. The network would relay each segment without any centralized control. He developed a rapid store-and-forward algorithm that indicates the best possible route to the destination. In addition, the table is constantly being updated by information on neighboring nodes.

The centralized network has all its nodes connected to a central switching node to allow simple switching, giving it a single point of high vulnerability; for example, a single explosion could destroy the point of control. The decentralized network, representative of the AT&T long-distance network at the time, is better. Instead of a single central switching node, the network comprises small-centralized clusters, with most traffic going to nearby neighbors, and only the longer-distance traffic routed to the longer links.

The distributed network is a network without any hierarchical structure; thus, there is no single point of vulnerability to bring down much of the network. Manhattan has streets organized in a semi-distributed network, while Paris is organized into a decentralized streets network.

The latter had been built by a police chef (Haussman) to stop revolutionary crowds. However, in today's environment, this network slows traffic, while it's still manageable in downtown New York City, due to its streets network.

The DoD wanted AT&T to develop Baran's network. AT&T replied that, "it's not going to work, and furthermore, we're not going into competition with ourselves." A few years later, Baran said: "The 'Net's biggest threat wasn't the USSR, it was the phone company" (Baran, 2003). Because of the roadblocks at AT&T and the Pentagon, it wasn't until the 1970s that the technology was finally adapted as the foundation architecture of ARPANET, the precursor of the Internet.

Baran's Vision of the Web and Projects

Around December 1966—when IBM had just introduced its famous IBM 360 series with disks and online capability of processing transactions and queries, the first mature solutions in the industry—Baran presented a paper at the American Marketing Association called "Marketing in the Year 2000." He described push-and-pull communication and how we are going to do our shopping via television set and virtual department store. This is pretty much what Web TV is today. Some in the audience were furious. They said, "People don't go shopping to buy things. They go there because of the enjoyment." Today, online shopping has not replaced traditional shopping, but it remains very popular.

The architect of the Internet, Baran, quit RAND and moved to the private industry as an entrepreneur. He and Millard started a string of companies specializing from consulting to satellites. In 1972, the two men founded CableData Associates, with an initial contract to study the divestiture of ARPANET into MILINET and INTERNET. The next set of companies is rich: The latest one is Com21 Inc., founded by him in 1992, which is a major supplier of cable modems and head ends for cable systems. Baran also works to preserve the history of technology as a member of RAND President's Council, as a trustee of the IEEE History Center, a trustee of the Charles Babbage Foundation and a trustee of the Marconi Foundation at Columbia University. He is recipient of many honors and awards. To mention a few: Armstrong Award (1987); Alexander Graham Bell Medal (1990); Electronic Frontier Foundation Pioneer Award (1993); IEEE's Life Fellow (1993); Franklin Institute Bower Award and Prize for Achievements in Science (2001; he received $250,000, later donated by Baran to education); and more.

The Next Milestones of the Internet's Development

The Information Processing Techniques Office (IPTO) at ARPA was supported by Congress generously. IPTO initiated the ARPANET project in 1966 to interconnect time-sharing computers at the 17 ARPA-founded academic, industrial and government computer centers around the country. This project had in mind the electric-generating station analogy to optimize capacity utilization through sharing of computer resources to meet demand. This was a time when the cost of large-scale computing could be in the tens of millions of dollars.

The future designers of ARPANET were supposedly more familiar with Leonard Kleinrock's dissertation (published in 1964) on "time slicing," which anticipated packet switching and distributed control in data networks, than with Baran's concept (Hughes, 1998). On the other hand, "time slicing" as a concept of time-sharing was implemented by General Electric (GE) in its "225" computer in 1962, which applied John Kemeny's interactive BASIC language. It is hard to accept the view that RAND's major project developed by Baran for the DoD was not known by the DoD's ARPA researchers.

The next milestones of future Internet solutions are as follows:

- **1967:** Interface Message Processors (IMP) are defined by Lawrence Roberts at ARPA.
- **1969:** IMP hardware and software are developed by Bolt Beranek and Newman (BBN) company, where the project was led by Frank Heart and Robert Khan. Also, Honeywell's crew adapted Honeywell 516 computer as an IMP.
- **1972:** Network Control Program (NCP), including host-to-host and host-to-IMP protocols, was defined and implemented by the Network Working Group at UCLA, led by Kleinrock.
- **1972, August:** 15 host-computer sites connected to the network were using the NCP protocol; however, the network ran at only 2% capacity.
- **1973:** E-mail constituted 75% of ARPANET traffic, giving the greatest stimulus for the growth of the 'Net.
- **1974:** Transmission Control Protocol/Internet Protocol (TCP/IP) was defined by Vinton Cerf and Robert Kahn.
- **1983:** The DoD decided that all ARPANET computers must apply TCP/IP and not the OSI standard.
- **1983:** The DoD divides ARPANET (with hundreds of host computers) into MILINET and a public net, after advice from Baran and Millard.

- **1984:** Internet is named and the TCP/IP protocol adapted.
- **1989:** World Wide Web (WWW) was created by Tim Berners-Lee at CERN in Geneva, Switzerland.
- **1990:** Information Superhighway – Al Gore.
- **1992:** The Internet Society, a private non-profit group, supports the Internet Activity Board (IAB), which handles much of the Internet's behind-the-scenes and architectural issues.
- **1993:** Mosaic, the first user-friendly software-oriented browser, was developed by Marc Andreseen at the University of Illinois.
- **1994:** Netscape, the first commercial-friendly software-oriented browser was developed by Andreseen at the Mosaic Communications Group (later renamed to Netscape), which was bought by America onLine (AoL) in 1998.
- **1995:** First version of Microsoft's Internet Explorer was launched, which in the 1990s has about 70+ percent of the browsers' market.
- **1997:** E-commerce takes off, Amazon.com – Jeff Bezos.
- **1998:** Growth of the New Economy (Global Economy based on the Net).
- **1999:** Internet2 created. It is a project led by 200+ universities working with corporations to develop a leading-edge network for the national research community.
- **2000:** Dot.Com crisis.
- **2001:** The rise of an e-republic.
- **2003:** The rise of an e-enterprise.
- **2004:** About 1 billion users of the Internet in Global Economy.
- **2005:** Emergence of Global Civilization and "flattened" world.

Political Consequences of the Internet

The development of a universal telecommunication network is of great importance for politics and civilization. As indicated, the Internet is a product of the Cold War, when at its peak in 1972 it reached the first phase of development, connecting 15 centers within the pilot system of ARPANET. It is necessary to mention that behind the Iron Curtain, a concept of the INFOSTRADA was launched in the same year, 1972. *La strada* means "highway" in Italian; hence, with an exception in Germany, all European highways are called "*autostrada*." The Polish INFOSTRADA was planned to transform Poland from an uninformed to informed society within the communist regime. Already in 1973, three nodes, Gdańsk – Warsaw – Katowice, had been interconnected via Singer 10 computers (IMP) within a "packet switch-

Figure 3. National Information System and INFOSTRADA (Targowski model, 1972)

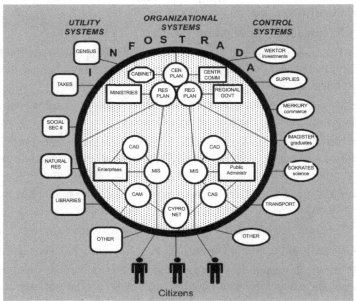

ing" network. Targowski learned about the technical solutions of ARPANET from Dr. L. Roberts during the Diebold Research Program Conference in Madrid in June 1971. The project, in addition to the Polish funds, was also sponsored by $1 million from the Singer Corporation, which wanted to apply tested solutions in its business in the U.S. However, ARPANET was designed to interconnect super-computers of scientific centers, while INFOSTRADA (Figure 3) was planned to support a flow of economic-social information among main organizations and citizens within the National Information System. Very soon, the communist authority found that IN-FOSTRADA led to the uncontrollable flow of information, and immediately the project was closed and its leaders, including the author, were put out of the job market (Targowski, 1991, 2001).

Of course, the INFOSTRADA project was not foreign to the Central Intelligence Agency (CIA), since it was widely publicized in the Polish press. At that time, a young Congressman—Albert Gore—was member of the Intelligence Committee and had to know all about the Polish project. When he became vice president of the U.S., he translated "INFOSTRADA" into "Information Superhighway" and admitted as much in the December 1995 issue of *Wired* magazine (Hellman, 1995). This idea soon became the leading concept for the development of all sorts of information infrastructures, triggering the emergence of the so-called New Economy in the U.S. as well as in the "new" Global World.

Figure 4. Relations among civilization revolutions

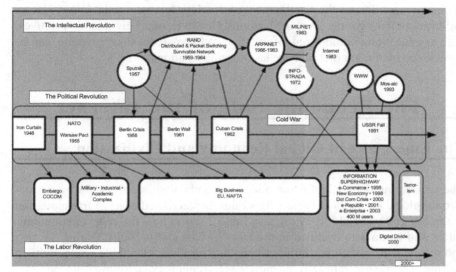

The Internet on the global scale supports the free-flow of info-communication and is positive for the expansion of democracy and negative for political or theocratic dictatorships. These types of dictatorships censor the info-communication flow on their servers. These attempts are reminiscent of the Pony Express strategy, where faster horses were introduced when the telegraph was introduced for the first time in America. Of course, the Internet enables the dissemination of criminal info-communications, including those among terrorists. The issue of practically applying ethics to the Internet is a hot topic among many societies. For example, in Russia, e-commerce cannot be applied due to dishonest practice of all involved parties, including gangsters.

Figure 4 illustrates the relationships among intellectual, political and labor revolutions. This model proves how these relationships are important for each type of revolution development.

The Social Consequences of the Internet

The use of the Internet requires access to a computer and an Internet service provider (ISP), which can be afforded by people with some resources. Hence, the digital divide issue takes place not only in underdeveloped countries but in developed ones, too. Nowadays, in the world there are 1 billion people with a password to a computer net and 5 billion without such a password. This leads towards the bifurcation of civilization and all of the negative consequences of it. One can say that the Internet accelerates the development of developed nations and relatively slows the development of underdeveloped nations. However, many civilization positives, such as education, training, and information and knowledge dissemination, can be accelerated by the Internet in those less-fortunate nations.

The Economic Side of the Internet

The Emergence of Global Economy and Civilization

These transportation and info-communication technologies provide the infrastructure for global operations. Table 1 illustrates the decreased costs of transportation in the last 160 years (1830-1990), and Table 2 shows how the costs of communication and computers declined in the last 40 years (1960-2000). During the first and second waves of globalization, technology provided incredible productivity in making and moving things. In the third wave, technology is driving the productivity of information itself.

Information and communication technology (ICT) triggers a shift in the post-industrial society's *modus operendi*, which is based on new key features (Bell, 1981):

1.   The shift from a goods-producing to a service economy

2.   The increasing reliance on theoretical knowledge

3.   Creation of a new "intellectual technology" based on computers and other smart machines

Table 1. Transport costs, 1830-1990 (Sources: Baldwin and Martin, 1999, World Economic Outlook, May 1997, Table 11)

Year	Ocean Transport		Average Air Transportation
	Wheat, Percent of Production Cost	Ocean Freight	Revenue per Passenger Mile (in 1990 US $)
1830	79		
1850	76		
1880	41		
1910	27.5		
1920		100	
1930		65	0.68
1940		67	0.46
1950		38	0.30
1960		28	0.24
1970		29	0.16
1980		25	0.10
1990		30	0.11

Table 2. Communication and computer costs, 1960-2000 (Sources: World Economic Outlook, May 1997, Table 11, updated to 2000; U.S. Commerce Department, Bureau of Economic Analysis and Masson [2001])

Year	Cost of a 3-Minute Telephone Call, New York to London (in 2000 US $)	Price of Computers and Peripheral Equipment Relative to GDP Deflator
1960	60.42	1,869,004
1970	41.61	199,983
1980	6.32	27,938
1990	4.37	7,275
2000	0.40	1,000

Manuel Castells (1996) observes that, "what has changed is not the kind of activities humankind is engaged in, but its technological ability to use as a direct productive force what distinguishes our species as a biological oddity: its superior capacity to process symbols." ICT technology does not replace agriculture and industry, but optimizes them. It leads towards the "informatization" of the Global Society, which by connecting all of us makes us the Global Open Society (Anderson, 2004). The emerging Global Digital Consciousness (GDC) as the symbiosis of humans and machines provides cognition and external memory systems that support Global Civilization and vice versa. Hence, the GDC is composed of:

- *infosphere* (computerized info-communication systems composed of databases, applications and networks),
- *cyberspace* (the Internet and Web applications),
- *mediasphere* (radio, TV, cable), and
- *mindsphere* (global ideas generated by previous global spheres).

The Globalization Index, which breaks down globalization into its most important component parts, indicates that the "most wired" countries in the world are beneficiaries of globalization. The Globalization Index tracks the movements of money in terms of investments and business transactions in the era of "electronic capitalism" (Bledsoe, 2001).

The fourth wave of modern globalization at the beginning of the 21st century leads towards the emergence of Global Civilization, because this civilization meets the general criteria of civilization (Targowski, 2004). For example:

- Human entity as the global society is composed of certain segments of the societies of eight autonomous civilizations (Western, Eastern, Islamic, Japanese, Chinese, Buddhist, Hindu and African), which apply global culture and infrastructures

- Culture has global character, which means that similar patterns of behavior are practiced (*de facto* by certain segments of those societies only) in those autonomous civilizations; for example, such ones as "English," professional and student dress code, music, movies, food, drinks and so forth

- Global Infrastructure of Information (1) (the Internet and global area networks) and of material (2) (transportation, finance, and business) are reaching every autonomous civilization and integrating them into an emerging global society and global economy. Furthermore, there are many international organizations (for-profit and non-profit, official and unofficial), such as United Nations (UN), UNESCO, GATT, World Trade Organization (WTO), World Bank (WB), IMF, NATO and others, which create the Global Infrastructure of Regulations (3). The last kind of infrastructure plays a paradoxical role, promoting justice and enhancing inequality, triggering world conflicts and instability. For example; globalization triggers the anti-globalization movement, putting emphasis on local forces and potential, which de facto can be called "glocal" (GLObal-lo-CAL), since their uniqueness is a product of global forces. Among anti-global forces, one that is becoming very violent is global terrorism, which can destroy huge parts of any civilization. In response, civilization develops security systems that protect global order against global chaos. Hence, the Global Infrastructure at the same time creates order and chaos!

The global economy is only possible because it is supported by global infrastructures, supporting; global communication (the Internet, global area networks); global transportation; global finance activities; global scientific knowledge creation and dissemination; global management practices; even global peace keeping (with less success). The solar model of global civilization is shown in Figure 5. The global civilization is controlled by an invisible power, composed of global financiers and banks, stateless corporations, outsourcing CEOs (receiving fat bonuses for better performing stocks), G7, IMF, WB, WTO. The evolution of this civilization is driven by the following process of wealth formation with the help of technology: The dynamics of global civilization is not limited to economic rivalries and financial operations only. This dynamics is more complex: Religious and sectarian forces for global harmony and conflict have become pervasive, and they are intensified on the Web. The accelerated migration of peoples and the speeding of e-communications, especially by means of the Internet, have led to the globalization of religion. This process has generated contradictory responses: Some communities are confrontational, insisting on their monopoly of truth and access to salvation, whereas others are more adaptive (Fred W. Riggs, *webdata.soc.hawaii.edu/fredr/faith.htm*).

Global culture develops to support a global flow of ideas, capital, goods, services and people. It interconnects different national cultures by common patterns of behavior.

Figure 5. The solar model of global civilization in the 21st century (Driven by info-communication and transportation technologies)

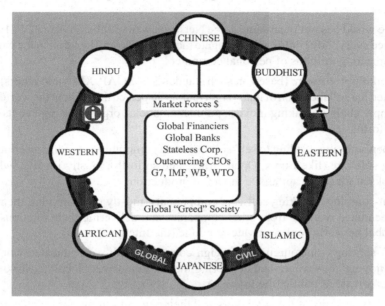

For example, English becomes the main language and the Western dress code, and international food is applied in global activities of business, politics, science, entertainment and art. Global communication culture is based mostly on the Internet and "CNN" culture. Global business transactions and political dialogs are supported by Western Culture's patterns of behavior, encoded in policies of the WTO, IMF, WB, UN and UE. In general, global culture interconnects national cultures to conduct Global Civilization's activities. However, because of the lack of the global society (or pseudo "global government"), global culture is very weak in regulating global economy and infrastructures.

The "Flattened" World

According to Friedman (2005), the world has been flattened by convergence of 10 major political events, innovations and companies:

1. The victory of Solidarity in Poland on August 1, 1989 and the fall of the Berlin Wall on November 9, 1989 unleashed forces that ultimately liberated all the

captive people of the Soviet Empire. It was caused by the impact of the underground press (information), which exceeded the readership of the official press.

2. The world has not been same since Netscape went public on August 9, 1995, since everybody could easily navigate the Internet to any location in the world, connecting millions of personal computers.

3. Work flow software (based on such standards as SOAP, XML and others) enabled the collaboration of many contributors dispersed throughout the world—a supply chain of making movies, publishing books, organizing big events and so forth.

4. Open sourcing, leading to self-collaborating communities producing competing software (like Linux, Open Office, and so forth), mostly for free, which looks at the post-capitalistic model of production.

5. Out-sourcing—making software components, mostly programming them by specialized workers from other companies and delivering their solutions via global networks, either private or public (the Internet).

6. Off-shoring—outsourcing to foreign countries, with well-educated workers "enjoying" low wages and delivering their solutions via global networks, either private or public (the Internet).

7. Supply-chaining—the computers and their networks allow for brand companies such as Wal-Mart to sell 1 million products through highly automated and computerized distribution centers. The high volume of business puts special pressure on subcontractors, who have to trim costs and keep good quality. In order to get "always" low prices, Wal-Mart is outsourcing and off-shoring its orders, mostly to China and other low-wage countries.

8. In-sourcing—based on asking world-oriented companies such as UPS or FedEX to carry the transportation processes inside of a company to speed up the delivery of goods and semi-products among units of a company or to its customers throughout the world.

9. Informing via Web search engines, such as Google, Yahoo and others, to speed up information-seeking users.

10. Mobile communication—a growing number of wireless gadgets (cell phone, iPaq, etc.), which can beam information to/from any location in the world, making people connected and informed with bullet train speed.

The Convergence I of all mentioned flatteners allows (according to Friedman, 2005) for multiple forms of collaboration at the level of knowledge production or project implementations in real time, without regard to geography and language. The Convergence II allows for the connection of all computers and involved workers/specialists into one virtual organization, which works productively and at low cost as one, but is spread out through the world. Convergence III allows for inclusion into the global economy/civilization people from developing or undeveloped countries, who without info-communication technology could be left behind the fast-progressing world. Of course, not everybody welcomes this working world, which takes advantage of weak partners, their discontent expressed under the form of anti-global activities.

Conclusion

1. Development of the Internet is the result of the Cold War, which has strong influence on the growth of the global economy and civilization.

2. Systems like the Internet are the results of many coincidences, where the most important one is the presence of exceptional research talent, such as Baran and others mentioned in this investigation.

3. Systems of the Internet's type are outcomes of many peoples' effort, similar to that which takes place when a cathedral is under construction for many centuries. Every new builder adds a new brick and says: "I built the cathedral." (Baran's statement in Hughes, 1998, p. 274). The Internet cathedral is shown in Figure 6.

4. The wide acceptance of info-communication systems depends on its "user friendliness." Therefore, the discovery of the WWW and Mosaic/Netscape browsers accelerated the acceptance of the Internet at the end of the 20th century and its influence on the further development of civilization.

5. The most unexpected influence of the Internet is on the conduct of war. For example, both sides of the battle can communicate via e-mail, as happened during the war in Iraq in 2003.

6. New capabilities of the Internet are constantly being discovered, and it seems that this process has not yet reached the point of saturation.

7. The close of INFOSTRADA/NIS in Poland in 1974 stopped the development of advanced info-communication systems for at least 25 years. In 2003, Poland created a Ministry of Science and Infomatization and launched the project to develop e-Poland.

8. Because global civilization at the same time creates order and chaos, it means that it becomes more "closed" and "undemocratic" than it looks at first glance, as can be explained by the II Law of Thermodynamics (closed systems generate more entropy, which is a measure of chaos-disorder). What does it mean? It means that global civilization should be more open, accepting not only one view ("Western View"), but many views, perhaps by development of another

Figure 6. The Internet cathedral

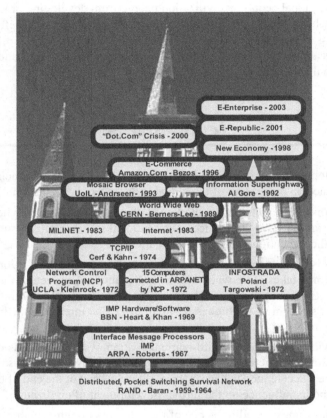

layer of world civilization, a universal-complementary civilization, which exchanges and accepts main and complementary values from all civilizations, as shown in Figure 7 (Targowski, 2004b).

References

Abbate, J. (1999). *Inventing the Internet*. Cambridge: MIT Press.

Anderson, W. T. (2004). *All connected now, the life in the first global civilization*. Boulder: Westview Press.

Baldwin, R., & Martin, P. (1999). *Two waves of globalization: Superficial similarities, fundamental differences* (NBER working paper).

Baran, P., et al. (1964). *On distributed communications* (RM 3420, 3103, 3578, 3638, 3097, 3762-7). Santa Monica: The RAND Corp.

Baran, P. (1964). *On distributed communications* (vol. V), History, alternative approaches, and comparisons (RM-3097-PR). Santa Monica: The Rand Corp.

Baran, P. (2002). The beginning of packet switching: Some underlying concepts: The Franklin Institute and Drexel University seminar on the evolution of packet switching and the Internet. *IEEE Communications Magazine*, July, 2-9.

Baran, P. (2003). *Inventor of packet switching and Internet pioneer.* A tribute to famous Polish-American, Gold Award Banquet. Detroit: American Polish Engineering Association.

Bledsoe, W. (2001). Globalization and comparative civilizations: Looking backward to see the future. *Comparative Civilizations Review, 45*, 13-31.

Castell, M. (1996). *The information age. Economy, society and culture (vol. 1): The rise of the network society.* Oxford: Blackwell.

Costa, J. (1966). RADC develops logic design for emergency broadcasting. *Electronic News*, January 10, 32.

Davies, D.W. (2001). An historical study of the beginnings of packet switching. *Brit. Cop. Sc. J., 44(3)*, 151-162.

Dyson, G. (1997). *Darwin among the machines.* Addison Wesley.

Friedman, L. Th. (2005). *The world is flat.* New York: Farrar, Straus and Giroux.

Hafner, K. (2001). A paternity dispute divides Net pioneers. *New York Times*, Nov 8.

Hafner, K., & Lyons, M. (1996). *Where wizards stay up late.* New York: Simon and Schuster.

Hughes, T. P. (1998). *Rescuing prometheus.* New York: Pantheon Books. Available at www.rand.org/publications/RM/baran.list.html

Kennan, G. (1947). X article, the sources of Soviet conduct. *Foraign Affairs*, July. Reprinted in Spring 1987.

Kissinger, H. (1994). *Diplomacy.* New York: Simon & Schuster.

Moczulski, L. (1998). *Geopolitics, power in time and space.* In Polish: Geopolityka, potęga w czasie i przestrzeni. Warsaw: Bellona.

Naughton, J. (1999). *A brief history of the future.* Woodstock: Overlook Press.

Norberg, A., et al. (2000). *Transforming computer technology.* Baltimore: John Hopkins University Press.

Selover, E. E. (1965). HF survivable communications system. *Proceedings of the IEEE Mohawk Valley Communication Symposium (NATCOM)* (pp. 35-40).

Soros, G. (2002). *On globalization.* New York: Public Affairs Press.

Soros, G. (2003). *The bubble of American supremacy*. New York: Public Affairs Press.

Spykman, N. J. (1942). *America's strategy in the world politics. The United States and balance of power*. New York: New Edition: Hamden, 1969.

Spykman N. J. (1944). *The geography of peace*. New York: Reprinted by Shoe String Press, 1969.

Targowski, A. (1991). Computing in totalitarian states: Poland's way to an informed society. *The Journal of Information Management, Information Executive, 4*(3), Summer, 10-16.

Targowski, A. (2001). *Informatics without illusions*. In Polish, Informatyka bez zludzen. Toruń: Adam Marszalek.

Targowski, A. (2004). A dynamic model of an autonomous civilization. *Dialogue and Universalism, XIV*(1-2), 77-90.

Targowski, A. (2004). A grand model of civilization. *Comparative Civilizations Review, 51*, 81-106.

Targowski, A. (2004b). From global to universal civilization. *Dialogue and Universalism, XIV*(3-4), 121-142.

Targowski, A. (2005). From the Cold War to Internet cathedral. *International Journal of Information and Communication Technology Education, 1*(2), 87-98.

Targowski, A., et al. (2000). *The fate of Poland and the world*. In Polish: Losy Polski i świata. Warsaw: Bellona.

Chapter VI

Writing-Across-the-IT/MIS Curriculum

Stephanie J. Etter, Mount Aloysius College, USA

Jeffrey W. Merhout, Miami University, USA

Abstract

Popular literature not only claims that college graduates are entering the work-force lacking sufficient writing skills but that companies must spend billions of dollars annually to train employees how to communicate effectively through writing (Canavor & Meirowitz, 2005; College Board, 2004). While writing across the curriculum is not a new concept, it seems that only certain areas of the curriculum have adopted it. The integration of writing into the management information systems (MIS)/information technology (IT) curriculum is an important and achievable goal necessary for the overall development of students in IT or MIS degree programs. While traditional IT/MIS programs rely heavily on technology-based courses, we argue that these technology courses must also promote effective writing habits needed for career growth in the IT/MIS fields. As business proposals, newsletters and reports are frequently being written by those in the information systems department of a corporation, rather than by those in the communication department, it is increasingly important that we prepare IT/MIS students with the appropriate writing skills needed for their careers. For example, in many cases we prepare students to create Web pages, a highly public information source, without providing any instruction on writing within the IT/MIS curriculum. This chapter illustrates how writing assignments can be used in many MIS/IT classes.

Introduction

The National Committee on Writing surveyed 120 major American corporations and found that the ability to write clearly significantly impacts the hiring and promotion process among salaried (i.e., professional) employees (College Board, 2004). While business majors may find writing integrated in the classroom at various academic levels, students majoring in IT and MIS are frequently focusing on technical material (e.g., hardware, software, communication technologies, programming languages, database management) rather than refining much needed communication skills like writing. While these students may find themselves employed at the same corporations as the business majors, they may not be granted the same opportunities for advancement.

A report in *Business Wire* (Technology Industry Suffers, 2005) states that writing activities account for an average of 37% of the typical professional's workday in the technology industry. The IT/MIS graduates entering today's workforce will be expected to write various communications, from business proposals and reports to online newsletters and Web sites. Even a simple e-mail requires clear and easily understood writing. In many cases, we prepare students to create Web pages, a highly public information source, without preparing them to fill the pages with appropriate text. IT/MIS students may be required to defend or explain a component of their technical work, either in a formal business proposal or as an answer to an online technical question.

In either instance, a written explanation that is hard to understand could hurt the bottom line. Canavor and Meirowitz (2005) argue that clear and easily understood writing provides a competitive advantage in this time of globalization. They state, "whatever the language, there's a critical need for clear, jargon-free writing that can easily be understood by non-native readers" (p. 31). According to *Business Wire* (Technology Industry Suffers, 2005), "Technology is new and complex by nature; therefore, technology companies depend on strong writing to clearly reveal the value of their products." This same report argues that unclear writing can dramatically affect the success of technology sales, customer service and overall customer satisfaction, as technology sales tend to be broad and frequently impact hundreds of thousands of users at a time. Effective writing and technical documentation is expected of today's IT workers. Without it, companies will find initials sales difficult and can expect an increase in the types and amount of support services it must provide after the sale.

Many writing deficient students may not get the chance to do any writing on-the-job as some companies now test writing skills as part of the hiring screening process. A 2004 survey concludes that "80% or more of the companies in the service and finance, insurance and real estate (FIRE) sectors, the corporations with the greatest employment growth potential, assess writing during hiring" (College Board, 2004,

p. 3). It is important to note that these industries employ a significant number of people in the IT and MIS fields. This same study reports that a "similar dynamic is at work during promotions. Half of all companies take writing into account when making promotion decisions" (College Board, 2004, p. 3). These decisions may be made on formal proposals or reports, but everyday communications such as e-mail may be considered, as well. E-mail has become the predominant writing activity for most business professionals, accounting for more than 2 hours per day on average for each employee (Business Professionals Unprepared, 2005).

The IT/MIS curriculum is often focused so intently on technology that students may fulfill degree requirements without fully learning other skills essential to successful career development. In an era of globalization, extremely competitive job markets and pockets of high unemployment rates, IT/MIS students need to graduate with skills that provide for employability and advancement. Communication skills, especially writing, should play an integral role in the IT/MIS curriculum. In order to accomplish this task, educators should strive to help develop IT/MIS students from a liberal education standpoint (e.g., development of critical thinking, illustrating critical thinking through writing, consideration of contexts, and engaging with other learners).

The purpose of this chapter is to argue that integrating writing at numerous stages throughout the IT/MIS curriculum is an important and achievable goal for the further development of our students and, more specifically, to illustrate how writing can be incorporated into IT/MIS courses at both the undergraduate and graduate levels. While much of the following discussion may be culturally specific to Western societies and principally to the United States (U.S.) (as discussed by Fox, 1994), educators in any country who are interested in developing well-rounded graduates may benefit from this chapter.

Importance of Writing

The decline in communication skills of college students is perhaps the best argument for including writing requirements in courses that traditionally do not have a writing component, such as those found in IT/MIS curriculums. Countless educators lament that many (or most) students cannot express themselves well (e.g., Bean, 2001; Epstein, 1999; Plutsky & Wilson, 2001), and this phenomenon threatens a nation's ability to develop citizens who can fully participate in political and economic processes. Moreover, when one cannot write well, it is often a symptom of a failure to think critically, which can be more damaging than just a lack of communication skills, especially for IT workers. In a 2003 survey, employers in the U.S. reported that many college students graduate without the communication and writing skills necessary to succeed in the workplace (Malveaux, 2003). The recent survey published by the College Board (2004) supports the earlier research by reporting that U.S. "corporations express a fair degree of dissatisfaction with the writing of recent college graduates" (p. 14). This problem is not specific to the U.S., however, as employers in the United Kingdom (UK) are also reporting a shortage of fundamental skills in job seekers who are recent graduates, specifically in the areas of communication and problem-solving abilities (Parrish, 1998).

Since many U.S. degree programs require only one or two composition courses, it is our working assumption that the skills learned in these courses are not sufficient to provide students with appropriate speaking and writing skills. Some institutions still count solely on language (e.g., English) or communications courses as the only sources for developing effective writing and speaking skills, part of a discipline-by-discipline approach in which courses rarely cover concepts outside of a specific discipline. Many institutions, however, have incorporated "writing across the curriculum" programs or, as they are known in Canada and Great Britain, "language across the curriculum programs." Writing across the curriculum calls for the inclusion of writing requirements in courses throughout a student's college curriculum (Bean, 2001). Carnes, Jennings, Vice and Wiedmaier (2001) further explain that a writing across the curriculum program "enables faculty of non-communication disciplines to build on the writing skills taught in communication courses, provides students with the opportunity to strengthen and reinforce communication skills and encourages consistency in communication training and assessment" (p.1). Moreover, this movement argues (and we concur) that the development of writing competence should be a shared responsibility between the various disciplines and the language departments within a college or university (Tynjala, Mason, & Lonka, 2001; Weimer, 2001).

While the push for writing across the curriculum has been around for several decades, a new push, this time for information literacy, is being brought into focus. Thompson (2005) argues that the teaching of writing should be a natural extension of our responsibility to teach information literacy. The teaching of writing and of information literacy both involve "ideas generated from information; both stress abundant and accurate information" (p. 48). By teaching information literacy, we are providing students with the skills needed to "recognize the need for information" and determine its "accuracy, relevance and comprehensiveness" (ALA, 1998). Obviously, these skills are also needed for writing.

We believe those responsible for educating tomorrow's information resources managers should share in the development of these future leaders' writing and critical thinking abilities by incorporating writing requirements throughout MIS/IT curriculums. This argument is supported by Nelson (1992), who contends that the development of key learning skills, including critical thinking and problem-solving abilities, is imperative for technical workers to keep up with rapid technological innovations.

This is not the same as supporting the concept of writing in the disciplines (WID), as WID programs prepare students for the discourse of a specific discipline by showing students discipline-specific models of writing (Ochsner & Flower, 2004). Since the IT/MIS fields are so intertwined in the day-to-day operations of business, students must learn to write for audiences outside of their discipline.

Bean (2001) convincingly argues that writing is a key way to develop critical thinking abilities and problem-solving skills, and notes that "integrating writing and other critical thinking activities into a course increases students' learning while teaching them thinking skills for posing questions, proposing hypotheses, gathering and analyzing data, and making arguments" (p. 1).

Similarly, Tynjala et al. (2001, p. 17) argue that "writing is a tool for thinking and a tool for learning." Bonwell and Eison (1991) add that informal in-class writing exercises, which can even be used in large class sections, can assist in student acquisition of course content. Hence, a compelling case can be made that improving MIS students' writing abilities by requiring and guiding written assignments can enhance their communication skills and critical thinking abilities while simultaneously assisting in the acquisition of the key concepts of a given course.

Challenges of Implementing Writing in the IT/MIS Curriculum

Implementing writing into any curriculum not traditionally considered to be writing intensive can be difficult on several levels. A 2001 study by Plutsky and Wilson found that faculties were especially concerned with their ability to provide appropriate feedback for writing and grammar. According to Bean (2001), in addition to feeling that their own writing skills are inadequate to provide appropriate feedback, faculty may hold other misconceptions about incorporating writing assignments, including the idea that time is taken away from coverage of content, that writing assignments are not appropriate for certain types of courses and that writing assignments will bury the instructor in paper grading. The challenges of incorporating writing into IT/MIS curriculums may also include, as Bean discusses, designing effective problem-oriented assignments, coaching students to be better writers and critical thinkers, commenting on and grading assignments, and dealing with grammar and sentence correctness.

To maximize the effectiveness of writing assignments, instructors must carefully design problem-based assignments that generate in-depth analysis of the course content and develop critical thinking skills while creating a finished product that can be fairly graded in a manageable fashion. Carnes et al. (2001) present a checklist for creating writing assignments: carefully planning the assignment and grading criteria; enumerating the assignment details in writing; explaining the grading criteria, preferably with a checklist; stating the details of when the assignment is due and in what format; providing opportunities for interim feedback; and using a detailed evaluation sheet that is very similar to the assignment grading criteria checklist. Gelinas, Rama and Skelton (1997) reiterate the importance of careful planning by identifying three critical planning decisions for integrating writing across the curriculum programs: defining measurements of quality for student writing, selecting forms of communication appropriate for the discipline, and selecting the appropriate mix of communication skills to teach in class.

Bean (2001) discusses the significance of coaching the writing process, of writing appropriate (and effective) comments on papers (e.g., positive feedback whenever possible) and of explicating and adhering to detailed grading criteria. The goal in coaching the writing process is to efficiently assist in the development of students' writing abilities by guiding the process without becoming overly burdened by grading requirements. Bean (p. 237) notes the traditional means of coaching writing by making "copious, red-penciled comments on finished student products [is] almost universally regarded among composition specialists as an inefficient use of teacher energy." Rather, the instructor should identify potential problems as early in the process as possible by having students submit early drafts to peers and/or to the instructor for feedback. Another idea in guiding the process is to refer students to a university writing center, assuming one exists. Once the writing process is near completion, the instructor can make high-level comments that require revision before the final draft is resubmitted. After receiving the final draft, the instructor

Table 1. Grading rubric

Requirement	YES	NO	Maybe
The problem statement is well-developed, and the problem is significant.			
The thesis statement is clear and succinct.			
Evidence to support the thesis statement is relevant (e.g., current) and strong.			
The paper makes a contribution.			
Arguments are logical.			
Ideas are well-developed and logically arranged.			
There are smooth transitions between sections, between paragraphs and between sentences.			
The voice, tone and style are appropriate for the assignment.			
Sentences are grammatically correct with zero misspelled words.			
The use and explanation of acronyms and abbreviations is appropriate.			
Peer review comments are attended to and/or responded to in a separate paper.			
Copies of sources are included (either hard copy or electronically).			
The paper is not plagiarized.			
Grade: Comments:			

should make minimal comments as it is unlikely students will benefit from this unless they are required to make revisions. Instead of making detailed notes on the paper to justify a grade, an instructor should use a grading or scoring scale, often called a scoring or assessment rubric, preferably based on the same scale presented to the students at the beginning of the assignment as criteria for evaluating their work. A rubric is an assessment tool that uses detailed criteria to evaluate content knowledge and process skills (Coray, 2000). An example of a rubric used to score a research paper for an MIS course is provided in Table 1.

Faculties often dislike the use of rubrics because they can be time consuming to create. With the help of Web sites that create modifiable rubrics for you, such as *teach-nology.com*, rubric creation should no longer be seen as a barrier for their use in assessment.

Examples of IT/MIS Writing Assignments

Bean (2001) classifies writing assignments as formal, or as informal, exploratory assignments. The use of informal assignments, such as in-class writing, journals, reading logs, creativity exercises, practice essay exams, early drafts of essays and memos to oneself (e.g., to explain a process), can serve as a writing component in any course without burdening the instructor with a heavy grading requirement. The goal of these assignments is to get the student thinking about the key concepts of the course. Bean (p. 118) argues that "exploratory writing, focusing on the process rather than the product of thinking, deepens most students' engagement with course materials while enhancing learning and developing critical thinking."

Informal writing assignments also have a place in the IT/MIS curriculum, such as 5-minute essays at the end of class that ask students to sum up the key points of the class in relation to another topic, such as a current event or their future career plans. Brief writing assignments during class time are one way to engage students in an active manner and seem to be appropriate for all types of courses, including IT education. For example, when teaching data modeling, we require our students to think about and summarize their thoughts on the process of creating a well-designed data model rather than just grading their finished product (such as their entity relationship model). The purpose of such an assignment is to help the student realize that data modeling is a creative process that often requires iteration and that the finished product should constantly be challenged as to its robustness. Even if an individual student did not actually make these exact points, an ensuing class discussion, perhaps in lieu of grading their writing, could help the student to understand that data modeling is just as much a process as it is an end product.

Formal writing assignments include short write-to-learn assignments (also called microthemes), thesis-based term papers, formal exploratory essays, reflection papers, essay questions on exams and a variety of other assignments that can be tailored to specific disciplines, such as poetry in psychology or creating word problems for mathematics class (Bean, 2001). Microthemes can be an effective way to assess how well the class as a whole is learning (or not learning) the key conceptual material in a course. Bean provides an example of a psychology professor presenting a scenario of cats reacting to being fed and then asking students to write an essay where the student applies several behavioral theories from psychology to explain the scene. Similarly, in a database course, we could ask our students to critique a database design that has several faults, such as not being properly normalized and/or omitting relationships between entities that would be needed to facilitate certain key queries.

Thesis-based term papers are very appropriate for MIS courses that survey the various information technologies and discuss the implications of these technologies from different perspectives, such as from a strategic, managerial and organizational impact standpoint. In thesis-driven papers, the thesis is usually presented near the beginning of the paper, where the purpose of the remainder of the essay is to present appropriate evidence and make persuasive (i.e., logical) arguments in support of the thesis. Assignments requiring a thesis are usually superior to simply asking students to write about a general topic appropriate for the class. Such a general course-related assignment likely would not require the student to develop the deep analysis and synthesis that is normally the product of effectively developing and defending a specific thesis about a topic. An example of a thesis-governed assignment used in a graduate course will be presented in the next section of this chapter.

Adding writing to the IT/MIS curriculum may also include using writing during exams. The addition of essay or short-answer questions to exams in the IT/MIS curriculum serves several purposes. First, it breaks up the cycle of rote memorization often required for successful completion of a multiple-choice exam, a very common exam method used in IT-related courses. Second, it allows the instructor to see if students really have an understanding of the material or if they have simply memorized the notes for the exam. Bloom, Englehart, Furst, Hill and Krathwohl's (1956) well-known taxonomy of learning (knowledge, comprehension, application, analysis, synthesis and evaluation) proposes that different levels of understanding can be achieved across subject areas. Short-answer or essay exam questions require higher levels of organizational skills to frame cogent answers, higher levels of recall about the subject matters, more integrative knowledge and, of course, good writing skills (Zeidner, 1987). Where an exam entirely made of short-answer or essay questions may not be considered practical, combining the common methods of multiple choice and true/false questions with one or two essay questions may not only help to evolve the communication skills of the student, but it may also help the instructor to evaluate the course by determining whether or not the student can actually synthesize working, productive output from the material provided in the course.

Detailed Examples of Writing Assignments

For the purposes of providing more specific examples of writing assignments incorporated into IT/MIS courses, this article describes assignments used in two postsecondary schools located in Ohio and Pennsylvania, as well as those found in literature. In MIS survey courses offered at both the undergraduate and MBA level, a semester term paper has proven to be a successful writing assignment. For undergraduate systems analysis and database courses, a semester group project with a final report write-up has been required. And in some cases, more than one writing assignment is appropriate. For example, a semester group project report and an individual term paper were both required in a graduate-level database course.

An example of a writing assignment currently used in an undergraduate database course is a short event summary paper. The objectives of the short paper are to give students more practice in writing and in critiquing their peers' writing, and to encourage their participation in extra-curricular activities. Students are required to attend at least one of the many outside speaker presentations sponsored by the Miami University Farmer School of Business during a semester. While many of these events have very informative speakers, the sessions are sometimes sparsely attended. Requiring students to attend one of these educational events and to write about their experience is intended to assist in their overall personal development. Students then write a short 300-400-word review of the event attended, including a synopsis of the presentation, an analysis and critique of the speaker's thesis, and a personal reflection about how the speaker's topic was relevant to their IT/MIS education. Moreover, a positive by-product of this assignment is that some students have become so enlightened by these presentations that they voluntarily attend more outside speaker events in the future.

Another example of a writing assignment in an undergraduate database course is a semester group project report. The objective of this assignment is to require students to think about the business purpose for investing in data management systems and to consider the organizational context of the problem domain for which they are designing a database. Students in the course are given explicit guidelines of the types of issues they must discuss and have a significant amount deducted off their project grade if they fail to address this requirement. While the main focus of their semester project is to properly design an effective relational database, this requirement forces them to think about how communications are part of every systems development project. One of the drawbacks realized up front is that this written part of the project package, which will also include items like data models and query results, will likely be composed by only one (or maybe a couple) of the team members. Hence, the entire group is also required to present their project to the class, which requires, at minimum, that each student practice his or her oral communication skills.

In a graduate program, it is often much easier to incorporate written assignments into the curriculum, as many students now have industry experience and are aware of the communication skills needed to succeed in the workplace. A research paper assignment has been successfully used in a graduate-level IT management course. The objective of the paper is to require students to research an appropriate IT topic beyond what is covered in their textbook and in class to focus on the strategic, managerial, organizational and social implications of investments in IT. These analytical components of the paper, when outlined and explained at the beginning of the assignment, can be used as part of a grading rubric (as discussed earlier) in addition to items such as a clearly defined thesis and argument. The requirement of a thesis forces the student to think in terms of organizational problems and research questions rather than just creating a "data dump" (Bean, 2001, p. 90). In essence, this format requires a deep analysis and synthesis, the type of higher-order thinking instructors should strive for in all IT/MIS courses.

In addition to a thesis, the assignment requires a sequence of deliverables that force students to work on the paper throughout the entire term. The first deliverable is to propose a topic and problem statement early in the semester that includes a discussion of the process of how they formulated their problem statement. Requiring students to write about how they formed their problem statements will force them to think about the development of a problem statement as a process rather than as a finished product. Moreover, it provides feedback so the instructor can guide and coach problem development as a process of asking researchable questions. It may also help to prevent or deter plagiarism, because the student will not be able to simply borrow or purchase (e.g., copy and paste from the Internet) a problem statement. The instructor then reviews the work and makes detailed, written comments about the topic and problem statement, which are then resubmitted with all subsequent submissions.

The second deliverable, due around mid-semester, requires an informal outline; a draft of their introductory paragraph(s), which include a thesis statement; and submission of all drafts created thus far in their writing process (as further protection against plagiarism). Once again, the instructor makes written comments that must be addressed in later submissions. The third deliverable, due 2 weeks before their final submission, is a draft of their complete paper for a fellow student to review and critique within the following week. The first student (i.e., the author) then has 1 week to attend to his or her cohort's comments (either in the paper or on a separate response sheet) before turning in their final draft for grading. This final draft must be part of a package of all prior submissions that have been reviewed by the instructor, including instructor comments.

By requiring all previous drafts and submissions, the instructor can assess whether students made an honest effort to improve their product as they went through this process. This explicit sequence of steps and deliverables will result in a deeper analysis of a student's chosen topic, which inevitably will enhance the student's learning of IT while helping to develop his or her writing and argumentation skills. Moreover, as suggested by writing advocates (e.g., Bean, 2001; Carnes et al., 2001), the instructor should provide a detailed set of grading criteria with the assignment outlining the requirements for an "A" paper and a grading rubric that provides the checklist to be used for a quick and clear assessment of the paper as it is read to determine the grade. Thus, the student will know up front what is expected. For example, one of the criteria in Table 1 is "the problem statement is well-developed." On the rubric, the instructor can check "yes," "no" or "maybe" and provide a brief explanation for answers other than "yes." This method is usually a much more effective (and efficient) means of assessing each paper rather than making detailed notes in the margins noting relatively minor issues, such as clarity and grammar.

Not all writing assignments have to be conducted outside of the classroom. If an already work-intensive course does not have time during the semester to include a formal paper or group project, smaller in-class writing assignments can be used. For example, an undergraduate introduction to computer security class occasionally includes short writing assignments at the end of a class based on the material discussed in that class or the past several classes. At the end of a class period spent on the discussion of password security and authentication tactics, for example, the instructor may ask students to write an explanation of the necessity of password security for an executive who has limited knowledge and IT background. In addition to practicing writing skills, students are also given the opportunity to try to explain these concepts in basic terms. This exercise also helps the instructor determine if the students truly understand the concepts or are just memorizing facts and figures.

Adding a personal reflective journal requirement to any IT/MIS course is an easy way to incorporate writing into the curriculum. Students may be asked to write in the journal weekly about things such as current events relating to the class or personal reflections on class materials or guest speakers. For example, students can be asked to contemplate how they might use relational databases in their careers, with the goal of having them realize the relevancy of taking a database design course (this is especially useful for non-MIS majors who might take such a course). Instructors can then collect the journals every few weeks to provide feedback. Again, a rubric can be used as a scoring method. Journals are often a successful way not only to further develop writing skills, but also for instructors to get a feel for student comprehension of the subject matter and perceptions of the course.

As previously noted, short writing assignments can also be used in exams. The same undergraduate computer security class requires students to answer at least one essay question per exam, providing students an opportunity to explain concepts in detail and often argue their opinion. For example, students may be given a brief biography of a company and are then asked to recommend a method of encryption based on the company's needs and line of business. This recommendation must be directed to a senior manager of a business, who may not be well versed in the need for encryption or computer security methods in general. Another assignment from this course has students designing a written brochure designed to inform middle-school students of ways to protect themselves and their computers while online. Both assignments allow students to provide an appropriate explanation of a topic to an audience outside of their field and demonstrate their comprehension of its application.

The 2004 survey published by the College Board (2004) reports that corporations express dissatisfaction with the writing of recent college graduates, including the academic styles of writing students are taught, which is often unsuited to workplace needs. While the assignments mentioned above do improve writing skills, it is important to focus also on writing that will help prepare students for the workplace. Kreth (2005) argues that assignments that reflect a client-based pedagogy can be useful for business students. We believe this applies to IT/MIS courses as well. A client-based pedagogy "focuses on helping students to understand and respond effectively to real-world clients and their organizational contexts" (Kreth, 2005, p. 52). Offering students the opportunity to write a proposal for an IT project for a specific company or in response to an organizational problem allows students to analyze the needs of a real-world audience, research relevant information related to the project and practice writing in a style appropriate for the business world, unlike a traditional term paper. One example of this type of writing assignment is taken from a 300-level application of e-commerce technologies course. Students are required to write a paper addressing an area of investigation of personal interest. Examples include an analysis of the presence of electronic markets in a given industry or an overview of an emerging technology not covered in the text. Students frame the report as a summary of research into the opportunities/problems associated with an emerging technology or electronic market applied to a specific consulting project scenario provided by the instructor. Additionally, students must write in a manner that persuades management that the conclusions/recommendations are sound and logically developed (including providing evidence that supports their thesis).

It is often easier to assign client-based assignments in graduate-level courses, because graduate students frequently have some experience in the industry. In a graduate-level impact of technology course, which discusses the influence of technology implementation, students are assigned to reflect on case studies from companies that describe a real-world technology implementation in the workplace. This reflection often allows students to think about the impact from a new perspective and focus on reasons why new technologies are not always adopted as planned, and helps to prepare students for another assignment later in the semester that is focused on planning for and managing an IT implementation project.

Avoiding Plagiarism

Faculty in non-writing-intensive areas have rarely had to deal with plagiarism, so adding a writing requirement to the IT/MIS curriculum often takes them into uncharted waters. An awareness of plagiarism and its hold on colleges and universities in today's Web-based world is necessary before jumping head-first into writing assignments.

In a recent *New York Times* article, a student from Duke University said that using a small paragraph that has been cut and pasted from the Internet and slightly altered as part of his research paper is "no big deal … it's not cheating" (Zernike, 2002, p. A10). This acceptance of cutting and pasting seems to be common among college students. The same Duke student explained that "as long as I can manipulate it to be my words, change a few, it's not cheating" (Zernike, 2002, p.10). Information technology, specifically word processing software and the Internet, has allowed students to copy full paragraphs, change a couple of words, and think that they have done nothing wrong. This form of plagiarism is identified by Iverson, Flanagin, Fontanarosa, Glass, Giltman, Lantz, Meyer, Smith, Winker and Young (1998) as "mosaic plagiarism," but it is also known as "patchwriting" (Howard, 1999) or "paraphragiarism" (Levin & Marshall, 1993).

Moreover, Western academicians indicate that international students often have different notions about plagiarism (Fox, 1994). Evans and Merhout (2004) explain that countries having a more collaborative work style may view plagiarism issues differently than Western countries that focus on individual contributions. Bean (2001) elaborates on Fox's discussion and further explains that some international students are surprised by the Western acknowledgement that other "individuals can 'own' [their original] words and ideas" (p. 43).

Given Western students' changing view of plagiarism thanks to the availability of Internet resources and the cultural views brought by international students, it is imperative to make a note on the course syllabus and discuss plagiarism with all students at the beginning of any class that contains writing assignments. It is also wise to check suspicious submissions by doing a Google search on strings of text that seem out of character for the student writer.

The best way to avoid plagiarism is in the design of an assignment where a statement against plagiarism is a necessary component to bring attention to the seriousness of this issue. Requiring multiple drafts of a document, creating assignments that are specific to a school or region and requiring students to use and cite library resources in the document also can be effective ways to avoid plagiarism. Another effective method is to teach proper citation in class or request a class session with a campus librarian.

Conclusion

Writing assignments are both appropriate and beneficial for students in MIS and IT courses. Specific examples of writing assignments that have been successfully implemented, including short papers, group projects, research papers and in-class writing, have been discussed. To create employable graduates, faculty must begin to take responsibility for the development of the whole student, and not simply accept responsibility for discipline-specific skills only. Key to the success of incorporating writing into a curriculum is providing clear grading requirements to students as well as feedback. Plutsky and Wilson (2001) suggest some critical success factors for writing across the curriculum, including developing standards for writing and assessment, and providing training programs for faculty. Accordingly, we offer this chapter as a resource that MIS/IT faculty can use as a starting point for incorporating writing into their own courses.

References

American Association of School Librarians (ALA) and Association for Educational Communications and Technology (AECT) (1998). *Information power: Building partnerships for learning.* Chicago: ALA.

Bean, J. C. (2001). *Engaging ideas: The professor's guide to integrating writing, critical thinking, and active learning in the classroom.* San Francisco: Jossey-Bass Publishers.

Bloom, B., Englehart, M., Furst, E., Hill, H., & Krathwohl, D. (Eds.). (1956). *Taxonomy of educational objectives: The classification of educational goals. Handbook I: Cognitive domain.* New York: David McKay Company.

Bonwell, C., & Eison, J. (1991). *Active learning: Creating excitement in the classroom* (ASHE-ERIC Higher Education Report No. 1). Washington, DC: The George Washington School of Education and Human Development.

Business professionals unprepared as writing responsibilities increase. (2005, October 12). *Business Wire.* Retrieved January 20, 2006, from the Lexis-Nexis Academic Universe database at http://web.lexis-nexis.com/universe/document?_m= 85e5491d2f2565ddaade097ca5a67119&_docnum=1&wchp=dGLbVzz-zSkVb&_md5=98e65ed2e4518f527729deb7c05ac21c

Canavor, N., & Meirowitz, C. (2005). Good corporate writing: Why it matters, and what to do. *Communication World, 22*(4), 30-33.

Carnes, L., Jennings, M., Vice, J. & Wiedmaier, C. (2001). The role of the business educator in a writing-across-the-curriculum program. *Journal of Education for Business, 76*(4), 216-219.

College Board. (2004). *Report of the National Commission on Writing for America's families, schools and colleges: Writing, a ticket to work or a ticket out.* Retrieved January 20, 2006, from www.writingcommission.org/pr/writing_ for_employ.html

Coray, G. (2000). Rubrics made simple. *Science Scope, 23*(6), 38-40.

Epstein, M.H. (1999). Teaching field-specific writing: Results of a WAC survey. *Business Communication Quarterly, 62*(1), 29-41.

Evans, D., & Merhout, J.W. (2004). Impacts of IT on human behavior in library settings. In M. Khosrow-Pour (Ed.), *Innovations through information technology* (pp. 112-114). Proceedings of the 2004 Information Resources Management Association International Conference, New Orleans, LA.

Fox, H. (1994). *Listening to the world: Cultural issues in academic writing.* Urbana: National Council of Teachers of English.

Gelinas, U.J., Rama, D.V., & Skelton, T.M. (1997). Selection of technical communications concepts for integration into an accounting information systems course: A WAC case study. *Technical Communication Quarterly, 6*(4), 381-401.

Howard, R. (1999). The new abolitionism comes to plagiarism. In L. Buranen & M. Roy (Eds.), *Perspectives on plagiarism and intellectual property in a postmodern world.* New York: State University of New York.

Iverson, C., Flanagin, A., Fontanarosa, P., Glass, R., Giltman, P., Lantz, J., Meyer, H., Smith, J., Winker, M., & Young, R. (1998). *American Medical Association manual of style: A guide for authors and editors (9th ed.).* Baltimore: Williams and Wilkins.

Kreth, M. L. (2005). A small-scale client project for business writing students. *Business Communication Quarterly, 68*(1), 52-59.

Levin, J., & Marshall, H. (1993). Publishing in the Journal of Educational Psychology: Reflections at midstream. *Journal of Educational Psychology, 85,* 3-6.

Malveaux, J. (2003). Workplace 2003: What's next for graduating seniors? *Black Issues in Higher Education, 20*(6), 35.

Merhout, J. W. (2004). Integrating writing requirements into MIS courses. In M. Khosrow-Pour (Ed.), *Innovations through information technology* (pp. 299-301). Proceedings of the 2004 Information Resources Management Association International Conference, New Orleans, LA.

Nelson, J. (1992). Case study: Teaching learning skills as a foundation for technical training. *Educational & Training Technology International, 29*(2), 1992, 89-93.

Ochsner, R., & Flower, J. (2004). Playing devil's advocate: Evaluating the literature of the WAC/WID movement. *Review of Educational Research, 74*(2),
117-141.

Parrish, D. (1998). One day, my son, all these key skills will be yours. *New States-
man, 11*(530), 21.

Plutsky, S., & Wilson, B.A. (2001). Writing across the curriculum in a college of
business and economics. *Business Communication Quarterly, 64*(4), 26-41.

Technology industry suffers as writing responsibilities increase by one-third. (2005, October 31). *Business Wire*. Retrieved January 20, 2006, from the Lexis-Nexis Academic Universe database at http://web.lexis-nexis.com/universe/document?_
m= fb37fa73b3172cfcec69f71e824ad360&_docnum=1&wchp=dGLbVzz-
zSkVb&_md5=26e32a3862cbed254ec79f84954b017c

Thompson, H. M. (2005). Ideas, information, and organization: Connecting information literacy and writing. *School Library Media Activities Monthly, 21*(7),
48-50.

Tynjala, P., Mason, L., & Lonka, K. (2001). Writing as a learning tool: An introduction. In G. Rijlaarsdam (Series Ed.), P. Tynjala, L. Mason, & K. Lonka (Volume
Eds.), *Studies in writing: Volume 7: Writing as a learning tool: Integrating
theory and practice* (pp. 7-22). Dordecht: Kluwer Academic Publishers.

Weimer, M. (2001). Foreword. In J.C. Bean (Ed.), *Engaging ideas: The professor's
guide to integrating writing, critical thinking, and active learning in the classroom* (pp. xvii-xx). San Francisco: Jossey-Bass Publishers.

Zeidner, M. (1987). Essay versus multiple-choice type classroom exams: The student's
perspective. *Journal of Educational Research, 80*(6), 352-358.

Zernike, K. (2002, November 2). With student cheating on the rise, more colleges
are turning to honor codes. *New York Times*, p. A10.

Chapter VII

Learning IT:
Where do Lectures Fit?

Tanya McGill, Murdoch University, Australia

Samantha Bax, Murdoch University, Australia

Abstract

Lectures are the traditional method of content delivery in undergraduate information technology degrees, yet concerns have been raised about their effectiveness. This chapter addresses the role of lectures within information technology (IT) degree programs from a student perspective; it examines the factors that influence lecture attendance, and student perceptions of the usefulness of a variety of possible lecture activities. Overall, the results suggest that students see the lecturer as contributing significant value to their learning experience through the lecture setting. Students appear to value the expertise of the lecturer and find activities that can best make use of the lecturer's expertise the most useful. The results also suggest that students recognize the importance of active learning within the constraints of traditional learning settings.

Introduction

The traditional lecture is one of the most common forms of teaching, and has long been the primary method of formally introducing subject material to the student population (Kumar, Kumar, & Basu, 2002), as well as providing opportunities for lecturers to guide students on how to study the courses' content (Khan, 1997). Yet the lecture is also considered to be one of the least effective forms of instruction for students (Bligh, 1972; Felder, 1992; Johnston, Moffat, Sondergaard, & Stuckey, 1996). Some problems reported with the lecturing approach include that lectures can promote passivity, feelings of isolation (Isaacs, 1994; Rosenthal, 1995) and boredom (Mukherjee, 2000). This could make them ineffectual as an approach to learning.

Despite these concerns and the increasing availability and popularity of online education (McCormick, 2000; Peffers & Bloom, 1999), the lecture is the traditional method of learning in undergraduate IT degrees and is still the standard for IT courses (Griffiths & Oates, 2003; Lynch & Markham, 2003). This raises the question of what the role of lectures can and should be within an IT degree program. The study described in this chapter meets Khan's (1997) call for more research on students' perceptions of the importance and benefits of attending lectures and explores the opinions of a group of IT students; examining the factors that influence their lecture attendance, and their perceptions of the usefulness of a variety of possible lecture activities.

Background

The majority of on-campus IT students today are assumed to attend lectures, which provide the main method of introducing IT content to students. However, lecture attendance is rarely mandatory and varies from course to course, with anecdotal evidence suggesting that there is a trend towards lower attendance. This lower attendance may reflect students' dissatisfaction with lectures as a tool for learning, but may also reflect the changing nature of student life, with students facing many completing demands on their time and requiring flexibility in learning.

Many lecture sessions take the format of traditional 'talking head' lectures. One concern associated with the passivity a lecture can encourage is that students who are not actively participating (whether physically or mentally) have a reduced level of concentration after the first 10 to 15 minutes of a lecture (Stuart & Rutherford, 1978), after which the amount of information retained by the student declines (Bligh, 1972). McKeachie (1986) reports that after a lecture, a student recalls 70% of the information presented in the first 10 minutes, but only 20% of the information presented within the last 10 minutes of lecture time.

Schank (1998) asserts that it is a difficult task to listen while someone else (i.e., the lecturer) talks, with the best case scenario being that a student will think about what has just been said, and then miss the points that follow in the lecture. What is required for learning to take place is for the student to stop listening and process what they have just heard before continuing with further points in the instruction (Rodger, 1995; Schank, 1998). Schank (1998, pg 23) goes so far as to state that, "lecturing is antithetical to learning."

In addition to problems with concentration and information retention, traditional lectures do not easily accommodate discussion, yet dialog and discussion are considered to be important elements in the promotion of higher-level cognitive processing (Mannison, Patton, & Lemon, 1994). Levels of effectiveness in learning are believed to be directly related to the participation of the student, with students tending to retain much of the material when their engagement with it is high—that is, when they are active learners rather than passive members of an audience (Dale, 1969).

Not all lecture sessions are alike. Lecture sessions may be utilized in a number of ways. In addition to the traditional 'talking head' session, today's IT lecture can involve multimedia demonstrations (e.g., Fagin, 1994; Makkonen, 1998; Robling & Freiseben, 2000), interactive case study analysis (Mukherjee, 2000), role playing exercises (Lynch & Markham, 2003; McConnell, 1996) and in-class problem solving (Rodger, 1995), as well as more unorthodox lecturing approaches, such as class singing as suggested by Siegel (1999). What these approaches have in common is an attempt to introduce active learning to the lecture situation.

One of the most common modifications to the traditional lecture format has been online availability of lecture notes. To reduce the amount of time students spend taking notes and hence make time available for more active learning, many academics have advocated making lecture slides available online prior to the lecture (e.g., Wirth, 2003). However, concerns have been expressed that online availability of lecture notes promotes lower attendance to the detriment of students concerned (Hunter & Tetley, 1999; Khan, 1997; Roosenburg, 2002).

While ideas for teaching innovations abound, very little empirical evidence is available to support them. This chapter addresses the role of lectures within IT degree programs from a student perceptive. It explores the opinions of a group of IT students, examining the factors that influence their lecture attendance, and their perceptions of the usefulness of a variety of possible lecture activities.

The Study

This study was conducted by survey. Participants in the study were students enrolled in a second-year IT course at an Australian university. They had experienced at least 1 year of IT lectures already, and these lectures would have been in classes of various sizes with a wide variety of lecturers. Participants were recruited during the first lecture of the semester and completed a questionnaire on the spot. It was stressed that completion of the questionnaire was voluntary and that it formed no part of their assessment in the course.

The first part of the questionnaire collected background information about participants and information about their lecture attendance. The participants in the study were 113 students (78.8% male, 21.2% female), with an average age of 24 (minimum age of 18 and maximum age of 49). The students were from two campuses of the university; 73.5% attended the larger main campus and 26.5% attended a smaller regional campus.

Students believed that they had attended around 80% of lectures during the previous semester, with a range from 5% to 100% attendance. Given anecdotal reports from academic staff who had previously taught this cohort of students, this average attendance figure might be an overestimate; however, it is consistent with figures reported by Hunter and Tetley (1999).

The second part of the questionnaire included questions that sought to determine the factors that influence whether students attend lectures. A list of factors that have been proposed to influence lecture attendance was provided and participants were asked to indicate if each factor influenced whether they attended lectures. The list of factors that have been proposed to influence lecture attendance was drawn from the literature (e.g., Hunter & Tetley, 1999; Isaacs, 1994; Khan, 1997; Roosenburg, 2002). Table 1 includes the list of factors.

The questionnaire also asked about student perceptions of the role of lecturers. The final questions asked students to rate the usefulness, in terms of their learning, of each of a list of possible lecture activities. This list was also drawn from the literature (e.g., Mannison et al., 1994; Mukherjee, 2000; Rodrigues & Atchison, 1996; Rosenthal, 1995; Wirth, 2003). The lecture activities were rated on a 5-point scale, where 1 was 'not useful' and 5 corresponded to the activity being 'extremely useful.' The Appendix contains a copy of the questions asked.

Results and Discussion

Factors Influencing Lecture Attendance

Various factors have been proposed to influence lecture attendance. Clashes with other classes are an obvious one, because if a student has more than one class scheduled for a particular timeslot, clearly they can be present only at one of them. The time of day in which a lecture is scheduled has been cited as a factor affecting lecture attendance by Khan (1997), who states that lectures timetabled for early morning or late afternoon appear to have a lower level of attendance. As discussed earlier, online availability of lecture notes is another factor that appears to affect lecture attendance, leading to a decrease in attendance as students have an alternative means of accessing at least some of the information provided in lectures (Hunter & Tetley, 1999; Khan, 1997; Roosenburg, 2002). The lecturer's style of teaching has also been suggested as a factor influencing lecture attendance, with approximately 50% of students citing poor-quality lecturing as a reason for non attendance in Khan's (1997) survey. The quality and accessibility of textbooks is another factor that has been suggested as a factor influencing attendance. It is considered that students will attend lectures to gain additional explanation and illustration of concepts presented within the text, especially if the textbook is difficult to understand or presents new or complex material.

Table 1 shows each of these factors ranked from most influential to least influential. Surprisingly, the style of the lecturer's teaching was the most commonly cited determinant of lecture attendance (57.4%). This result is consistent with Khan's (1997) comment that students will be attracted to well-prepared and delivered lectures that are engaging, easy to follow and relevant to their studies. However, this result also implies that while the student may consider that a lecture adds value to his or her learning experience, if the style of the lecturer is not one that suits the student, attendance will fall.

The time of day at which the lecture is scheduled was ranked second (40.7%) among the five factors influencing lecture attendance. This appears to be consistent with

Table 1. Ranked list of factors influencing lecture attendance

Rank	Factor	No. responses citing factor	Percentage of responses
1	Lecturer's style of teaching	62	57.4
2	Time of day lecture scheduled	44	40.7
3	Online availability of lecture notes	35	32.4
4	Clashes with other classes	33	30.6
5	Quality and accessibility of the textbook	22	20.4

Khan (1997), who noted that students prefer classes that are not scheduled during late afternoon or early morning.

Online availability of lecture notes was ranked third among the factors (32.4%) influencing lecture attendance. While not the most influential factor, online availability of lecture notes played a major role in influencing whether or not approximately one-third of the students attended lectures. This is consistent with the results of Hunter and Tetley's (1999) study of the reasons for nonattendance of lectures. Nevertheless, a substantial proportion of students (67.6%) were not influenced by availability of online lecture notes and presumably believe that attending lectures can add further value to their learning experience.

Clashes with other classes were ranked fourth (30.6%). This relatively low ranking may result from careful lecture scheduling in the past, ensuring that a minimal number of classes are timetabled for the same timeslot for this cohort of students. However, a lecture at which some of this data was gathered was inadvertently scheduled to clash with two other classes during the semester, and this fact was noted by a number of students within the comments section of the survey.

The quality and accessibility of the textbook was the least-cited determinant of lecture attendance (20.4%). This may indicate that many students believe that the lecturer adds substantial value to the material available to them, regardless of the quality of the textbook. It may also be that attendance is influenced by a number of these factors in combination. For example, the quality of the textbook might not be such an influential factor if the related lecture notes are available online.

The results were further examined to determine whether gender, age or the campus a student attended had an influence on the factors determining lecture attendance. Possible differences due to gender, age or campus were explored using chi-square tests, as the variables were all measured on nominal scales. Significantly more male students than female students identified teaching style as an influence on their attendance ($\chi^2(1) = 5.004$, $p = 0.025$). One explanation for this is that female students are more likely to view lectures as adding value to their learning regardless of teaching style. However, an alternative explanation might be that lecture attendance meets other needs of female students, such as face-to-face interaction before and after the lecture presentation. No other gender differences were found.

Age appeared to have a significant effect on whether the time of day the lecture was scheduled influenced lecture attendance. Approximately 31% of the sample was at least 24 years old and these students were less influenced by the time of day at which the lecture took place ($\chi^2(1) = 10.137$, $p = 0.001$). It may be that older students, having made the decision to return to study, are more dedicated to completing the course than younger students, and so they will attend the lectures regardless of the time at which they are scheduled. Further research is required to confirm this possibility. No other age differences were observed, nor were any differences noted between the two campuses regarding factors that influenced students' attendance.

Students also identified other factors that might influence lecture attendance. These included the length of the lecture (the lecture for the course in which the survey was administered was at this time scheduled for a 3-hour block, and the majority of students were noted as being opposed to this) and the students' work commitments. However, several students noted that they would always attend lectures both as a preparation for the tutorial work and as an aid in staying up to date within the class, while others claimed laziness and lack of motivation as other factors influencing their attendance at lectures.

Role of the Lecturer

Students were asked to indicate whether they consider the role of lecturers to be 'to teach you' or 'to help you learn.' Despite being asked to select the statement that most accurately reflected their perceptions, a number of students selected both statements. Thus, 19.4% considered the role of lecturers to be to teach students, 51.9% considered it to be to help students learn and 28.7% considered the role of the lecturer to be that of both teaching and helping the student to learn. The results indicate that lecturers are increasingly considered to be guidance or learning support personnel, indicating that students at university have a heightened sense of responsibility for their own scholarship. Thus, student-centered learning appears to be a goal being accepted by university staff and students alike (e.g., Griffiths & Oates, 2003; Lynch & Markham, 2003; McConnell, 1996; Mukherjee, 2000; Rodger, 1995).

Possible differences in perceptions of the role of the lecturer due to gender, age and the campus attended were examined using the chi-square test. While the majority of students saw the role of lecturers to be primarily to help students learn, significantly more male students than female students ($\chi^2 (2) = 7.507$, p = 0.023) still believed the role of lecturers is to teach students (25% of male students compared to 0% of female students). Thus, female students appear to have accepted the responsibility for their learning more readily than male students. This is consistent with the gender difference in response to teaching style discussed above. That is, the lecture attendance of female students is less likely to be affected by their perception of the lecturer's teaching style.

No significant differences were noted between age groups for the perceived role of the lecturer. It thus appears that a student's view of the role of the lecturer does not significantly change as they mature. This result is surprising, given that older students might be expected to take a more mature and self-motivated approach to learning (Piccoli, Ahmad, & Ives, 2001).

A significant difference did exist however, between the two campuses of the university ($\chi^2 (2) = 6.433$, p = 0.040). A much larger percentage of students attending the smaller regional campus (35.7%) considered that the role of the lecturer was to teach them, compared to 13.8% of the students at the main university campus. This result was surprising, as we had anticipated that students attending the larger, more anonymous lectures at the main campus would be predisposed to seeing their own role as a more passive one. However, the difference may be due to the students at the regional campus having a more traditional working class background, and hence being less familiar and comfortable with the technological innovations that tend to support student-centered learning.

Lecture Activity Usefulness

The final part of the questionnaire asked students to rate the usefulness, in terms of their learning, of each of a list of possible lecture activities. All suggested activities were ranked relatively high, indicating that students want more than just the traditional style of lectures. Table 2 shows each of the activities ranked by perceived usefulness.

The lecture activity identified as most useful to learning was practical demonstration. The fact that a number of students also specifically commented that they would like to see practical or 'real-life' applications of the theory covered within lectures provides further evidence of this. The importance of the use of real-world illustrations of course material has also been highlighted by Orngreen and Bielli (2002), Mukherjee (2000), and Rodrigues and Atchison (1996).

Reviewing of exam questions was ranked second in terms of usefulness as a lecture activity. This result may be related to the students' recognition that reviewing exam questions is a useful revision aid for the current lecture topic, particularly when having access to the knowledge of the lecturer while the revision activity is occurring. This result highlights how focused students are on passing courses. With increases in education costs, this is to be expected.

Coverage of the topic material was listed as the third most useful lecture activity. Despite the increased flexibility in approaches to study available to students, many appear to still consider the lecture, and its related additional explanations and clarifications, as a valuable addition to their learning.

Table 2. Perceived usefulness of lecture activities

Rank	Lecture activity	Mean	SD	Min.	Max.
1	Practical demonstrations	4.47	0.74	1	5
2	Reviewing previous exam questions	4.29	0.90	1	5
3	Coverage of topic material	4.12	0.88	1	5
4	Questioning the lecturer	3.78	1.04	1	5
5	Class discussion	3.64	1.06	1	5
6	Videos/Multimedia	3.58	1.04	1	5
7	Small group activities/exercises	3.49	1.05	1	5

Questioning the lecturer was considered fourth in usefulness as a lecture activity. This is further evidence that students view the lecture as an opportunity to add value to their learning experience, and that the expertise of the lecturer is considered to be a significant addition to both their lecture time as well as to their education.

Class discussion was ranked fifth. This relatively low ranking of class discussion as a lecture activity can be explained by the fact that many IT classes are large (Johnston et al., 1996), and group discussion is impractical for large groups. Many students feel uncomfortable expressing themselves in a large public setting, and it is difficult to hear individual contributions within a large lecture theatre. In addition, in Australian universities, class discussion is traditionally an activity performed during tutorial classes. Thus, undertaking an activity already being completed within other learning sessions may not be considered by students to be a useful activity during lecture time. Despite this, Rodger (1995) reported on the value of class discussion in IT lectures, stating that, "Although less material is covered during class, students obtain a deeper understanding of this material and can expand on this understanding outside of class" (p. 278).

Use of videos and multimedia was ranked second lowest. Computer-based activities are perhaps perceived as activities that students can undertake on their own time. Thus, time during lectures could be better spent in activities that are less flexible time-wise and that can take advantage of the expertise of the lecturer while he or she is present. The lowest-ranked lecture activity was that of small group activities and exercises. This result might be explained by small group activities also being prevalent within tutorial classes, and thus the students may not consider this to be a useful addition to the lecture timeslot.

Overall, it appears that activities that provide access to the knowledge and expertise of the lecturer are those most valued during the lecture timeslot. However, it also appears that the students wish to have a greater control of these activities to ensure that the activities undertaken during lecture time suit their perceived needs.

The responses were further examined to determine if differences occurred in perceptions of the usefulness of the suggested lecture activities based on gender, age or the campus surveyed. This analysis was undertaken using independent sample t-tests. The results indicated that on average females overall ranked most of the activities as more useful than males (except for practical demonstrations). However, the only significant differences existed for small group activities/exercises ($t = 0.276$, $p = 0.007$) and questioning the lecturer ($t = 2.35$, $p = 0.021$). This may be an indication that females desire a more personalized approach to learning, relative to their male counterparts. However, more research is required to further explore this finding.

Videos and multimedia were seen as significantly more useful additions by students who were younger (younger than 24 years of age) ($t = 2.35$, $p = 0.021$). One explanation for this finding may be that younger students are more comfortable with the use of technology in education and, hence, perceive it to be more useful. However, future research is required to better clarify this finding.

The only significant difference in preference for lecture activities between campuses was that of class discussion (t = -0.201, p = 0.047), where the students attending the smaller regional campus indicated this as a more useful lecture activity. This difference can be explained by the fact that class discussion during lecture times is more feasible with the smaller class sizes of the regional campus.

Conclusion

The results of this research suggest that students can see the importance of attending lectures, and that they see the lecturer as contributing significant value to their learning experience through the lecture setting. Students appear to value the expertise of the lecturer, and wish to take advantage of this knowledge during lecture time. Thus, despite the influence of the lecturer's teaching style on attendance, the activities that can best make use of the lecturer's expertise are those most preferred to be undertaken during the lecture timeslot.

It also appears that the role of the lecturer is perceived as more than just that of a teacher. Many students have adopted a student-centered view of education and perceive the role of the lecturer as facilitating their learning. The results of the study also suggest recognition of the importance of active learning within the constraints of traditional learning settings. Active learning has received attention among both trainers and academics for its role in aiding learning (Mukherjee, 2000) and encouraging students to become self-directed learners throughout their lifetimes (Meyers & Jones, 1993). Therefore, it should be a goal of all lecturers to involve active learning in their lectures.

This chapter attempted to explore the role of lectures within IT education. As discussed above, many students do see the importance of attending lectures, and see the lecturer as contributing significant value to their learning experience through the lecture setting. However, if lectures are to continue to play a role in IT education, they must facilitate active learning in ways that are appropriate for the size and nature of the course. Given the prevalence of online availability of lecture notes, and the flexibility this provides to students, lecturers must ensure that lecture sessions provide added value. They must provide varied opportunities for students to take advantage of the lecturer's expertise, and also encourage students to become active and self-directed learners.

References

Bligh, D. A. (1972). *What's the use of lectures?* Hammondsworth: Penguin.

Dale, E. (1969). *Audio visual methods in teaching.* New York: Holt, Rinehart, Winston.

Fagin, B. (1994). Two years of "The Digital World": Portable courseware for technological literacy. *SIGCSE Bulletin, 26*(1), 97-101.

Felder, R. (1992). How about a quick one? *Chemical Engineering Education, 26*(1), 18-19.

Griffiths, G., & Oates, B.J. (2003). Lecture-free teaching for systems analysis: An action research study. *Proceedings of the 2003 Informing Science + Information Technology Education Joint Conference,* June.

Hunter, S., & Tetley, J. (1999). Lectures. Why don't students attend? *Cornerstones: What We Value in Higher Education*, 1-8.

Isaacs, G. (1994). Lecturing practices and note-taking purposes. *Studies in Higher Education, 19*(2), 203-216.

Johnston, R., Moffat, A., Sondergaard, H., & Stuckey, P. (1996). Low-contact learning in a first year programming course. *Proceedings of the 1st Australasian Conference on Computer Science Education* (pp. 19-26).

Khan, S. (1997, February). Why don't they come to the lecture? In *Learning Through Teaching: Proceedings of the 6th Annual Teaching Learning Forum,* Perth, Australia (pp. 163-165).

Kumar, A., Kumar, P., & Basu, S.C. (2002). Student perceptions of virtual education: An exploratory study. In M. Khosrow-Pour (Ed.), *Web-based instructional learning* (pp. 132-141). London: IRM Press.

Lynch, K., & Markham, S. (2003). The winds of change: Students' comfort level in different learning environments. *SIGCSE Bulletin, 35*(3), 70-73.

Makkonen, P. (1998). WWW-based presentations as a complementary part of conventional lectures in the basics of informatics. *SIGCSE Bulletin, 30*(3), 162-165.

Mannison, M., Patton, W. & Lemon, G. (1994). Interactive teaching goes to uni: Keeping students awake and learning alive. *Higher Education Research and Development, 13*, 35-47.

McConnell, J. J. (1996). Active learning and its use in computer science. *SIGCSE Bulletin, 28*, 52-54.

McCormick, J. (2000). The new school. *Newsweek, 135*(17), 60-62.

McKeachie, W. J. (1986). *Teaching tips.* Lexington: D.C. Health & Co.

Meyers, C. & Jones, T. B. (1993). *Promoting Active Learning: Strategies for the College Classroom*. San Francisco: Jossey-Bass.

Mukherjee, A. (2000). Effective use of in-class mini case analysis for discovery learning in an undergraduate MIS course. *Journal of Computer Information Systems, 40*(3), 15-23.

Orngreen, R., & Bielli, P. (2002). Learning with multimedia cases in the information systems area. In M. Khosrow-Pour (Ed.), *Web-based instructional learning* (pp. 242-251). London: IRM Press.

Peffers, K., & Bloom, S. (1999). Internet-based innovations for teaching IS courses: The state of adoption, 1998-2000. *Journal of Information Technology Theory and Application, 1*(1), 1-6.

Piccoli, G., Ahmad, R., & Ives, B. (2001). Web-based virtual learning environments: A research framework and a preliminary assessment of effectiveness in basic IT skills training. *MIS Quarterly, 25*(4), 401-427.

Robling, G., & Freiseben, B. (2000). Experiences in using animations in introductory computer science lectures. *SIGCSE Bulletin, 32*(1), 134-138.

Rodger, S. H. (1995). An interactive lecture approach to teaching computer science. *SIGCSE Bulletin, 27*(1), 278-282.

Rodrigues, C. & Atchison, M. (1996). A case-study based approach to assessment of systems design and implementation. *Proceedings of the 1st Australasian Conference on Computer Science Education* (pp. 95-102).

Roosenburg, A. (2002). *Attention, attendance sliding away*. Retrieved July 1, 2004, from www.cavelierdaily.com/CVarticle.asp?ID=12944&pid=895

Rosenthal, J. (1995). Active learning strategies in advanced mathematics classes. *Studies in Higher Education, 19*(2), 223-228.

Schank, R.C. (1998). Horses for courses. *Communications of the ACM, 41*(7), 23-25.

Siegel, E.V. (1999). Why do fools fall into infinite loops: Singing to your computer science class. *SIGCSE Bulletin, 31*(3), 167-170.

Stuart, J., & Rutherford, R. (1978). Medical student concentration during lectures. *The Lancet, 2*, 514-516.

Wirth, M.A. (2003). E-notes: Using electronic lecture notes to support active learning in computer science. *SIGCSE Bulletin, 35*(2), 57-60.

Appendix

1. How old are you? _____ Years

2. What gender are you?
   ☐ Female
   ☐ Male

3. Do you normally attend lectures?

   Rarely   *Always*
   1   2   3   4   5

4. Approximately what percentage of your lectures did you attend last semester? _____ %

5. What factors influenced whether you attended lectures? (tick all that apply)
   ☐ Clashes with other classes
   ☐ Time of day
   ☐ Whether lecture notes could be downloaded
   ☐ Lecturer's style of teaching
   ☐ Quality and accessibility of the textbook
   ☐ Other (add as many as you like)
   _____
   _____

6. Which of the following statements more accurately reflects your perception of the role of a lecturer?
   ☐ To teach you
   ☐ To help you learn
   ☐ Other (add as many as you like)
   _____

7. Please rate the usefulness of each of the following lecture activities in helping your learning.

	Not useful				Extremely useful
Detailed coverage of topic material	1	2	3	4	5
Practical demonstrations	1	2	3	4	5
Videos/multimedia	1	2	3	4	5
Class discussion	1	2	3	4	5
Small group activities/exercises	1	2	3	4	5
Questioning the lecturer	1	2	3	4	5
Reviewing previous exam questions	1	2	3	4	5

Chapter VIII

Training Sequences and their Effects on Task Performance and User Outcomes

Clive Sanford, Aalborg University, Denmark

Anol Bhattacherjee, University of South Florida, USA

Abstract

This chapter introduces the concept of information technology (IT) training sequences and examines how sequencing of conceptual and procedural training impact IT task performance, user satisfaction and users' self-efficacy. Using assimilation theory, we develop four hypotheses related to training sequences. These hypotheses were then tested in a database design context using a quasi-experimental study involving student subjects. Empirical results demonstrate improved far-transfer and near-transfer task performance and higher self-efficacy for subjects trained in the conceptual-procedural sequence vs. the reverse sequence, though user satisfaction was not significantly different between the two sequences. Implications for IT training research are discussed.

Introduction

As IT has been widely adopted by firms as a potent means of improving task performance and user productivity in today's IT-dominated workplace, such adoption has also imposed substantial pressure on firms to continuously train internal users in the knowledge and skills needed to use these systems effectively. Despite innovations in the training domain, such as computer-based, CD-based and online training, the core issue still remains how training programs should be structured to improve IT users' knowledge retention and task performance given predefined technologies, tasks and potential users (Davis & Bostrom, 1993).

Several approaches to IT training have been proposed in the literature, such as instruction-based vs. exploration-based training (Davis & Bostrom, 1993), applications-based vs. construct-based training (Olfman & Bostrom, 1991), and conceptual vs. procedural training (e.g., Olfman & Mandviwalla, 1994; Santhanam & Sein, 1994). Of these, the last taxonomy seems to have gained the broadest acceptance. *Conceptual training* is a "top-down" approach where IT users are trained in the nature and associations of semantic objects required for comprehending and solving a problem, while *procedural training* is a "bottom-up" approach focusing on action-plan sequences that users should learn to complete specific tasks. Because of the direct and immediate applicability of procedural knowledge in specific task situations, procedural training has emerged as the approach of choice for many corporate IT training programs (Atlas, Cornett, Lane, & Napier, 1997).

Prior research on conceptual and procedural training has compared the relative effects of these approaches on IT task performance, reporting mixed results (e.g., Olfman & Mandviwalla, 1994; Santhanam & Sein, 1994). However, researchers tend to agree on the importance of both forms of training. Santhanam and Sein (1994) note that procedural training is more useful when the target system is easy to operate; however, these users tend to perform poorly on novel tasks. They also note, "conceptual training is likely to provide a better opportunity for a user to form a coherent mental model compared to procedural training" (p. 382). Elaborating the gaps in extant IT training research, Olfman and Mandviwalla (1994, p. 407) state, "some *combination* of concepts and procedures is needed … It is the relative quantity and *sequencing* of the two kinds of content that has not been fully established" (emphasis added).

Defining *training sequence* as the ordering of conceptual and procedural training, the objective of this study is to examine whether the conceptual-procedural sequence improves IT task performance and user outcomes, such as satisfaction and self-efficacy, compared to the reverse sequence. Though the importance of training sequences was noted by Olfman and Mandviwalla (1994), to date, empirical analysis of such sequences has remained unexplored in the IT training literature. The idea of training sequences, however, has some support in learning theory (Glaser, 1990) and instructional design theory (Reiguluth & Stein, 1983), where leading proponents have long advocated that user training be conducted in a holistic manner to include both conceptual and procedural components. The rationale is that this strategy integrates two complementary forms of knowledge (concepts and procedures) that are both required for the performance of many complex organizational tasks.

To examine the above research objective, we draw on Ausubel's (1978) assimilation theory in the educational psychology literature to develop four research hypotheses relating training sequences to near- and far-transfer IT task performance (defined later), user satisfaction and user self-efficacy. These hypotheses are then tested empirically via a quasi-experimental laboratory study in a database design context. Results of the analysis confirm that the conceptual-procedural training sequence improves task performance and self-efficacy more than the reverse sequence, though user satisfaction is not significantly different between the two sequences.

The rest of this chapter proceeds as follows: The next section formulates research hypotheses by drawing on assimilation theory and prior IT training research. The third section describes experimental research design, subjects, treatments and measurement. The fourth section describes statistical data analysis techniques and results. The fifth section discusses the study's key findings, limitations and implications for research and practice.

Theory and Research Hypothesis

Assimilation Theory

The individual learning process is presumed to proceed in three stages (Mayer, 1981). In the reception stage, learners acquire new information from the external environment and store it in their short-term memory. The short-term memory is a temporary and limited-capacity storage space where information is stored as distinct entities (instead of integrated knowledge structures). Next, in the availability stage, learners search their long-term memory for knowledge structures (or "schemas") potentially related to the new information. The long-term memory is a permanent and virtually unlimited storage space for classifying, organizing and archiving information using preexisting or new schemas. Finally, in the activation stage, the new information is transferred from the short-term memory to appropriate knowledge structures or "anchors" in the long-term memory, where it is mapped and integrated with prior schemas and preserved for future use.

Assimilation theory defines two types of human learning: meaningful learning and rote learning (Ausubel, 1978). *Meaningful learning* (or assimilation) occurs when learners relate, connect and integrate new information with that already stored in existing knowledge structures or schemas in their long-term memory. In contrast, *rote learning* (or memorization) occurs when learners store new information in their short-term memory in a disjointed manner, without integrating that information within schemas in their long-term memory. While rote learning requires the completion of only the reception stage in Mayer's (1981) three-stage learning process, meaningful learning occurs only when all three stages are completed.

Rote learned information, such as procedural rules, is often useful in performing tasks that are simple, routine or structurally similar to that of the learning context (termed *near-transfer tasks*), but provides little assistance in performing novel, creative or structurally dissimilar tasks (*far-transfer tasks*). Further, this information is difficult to retain over the long term because of its lack of organizing structure. Being stored in the short-term memory, it is also susceptible to interference from new information. However, meaningfully learned information residing in the long-term memory is often useful in performing novel, dissimilar or far-transfer tasks, is temporally stable and is retained for a longer period of time (Davis & Bostrom, 1993). Moreover, meaningful learning takes advantage of the knowledge already possessed by the learner, which is purportedly the single most important driver of individual learning (Ausubel, 1978).

Many organizational IT tasks, such as transaction processing and electronic mail (e-mail) usage, are of the near-transfer type, requiring users to learn procedural know-hows, such as event sequences and screen layouts. However, other tasks, such as decision-making and executive planning, are of far-transfer type, requiring conceptual know-whats, such as what-if analysis and ad hoc data mining. Complex knowledge work, such as system development, often involve both components, in that the designers should not only learn near-transfer details such as program coding, application program interfaces and integrated development environment (IDE) features that are easily transferable across projects, but also less transferable far-transfer knowledge, such as requirements planning, systems analysis and integration test planning. Hence, successful comprehension and performance of such tasks are best supported by a combination of conceptual and procedural approaches, which we call a "training sequence."

Prior research have compared conceptual vs. procedural training for Windows accessories (Write and Paintbrush) (Olfman & Mandviwalla, 1994) and the VAX e-mail system (Santhanam & Sein, 1994), and found no significant difference in effects between the two approaches. Though these studies contrasted training *approaches*, no studies to date have empirically studied training *sequences*. Further, prior research has mostly focused on relatively simple IT tasks, such as e-mail or spreadsheet usage, where training sequence may have marginal impact. As described next, training sequences are likely have a greater impact on more complex tasks of the type examined in this study (database design).

IT Training Sequences

In complex IT tasks requiring both conceptual and procedural knowledge, do users perform better if they are trained conceptually first, then procedurally, vs. the reverse sequence? Assimilation theory suggests that training sequences are not commutative and that the two sequences have differential effects on users' ability to retain and apply knowledge (Ausubel, 1978). In the conceptual-procedural sequence, the knowledge structures or schemas developed during initial conceptual training provide a meaningful context or "ideational scaffolding" (Ausubel, 1978) for interpreting and assimilating action-plan details acquired later, aiding near-transfer task performance. In contrast, in a procedural-conceptual sequence, lack of mental schemas during initial procedural training may hinder appropriate "anchoring" of concepts during subsequent conceptual training, hurting far-transfer task performance. Anderson (1995) noted that some users may be able to infer conceptual knowledge from procedural details learned earlier. However, we argue that such inference is more likely for simple (primarily procedural) IT tasks/technologies, such as e-mail or word processor usage, but less so for more complex tasks, such as database design or system development, requiring substantial levels of both conceptual and procedural knowledge. Training sequences, therefore, are expected to be more relevant in the performance of complex IT tasks (i.e., IT-based knowledge work).

In the conceptual-procedural sequence, the need for assimilative schemas or "advance organizers" (e.g., high-level ideas, diagrams, abstracts) was highlighted by Ausubel (1978), who found that learners' recall of ambiguous textual content improved significantly when an organizing title was provided prior to the actual textual material, while the organizing title had no effect on subjects' learning or retention if presented after the learner had read the text. Likewise, Reigeluth and Stein (1983) recommended designing instructional content as "elaborative sequences," where the general concepts are presented first, followed progressively by differentiated levels of procedural details and specificity. Hence, we hypothesize:

H1:   IT users trained in a conceptual-procedural sequence perform *near-transfer* IT tasks better than those trained in a procedural-conceptual sequence.

H2:   IT users trained in a conceptual-procedural sequence perform *far-transfer* IT tasks better than those trained in a procedural-conceptual sequence.

Though task performance is the primary dependent variable of interest to corporate IT trainers and managers, we also examine two user-related outcomes – user satisfaction and self-efficacy—that are increasingly being viewed as key motivators of user learning/training circumstances. *Satisfaction* refers to users' affective evaluation of their own task performance, and *self-efficacy* is the cognitive belief in their ability to perform similar tasks in the future. Bandura's (1986) social cognitive theory provides theoretical support for the self-efficacy construct, which is theorized to be directly related to satisfaction and future task performance. Empirically, Yi and Davis (2003) demonstrate that post-training software self-efficacy is related to intermediate-term and long-term task performance; Compeau and Higgins (1995) justify the linkage between IT training and self-efficacy; and Compeau, Higgins and Huff (1999) validate the association between self-efficacy and affect (e.g., satisfaction). Following a meta-analysis of the training literature, Colquitt, LePine and Noe (2000) show that pre-training self-efficacy positively impacts motivation to learn, which in turn affects post-training self-efficacy and task performance.

Most users tend to favor procedural training because of its technology-focused and hands-on nature and its ability to quickly initiate a user to a specific task at hand. Carroll and Rosson (1987) contend that users prefer learning quick procedures that can help them get started with system usage and thereby minimize the "IT productivity paradox," rather than "waste" their time understanding concepts. Since procedural-conceptual sequence initiates users to procedural training faster, users are more likely to be satisfied with this sequence than with the reverse sequence. In contrast, self-efficacy should be higher for the conceptual-procedural sequence, because as these users perform near-transfer and far-transfer tasks better (per assimilation theory); they gain confidence in their ability to perform similar tasks in the future. Hence, we hypothesize:

H3:   IT users trained in a conceptual-procedural sequence experience *lower* satisfaction with IT task performance than those trained in a procedural-conceptual sequence.

H4:   IT users trained in a conceptual-procedural sequence experience *higher* self-efficacy regarding their IT task performance than those trained in a procedural-conceptual sequence.

Control Variables

Extraneous variables that can potentially confound the above hypotheses can be grouped into four categories: (1) technology attributes, (2) training context (e.g., trainer, setting), (3) task attributes, and (4) trainee attributes (individual differences). The first three categories can be partially controlled via appropriate research designs; for example, by employing a single IT (technology attributes); a common training approach, duration and trainer for all sessions (training context); and common IT tasks (task attributes). We control for individual differences by adding prior IT experience and attitude toward IT as control variables in our study, for reasons described below.

Users' prior IT experience may be an alternative source of assimilative schemas (as opposed to conceptual training) driving the meaningful learning process (Santhanam & Sein, 1994). Ex ante availability of such schemas in long-term memory (from prior experience) can help more experienced IT users anchor and assimilate new procedural information without additional conceptual training. Programmers already familiar with one programming language often find it easier to learn a second similar language, because they can assimilate the procedural details (e.g., syntax) of the second language within schemas (e.g., branching, iteration, arrays) acquired from the first. In contrast, lack of such schemas may force relatively novice or inexperienced users to rely on rote learning for retaining procedural details for near-transfer task performance. Prior IT experience, therefore, can confound the impact of training sequence on near-transfer task performance and is included in this study as a control variable.

IT users' task performance may also be confounded by their attitude (affect) toward IT tasks (Bostrom, Olfman, & Sein, 1990; Olfman & Pitsatorn, 2000). Users with positive attitudes (e.g., enthusiastic users) often put in more effort in task performance, irrespective of their prior conceptual and/or procedural training, resulting in improved task performance. In contrast, users with negative attitudes (e.g., less motivated users) may be reticent to put forth their best effort despite extensive prior training, leading to poor performance. In order to tease out the effect of IT training sequences on task performance, we include attitude as a second control variable.

Research Methodology

Experimental Design, Subjects and Treatments

A quasi-experimental laboratory study (see Figure 1) using student subjects was conducted in a database design context to empirically test our four research hypotheses. Entire class sections were randomly assigned to one of the two treatment groups (conceptual-procedural or procedural-conceptual training sequence); hence the quasi-experimental design. A mixed-model research design was employed, where (1) different subjects experience different treatments, and (2) all subjects experience each treatment (Myers, 1977). An explicit control group (with no treatment) was not required, since each group acted as a control for the other group. All treatments were administered by the same instructor, using a combination of lectures, discussions, in-class exercises and graded assignments.

Subjects for this study were drawn from undergraduate and graduate students (approximately 50% in each category) enrolled in four sections of a database management class at a large public university. The subject pool had a mean age of 26

Figure 1. Research design

	Week 0	Weeks 1-3	Weeks 4-6	Week 7	
Group A	O_{PRE}	X_{CT}	X_{PT}	O_{FT+NT}	O_{POST}
Group B	O_{PRE}	X_{PT}	X_{CT}	O_{FT+NT}	O_{POST}

Legend: O_i = Observations (questionnaires: PRE, POST;
tasks: near transfer [NT], far transfer [FT])
X_i = Training (conceptual [CT], procedural [PT])

years, full-time work experience of 3.7 years, computer-related work experience of 2.8 years, and database usage (but not design) experience of 0.9 years. Forty-one percent of these subjects were previously or currently employed in the IT industry, being somewhat representative of the target population of IT professionals. Though student and non-student subjects may differ in their intrinsic motivation toward learning database design, we attempted to control for this difference by including subjects' attitude as a covariate in our research design. Further, our use of student subjects was consistent with much prior IT training research (e.g., Ahrens & Sankar, 1993; Davis & Bostrom, 1993; Santhanam & Sein, 1994).

The database design task was selected because this is a typical example of a complex IT task that included elements of both conceptual and procedural knowledge, which rendered it well to the research objectives of this study. Though this particular task has seen very limited use in prior IT training research (one exception being Ahrens and Sankar, 1993), it is a fairly common task domain for real-life IT professionals and hence, was deemed appropriate.

Prior to the experimental treatments, subjects were administered a short pre-treatment questionnaire soliciting demographic information, prior work experience (general and IT related) and attitude toward learning database design. For the next 3 weeks, about half of the subject pool (Group A in Figure 1) received conceptual training on database design, while the other half (Group B) received procedural training. The conceptual training focused on abstracting a conceptual data model from a textual narrative of users' data needs, documented in the form of an entity-relationship diagram (ERD). This training included: (1) identifying data objects (entities), (2) specifying relationships between entities, (3) identifying attributes for each entity, and (4) establishing relationship cardinalities (e.g., one-to-many, subtype-supertype, mandatory-optional). Procedural training focused on converting an existing ERD into a logical data model (LDM) (a set of third normal form relations or tables for relational implementation) using procedural rules. Specific activities included: (1) mapping entities into relations, (2) specifying primary keys, (3) normalizing relations into third normal form, and (4) specifying relationships using foreign keys or associative relations.[1] For weeks 4-6, the training approach (and content) was reversed for the two groups, so that Group A subjects received procedural training and Group B received conceptual training. Each 3-week training period ended with an in-class database design exercise intended to help subjects internalize their recent learning experience, which was graded and returned to the subjects. On the 7th week, subjects were asked to complete an in-class database design task that involved both far- and near-transfer components (i.e., design an ERD and LDM from a given user narrative), following which, they recorded their post-training satisfaction and self-efficacy in a post-treatment questionnaire.

Construct Measurement

Training sequence (independent variable) was manipulated via treatment assignment. Prior IT experience and attitude (control variables) were measured via the pre-treatment questionnaire. Among dependent variables, IT task performance was assessed by three independent judges, and IT user satisfaction and self-efficacy were assessed perceptually using the post-treatment questionnaire. A combination of fill-in, Likert-scale, semantic differential and externally evaluated measures were employed to reduce common methods bias. Scale items were adapted from pre-validated measures, appropriately modified for the database design context, and are listed in Appendix A.

Prior IT experience was assessed using three fill-in questions that asked subjects the number of years they had worked with (1) computers, (2) databases, and (3) programming (item means were 2.8, 0.9 and 1.2 years, respectively). Databases and programming are two typical functional domains of IT tasks, and thus were considered appropriate for this scale. The overall experience measure was computed as the average of these three items.

Attitude was measured using three seven-point semantic differential items anchored between adjective pairs: (1) extremely bad ... extremely good, (2) extremely desirable ... extremely undesirable, and 3) strongly dislike ... strongly like. These items were adapted from Mathieson (1991) and reworded to relate specifically to the database design context.

Near-transfer and far-transfer task performances were evaluated by a panel of three independent judges. The panel consisted of one teaching faculty, one research faculty and one graduate assistant experienced in database design. A diverse panel was purposely chosen to reduce potential judgment biases among judges. However, to ensure consistency in judges' performance assessment, assessment rules were discussed and agreed upon prior to actual grading.[2] Each judge assigned a score of 1 (completely incorrect), 2 (mostly incorrect), 3 (about half-correct), 4 (mostly correct) and 5 (completely correct) for each task, which were later averaged across judges for an overall score for that task. External assessment helped avoid subjectivity often inherent in self-reported performance measures.

Satisfaction, referring to subjects' overall emotional state following IT task experience, was assessed using three seven-point semantic differential items from Bhattacherjee (2001). These items were anchored between adjective pairs: (1) extremely dissatisfied ... extremely satisfied, (2) extremely frustrated ... extremely contented, and (3) extremely terrible ... extremely delighted. A fourth item in the original scale (extremely displeased ... extremely pleased) was dropped because of its semantic proximity with the first item.

Self-efficacy was measured using five seven-point Likert-scaled items (anchored between "strongly disagree" and "strongly agree") taken from Compeau et al.'s (1999) computer self-efficacy scale. These items examined subjects' confidence in their ability to design databases (1) without help from anyone, (2) using only database manuals for reference, (3) using only an online help facility for assistance, (4) if adequate time is available to complete the tasks, and (5) if someone can be reached for assistance. Compeau's scale had five additional items that were not applicable to our study, given that we were measuring post-usage self-efficacy (while Compeau et al. measured pre-usage self-efficacy), and thus were dropped from our scale.[3]

Data Analysis and Results

Pilot Study

Since IT experimental studies are often plagued with inadequate treatments, unreasonable tasks (for target subjects) and unclear instrumentation (Jarvenpaa, Dickson & DeSanctis, 1985), a pilot study was conducted prior to the actual empirical study to examine these issues. This study involved 19 undergraduate subjects, 10 of whom were trained using the conceptual-procedural sequence, while the remaining nine were trained in the reverse sequence. Subjects completed the near-transfer and far-transfer tasks and the pre- and post-questionnaires as shown in Figure 1. In addition, they were asked to comment on the reasonableness of tasks, the adequacy of the preceding training, and the clarity and understandability of scale items.

Subjects confirmed that the assigned far-transfer and near-transfer tasks were indeed reasonable (most scores ranged between 3.5 and 4.5 on a 5-point task performance scale) and that a 3-week training duration for each task type was adequate for acquiring the necessary database design skills for performing these tasks. However, based on their inputs, some of the scale items and task descriptions were slightly reworded to improve understandability. Since IT task performance was a key dependent variable in this study, we also examined correspondence between judges' ratings of this variable using Pearson's correlation coefficients. This statistic ranged between 0.61 and 0.72 for pairs of judges, with a mean correlation of 0.67. All correlations were significant at $p < 0.01$, indicating a high level of agreement between judges.

Finally, effect size estimates (means and standard deviations) obtained from the pilot study was used to estimate optimal sample sizes required to detect the hypothesized effects in the main study. Power calculations based on a two-sample, normal, equal variance distribution, desired statistical power of 0.80 and significance level of 0.05 yielded a minimum sample size of 52 to detect the hypothesized far- and near-transfer task performance effects. To be on the safe side, we decided to target a desired sample size of 100.

Instrument Validation

The final empirical study consisted of a total of 121 subjects. This subject pool consisted of 59 graduate and 62 undergraduate students. Sixty subjects were trained using the conceptual-procedural sequence and 61 subjects were trained in the reverse sequence. Comparison of means tests revealed that the two treatment groups were not significantly different with respect to age (means 25.35 and 25.94 years, t=0.88, df=138), prior work experience (means 3.41 and 3.82 years, t=0.77), prior computer-related work experience (means 2.61 and 2.71 years, t=0.21) and prior database usage experience (means 0.70 and 0.99 years, t=1.09), assuring equivalency between groups. Approximately equal-sized treatment groups also improved the statistical power of our analysis (described later).

The first step in our statistical data analysis was to examine the psychometric properties (validity and reliability) of scale items. For this purpose, the three perceptual scales in this study—IT user attitude, satisfaction and self-efficacy—were factor analyzed using the principal components technique with direct oblimin rotation (oblique rotation was chosen because the scales were expected to be correlated). Prior IT work experience was excluded from this analysis since it consisted of three self-reported fill-in items. Three factors were identified based on a visual examination of the scree plot and a minimum eigenvalue criterion of 1.0, which respectively extracted 41%, 22%, and 18% of the total variance (cumulative variance of 81%). Item factor loadings, along with item means and standard deviations, are listed in Table 1.

For convergent validity, hypothesized scale items should have factor loadings exceeding 0.60 on their underlying scales (SAS Institute, 1990). This condition was met by all items in the attitude and satisfaction scales, and four out of five self-efficacy items, except SE5 ("… if I can call someone for help"). For discriminant validity, cross-factor loadings (on other scales) should be less than 0.30 (SAS Institute, 1990). This condition was also met by all items except SE5. In light of the above problems, item SE5 was dropped from the self-efficacy scale. Cronbach alpha for the remaining scales were 0.88 for attitude, 0.91 for satisfaction and 0.92 for self-efficacy—all exceeding the minimum of 0.80 required for confirmatory research.

Table 1. Scale reliabilities and validities

Scale Item	Mean	Std. Dev.	Factor Loadings (Direct Oblimin Rotation)		
			Factor 1 (Self-Efficacy)	Factor 2 (Attitude)	Factor 3 (Satisfaction)
ATT1	5.78	1.30	0.07	**0.90**	-0.08
ATT2	5.89	1.16	0.12	**0.89**	0.08
ATT3	5.93	1.11	0.02	**0.90**	-0.01
SAT1	5.22	1.45	0.23	-0.01	**0.84**
SAT2	5.31	1.58	0.19	-0.04	**0.94**
SAT3	5.11	1.58	0.21	0.06	**0.92**
SE1	4.94	1.67	**0.94**	0.10	0.14
SE2	4.90	1.69	**0.93**	0.07	0.15
SE3	5.14	1.60	**0.87**	0.10	0.02
SE4	4.98	1.71	**0.86**	-0.03	0.27
SE5	5.02	1.47	*0.33*	0.10	*0.58*
Eigenvalue			4.51	2.43	1.97
Variance extracted			40.95%	22.10%	17.86%
Cronbach alpha (reduced scales)			0.92	0.88	0.91

Inter-rater reliability for IT task performance (rated by three judges) was assessed by pooling together the near-transfer and far-transfer task performance scores and examining Pearson correlations between pairs of judge ratings. All correlations were significant at $p < 0.01$ (two-tailed), and the mean correlation was 0.713. High agreement between judges was proof of the quality of this measure.

Hypotheses Testing

Means and standard deviations of aggregated dependent variables for the overall sample and for each treatment group are listed in Table 2. Group A (conceptual-

Table 2. Group means and standard deviations

	Means (Standard Deviations)		
	Conceptual-Procedural (N=60)	Procedural-Conceptual (N=61)	Overall (N=121)
Near-transfer task performance	4.57 (0.46)	4.09 (0.54)	4.33 (0.55)
Far-transfer task performance	4.31 (0.37)	3.79 (0.45)	4.04 (0.49)
Satisfaction	5.13 (1.41)	5.29 (1.42)	5.21 (1.41)
Self-efficacy	5.30 (1.40)	4.68 (1.56)	4.99 (1.51)
Note: Far- and near-transfer task performance was assessed on 5-point scales (by external judges); satisfaction and self-efficacy was assessed on 7-point Likert scales (by subjects).			

Table 3. MANCOVA results

	Hotelling's Trace	Wilks' Lambda	F-statistic	p-value	Power*
Intercept	3.50	0.22	99.87	0.00	1.00
Treatment Group	0.41	0.71	11.59	0.00	1.00
Prior IT Experience	0.06	0.94	1.76	0.14	0.52
Attitude	0.02	0.98	0.48	0.75	0.16

Design: Dependent variables = Intercept + Treatment group + Prior IT experience + Attitude
Dependent variables: Far-transfer task performance, Near-transfer task performance, Satisfaction, Self-efficacy – all measured at time T_3
Hypotheses DF was 4 and error DF was 114 in all cases.
*Power estimated using α=0.05.

procedural sequence) experienced higher far- and near-transfer task performance means on Week 7 (4.31 and 4.57, respectively, on 5-point scales) than Group B (procedural-conceptual sequence) (3.79 and 4.09, respectively), as expected from Hypotheses H1 and H2. Satisfaction was lower and self-efficacy was higher for Group A (5.13 and 5.30, respectively, on 7-point scales) compared to that of Group B (5.29 and 4.68, respectively), in accordance with Hypotheses H3 and H4. Hence, the directionality of empirically observed effects is consistent with theory.

The multiple analysis of covariance (MANCOVA) technique, followed by univariate analysis of covariance (ANCOVA) for each dependent variable, was used to examine whether the above differences were significant. This approach was appropriate, since our independent variable (training sequence) was categorical, the four dependent variables (far- and near-transfer task performance, self-efficacy and satisfaction) were interval-scaled, and covariates (prior IT experience and pre-training attitude) were also interval-scaled. Per the multivariate central limit theorem, two-group comparison analysis is robust to violations of the multivariate normality and equality of variance/covariance assumptions for large samples (> 20 per group), as was the case in our study.[4]

MANCOVA was performed using the general linear model approach; the results are presented in Table 3. Four multivariate significance tests were performed: Hotelling's Trace, Wilks' Lambda, Pillai's Trace and Roy's Largest Root test.[5] Each test reported a significant treatment effect (training sequence), with an F-statistic of 11.59 ($p<0.01$) and statistical power close to 1.00, confirming a multivariate treatment effect of training sequence on four dependent variables: far-transfer task performance, near-transfer task performance, satisfaction and self-efficacy. The covariates, prior IT experience and attitude, had non-significant effects (p-values of 0.14 and 0.75,

Table 4. ANCOVA results

	Sum Squares	DF	F-statistic	p-value	Power*
Hypothesis H1: Dependent variable=Near-transfer task performance; Supported					
Intercept	62.03	1	247.95	0.00	1.00
Treatment Group	6.73	1	26.89	0.00	0.99
Prior IT Experience	.47	1	1.87	0.17	0.27
Attitude	.17	1	0.69	0.41	0.13
Error	29.27	117			
Hypothesis H2: Dependent variable=Far-transfer task performance; Supported					
Intercept	54.03	1	318.96	0.00	1.00
Treatment Group	7.77	1	45.88	0.00	1.00
Prior IT Experience	0.03	1	0.20	0.65	0.07
Attitude	0.33	1	1.92	0.17	0.28
Error	19.82	117			
Hypothesis H3: Dependent variable=Satisfaction; Not Supported					
Intercept	94.98	1	47.02	0.00	1.00
Treatment Group	0.73	1	0.36	0.55	0.09
Prior IT Experience	1.49	1	0.74	0.39	0.14
Attitude	0.02	1	0.01	0.92	0.05
Error	236.36	117			
Hypothesis H4: Dependent variable=Self-efficacy; Supported					
Intercept	78.99	1	35.52	0.00	1.00
Treatment Group	10.76	1	4.84	0.03	0.59
Prior IT Experience	0.28	1	0.13	0.72	0.06
Attitude	0.53	1	0.24	0.63	0.08
Error	260.23	117			
Design: Dependent variable = Intercept + Treatment group + Prior IT experience + Attitude					
*Power estimated using α=0.05.					

respectively) on the dependent variables; however, these lack of effects may have been masked by low power (presumably due to small effect sizes).

Results of follow-up univariate ANCOVAs (tests for individual hypotheses) are reported in Table 4. These results indicate that the treatment effect was significant for near-transfer task performance (F=26.89, p<0.01) when controlled for users' pre-treatment IT experience and attitude. Coupled with the higher mean for Group A (4.57) than for Group B (4.09) (see Table 2), this indicates that the conceptual-procedural training sequence resulted in significantly better near-transfer task performance than the procedural-conceptual sequence. Likewise, the significant treatment effect for far-transfer task performance at time T_3 (F=45.88, p<0.01) combined with the higher mean for Group A (4.31) than that of Group B (3.79), demonstrates the superiority of the conceptual-procedural training sequence in far-transfer task performance. Hence, Hypotheses H1 and H2 were both supported. Note that the statistical power of both effects equaled or exceeded 0.99, providing high confidence in our empirical findings.

Post-training satisfaction was expected to be significantly lower for Group A than for Group B (Hypothesis H3), while the reverse effect was expected for self-efficacy (Hypothesis H4). In conjunction with the self-efficacy means (5.30 and 4.58 for Groups A and B, respectively), ANCOVA results supported H4 (F=4.84, p=0.03), though the statistical power of this test was lower than desired (0.59). However, H3 was not supported (F=0.36, p=0.55), despite the group means for satisfaction being in accordance with the stated hypothesis (5.13 and 5.29 for Groups A and B, respectively), indicating that satisfaction may not differ significantly across training sequences. Even if users value procedural training more than conceptual training, the above results indicate that they may be indifferent to whether the procedural training is received earlier or later in the training sequence. Implications of these findings are discussed in the next section.

Discussions and Conclusion

Key Findings and Implications

The goal of this study was to examine whether conceptual-procedural or procedural-conceptual training sequence was most effective in achieving the best IT task and user outcomes. Drawing from assimilation theory (Ausubel, 1978), we postulated that a conceptual-procedural training sequence can provide better near-transfer task performance, far-transfer task performance and user self-efficacy but lower user satisfaction than a procedural-conceptual sequence. These hypotheses were empirically tested using a quasi-experimental study of 121 subjects in a database design context, while controlling for subjects' pre-treatment attitude and IT experience.

Assimilation theory predicted that the conceptual-procedural sequence is better for near-transfer and far-transfer task performance because prior conceptual training creates mental schemas that help assimilate procedural details during subsequent procedural training. Since IT users trained in the conceptual-procedural sequence experience better task performance, they gained confidence in their ability to perform similar tasks and, hence, increased their self-efficacy. In contrast, the reverse sequence was expected to be more satisfying, because users can directly relate to action-plan knowledge gained during the procedural training but not necessarily to the abstract schemas acquired during conceptual training.

Our empirical findings supported the predicted effects for far- and near-transfer task performances and user self-efficacy, but not for user satisfaction. The satisfaction mean was slightly higher for procedural-conceptual sequence as expected, but this difference was non-significant. Hence, procedure-first IT training programs, often employed to maximize user satisfaction, are marginally useful in enhancing satisfaction while adversely impacting near-transfer and far-transfer task performance and self-efficacy. Instead, scarce training resources are best utilized in designing training programs where conceptual training precedes (rather than follows) procedural training, especially for complex IT tasks involving both conceptual and procedural knowledge.

Limitations of the Study

Like most experimental studies, this study is not without limitations. First, one may question whether the study's findings, inferred using student subjects, are generalizable to the general population of IT users because of differences in intrinsic motivation between the sample and the population. However, the mean work experience of 3.7 years and mean computer-related work experience of 2.8 years make our sample somewhat representative of the target population. Further, many of our subjects were also employed in the local IT industry at the time of the study. The key difference between student subjects and the IT workforce at large is often prior IT experience, which was controlled for in this study.

Second, though our post-test-only design alleviated several threats to internal validity—such as pre-test/post-test sensitization, statistical regression (toward the mean), and subject mortality—it may still have been susceptible to novelty effect (subjects' newness of database design task), Hawthorne effect (subjects' awareness that they were participating in an experiment) and Rosenthal effect (the researcher's physical proximity to subjects during task performance) (see Huck, Cormier, & Bounds, 1974).

Third, since we used both undergraduate and graduate students in our sample, one may argue whether these two groups were systematically different in their response patterns. Graduate students tend to be older and have more work experience than undergraduate students, and may even demonstrate a more positive attitude toward IT learning. We eliminated these concerns by controlling for prior IT experience and pre-training attitude in our research design. The F-statistics and p-values of these effects (see Table 4) suggest that even if undergraduates differed from graduate students on these dimensions, such differences did not significantly influence their task performance or personal outcomes.

Finally, it may be questioned whether our findings, based on a database design task, can be generalized to other types of IT tasks. A database task was chosen in this study because of its combination of conceptual and procedural content typical of most complex IT tasks. While this is different from simpler and more procedurally oriented tasks examined in prior training research (e.g., e-mail or spreadsheet usage), we expect our findings to be generalizable to other complex tasks, though this assertion cannot be validated without additional studies. Further, we expect task complexity to moderate the effects of training sequences on task and user outcomes, which is also left open for future research.

Contributions for Research and Practice

The study makes several important contributions for IT training research and practice. First, it introduces the concept of IT training sequences and describes how training sequences should be structured for optimal task and user outcomes. For IT tasks that require both conceptual and procedural knowledge, we demonstrate that conceptual training should precede procedural training, so that IT users can form conceptual schemas prior to assimilating action plan sequences using these schemas. Even if the conceptual-procedural training sequence marginally decreases user satisfaction, it is still preferable by virtue of its positive impacts on near-transfer and far-transfer task performance and user self-efficacy. For practitioners, this finding offers some guidelines on how to allocate scarce training resources for the best outcomes. For researchers, this study empirically validates the expectation from prior research that conceptual training prior to procedural training helps form better mental models (e.g., Santhanam & Sein, 1994) and extended this logic to demonstrate its effects on task performance and user outcomes.

Second, this study was one of the earliest to examine multiple types of training outcomes. Specifically, we examine two task outcomes (near-transfer and far-transfer task performances) and two user outcomes (self-efficacy and satisfaction), and demonstrate that these constructs do not necessarily covary. We did not fully explore the theoretical linkages between these outcomes, but this presents an opportunity for future researchers to extend the current study.

Finally, while prior studies examined training involving simple IT tasks/technologies such as e-mail, spreadsheet or word processing usage, this study was one of the earliest focusing on complex IT tasks, such as database design, typical of today's knowledge-based work. Appropriate training sequence is more critical in the latter context, given its higher conceptual and procedural knowledge requirements. As IT tasks/technologies become more complex, it will be important to broaden our range of training contexts to examine areas such as database design. Further, consideration of task complexity may help reconcile some of the mixed empirical findings reported in prior training research and build a cumulative body of knowledge in this area.

References

Ahrens, J. D., & Sankar, C.S. (1993). Tailoring database training for end users. *Management Information Systems Quarterly, 17*(4), December, 419-439.

Anderson, J. R. (1995). *Cognitive psychology and its implications* (4th ed.). New York: Freeman.

Atlas, R., Cornett, L., Lane, D.M., & Napier, H.A. (1997). The use of animation in software training: Pitfalls and benefits. In M. Quinoñes & A. Dutta (Eds.), *Training for 21st century technology: Applications of psychological research.* Washington, DC: American Psychological Society.

Ausubel, D. (1978). *Educational psychology: A cognitive view* (2nd ed.). New York: Holt, Reinhart & Winston.

Bandura, A. (1986). *Social foundations of thought and action.* Englewood Cliffs: Prentice Hall.

Bhattacherjee, A. (2001). Understanding information systems continuance: An expectation-confirmation model. *Management Information Systems Quarterly, 25*(3), 351-370.

Bostrom, R.P., Olfman, L., & Sein, M.K. (1990). The importance of learning style in end-user training. *Management Information Systems Quarterly, 14*(1), 101-119.

Carroll, J. M., & Rosson, M. B. (1987). Paradox of the active user. In J. M. Rosson (Ed.), *Interfacing thought: Cognitive aspects of human-computer interaction.* Cambridge: Cambridge Press.

Colquitt, J. A., LePine, J. A., & Noe, R. A. (2000). Toward an integrative theory of training motivation: A meta-analytic path analysis of 20 years of research. *Journal of Applied Psychology, 85*(5), 678-707.

Compeau, D. R., & Higgins, C.A. (1995). Application of social cognitive theory to training for computer skills. *Information Systems Research, 6*(2), 118-143.

Compeau, D. R., Higgins, C. A., & Huff, S. (1999). Social cognitive theory and individual reactions to computing technology: A longitudinal study. *Management Information Systems Quarterly, 23*(2), 145-159.

Davis, S. A., & Bostrom, R. P. (1993). Training end users: An experimental investigation of the roles of the computer interface and training methods. *Management Information Systems Quarterly, 17*(1), 61-85.

Glaser, R. (1990). The reemergence of learning theory within instructional research. *American Psychologist, 45*(1), 29-39.

Huck, S. W., Cormier, W. H., & Bounds, W. G. (1974). *Reading statistics and research.* New York: Harper Collins.

Jarvenpaa, S. L., Dickson, G. W., & DeSanctis, G. (1985). Methodological issues in experimental IS research: Experiences and recommendations. *Management Information Systems Quarterly, 9*(2), 141-156.

Johnson, R. A., & Wichern, D. A. (2002). *Applied multivariate statistical analysis* (5th ed.). Upper Saddle River: Prentice Hall.

Mathieson, K. (1991). Predicting user intentions: Comparing the technology acceptance model with the theory of planned behavior. *Information Systems Research, 2*(3), 173-191.

Mayer, R. E. (1981). The psychology of how novices learn computer programming. *ACM Computing Surveys, 13*, 121-141.

Myers, J. (1977). *Fundamentals of experimental design* (2nd ed.). Boston: Allyn and Bacon.

Olfman, L., & Bostrom, R. P. (1991). End-user software training: An experimental comparison of methods to enhance motivation. *Journal of Information Systems, 1*(4), 249-266.

Olfman, L., & Mandviwalla, M. (1994). Conceptual versus procedural software training for graphical user interfaces: A longitudinal field experiment. *Management Information Systems Quarterly, 18*(4), 405-426.

Olfman, L., & Pitsatorn, P. (2000). End-user training research: Status and models for the future. In R.W. Zmud (Ed.), *Framing the domains of IT management.* Cincinnati: Pinnaflex Educational Resources.

Reigeluth, C. M., & Stein, F. (1983). The elaboration theory of instruction. In C. Reigeluth (Ed.), *Instructional design theories and models.* Hillsdale: Lawrence Erlbaum Associates.

Santhanam, R., & Sein, M.K. (1994). Improving end-user proficiency: Effects of conceptual training and nature of interaction. *Information Systems Research, 5*(4), 378-399.

SAS Institute Inc. (1990). *SAS/Stat users guide* (Vols. 1 and 2). Cary, NC: Author.

Yi, M. Y., & Davis, F. D. (2003). Developing and validating an observational learning model of computer software training and skill acquisition. *Information Systems Research, 14*(2), 143-169.

Endnotes

[1]   To conserve space, the training script is not provided here, but is available from the authors on request.

2   To avoid possible confounding between near-transfer (LDM) and far-transfer (ERD) task performance, since the former followed the latter, LDM was evaluated based on subjects' depiction of ERD, even if the ERD was incorrect.

3   The five dropped items were: (1) "if I have never used a software package [performed similar tasks] like it before," (2) "if I had only seen someone else using it before trying it myself," (3) "if someone else had helped me get started," (4) "if someone showed me how to do it first," (5) "if I had used similar packages before this one to do the same job." These were not relevant in our context since subjects have already seen the instructor perform similar tasks during the training process, had been shown how to perform such tasks by the trainer, and had gotten started on (and completed) similar tasks during the training process.

4   Multivariate central limit theorem states that test statistics in two-group analysis can be assumed to be normally distributed if: (1) the samples are drawn randomly, (2) the groups are independent, and (3) the groups are large (> 20) (Johnson & Wichern 2002, p. 282-283). Tests of multivariate normality and equality of variance/covariance of sample data are required to assure normal distribution of test statistics only if the samples are small or more than two groups are being considered, or the independent variable is continuous or interval-scaled.

5   Results from Pillai's and Roy's tests were similar to that from Hotelling's and Wilks' tests and, hence, are not reported in Table 3.

Appendix A: Measurement Items

Training Sequence:

Manipulated via experimental treatment (conceptual-procedural versus procedural-conceptual).

Prior IT Experience (fill-in):

EXP1.   Number of years of experience working with computers: _____ years

EXP2.   Number of years of experience working with databases: _____ years

EXP3.   Number of years of programming experience: _____ years

Attitude (seven-point semantic differential scale):

ATT1.   I strongly (dislike...like) the idea of learning about database design.

ATT2.   Learning about database design is an extremely (bad...good) idea.

ATT3.   Learning how to design databases is an extremely (undesirable…desirable) idea.

Task Performance (five-point assessment scale):

Assessed independently by three judges.

Satisfaction (seven-point semantic differential scale):

SAT1.   I am extremely (dissatisfied…satisfied) with my overall performance in this   assignment.

SAT2.   I am extremely (frustrated…contented) with my overall performance in this   assignment.

SAT3.   I feel extremely (terrible…delighted) with my overall performance in this   assignment.

Self-Efficacy (seven-point Likert scale):

SE1.   I can now design databases even if there is no one around to help me.

SE2.   I can now design databases using only database manuals for reference.

SE3.   I can now design databases using only online help facility for assistance.

SE4.   I can now design databases if I have enough time to complete the task.

SE5.   I can now design databases if I can call someone for help if needed (dropped).

Appendix B:
Final Database Design Task

Prepare (1) an entity-relationship diagram (ERD), (2) a logical data model as a set of third normal form (3NF) relations reflecting the data and relationships of the following narrative. Your ERD should contain appropriate cardinality and mandatory/optional symbols. Your logical data model should have appropriate primary (identifier) and foreign keys, referential integrity constraints, and associative relations.

A cable television (CTV) company desires a database to manage customer data. CTV offers three services (monthly charges in parentheses): (1) Basic ($30), (2) Movie Channels A, B, or C ($15 per channel), and (3) Children's Channel ($10). In addition, it rents two types of equipment (serial numbers and monthly charges in parentheses): (1) Decoder (1237810, 484965, 319542; $5 per decoder), and (2)

Remote (432, 947, 376; $4 per remote). Two typical customers are:

Account Number: 101
John Lamb
123 Lanai Court
Gotham City, NY 10023
Phone: 203-247-5195
Service: Basic, Movie Channel B
Equipment: Decoder(1237810), remote control(947)

Account Number: 102
Mary Jones
4443 8th Ave
Gotham City, NY 10043
Phone: 203-232-6243
Service: Basic, Children's Channel
Equipment: Decoder (319542)

The following business rules apply to this company:

- Each customer is assigned one account number only, which can be used for multiple services.
- The company can have a service that has no assigned customers.
- The company maintains an inventory of equipment, which may or may not be used.
- It is possible for a customer to have established service without any assigned equipment.

Section II

Distance Learning Technology Education

Chapter IX

Group Process and Trust in Group Discussion

Lorna Uden, Staffordshire University, UK

Linda Wojnar, Duquesne University, USA

Abstract

Successful group discussion plays a crucial role in online learning. Teachers normally assume that students automatically transfer their learning of group process from group to group. Our experience found that for group discussion to be effective, it is important that we consider group process and the role of trust within groups. This chapter begins with an introduction to group process and trust, followed by a brief review of the benefits of group discussion for online learning. Then, we describe the role that teachers play in initiating environments that promote trust and group empowerment. Through our experience of the implications of group process and trust, we will discuss how this environment fosters trusting relationships. We will also discuss the value of reviewing trust in the group process for each class before assigning group work. The chapter concludes with the outcomes of our experience and suggestions for further work.

Introduction

Students are taught at a very early age about group process, which includes teaching the importance and value of internalizing and distributing roles among group members to maximize the results of the task. Knowing that group process is taught in a specific grade level, succeeding teachers make assumptions that these students will automatically transfer their skills, and the teachers do not first check with the students to learn about what they do remember. Although some groups of students may recall and follow the process as they were instructed, our experience showed that most of them do not. More importantly, when most teachers, who are quite experienced in teaching group process, become learners themselves, they, too, do not automatically follow the procedure of assigning roles to group members when working in groups. For group process to work effectively, it is also important to consider trust.

Group Processes

Tasks and activities performed in a group discussion generally can be known as a process. Group process is a crucial part of computer-supported collaborative work (CSCW) concepts that specify the goals and structure of the team, as well as the progress of the cooperation between team members (Borghoff & Schlichter, 2000). According to Borghoff and Schlichter (2000), a group process is the specification of information, activities and characteristics of an electronically supported team, including the context for group interaction. It usually consists of a static part and dynamic part. The static part describes the team and its environment for performing activities, whereas the dynamic part specifies the progress of the group work and its respective state. The static part of the group process consists of: goals, organization, protocols and environment of the group. On the other hand, the dynamic part is made up of shared documents, group activities, the current group state and group sessions (Borghoff & Schlichter, 2000).

Group goals describe the global goals to be achieved by a predefined team. Individual goals can differ from group goals. Group goals have priority over individual goals. Group organization describes team members according to profiles (their skills and competencies) and their position within the team and the organization in which the team is embedded. The role of the team within the group may depend on their roles within the organization. It may also change dynamically as the group progresses. There are active and dynamic participants within a group discussion. The group protocol describes the way in which the team members cooperate and communicate with each other. Two types of protocols exist: technical and social. A technical protocol is based on hardware or software, while a social protocol is one controlled by team members. It helps to determine how the flow of conversation will occur during a session. Two approaches can determine the flow of the conversation: informal and formal. In the case of an informal approach, each participant can feel free to speak according to predefined rules. In the formal approach, a moderator is appointed. Group environment is determined by the context of the group work, and includes the hardware and software systems, room equipment and room layout.

Group documents belong to the dynamic part of the group process. A meeting session is one example where a group shares information and relates to a group process. Activities taking place during a group process can have temporal or causal dependencies on each other. It must be dynamically adaptable to new situations. Borghoff and Schlichter (2000) suggest that a group session is performed as part of a group activity. It can be both synchronous and asynchronous. Participants may include one or several or all team members. A variety of operations is performed within a group session. According to Borghoff and Schlichter (2000), group process is dynamic and passes through several stages during the group's life. It consists of two main phases: creation and consolidation, which are subdivided into seven phases:

- **Creation phases:**
    1. **Orientation:** This phase represents the beginning of the group process. Team members discuss the overall goals of the group and then ask, Why was the team created? What is the purpose of the team?
    2. **Trust building:** Next, the integration of individual persons into the group process is of interest: What is expected of me? Who are my direct contacts? What amount of work am I expected to do? Trust building is important, because it leads to an open atmosphere and mutual respect. Disorientation or uneasiness of team members requires back-tracking to the previous phase.
    3. **Goal/role clarification:** In this phase, the goals and tasks of a group are defined.
    4. **Commitment:** The procedure for achieving group goals is outlined. Discussions are made with respect to problem structure and the assignment of resources. All team members must agree to support that procedure. Unresolved dependencies and responsibilities may require the group's return to Phase 3.
- **Consolidation phases:**
    5. **Implementation:** Individual tasks are assigned to people after team members have agreed on a problem. Temporal and causal dependencies during task execution must be taken into consideration. Conflicts between tasks and confusion of team members could result in back-tracking to the goal/role of clarification phase.

Figure 1. Group process model of Drexler and Sibbet

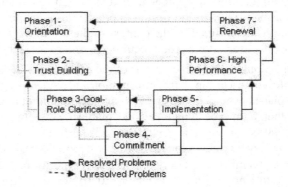

6. **High performance:** When methods and procedures are defined, it is no longer necessary for the team to convene to discuss and determine each and every step. Instead, activities occur intuitively and flexibly.

7. **Renewal:** The high performance phase is only of limited duration. Team members become less motivated as time goes on.

The structuring of a group process into phases and interdependencies helps us pinpoint the potential of group work to support the tasks of the individual steps. The first two phases require direct contact (e.g., face to face) between team members. Synchronous conferencing systems or electronic meeting rooms are acceptable alternatives. A mixture of synchronous and asynchronous group work can support activities within the goal/role clarification phase. According to Borghoff and Schlichter (2000), fast communication is indispensable for mutual understanding. During the phases of commitment, implementation and high performance, focus is on the determined and agreed-upon group activities. For the renewal phase, direct contact between team members is necessary.

Trust

Another important factor that contributes to the success of group discussion is that of trust. Trust is essential if teamwork is to be successful, especially in online learning, where group members are geographically separated. The level of trust between individuals, organizations and within society as a whole influences the nature of trust in online learning, both in terms of the contributions made by individuals and the productivity of the discussions within the learning environment.

There are different types of trust, depending on the length of time that the team members have known each other. These are (Jarvenpaa & Shaw 1998):

- **Identification-based trust:** The individuals are convinced that they have similar intensions and goals.

- **Deterrence-based trust or calculus-based trust:** Results from a fear of the consequences of behaving in an untrustworthy matter. Calculus process is where a trustor calculates the costs and/or rewards for another party to be opportunistic. In the prediction process, the trustor forecasts another party's behavior from historical data. The individual recognizes the consequences for not doing what he or she said he or she would do.

- **Swift trust:** The time available does not allow trust to be built up in the normal way, and team members simply assume that the other team members embrace similar values to their own.

- **Knowledge-based trust:** The individuals trust each other, as they know each other sufficiently well to be able to predict each other's behavior and have shared experiences. The trustor uses information about how the trustee has carried out tasks in the past to predict future action.

- **Transferred trust:** May occur when the trustor knows and trusts a person or institution that recommends the trustee. This is a form of swift trust.

- **Psychological or behavioral trust:** A predisposition towards having confidence that others will carry through on their obligations (Warrington, Algrab & Caldwell, 2000).

- **Technological trust:** A belief that technologies will perform reliably and will not be used for untoward purposes (Chiravuri & Nazareth, 2001).

- **Organizational trust:** The belief that an organization will carry through on its obligations (Cummings & Bromiley, 1996).

- **Situational trust:** Dependence on cues and clues in the immediate social environment when deciding whether to trust another group, organization or institution (Karake-Shalhoub, 2002).

- **Interpersonal trust:** An expectation that others will behave in a predictable way, and a willingness to be vulnerable during the trust relation (Dibben, 2000).

Shapiro and others (1992) identified three consecutive stages through which trust develops: calculus-based, knowledge-based and identification-based. In the beginning, calculus-based trust exists when neither party is familiar with the other. The knowledge-based stage is entered when information flow increases and behavior becomes more predictable, therefore adding more mutuality to the relationship. Finally, trust develops into the information-based stage. By that time, there should be complete empathy within the relationship and a full understanding of each other's needs, wants and intentions (Ashleigh, Connell & Klein, 2003).

According to Fukuyama (1995), trust is the expectation that arises within a community of regular, honest and cooperative behavior, based on commonly shared norms, on the part of the other members of that community. What is the role of trust in synchronous group discussion? We believe that knowledge transfer in group discussion is embedded in a social context. Participation in the relevant social context is essential for the successful transfer of learning in productive synchronous group discussion. The very existence of a relationship between participants in productive group discussion exchange requires the presence of trust. The transfer of knowledge through education in group discussion requires trust between the teacher and the student. We also believe that trust, familiarity and mutual understanding, developed in a person's social and cultural contexts, are prerequisites for the successful transfer of learning in group discussions. Trust within and between members of the group can assist the dissemination of knowledge in group discussion. However, it is also important for us to recognize that issues of control and power also shape social interaction and, therefore, influence the processes of learning in group discussion. When a teacher structures the discussions, his or her control has an important impact on the participation and contributions of the learners.

Two types of trust are necessary for knowledge sharing: benevolence-based trust and competence-based trust (Levin, Cross, Abrams, & Lesser, 2002). Benevolence-based trust is one in which an individual will not intentionally harm another when given the opportunity to do so. Competence-based trust describes a relationship in which an individual believes that another person is knowledgeable about a given subject area. Both types of trust were necessary for students to work effectively and share knowledge.

Benefits of Online Learning: With Respect to Group Discussion

There are many benefits to online learning. For learners, benefits include easy access to global resources; learning at a time during the day, evening or night when learning is best for the learners; learning at the place that is most convenient to the student without the need to travel to universities to attend classes; and learning without any interruptions to their work schedules, appointments or family events. For teachers, information and communications technology (ICT) embraces the design of learning environments that permit deeper learning using multimedia facilities. Teachers have an online location where they can add additional resources to meet the learning needs for all students, who learn through a variety of modalities. Given all the benefits, the heart of online learning is located in the online discussions. Online discussions facilitate learning on a scale not practicable in the past. In residential classrooms, while traversing the room from group to group, teachers can only listen to one group of students at a time. In some online learning systems, teachers have the ability to open and view the chat rooms for all of the groups at the same time, where they may take advantage of 'teachable moments' that occur in synchronous group discussions, to provide explanations when needed or to challenge students to think at higher levels while the discussions are in action. In most learning management systems today, online discussions are automatically archived. A benefit of an archived discussion is that the transcript could be viewed by students who were not able to take part in the discussion. Another benefit is that the chat logs from all of the groups could be posted to a discussion thread, where the entire class could access and learn from them, adding to the richness of the class. Online discussions provide the medium for teachers to observe the level of community building within in each group, within the entire class, and to add more scaffolding to move the community building to higher levels.

We believe that trust and performance are interrelated in online learning. The reason given is that much learning happens through social interaction. According to Sousa (2003), the trust students put in three main components of an online distance learning scenario is the common denominator of several related problems, such as motivation, retention and technology difficulties, which normally lead to low academic performance. The three factors identified by Sousa and others (2003) are:

- Students' trust toward the teacher's interaction;
- Students' trust toward the virtual leaning environments (VLE); and
- Students' trust toward the technology.

The work by Jarvenpaa and Leider (1998) also pointed to the relationship between trust and performance in online distance learning. They suggested that responses to positive trust building activities have an increasing trust in team members. In the paper *Trust, Safety and Confidence: Building the Foundation for Online Interaction*, Klecka (2003) shows that besides safety and confidence, trust is the basis for interaction in online learning. In her research, Klecka (2003) found that users need to establish trust before they feel confidence to participate in group discussion and sharing.

Online Learning at Duquesne

GITED516: Distance Learning Course Design is a graduate course purposefully designed for educators who aspire to teach online. This course was designed to place teachers in the role of a learner so they could experience and gain an appreciation of what it was like to learn online from a learner's perspective. In this blended course, learners meet residentially for a total of four sessions during the 15-week semester: two sessions at the beginning of the course and two sessions at the end of the course.

From the moment the students enter a class, when they meet the teacher and other students for the first time, they develop an intuition about how they feel about the culture of the class. Initial Online Trust (IOT) is the initial stage of a user's trust in the online learning system. It inherits the essential nature of general trust. IOT is the trust that surfaces when parties first meet or interact. It is based on an individual's disposition to trust or an institutional cue that enables one person to trust another without firsthand knowledge (McKnight & Cummings, 1998). Initial trust is also the trust in an unfamiliar trustee, a relationship in which the actors do not yet have any credible, meaningful information about or affective bonds with each other. We believe it is important to identify the type of knowledge a trustor has before the first interaction. Differentiating users based on their knowledge is the first step to understanding their trust.

Even if students do not verbalize their thoughts, they enter a classroom concerned whether they are enrolled a safe risk-taking course, where they can trust the teacher and the students, where they can take risks, possibly even make mistakes, and still be accepted by others. In this course, during the first face-to-face session, the teacher took the first step in setting the tone of the environment. The teacher and the students briefly introduced themselves to the class, since one of the homework assignments for the first class was for the students to upload their autobiography, adding more details into the Learning Management System (Blackboard) than they shared in class. The bio is an important activity. Students from past courses frequently commented that they referred back to the photos and personal information about their peers several times during the course after they began to read each others' postings. Following the brief introductions, the students performed an activity where they completed an unannounced 1-minute typing test, using an authentic secretarial typing test, to identify their typing speeds. The purpose of this activity was to identify the typing speeds of each student so that the teacher could combine this information along with the knowledge learned from the students' bios, so that the teacher could place them in groups for the next two activities: an unstructured and structured synchronous chat. The ability to communicate can be hindered by limited typing skills. Clear communication is essential for online teams to function effectively (Larson & La Fasto, 1989). Building trust fosters effective online communication. A synchronous chat is similar to on-ground small-group discussions, which happen in real time.

The class was divided into groups consisting of no more than three to four students per group. As other previous GITED 516 classes, the average typing for this class was 30-40 words per minute. Once the groups were formed, the teacher shared this information with the class and then taught the class about the 'mechanics' of entering and posting their thoughts into a virtual classroom, called a 'chat room.' This is where the students only learned about the tool. Intentionally, information was shared with the students at this time.

The first synchronous activity was called an unstructured chat. In the unstructured chat, the teacher provided no rules of online etiquette (netiquette) and she did not provide any reference to group processes. The purpose of the chat was to observe the interactions of the group members, to witness whether their typing speeds were exchanged without prompting, to check for group organization and productivity, to observe for equal participation of all group members, and particularly to see whether the groups assigned roles. The teacher timed the activity to last 15 minutes. The group was tasked to answer two questions, which the teacher knew they could answer from their past experience. The two questions for this assignment were:

1.   Discuss your most favorite teacher and the reason you remember the teacher so well.
2.   Discuss what you either heard from others, experienced yourself or perceive about the characteristics and qualities of successful online students.

The teacher assured the students that there were no right or wrong answers to this activity, hoping that the students would be more willing to express their thoughts in a public forum (but in a password-protected Learning Management System) to their peers they met that evening.

Once the unstructured chat was over, the students were allotted 15 minutes to discuss their unstructured synchronous chat experience. As with other classes, the groups said they felt like they were on a treadmill, where they had difficulty keeping up with reading and typing at the same time. Some students said they stopped participating in the discussion because of their limited typing speeds or because English was not their first language, feeling excluded because the American students used a lot of slang or local terminology they did not know. Following the discussion, the teacher spent the next 15 minutes reviewing the group process, structure, rules of netiquette and the group roles the students would be expected to assign for each succeeding synchronous chat. The five roles communicated to the students were: *Organizer, Communicator, Timekeeper, Recorder and Remediator.*

- **Organizer:** Monitors the group's progression, keeps the group on task, and checks for accuracy in the posted information.

- **Communicator:** Substantiates that all participants in the group had an equal opportunity to voice their thoughts, opinions and ideas during the discussion and assures that the diversity of thoughts is respected. *Communicators* must know the typing speeds of each member to decrease the pace of the conversation, when necessary, to keep all members participating at an achievable level.

- **Timekeeper:** Monitors and manages the assigned tasks to assure that all questions or assignments have been addressed.

- **Recorder:** Reviews the online chat log following the discussion, summarizes the important points addressed, sends the analysis to all team members to be sure the summary is reflective of everyone's thoughts, and posts the summary to the discussion board for the other groups to read so that everyone in the class has the opportunity to learn from the discussions of all groups.

- **Remediator:** Recaps the group's agenda, tasks or assignments, updates the member briefly of the group's progress, and asks the member for his or her input.

From the author's experience, building trust within a community of learners (Phase 2: Trust in Borghoff and Schlichter's model, 2000) evolves within an eight-step hierarchical model. If teachers want groups to attain their highest levels of trust that leads to sustaining online dialog, the teacher's role must evolve from leading and directing the conversation to a facilitator's role, which becomes supportive and fosters group empowerment, culminating in the facilitator stepping aside, letting the group take the lead, and only intervening in the conversation on occasion and when appropriate. The eight-step hierarchical model to aid in sustaining online discussions and building trust involves:

- **Step 1:** Facilitator learns about the audience and sets everyone up for successful dialog.

- **Step 2:** Facilitator individualizes the setting—links content to the context and culture of the audience.

- **Step 3:** Facilitator sets up a risk-taking environment for the group to respect each others' thoughts.

- **Step 4:** Group depends on the facilitator to raise the comfort level of the group and begin the discussion, rarely taking risks when they speak.

- **Step 5:** Group begins the dialog, but superficially shares their thoughts. The group begins to formulate thoughts about the trustworthiness of the group. Learners are less vulnerable in conversations when they begin their dialog with the word "They."

- **Step 6:** Group leads the dialog, but increases their trust slowly—taking one risk at a time (Trust builds on small successes) and testing the trustworthiness of the group by taking more risks with the more acceptance they receive from the group. Learners are more vulnerable and generally progress from beginning their thoughts with the word "They" to the word "We."

- **Step 7:** Group sustains the dialog and shares deeper thoughts with the group. The group depends on each other to drive the dialog. This is where the learners are most vulnerable, and they generally begin their conversations with the word "I."

- **Step 8:** Group sustains the dialog and the group members speak with a unified voice, understanding each other when they speak. This level demonstrates that the highest levels of trust are evident. The group speaks openly and honestly, and refrains from group think.

Online dialog has the potential for groups to form deeper relationships, because in an online environment learners who do not speak (by typing their responses) are considered absent. Learners cannot remain passive in an online environment or no one will know they are present. The first four steps in the model described above are initiated and implemented by the teacher. The remaining four steps are led by the group members. Building trust evolves over time and is accomplished through a hierarchical approach. For example, when trust is breached, learners may regress at least one or two more steps. Depending on the learner's trust established in prior relationships, the length of time it takes for learners to trust the group members will vary. This factor must be taken into consideration in the group process. Some students will not openly share their thoughts until trust among the group members has been achieved.

One of the homework assignments for the first session was for students to answer a 20-question self-assessment questionnaire related to *Making Informed Decisions About Online Learning*. This survey was another tool that further assisted the teacher in learning more about the students before they worked online and outside of the residential setting. The questions below were selected from the survey because of their direct implication in providing more knowledge about each student's past experiences, which may impact their performance in the group. In the survey, students rated themselves using the metaphor of a traffic light, implicating their answers in a green (benefit), yellow (caution) or red (risk) category. For any markings in the yellow (caution) or red (risk) categories, students were asked to provide an explanation for their answers. Our experience has shown that many students rated themselves more critically than the teacher would have rated them. This survey was used to identify potential and proactive "red flags" that may indicate potential problems the students may experience in the course and group work. The questions most appropriate for this chapter and the students working in groups in general were:

- Rate your leadership skills;
- Rate your history of verbal participation in class;
- Rate your pattern of focusing and answering questions/dialoging on task;
- Rate whether you prefer to work in groups or to work alone;
- Rate your individual productivity completing group work;
- Rate your level of active listening during a conversation;
- Rate your level of comfort sharing your work with others; and
- Rate your ability to read carefully.

The Case Study

In this section we describe how the group process of Borghoff and Schlichter (2000) is used in our case study for our online learning course at Duquesne.

Phase 1: Orientation

Following the Best Practice Model of Online Teaching and Learning in the article by Wilcox and Wojnar, *Best Practice Goes Online* (2000), getting to know the audience is an important starting point to building trust and individualizing instruction for all learners. In this phase, the teacher and students met in a residential classroom. Meeting their peers in a face-to-face (on-ground) classroom before conducting online discussions in a virtual classroom, where the students were meeting online from various geographical locations, helped the students to feel more at ease with their peers. They were able to connect names with the faces of their peers they re-membered from the first session. Online, students will be communicating in text-based synchronous discussions and asynchronous discussions. The instructor guided the students through the unstructured chat, the teaching portion of group process, expectations and netiquette guidelines, and then through the structured chat. For homework, students were tasked to complete a 20-question survey. The orientation aims to prepare the class for a problem-solving synchronous discussion the groups will conduct themselves, without the presence of the teacher, using the content of the *Six Thinking Hats* book by Dr. Edward De Bono in Session/Week 4.

Phase 2: Trust Building

Teachers and students evolve into communities of learners over time. Trust begins on the first day the teacher and students meet. In our model, the teacher facilitates the first four steps toward building a community of learners. Steps four through eight focused on the group's role in this process. The goal is to keep increasing the levels of trust within the group so that the discussions will become rich and will be sustained by the group. *Trust is the most fluid and most critical level in the group process to keep learners involved in the learning process.* As long as group members continue trusting each other, by acquiring small successes to what they post and gaining acceptance by their peers, the members will be more willing to share their thoughts in a public forum, which in turn aids the progression of the dialog, where students are comfortable sharing their true thoughts without the fear of rejection. Facilitating and nurturing the process where students depend on each other, rather having them depend on the teacher to provide the knowledge and guidance they need to be successful in online discussions, assists students in taking ownership and responsibility for their own learning.

Phase 3: Goal-Role Clarification

The agenda for the group work is clearly articulated and understood by all group members. Discussions proceed smoother and on-task faster when one person in the group posts the objectives and tasks the group is expected to complete. It is important to review netiquette guidelines and assign roles to each member of the group. Initially, the teacher should assign the roles to the group members. The more clearly the objectives and tasks are articulated and understood at this time, the easier it will be for the group to begin to focus their thinking and move forward in their discussion.

Phase 4: Commitment

The teacher selected the groups. In this assignment, students were provided with a link to an online case study in advance of the discussion. The entire class read the *Six Thinking Hats* book. The teacher assigned a different colored hat to each student. There were six students per group. Students were expected to lead the discussion when their group requested a response of the thinking of their colored hat to solve a problem. The group was tasked to problem solve a case study using all of the colored hats.

Phase 5: Implementation

The synchronous discussion took place over 1-1½ hours. Our experience has shown that a discussion lasting longer than 1½ hours causes a decline in the students' concentration and reading abilities, because the thinking and concentration of reading text online was so intense.

Phase 6: High Performance

Reports and comments from students have shown that this activity is very meaningful. Most of the students had been involved in work or life situations that required problem-solving skills. In prior situations, students had recognized they generally do their problem solving with some, but not all, of the colored hats. Because students found this activity so interesting and practical, they were able to see how this activity could transfer to problem-solving issues in their workplace. The group's concentration was very intense, but sustainable by the group.

Phase 7: Renewal

Limiting the time frame to conducting the discussion to a manageable time frame (no longer than 1½ hours), the group was able to sustain the momentum of the discussion without getting tired or becoming less motivated. In past classes, when the chat lasted more than 1½ hours, renewal time was required.

The Role of Trust in Synchronous Group Working

How do we facilitate trust?

1.   Creating a common understanding of how the online learning course works, we found it important to develop a common context or common understanding among students regarding the nature and goals of the course. Factors that were significant in building benevolence and competence-based trust include: a shared language and goals; and relating to the importance of building a shared view of how learning was accomplished, how it is measured and how it is ultimately rewarded. Creating this common understanding makes it easier to

focus on mutually held goals and values. This helps to reduce the time and effort spent on individual issues and motivation.

2.   Help build trust-building behavior. As teachers, we can influence the level of trust by modeling and recognizing trust-building behavior, such as receptivity and discretion.

Teacher support is vital to the success of online learning. Teachers should support their students at the start of their learning. What type of support is appropriate? It is our belief that support should include providing information, encouragement and resources to the students. Teachers should respond promptly to students' queries and provide direction to them, acting as an arbitrator and backing decisions of teams.

Until students get to know one another, the benefits of learning through group discussion may require a leap of faith. New online learners will not know whether what they are learning is of value until they fully experience several discussions. The ability to share a high degree of mutual understanding, built on a common appreciation of a shared social and cultural context, is essential to building trust between individuals.

Trust is widely recognized as a major issue affecting the uptake of online learning. We know that although ICT can be used to facilitate the transfer of knowledge through online learning, it should also be capable of reinforcing trust by providing mechanisms of validation and protection through necessary regulatory and institutional framework. In addition, trust should also depend on the sharing of a set of socially embedded values, cultural institutions and expectations. This may be facilitated through the establishment and maintenance of a strong institutional culture. It is possible with the aid of ICT through the virtual learning environment of the discussion group to build a relationship of trust and mutual understanding.

While mutual goals are necessary, they are not sufficient to gain mutual trust for collaboration (Dodgson, 1993). With mutual trust, participants will reciprocate openness and sharing of information and knowledge over time. Other conditions that impact mutual trust are rivalries and occupational communities. We believe that it is necessary to understand the philosophy of group process with trust built in as part of the process.

It is our belief that cooperation is an essential part of online learning. Borghoff and Schlichter (2000) believe that cooperation in a group is both a repeated alternate between synchronous and asynchronous cooperation and a process during which subgroups constitute themselves for solving individual subprograms. For example, a seminar on a paper can exemplify alternation between the different cooperation modes, as shown in Figure 2 (Borghoff & Schlichter, 2000).

The synchronous environment demonstrates students' ability to demonstrate thinking using both preparatory and impromptu techniques (Wallace & Wojnar, 2002).

In our case study, students were assigned a Universal Resource Locator (URL) to locate an article for their case study. Students were expected to identify the issues and then to problem solve each issue using all six hats. Since students had time to prepare and formulate or process their thoughts, they used a preparatory technique. As the discussion continued and the group posed questions to each other, students responded to the questions without any prior preparation. This technique is called the impromptu question-and-answering technique. The asynchronous environment is more reflective than the synchronous environment and allows for students who are processors of information to think through and rewrite their original thoughts once they have had ample time to process the information. Incorporating both synchronous and asynchronous discussions in an online course are the closest means to replicating a residential learning environment. Residential classrooms are filled with rich discussions because they include both group and individual work.

During the 15 weeks the course was taught, there were only two synchronous discussions scheduled with each discussion lasting no longer than 1-1½ hours. Too many synchronous discussions during a course defeat the purpose most learners enroll in online classes—flexibility, leading to a fixed ourse schedule.

Learning is a social process involving teams of people working together. Building relationships for online learning is vital to the effectiveness of the team (DeNigris & Witchel, 2000). This is a positive link between member relations and team performance for both short-term teams and long-term teams (Druskat, 1996; Druskat & Kayes, 2000).

Conclusion

Group discussion is a crucial part of online learning. For effective group discussion, it is important that we understand group process and trust in collaborative work. According to Borghoff and Schlichter (2000), a group process is the specification of information, activities and characteristics of an electronically supported team, including the context for the group interaction. Included in the group process is the issue of trust. Trust is vital if we want students to be fully active and participate in the group discussion. The outcome of the trust building process in the group discussion leads to a student's ability to learn from other each and from the teacher. Because students began to trust each other and their teacher, they became more open and able to share their thoughts without fear of being rejected. This allows them to learn problem solving from each other that will lead to solving related issues in their workplace. The trust that individual members develop within their team helps them to predict others' behaviors. The initial getting-to-know-you session encompasses sharing of cultural information. These individuals exchange information about shared values, assumptions, opinions and beliefs. There is also a sharing of personal information, such as hobbies, interests, family life, work life, personal expectations of team, equipment, resources and so forth.

Our experience has shown that for online discussions to be productive and goal oriented, teachers should review the group process with students before they assign group work. Students need to know the value and impact they have on making groups functional and high performing. Surveys that could identify past experiences within group work may help to identify "red flags" that may proactively make a difference between student satisfaction and frustration in online discussions. Trust is one of the most fluid yet critical elements that either led groups to share or to hold back their thoughts in any setting. By taking the time to explain the rules of online engagement, teachers will increase the probability that the discussion will be content-rich, productive and on-task, and meets or exceeds the objectives and tasks assigned, rather than being disappointing, non-productive and demonstrating no viable results.

Once students are skilled in the procedure for conducting online discussions, generally with secondary students or adult learners, teachers may empower their groups to monitor and manage a synchronous discussion without their presence. By carefully following the model of Borghoff and Schlichter (2000) from orientation to renewal, higher-quality and more productive discussions that actively engage all learners are possible. Students who have multiple classes together may be more inclined to experience all eight steps in our community building model. We have demonstrated in this chapter how we have utilized both group process and trust in our online course.

Future Research

We would like to conduct further research in how group process and the issue of trust impacts online learning discussions, the limitations of the current model, the process of identifying the types of audiences that would be most suitable for online group discussion, online chat logs from the course to identify whether groups automatically assign roles to their group members and the group process they follow, and group online productivity through a variety of assignments.

References

Ashleigh, M., Connell, C., & Klein, J.H. (2003, October 23-24). *Trust and knowl-edge transfer: An explanatory framework for identifying relationships within a community of practice.* Proceedings of the EIASM second workshop on trust within and between organizations, Amsterdam.

Borghoff, U. M., & Schlichter, J.H. (2000). *Computer-supported cooperative work: Introduction to distributed applications.* Berlin: Springer-Verlag.

Chiravuri, A., & Nazareth, D. (2001). Consumer trust in electronic commerce: An alternative framework using technology acceptance. *Proceedings of the Seventh Americas conference on information systems* (pp. 781-784).

Cummings, L. L., & Bromiley, P. (1996). The organizational trust inventory (OTI): Development and validation. In R. M. Kramer & T. R. Tyler (Eds.), *Trust in organizations: Frontiers of theory and research.* Thousand Oaks: Sage Publications.

De Bono, E. (1999). *Six thinking hats.* Boston: Little, Brown and Company.

DeNigris, J., & Witchel, A. (2000). *How to teach and train online.* Needham Heights: Pearson Custom Publishing.

Dibben, M. R. (2000). *Exploring international trust in the entrepreneurial venture.* London: Macmillan.

Dodgson, M. (1993). Learning, trust and technological collaboration. *Human Relations, 46*(1), 77-96.

Druskat, V. U. (1996, August 13). *Team-level competencies in superior performing, self managing work teams.* Proceedings of the annual meeting of the Academy of Management, Cincinnati, OH.

Druskat, V. U., & Kayes, D.C. (2000). Learning versus performance in short-term project teams. *Small Group Research, 31*(3), 328-353.

Fukuyama, F. (1995). *Trust: The social virtues and the creation of prosperity.* London: Penguin Books.

Jarvenpaa, S., & Leidner, D. (1998). Communication and trust in global virtual teams. *Journal of Computer-Mediated communication and Organization Science: A Joint Issue, 3,* 1-38.

Jarvenpaa, S. L., & Shaw, T. R. (1998). Global virtual teams: Integrating models of trust. In P. Siober & J. Griese (Eds.), *Organizational virtualness* (pp. 35-51). Bern: Simowa Verlag.

Keccka, C. (2003). *Trust, safety and confidence. Building the foundation for online Interaction.* University of Urbana-Champaign. Retrieved from www.ed.uiuc. edu/meter/Publications/Documents/klecka_Trust_AERA03.pdf

Larson, C., & La Fasto, F. M. (1989). *Teamwork: what must go right/what can go wrong*. Newbury Park: Sage.

Levin, D. Z., Cross, R., Abrams, L. C., & Lesser, E. L. (2002). *Trust and knowledge sharing: A critical combination*. IBM Institute for Knowledge-Based Organizations.

McKnight, D. H., & Cummings, L. (1998). Initial trust formulation in new organizational relationships. *The Academy of Management Review, 23*(3), 473-495.

Shapiro, D., Sheppard, B. H., & Cheraskin, L. (1992). Business on a handshake. *Negotiation Journal, 8*, 365-377.

Sousa, S. (2003). *Trust and performance in online distance learning*. Retrieved from www.pa-linz.ac.at/international/Alert/Tntee/Tntee_publication/ELHEII/sonja.pdf

Wallace, R., & Wojnar, L. (2002, September). How to use chat. *EC & T Journal*, September, 37-38.

Warrington, T. B., Algrab, N. J., & Caldwell, H. M. (2000). Building trust to develop competitive advantage in e-business relationships. *Competitive Review 10*(2), 160-168.

Wilcox, B., & Wojnar, L. (2000, August). Best practice goes online. *Reading Online, 4*(2). Retrieved March 8, 2004, from www.readingonline.org/articles/art_index.asp?HREF=/articles/wilcox/index.htm

Chapter X

Task-Orientation Online Discussion:
A Practical Model for Student Learning

Byron Havard, University of West Florida, USA

Jianxia Du, Mississippi State University, USA

Anthony Olinzock, Mississippi State University, USA

Abstract

A dynamic task-oriented online discussion model for deep learning in distance education is described and illustrated in this chapter. Information, methods, and cognition, three general learning processes, provide the foundation on which the model is based. Three types of online discussion are prescribed: flexible peer, structured topic, and collaborative task. The discussion types are paired with tasks encouraging students to build on their adoptive learning, promoting adaptive learning and challenging their cognitive abilities, resulting in deep learning. The online discussion model was applied during two semesters of an online multimedia design for instruction graduate-level course. The strategies for creating dynamic discussion serve to facilitate online interactions among diverse learners and assist in the design of assignments for effective interactions. The model proposed and the strategies for dynamic task-oriented discussion provide an online learning environment in which students learn beyond the course goal.

Introduction

The purpose of this study was to apply a theoretical model in an actual online discussion context. Deep learning, the holistic acquisition of higher-order skills (such as analyzing, interpreting and evaluating) exhibited through higher-order problem solving (Entwistle & Ramsden, 1983), serves as the educational goal for this model. Deep learning, according to Weigel (2001), is "learning that promotes the development of conditionalized knowledge and metacognition through communities of inquiry" (p. 5). The theoretical underpinnings of the model may be applied to many diverse educational environments. This chapter offers distance learning educators strategies within the proposed model that will enhance online courses. The model reveals an approach to distance learning that fosters and encourages deep learning for higher-order thinking. Application of this model in distance learning may be applied to a variety of online courses to enhance student learning.

Theoretical Framework

Several researchers have contributed to the effort of understanding the learning process. Their conclusions can help in the process of developing models for analyzing the distance learning process. Henri (1992) developed an analytical model that can be used by educators for a better understanding of the learning process. This model was developed to emphasize five dimensions of the learning process exteriorized in the message: participation, interaction, social, cognitive and metacognitive dimensions. Henri's model provides information on participants as learners and on their ways of dealing with a given topic. Oliver and Mcloughlin (1996) suggested some changes to Henri's analytical model. They recognized five kinds of interactions: social, procedural, expository, explanatory and cognitive. Oliver and Mcloughlin's model has been used for analyzing the different kinds of communication in distance learning and traditional teaching.

The model of deep learning for distance education (see Figure 1) is established through the categorization of the five kinds of interactions proposed by Oliver and Mcloughlin (1996) into three general processes: information, methods and cogni-

Figure 1. The information, methods and cognition model with two layers

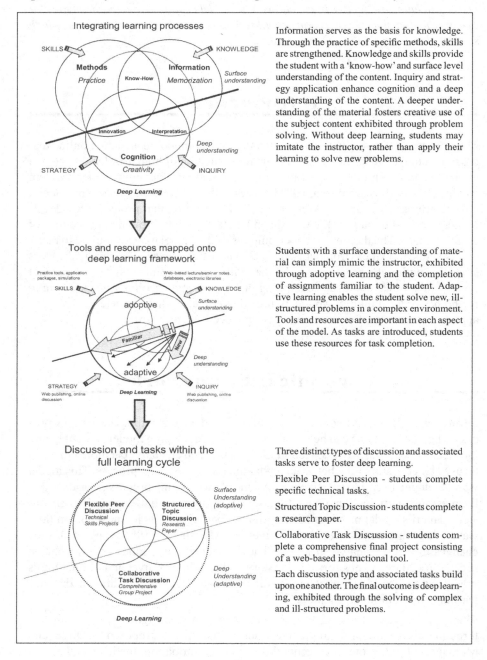

Information serves as the basis for knowledge. Through the practice of specific methods, skills are strengthened. Knowledge and skills provide the student with a 'know-how' and surface level understanding of the content. Inquiry and strategy application enhance cognition and a deep understanding of the content. A deeper understanding of the material fosters creative use of the subject content exhibited through problem solving. Without deep learning, students may imitate the instructor, rather than apply their learning to solve new problems.

Students with a surface understanding of material can simply mimic the instructor, exhibited through adoptive learning and the completion of assignments familiar to the student. Adaptive learning enables the student solve new, ill-structured problems in a complex environment. Tools and resources are important in each aspect of the model. As tasks are introduced, students use these resources for task completion.

Three distinct types of discussion and associated tasks serve to foster deep learning.

Flexible Peer Discussion - students complete specific technical tasks.

Structured Topic Discussion - students complete a research paper.

Collaborative Task Discussion - students complete a comprehensive final project consisting of a web-based instructional tool.

Each discussion type and associated tasks build upon one another. The final outcome is deep learning, exhibited through the solving of complex and ill-structured problems.

tion (Du & Havard, 2003). The first stage of integrating these learning processes is the acquisition of knowledge, representing a surface level of understanding. Skill development, the second stage of the model, is often accomplished through drill and practice. Students operating at these two levels develop a 'know-how' of the material, but on a very limited basis. The third stage represents cognition, where inquiry and strategy application assist students in learning to solve problems. A deeper understanding of the material fosters creative use of the subject content. Without deep learning, students will simply imitate the instructor, rather than apply their learning to new problems.

New and complex assignments require students to build on their existing knowledge of a topic, challenging them to systematize this information with newly acquired information in a variety of ways (Laurillard, 1984). Greene (1995) emphasizes that imagination can help people create new orders, bring pieces together, assemble or reassemble patterns. The foundation of deep learning relies on assignments that encourage inquiry and creativity. Thayer-Bacon (2000) stresses that "reason is an invaluable tool to help us construct quilts of knowledge" (p. 148). Reason can aid one to filter useful and useless information, organize them into meaningful entity, retrieve previous knowledge and ultimately gain new or deeper understanding.

Problem-based learning provides the rich context in which higher-order thinking is essential for problem resolution. Students working through a difficult ill-structured problem have more opportunity to develop a much deeper understanding than students who simply memorize information or develop specific skills without context (Tiene, 2002). Through innovative assignments, students can inquire about the process they are using rather than inquire about the product or answer to a specific question (Ruberg, Moore, & Taylor, 1996).

Two fundamental concepts inherent in the proposed model are adopt and adapt (see Figure 1). Students with a surface understanding of material can effectively adopt what the instructor does. They may simply mimic the instructor. Students are unable to adapt their learning to unique situations because they have not developed a deeper learning of the material. They lack the strong grasp of the material required to adapt to a complex problem-based environment. Assignments familiar for the student measure surface learning, while new and innovative assignments measure a student's deep learning. Adoption and adaptation become very important when change is introduced in the distance learning environment regarding the material students are learning. It is not enough to adopt what the instructor teaches. Encouraging students to effectively adapt to changes in the distance learning environment requires students to think for themselves rather than rely on learning guidance from the instructor (Brookfield, 1982). In this type of distance learning environment, the instructor acts as a facilitator, requiring students to take more responsibility in the learning process. The role of facilitator is complex, but through the proposed model, techniques and student activities are diagrammed to assist in reducing this complexity.

Application of the Model

Distance learning requires special course design techniques, special methods of communication, as well as special organizational and administrative arrangements (Moore, 1989). To further explore the model of deep learning for distance education, we applied the model during two semesters of a graduate-level multimedia design for instruction course. Learning technologies were mapped to learning processes. Students began the full learning cycle with resources supplied by the instructor. These include: (a) Web-based lecture with seminar notes, (b) databases for details related to specific concepts, (c) electronic libraries for additional reference material, and (d) CD-ROMs as supplemental information, in addition to the formal course content. These resources served to provide the foundation on which knowledge of the course topics were based. This multimedia design for instruction course is required for all students enrolled in the Master of Science in Instructional Technology (MSIT) program. Students enrolled in the MSIT program and in this course represent a wide range of diverse backgrounds. They reside throughout the state of Mississippi, Tennessee and Alabama. Each semester, approximately 30 students are enrolled in this course. The purpose of this course is to provide students with an overview of hypermedia/interactive multimedia technology through working with various hypermedia/multimedia tools. Students are introduced to the design and production process of developing multimedia applications and are provided the opportunity to learn various tools, concentrating on different aspects of the technology: text, graphics, audio, animation and video. Through working with these tools, students are expected to develop an understanding and the skills required for the creation of instructional tools for application in education and industry settings. Students are required to apply design principles necessary for the creation of hypermedia/multimedia when developing multimedia-based applications.

Learning Environment

The course simulates practices in the multimedia industry. Students work in groups and take on different roles in the multimedia development process. The contexts for learning in this course are primarily interactive, collaborative, multi-disciplinary and student-centered. Students are required to actively participate in weekly discussions regarding specific multimedia development topics. Assignments on learning different tools are given to assess application skills. Students must write a research and reflective paper on hypermedia/interactive multimedia instruction. Group projects for the semester both develop and assess students' ability to comprehensively apply the theoretical and technical requirements for multimedia design for instruction. Through these activities, we have observed students developing deep thinking in higher-order problem solving, from the foundation of surface understanding to deeper understanding exhibited by problem resolution.

WebCT served as the online learning environment for this course. WebCT is a database-driven, Web-based course management system designed to support online learning environments (Hutchins, 2001). The database elements available in WebCT enable the instructor to record, manage and support the activities and interactions of a large number of students. There are several important aspects about this environment regarding skill development, theoretical and technical issues, and the application skills and knowledge towards the successful development of a comprehensive multimedia instructional tool (Popolov, Callaghan, & Luker, 2002). Through online group communication using the asynchronous discussion feature and synchronous chat available through WebCT, students' skills and knowledge regarding multimedia development are enhanced. The social aspect of the learning environment is critical (Vygotsky, 1978). This requires focused attention by the instructor, as knowledge is socially constructed and enhanced through peer-to-peer and instructor-to-peer communication (Boud, Cohen, & Sampson, 1999; Kitchner, 1983; Kitchner & King, 1981).

Application of the model within the context of a distance learning environment will be described. The strategies used through model application may assist others in implementing the model within their own distance learning environments. The information, methods and cognition model serves to foster and encourage learning and, specifically, deep learning in an online environment. Through implementation of the three-stage model, we have established a learning environment that supports problem-based learning with synchronous and asynchronous tools for students to collaborate on set problems, share resources, post solutions, and compare and review answers from other groups (Graham & Scarborough, 1999; Popolov, Callaghan, & Luker, 2002).

Online Discussion and Tasks

A structured and moderated online discussion may be defined as a Web-based bulletin board for peer learners to communicate and collaborate, where the instructor takes active responsibility to structure, scaffold and moderate the collaboration. The proposed model of information, methods and cognition involves a number of activities and assignment tasks that provide powerful contexts for learning course content. The structure of the bulletin board is divided into the three processes related to the model. Through this structure, a number of key skills are demonstrated by students in the higher-order problem-solving process; from surface understanding to deeper understanding.

Students complete assignments requiring them to apply their surface learning and develop their deeper learning. The difficulty of the assignments progresses, challenging students to hone their abilities and problem-solving skills. Scaffolding is important throughout the process, and is most pronounced during the first two assignments. As students' deep learning develop and their competence to accomplish the assignments increase, the necessity to scaffold is reduced (Gredler, 1997). The assignments in this course consist of two technical projects, a theoretical research paper and a comprehensive technical and theoretical final group project. The purpose of these assignments and their structure is to scaffold students' learning from surface to deep. Online discussion is used extensively in this course as a means to develop deeper learning. The WebCT bulletin board is composed of three categories; technical, theoretical and comprehensive, corresponding to the three general process of the model; information, methods and cognition.

Flexible peer discussion. Students use Dreamweaver and Fireworks as the multimedia development tools for this course. Within the technical category of the bulletin board, discussion points are further categorized into topic technical issues, practice issues and peer discussion. Students are presented two questions per week within the topic technical issues related to the technical aspects and use of Dreamweaver and Fireworks. Students must respond to the question presented and must also critique one other peer's response. Students are also presented with weekly practice assignments, progressing in difficulty. As they work through the assignments they must post one question regarding an issue they encountered while working on the assignment. They must also answer at least one peer's question that was posted. The peer discussion category of the bulletin board is available for open discussion about Dreamweaver and Fireworks, and students are required to post at least one new item they learned while using either of these multimedia development applications.

Structured topic discussion. The theoretical category of the bulletin board consists of three questions posed to the students over a 3-week period prior to the middle of the semester. Through focused and concise answers, students are able to develop the foundation for their theoretical research paper. Students are encouraged to discuss the question and offer opinions on how the question may be addressed. Responses do not occur immediately; instead, students spend time clarifying the questions among themselves. Discussion occurs during the week. Towards the end of the week, students begin to formulate and post their responses. Discussion continues as students submit their responses. Students must also critique two other peers' responses each week. In the critique, students must provide constructive criticism and assist in further developing each peer's topic. The questions are meant to be a guide to assist students in topic development. The first question guides students towards describing how the specific multimedia development tools in the course may be used. They must cite their reading assignments within their response to support their claims. The second question focuses on instructional design principles. There are two required textbooks for this course and journal articles provided by the instructor, posted online, which serve as additional reading. Students must describe how the instructional design principles are applied in an actual multimedia development project, including details related to learner and context. Students must work together in groups to complete the final comprehensive project. The third question requires students to propose a group project they will collaborate on and submit as their final comprehensive project. Their responses must include details regarding the learner, instructional context, subject content and the needs for the proposed multimedia instruction. They must provide a rationale for the development tools they wish to use. They must also describe the instructional strategy they will use and describe why they chose that particular strategy. After submitting responses to all three questions, students must then complete a theoretical research paper.

Collaborative task discussion. The outcome of the comprehensive final project is a Web-based instructional tool. The project combines the technical aspects and theoretical issues discussed online during the semester. The groups must apply the instructional design principles towards the development of a "real" Web-based educational product. Three progress points during final project development are meant to focus students towards the desired outcome in a professional manner. These points consist of a proposal presentation, progress report and a final project and presentation with documentation. The groups are composed of five students, with one serving as the coordinator. Asynchronous and synchronous discussion occurs among the groups. The bulletin board is used by the group for introductions. The group must decide which member will accomplish what task based on the proposed project. The topic is decided on through discussion and deliberation among the group members. Each member proposes a topic and must negotiate online to determine which topic the group will agree on for the final product. As group members begin gathering information on their chosen topic, they post this for other group members. Discussion and clarification is often necessary as the information is refined (Flynn & La Faso, 1972). Synchronous chat offers the group opportunities to discuss issues in real time. Specific chat dates and times are decided on through the bulletin board. Students meet in their group's chat room to discuss issues with the instructor and to present their proposal and progress report. Each group conducts their final presentation through chat with the instructor present. Students receive immediate feedback from the instructor and must respond to questions posed by the instructor regarding the final product.

The proposed model and the design of the discussion activities applied within the model provide students both adoptive and adaptive learning opportunities. The technical and theoretical discussion aspects occur as students complete the first two assignments. This provides a strong surface level of understanding regarding the multimedia development tools used in this course. The theoretical portion of the discussion, as students respond and critique one another's responses to the three questions posed by the instructor, provides students with a strong surface understanding of the instructional design principles for multimedia development. Students begin moving towards adaptive learning as they begin focusing their efforts on the final comprehensive project. Through asynchronous and synchronous discussions regarding the development of the instructional product, students move from surface to deep learning. The learning is adaptive, as they are creating a product to fulfill an instructional need where no right or true answer exists.

Findings

The information, methods and cognition model provides very powerful contexts for learning the course content. The assignments encourage students to interact with the course content, to read and explore beyond the immediate setting and to reflect on what is being read (Warschauer, 1997). At the same time, the assignments encourage and support many other useful skills, including negotiation, written communication, diversity, constructive criticism, strategy development and execution, and reflection.

When the assignments undertaken by the students exposed to this form of learning environment are examined in the light of a model proposed by Bennett, Dunne, and Carre (1999), its capacity to support students achieving deep understanding immediately becomes evident. Based on the model we have proposed, the distance learning setting helped and encouraged students to practice and develop higher-order thinking across the full range of information, methods and cognition. The following major points emphasize the importance of the activities when applying the model in a distance learning course.

The assignments required learners to plan their steps, explore the domain and work towards a goal. Similar to Fenwick (2002), students perceived their most valuable learning was related to two main areas: group process and self-knowledge. In the process, they needed to confront unexpected outcomes and hurdles, reflect and judge their progress, and use a variety of learning strategies to develop their solution. In the group setting, students were required to work with others and maintain a good working relationship throughout the semester. On a day-to-day basis, they needed to be cooperative and attentive to the group's needs, defend their own stance, negotiate, and give and accept criticism.

The assignments required students to apply various technologies available to them in the learning environment. These include e-mail, chat and bulletin board. Through the strategies for dynamic discussion, students consolidate the large amounts of information obtained and discuss how to delineate the importance and value of the information towards assignment completion. They needed to interpret the information and balance the multiple perspectives presented. Succinct summaries of the information required reflection and critical thinking.

Students' reflections on the course based on e-mail, collaborative discussion and chat demonstrate their positive attitudes regarding the course. Their satisfaction with the structure of the online environment was expressed in the individual student evaluations gathered at the end of the semester. Through their final documentation submitted with their final product, students described their appreciation for their diligent work.

Finally, in terms of managing assignments, these activities compelled students to identify sub-tasks and conceptualize the problem they were required to solve and how it could best be managed. The activities required the students to formulate a plan and execute the course of action, and reflect on the directions and outcomes. Each member of the group takes on specific responsibilities, executes tasks to benefit the group, and works together with team members towards achieving a common goal; a finding similar to other research (Hinds & Weisband, 2003; Dehler & Parras-Hernandez, 1998). Amid differing opinions and perspectives, groups were highly capable of resolving the problems assigned throughout the course.

Conclusion

Online discussion strategy is imperative for student learning. Many distance learning courses experience high attrition rates that result from factors such as students feeling isolated, unmotivated, overwhelmed or unchallenged in online courses. Based on the model proposed in this chapter, dynamic task-oriented discussions (e.g., flexible peer, structured topic and collaborative task) in these two classes encourage participation in all aspects of the requirements for course completion. Students are made to feel as if they are part of a community, where their input is valued by their peers and where their suggestions are encouraged (Blumenfeld, Marx, Soloway, & Krajcik, 1996). The supportive environment created in this type of discussion serves to assist students that may feel overwhelmed by the course requirements. Motivation to learn and share ideas is encouraged and evolves naturally as the course progresses. Continuous peer review of posted responses to items challenges each student to provide their best input for the learning community created through dynamic task-oriented discussion.

Discussion is an integral part of an online course. As students work through the assignments, the importance of discussion and the sharing of ideas and opinions cannot be ignored. The assignments in this course require extensive peer-to-peer discussion throughout the semester to achieve the desired outcomes for the course. Through the structure of the dynamic task-oriented discussion presented in the model, students engage in discussion as part of assignment completion. In a sense, the discussion and the assignment cannot be separated; both act as a means for attainment of the course goal. The nature of online interactions and communications must be understood by both instructors and instructional designers (Pincas, 1998).

The strategies we have proposed for creating dynamic task-oriented discussion serve to facilitate online learning among diverse individuals and assist in the design of assignments for effective interactions.

Providing students with a learning environment that will assist them in achieving the course goal is important, but we must look beyond the boundaries of a single course. The model proposed and the strategies for dynamic task-oriented discussion provide an environment in which students learn beyond the course goal, paving the way from surface to deep learning. Students build on the adoptive learning taking place through assignments designed to promote adaptive learning and challenge their cognitive abilities, resulting in deep learning. Students' cognitive process is challenged through learning to use collaborative tools, learning to work collaboratively on complex learning assignments, and learning how to collaborate at a distance both asynchronously and synchronously.

References

Bennett, N., Dunne, E., & Carre, C. (1999). Patterns of core and generic skill provision in higher education. *Higher Education, 37*(1), 71-93.

Blumenfeld, P. C., Marx, R. W., Soloway, E., & Krajcik, J. (1996). Learning with peers: From small group cooperation to collaborative communities. *Educational Researcher, 25*(8), 37-42.

Boud, D., Cohen, R., & Sampson, J. (1999). Peer learning and assessment. *Assessment and Evaluation in Higher Education, 24*(4), 413-426.

Brookfield, S. (1982). Independent learners and correspondence students. *Teaching at a Distance, 22,* 26-33.

Dehler, C., & Parras-Hernandez, L.H. (1998) Using computer-mediated communication (CMC) to promote experiential learning in graduate studies. *Educational Technology, 38*(3), 52-55.

Du, J. X., & Havard, B. (2003). A framework for deep learning in distance education. *Delta Pi Epsilon, 45*(3), 204-214.

Entwistle, N., & Ramsden, P. (1983). *Understanding student learning.* London: Croom Helm.

Fenwick, T. J. (2002). Problem-based learning, group process and the mid-career professional: Implications for graduate education. *Higher Education Research & Development, 21*(1), 5-21.

Flynn, E. W., & La Faso, J. F. (1972). *Group discussion as a learning process.* New York: Paulist Press.

Graham, M., & Scarborough, H. (1999). Computer mediated communication and collaborative learning in the undergraduate distance education environment. *Australian Journal of Educational Technology, 15*(1), 20-46.

Gredler, M. E. (1997). *Learning and instruction: Theory into practice* (3rd ed.). Upper Saddle River: Prentice-Hall.

Greene, M. (1995). *Releasing the imagination: Essays on education, the arts, and social change.* San Francisco: Jossey-Bass.

Henri, F. (1992). Computer conference and content analysis. In A. Kaye (Ed.), *Collaborative learning through computer conferencing* (pp. 117-136). Berlin: Springer-Verlag.

Hinds, P., & Weisband, S. (2003). Knowledge sharing and shared understanding in virtual teams. In C.B. Gibson & S.G. Cohen (Eds.), *Virtual teams that work: Creating conditions for virtual team effectiveness* (pp. 21-36). San Francisco: Jossey-Bass.

Hutchins, H. M. (2001). Enhancing the business communication course through WebCT. *Business Communication Quarterly, 64*(3), 87-94.

Kitchener, K. S. (1983). Cognition, metacognition, and epistemic cognition: A three-level model of cognitive processing. *Human Development, 26*, 222-232.

Kitchener, K. S., & King, P. M. (1981). Reflective judgment: Concepts of justification and their relationship to age and education. *Journal of Applied Developmental Psychology, 2*, 89-116.

Laurillard, D. (1984). Styles and approaches in problem-solving. In F. Marton, D. Hounsell, & N. Entwistle (Eds.), *The experience of learning* (pp. 124-143). Edinburgh: Scottish Academic Press.

Moore, M. (1989). Three types of interactions. *The American Journal of Distance Education, 3*, 1-6.

Oliver, R., & Mcloughlin, C. (1996). *An investigation of the nature and form of interactions in live interactive television.* Melbourne: Australian Society for Educational Technology. (ERIC Document Reproduction Service No. ED396738).

Pincas, A. (1998). Successful online course design: Virtual frameworks for discourse construction. *Educational Technology and Society, 1*(1), 14-25.

Popolov, D., Callaghan, M., & Luker, P. (2002). Tying models of learning to design of collaborative learning software tools. *Journal of Computer Assisted Learning, 18*(1), 46-47.

Ruberg, L. F., Moore, D. M., & Taylor, C. D. (1996). Student participation, interaction, and regulation in a computer-mediated communication environment: A qualitative study. *Journal of Educational Computer Research, 14*(3), 243-268.

Thayer-Bacon, B. J. (2000). *Transforming critical thinking: Thinking constructively*. New York: Teachers College Press.

Tiene, D. (2002). Exploring current issues in educational technology using a problem-based approach to instruction. *Educational Technology, 42*(1), 14-22.

Vygotsky, L. S. (1978). *Mind in society*. Cambridge: Harvard University Press.

Warschauer, M. (1997). Computer-mediated collaborative learning: theory and practice. *Modern Language Journal, 81*(4), 470-481.

Weigel, V. (2001). *Deep learning for a digital age: Technology's untapped potential to enrich higher education*. San Francisco: Jossey-Bass.

Chapter XI

Addressing the Cultural Dimensions of E-Learning:
Where to Begin?

Andrea L. Edmundson, eWorld Learning, USA

Abstract

In an exploratory study, the researcher examined the effects of cultural dimensions on e-learning outcomes for employees in functionally equivalent jobs in Western and Eastern cultures. Participants from the United States (U.S.) and India completed a Level 1 e-learning course designed in the U.S. In addition, randomly selected completers then reported their interactions with the e-learning course in a survey. Learners from the two cultures achieved equitable learning outcomes, suggesting that characteristics of Level 1 e-learning courses mitigate the effects of culture. In addition, while cultural dimensions did appear to affect learners' preferences for and perceptions of e-learning, both Eastern and Western participants were willing to try new approaches to learning that did not align with their cultural profiles. Based on these results and practical usage, the revised (v.2) cultural adaptation process (CAP) model is presented as a guideline for adapting e-learning courses for other cultures.

Introduction

The term *globalization* gained currency in the 1970s as Western corporations rapidly expanded into other parts of the world (Jarvis, 2002), accelerating cultural exchanges (Walker & Dimmock, 2002). Industrial anthropologists have identified *cultural dimensions*—categories of characteristics across which cultures can be compared and contrasted, such as how members of a culture communicate, perceive time or view themselves in relation to the environment. As e-learning options proliferate and globalization continues, an expanding audience of learners is more likely to encounter courses created by another culture. Most e-learning courses are designed in Western cultures; however, the largest and fastest-growing consumer groups live in Eastern cultures, such as China, Japan and India (Van Dam & Rogers, 2002). "Over the next 20 years, the global market for online learning is estimated to exceed $215 billion, with rapid growth expected from cross-border delivery of higher education (an institution in one country delivers courses to students in other countries)" (Hezel & Mitchell, 2005, para. 1). Educators thus will be challenged to provide e-learning opportunities that result in equitable learning outcomes for new groups of learners from other cultures.

Learning outcomes were defined by Henderson (1996) as any results that reflect the acquisition of skills and knowledge, the effectiveness of instructional techniques and students' perceptions or attitudes. Educational practitioners have begun to apply the concepts of cultural dimensions to instructional design, presuming that selecting or adapting courses to suit the cultural profiles of learners will generate equitable learning outcomes. However, empirical research has neither conclusively supported nor disproved them. The purpose of this study was to understand better the effects of cultural dimensions on e-learning in the globalized environment.

The problem is: "Are e-learning courses designed in a Western culture equally effective when used in an Eastern culture?" The research questions used to address this problem were as follows:

1.   When taking an e-learning course designed in a Western culture, do participants from Eastern and Western cultures experience *equitable learning outcomes*?

2.   Do they have different *preferences for or perceptions of* e-learning?

3.   If there *are* strong similarities or significant differences in learning outcomes between the two cultures, in participants' use of features or in their preferences or perceptions, are these similarities or differences *related* to the cultural dimensions described in the literature?

Importance

According to a United Nations Development Program report (UNDP, 2001), the most developed, progressive and economically stable countries in the world are those that are technologically advanced. Technological change and the building of human capabilities are interrelated: Each requires the development of the other for success. Thus, the UNDP report (2001) promoted "rethinking educational systems to meet the new challenges of technology" (p. 84) through improved technology and technological education at a global level. Interest in promoting education and technologies continues to be addressed by the U.N. Millennium Development Goals (United Nations, 2005). Domestically, "At a time when many institutions in the U.S. must explore new markets for enrollment growth, other countries face a shortage of higher education campuses and student seats" (Hezel & Mitchell, 2005, para. 3).

From an instructional point of view, incompatibilities between the cultural characteristics of e-learning courses and learners could cause inequitable learning outcomes (Henderson, 1996). For example, members of cultures may prefer to learn in a particular manner (Gardner, 1989; Horton, 1999), or they may have specific approaches to problem solving (Lave, 1988; Soh, 1999) and creativity (Gardner, 1989). Or, a pedagogical paradigm espoused by one culture could alienate or confuse targeted learners (Hall, 1981), as could unintentional cultural biases in instructional design (McLoughlin, 1999). Learning styles may also be influenced by culture. Through their use of research on cultural dimension, practitioners propose that e-learning be designed to match to the cultural profiles of the targeted learners (Marcus & Gould, 2001; Marinetti & Dunn, 2002).

Theoretical Foundations

Hofstede (1984, 1997, 2001), Trompenaars and Hampden-Turner (1998) and Hall (1953, 1981) identified and characterized cultural dimensions at the national level, primarily with respect to corporate business and communication. While they posited the probable effects of many of these dimensions on education, researchers Gardner (1983, 1989), Henderson (1996) and others have explored similar concepts within the discipline of education. Jaju, Kwak, and Zinkhan's (2002) study related learning styles and preferences to cultural dimensions, a step towards confirming a definitive relationship of culture to e-learning and its importance.

Hofstede and Cultural Dimensions at the National Level

Hofstede (1984, 1997) established the practice of using *national cultures* in quantitative studies: Samples of people living and working in the same country are reasonable representations of the national culture. He gathered data from questionnaires administered to 116,000 participants in 50 countries and three regions, identifying five cultural dimensions that he portrayed as continua bounded by polar extremes. He calculated indices of these dimensions for each country, described below, across which cultures could be compared and contrasted.

Power Distance Index (PDI)

The PDI—"the extent to which the less powerful members of institutions and organizations expect and accept that power is distributed unequally" (Hofstede, 1997, p. 27)—has ramifications in educational organizations. In nations with low PDI scores, such as the U.S. (PDI = 40), teachers and students tend to be perceived as equals. Teachers are facilitators of student-centered education rather than authoritative subject matter experts (SMEs). Students are expected to show initiative, solve problems, build their own knowledge base, question teachers and initiate discussions. In high PDI nations, such as India (PDI = 77), relationships between teachers and students are accepted as inequitable: Teachers are authorities and SMEs; thus, students tend not to question their knowledge (Hofstede, 1997).

Individualism Index (IDV)

Hofstede (1997) defined individualistic societies as those "in which ties between individuals are loose" (1997, p. 51). By contrast, collectivist societies are those "in which people from birth onwards are integrated into strong, cohesive *ingroups*, which throughout people's lifetime continue to protect them in exchange for unquestioned loyalty" (Hofstede, 1997, p. 51).

Members of collectivist societies tend to rely on their ingroups to determine social relationships in educational settings, and may even expect differential treatment dependent on their social class. In contrast, students in high-IDV societies expect to be treated as equals among peers and faculty. They prefer to work as individuals and expect recognition for individual merit.

Globally, collectivist societies are predominant (Hofstede, 1997). From the perspective of education, this represents an important consideration. The U.S. and other high-IDV countries produce most instructional artifacts, including e-learning. Characteristics of these courses could significantly conflict with the values of collectivist societies that import them. The U.S. has the highest IDV (91) in Hofstede's study, while India has a much lower IDV of 48 (Hofstede, 1997).

Masculinity Index (MAS)

Hofstede (1984) defined the dimension "masculinity vs. femininity" in terms of how a culture socializes its members to perform gender roles. In a masculine culture, men are expected to be tough and assertive, while women are perceived as tender and modest. In a feminine culture, men and women are more likely to have similar roles; both are expected to be tender and modest, even if men also express some assertiveness.

Hofstede (1997) contended that, in high-MAS countries, students compete openly, are achievement conscious and are disappointed by failure. An instructor's academic excellence and reputation are important. In a low MAS culture, teachers and students have more relaxed expectations. The U.S. and India yielded similar MAS indices in Hofstede's work (62 and 56, respectively).

Uncertainty Avoidance Index (UAI)

Uncertainty avoidance is "the extent to which the members of the culture feel threatened by uncertain or unknown situations" (Hofstede, 1997, p. 113). Uncertainty avoidance is not risk avoidance; rather, it refers to a pattern of reducing ambiguity.

Hofstede (1997) felt that, in a high-UAI environment, the teacher is an expert and unquestionable authority. Students prefer a structured learning environment, precise objectives, strict timetables, precise answers and rewards for accuracy. In contrast, in low-UAI cultures, teachers act as facilitators of learning. Students are comfortable with vague objectives, loose timetables and multiple solutions to problems, and they seek to be rewarded for originality. The U.S. and India have similar, mid-range UAI scores of 46 and 40, respectively.

Long-Term Orientation (LTO)

Hofstede's fifth cultural dimension, "short-term vs. long-term orientation to time," was theorized after his original 1984 study. In general, Hofstede found that Eastern countries had relatively high LTOs, while Western countries yielded relatively low LTO scores. Hofstede did not propose specific ramifications of the LTO dimension on education, and it was not included in this study.

Trompenaars and Hampden-Turner's Cultural Study

Trompenaars and Hampden-Turner (1998) also researched cultural dimensions at the national level; like Hofstede, they were primarily interested in the effects on business. Their analysis of surveys (more than 30,000 corporate managers from more than 100 countries) identified eight cultural dimensions, some of which were similar to Hofstede's. Each of their dimensions, like Hofstede's, was described as a continuum bounded by two extreme, opposing characteristics. However, in contrast to Hofstede, they held that in practice, cultural groups display both extremes of all dimensions but show a preference or tendency toward one extreme in most situations. Unlike Hofstede, they rarely speculated on the implications of cultural dimensions in education.

In the first category, "relationships and rules," Trompenaars (1998) identified five dimensions across which cultures could be compared and contrasted. *Universalism vs. particularism* relates to the balance between rules and relationships. Universalists tend to adhere to rules. In a particularist society, rules are flexible guidelines over which relationships always take precedence. This dimension is not dissimilar to those delineated by Hofstede; however, attitudes towards relationships and rules could prove to be important in an educational environment. For example, a teacher from a universalist culture conforms to the rules: "You did less than C average work; thus, you have earned the failing grade." However, a teacher from a particularist society might bend the rules to allow the student to pass, acknowledging that the student has put forth effort; or the teacher might be more lenient if he or she is acquainted with the student's family.

The *individualism vs. communitarianism* dimension, similar to Hofstede's IDV index, refers to the tendency to perceive oneself primarily either as an individual or as a member of a group. In an individualistic culture, members value personal achievement and responsibility. The communitarian society, meanwhile, privileges the achievement of group goals. They frequently make decisions via consensus or defer decisions to an authoritative entity.

Members of *affective vs. neutral* cultures may be, respectively, emotionally expressive or emotionally detached and objective in verbal or non-verbal communication. This dimension is reflected in communication through forms of humor, styles of speaking, tone of voice, frequency and type of touch, amount of eye contact and the ratio of nonverbal (contextual) to verbal (content) communication. Characteristics of this dimension are similar to those described by Hall's (1981) concept of high-context vs. low-context cultures and could, conceivably, affect learning preferences or outcomes.

Specific vs. diffuse relates to "the degree to which we engage others in *specific* areas of life … or *diffusely* in multiple areas of our lives" (Trompenaars & Hampden-Turner, 1998) and accounts for the degree and level of interaction between people. In *specific* cultures, for example, the "boss" is the authority in the office, but beyond that environment, he or she is no longer granted the same deference. Conversely, in *diffuse* cultures, members confer authority to superiors across most environments. Members of specific cultures tend to use direct and purposeful communication, while diffuse cultures tend to be less direct, often to the point of appearing evasive. Such differences in communication could, conceivably, interfere with learning in a globalized environment.

The *achieved status vs. ascribed status* dimension relates to whether a culture determines status according to accomplishments or according to markers of group membership. In achievement-oriented cultures, according to Trompenaars and Hampden-Turner (1998), authority is tied to one's task or job, whereas in an ascription-oriented culture, titles clarify status. This dimension shares characteristics with Hofstede's PDI.

Trompenaars and Hampden-Turner (1998) also identified two dimensions in the category "attitude toward time." *Orientation to past, present and future* reflects to how cultures perceive the importance of each of these periods. The dimension *sequential vs. synchronic* is related to whether time is perceived as linear and composed of discrete events or as circular and composed of integrated, overlapping events.

Lastly, Trompenaars and Hampden-Turner (1998) categorized "attitudes toward the environment." Members of *inner-directed* cultures believe they have significant control over the outcome of events, aggressively trying to manage situations; whereas members of *outer-directed* cultures believe they are subject to an external locus of control, and thus are more comfortable and flexible when confronted with change.

Hall's Perspectives of Cultural Differences

In Hall's (1981) words, "culturally based paradigms place obstacles in the path to understanding because culture equips each of us with built-in blinders, hidden and unstated assumptions" (p. 220). Hall envisioned cultural differences as poles on opposite ends of continua that resemble the indices and characteristics, respectively, of Hofstede (1984, 1997) and Trompenaars and Hampden-Turner (1998).

According to Hall (1981), members of *M-time* (monochronic) cultures tend to emphasize schedules, promptness and segmentation of activities. Their communication is low context, depending more on direct language than on subtle signals. In contrast, members of *P-time* (polychronic) cultures engage in multiple activities simultaneously and tend to focus on relationships and the completion of transactions rather than on scheduled events. Their communication is high context, as it is dependent on what they already know about their culture.

According to Hall (1981), American education tends to be linear, compartmentalized and lacking in creativity and problem-solving techniques. As members of a low-context culture, Americans tend to use sparse communication, especially in technologically driven environments. However, such direct communication may be advantageous in globalized e-learning.

Applications of National Level Cultural Dimensions in Education

Educational researchers and practitioners have begun to incorporate the findings of national-level studies into e-learning. Marcus and Gould (2001), for instance, proposed redesigning the user interface of Web pages to match the known cultural dimensions of the target culture as described by Hofstede (1997).

Marinetti and Dunn (2002) proposed adapting courses of varying complexity to the cultural dimensions of learners as identified in the literature to accommodate the presumed preferences of different groups. Their adaptation strategies are summarized in Table 1. For the purpose of discussion, each level of course complexity has been assigned a number, ranging from Level 1 to Level 4, also indicating the level of cultural influence on the course design.

For example, based on their table, for Level 1 courses, simple *translation* of content would be adequate as a cultural adaptation technique, because the content and method of presentation is straightforward, indicating little if any cultural impact. Translation could encompass simple conversion to 'global English' or to British English, or to full-scale translation to another language. For Level 2 courses, in which content or tasks are more complex but universally familiar, in addition to

Table 1. Descriptions of course levels 1-4 (Marinette & Dunn, 2002)

Complexity Level	Level 1	Level 2	Level 3	Level 4
Content Type	Simple information, knowledge, news	Low level, cognitive "hard skills"; simple knowledge and core concepts	Some soft skills; complex knowledge, such as regulatory or financial information; business strategy and most business skills	Mostly "soft skills," such as attitudes and beliefs; many complex management skills
Content Examples	Product knowledge, company procedures	Application software, other electronic skills	Project management, presentation skills, marketing strategy	Negotiation skills, motivation, teamwork, conflict resolution
Content Adaptation: What people learn	Translation only; content and context culturally neutral	Translation plus context adaptation, examples as required	Translation plus context adaptation, examples and some modular content	Significant proportion of content and context is unique per culture
Instructional Strategy Adaptation: How people learn	None	Minor changes	Required at key points; re-ordering information, representation of concepts, alternative media, etc.	Significant proportion unique per culture; may require alternative course architectures
Adaptation Strategies	Translation	Localization	Modularization	Origination

potential translation, *localization* could ensure that concepts and technical tasks are achievable by the targeted culture.

Localization may be described as "the process of converting material ... into a format that is technically, linguistically and culturally appropriate for countries outside the original market" (Transware, 2002). These superficial changes, called *soft-multiculturalism* by Henderson (1996), include slang, humor, gestures, units of measure, law, taboos, etiquette and so forth. For Level 3 courses, Marinetti and Dunn (2002) proposed *modularization*. Modularization entails adapting only those components of the e-learning course that vary between the designing and recipient culture, and that could affect learners' outcomes. These components, referred to as *reusable learning objects* (RLOs), may also be called *cultural learning objects* (CLOs) in this context (Alberta Online Consortium, 2004) or cross-cultural learning objects (XCLOs). Finally, for course content that is complex or culturally differentiated, Marinetti and Dunn recommended *origination*—creating a new course with the full participation of the target culture to meet its very specific needs and preferences.

Any of the above techniques, singularly or in combination, could simplify the adaptation process and reduce the costs of redesign, subsequently improving the cultural compatibility of e-learning courses. However, the presumed need to adapt e-learning courses to the cultural dimensions of targeted learners remains unproven by research. In addition, the possibility that a cultural group could accept or adapt to the dimensions of the culture in which an e-learning artifact originated remains unexplored.

Cultural Dimensions in Education

At a high level, culture influences multiple aspects of education, from the obvious, such as educational structures, governance, delivery systems and teaching styles (Thomas, 1990), to the subliminal, such as values or the purpose of education (Gardner, 1989; Mosa, 1999; Jarvis, 2002).

Gardner (1983) argued that cultures value different types of intelligence and different forms of knowledge. These intelligences are not cultural dimensions per se, but Gardner's theory of multiple intelligences suggests that one culture could prefer one cluster of intelligences to another, and that education could be designed to accommodate those intelligences. In another study (1989), he found that the Chinese prefer a *mimetic* approach to education: Teachers (and educational materials) are treated as unquestioned repositories of knowledge. In contrast, Americans were moving toward a *transformative* approach to education: Teacher act as coaches, eliciting desired qualities from students.

Henderson (1996) proffered a comprehensive *multiple culture model* (MCM) specifically for investigating cultural characteristics in education, with 14 dimensions represented as continua with polar extremes, reminiscent of those used by Hall (1981), Hofstede (1984, 1997) and Trompenaars and Hampden-Turner (1998). In the model, the course features and characteristics represented on one side reflect the objectivist-instructivist pedagogical paradigm, while those on the other side reflect the constructivist-cognitive paradigm, bearing similarities to the descriptions of Level 1 through Level 4 courses (Marinetti & Dunn, 2002).

Study Methodology

For this study, the 14 dimensions on the MCM were reduced to nine, thereby creating the *simplified multiple cultural model* (SMCM) (Edmundson, 2004):

1. **Pedagogical Paradigm:** *Instructivist/Objectivist – Constructivist/Cognitive.* Four closely related dimensions—*Epistemology*, *Pedagogical Philosophy*, *Underlying Psychology* and *Goal Orientation*—were combined to create a singular dimension, Pedagogical Paradigm.

2. **Experiential value:** *Abstract – Concrete.* When instruction has abstract experiential value, learning is removed from reality. Instruction with concrete experiential value integrates the learning process with the learner's world.

3. **Teacher role:** *Didactic – Facilitative.* A didactic exposition of knowledge, such as a lecture, contrasts with facilitative pedagogical techniques that enable exploratory learning without controlling outcomes.

4. **Value of errors:** *Errorless learning – Learning from experience.* Under an errorless learning paradigm, students learn until they generate no mistakes, or the instructional method does not allow for errors. In contrast, the learning from experience approach to instruction uses errors in the educational process.

5. **Motivation:** *Extrinsic – Intrinsic.* Extrinsic motivation originates from factors outside the learner, such as the need for high grades or the presence of engaging materials. Intrinsic motivation comes from an internal desire to learn.

6. **Accommodation of individual differences:** *Non-existent – Multifaceted.* In some contexts, learning and knowledge are structured so that there is no need for accommodation of individual differences. When accommodation of individual differences is existent, on the other hand, knowledge and learning are presented in a variety of ways so that learners can utilize the tools that most suit their preferences.

7. **Learner control:** *Non-existent – Unrestricted.* In this dimension, the student either learns along a predetermined path or by independent discovery.

8. **User activity:** *Mathemagenic – Generative.* A mathemagenic approach permits learners to access the same content in different ways, while a generative approach encourages learners to engage in the process of creating and elaborating content.

9. **Cooperative learning:** *Unsupported – Integral.* In this dimension, learners work independently, or learning is encouraged through cooperative activities.

Certain SMCM dimensions (e.g., cooperative learning) may be manifestations of cultural dimensions at the national level, while others may simply reflect learner preferences or subliminal effects of culture. To date, however, relatively few studies have examined cultural dimensions within e-learning courses. Likewise, few researchers have administered an e-learning course designed by one culture to individuals in another culture with the intention of measuring potential differences in learning outcomes.

The Study

The experimental design best suited to part one of this study was the posttest-only control group design (Campbell & Stanley, 1963; Leedy & Ormrod, 2001; Tuckman, 1978) diagrammed in Figure 1.

Pre-testing was neither desirable nor useful in this study, as the researcher was interested in the differences between learning outcomes caused by the culture, rather than the knowledge or skills generated by the e-learning course.

Figure 1. Posttest-only control group design

```
R1   X   O1
R2       O2
```

Note:

R = randomly selected members of the groups under study

X = the treatment (i.e., the culture of each of the two groups)

O = the observations or measurements of differences between the two groups (i.e., tutorial results and questionnaire responses)

Seven hundred fifty-seven technology workers in functionally equivalent roles were required by their company to take a western-designed e-learning course. The Software Upgrade Tutorial was designated as a Level 1 course, according to the criteria described by Marinetti and Dunn (2002). From this group, 250 were randomly selected (for a confidence interval of 95%) to participate in the study: 204 from a Western culture (U.S.) and 46 from an Eastern culture (India). Data on learning outcomes were analyzed using students' t tests for unequal n using Stat-Disk (Triola, 2001).

In part two of the study, the 250 participants were invited to complete an online post-course questionnaire, which included questions based on the SMCM dimensions, to identify (a) learning outcomes not recorded by the learning management system, and (b) the participants' preferences for and perceptions of e-learning, based on potential cultural differences and their overall experiences with the genre. The students' mean (coded) responses were analyzed using students' t tests for unequal n using StatDisk (Triola, 2001).

Finally, the researcher explored possible relationships between the learning outcomes and participants' preferences and perceptions to the cultural dimensions described in national-level research.

Summary of Findings

Members of both groups, completing a Level 1 course, achieved equitable learning outcomes when they took the Software Upgrade Tutorial. There were no significant differences $(\alpha = .05)$ between learning outcomes (number of attempts needed to complete the course, scores of each attempt and time needed for each attempt). Responses on the questionnaire provided additional information on how they navigated and used the course and their perceptions of its effectiveness. Both groups needed no more than three attempts to complete the course. An average of 85% of the participants completed the course on the first attempt in an average of 68 minutes, with an average score of 85.5%. While the U.S. participants felt that the tutorial did not completely meet its objectives, both groups agreed that they had *applied* most of what they had learned to their work. Both groups used the course features, in the form of simple media (demonstrations, handouts and navigation tools), in the same manner, although Americans tended to print more handouts than Indian participants. Both groups acknowledged that they had experienced confusion in the past with language and format in e-learning, which indicated that they had taken e-learning courses more complex than the Level 1 tutorial used in this study.

Participants expressed equal acceptance of the course characteristics manifested in behavioral/objectivist and cognitive/constructivist paradigms. This acceptance may have been related to characteristics of this particular group, but should be considered when working with members of other cultural groups, as well. With respect to those features and characteristics, participants preferred that the instructor/course designer manage the design elements; establishment of course objectives; selection of activities, instructional methods; examples; and determination of the best path to learning. These features are typically selected during the *design process*.

Participants also indicated that they preferred being guided by a facilitator rather than instructed by an expert, controlling the pace of learning, testing themselves by experimentation, learning from their mistakes, and applying course knowledge and skills to their own activities. In other words, participants expected to control *how they interacted with the course*, although both groups indicated that they would be open to trying other approaches to learning.

Participants' responses indicated that two of the nine dimensions of the SMCM are related to certain cultural dimensions described at the national level. The dimension of *cooperative learning* on the SMCM shares characteristics with Hofstede's IDV dimension, Trompenaars and Hampden-Turner's individualism vs. communitarianism dimension, and Hall's M-time vs. P-time dimension (M-time stressing independence and individualism). The *origin of motivation* on the SMCM shares characteristics with Hofstede's IDV and MAS dimensions (why students chose to participate and achievement consciousness, respectively), as well as to Trompenaars and Hampden-Turner's individualism vs. communitarianism dimension (motivation toward personal achievement or group goals).

Two other SMCM dimensions seem potentially related to those identified at the national level, though not as strongly as *cooperative learning* and *origin of motivation*. *Teacher role* from the SMCM appears to share characteristics with Hofstede's MAS dimension (teacher's status) and with Trompenaars and Hampden-Turner's specific vs. diffuse dimension (the range of authority conferred). *Learner control* on the SMCM appears to share characteristics with Hofstede's PDI (degree of authority or control conferred) and Trompenaars and Hampden-Turner's inner-directed vs. outer-directed dimension (one's need for control over the environment). *Value of errors* on the SMCM seemed weakly related to Trompenaars and Hampden-Turner's universalism vs. particularism, the dimension encompassing the value of rules.

Thus, while this study did not explore statistical correlations between cultural dimensions and learner preferences, there appear to be potential relationships between at least four dimensions of the SMCM and dimensions identified by other researchers. These findings suggest the need for studies of cultural dimensions in Level 1 to 4 courses, as greater course complexity may trigger stronger responses, indicate more cultural preferences or infer more obvious relationships to national-level cultural dimensions.

Results

New Perspectives on E-Learning

The findings in this exploratory study offer five new perspectives on the e-learning environment that could change how instructors/designers create courses, how consumers adapt and/or export Western-designed e-learning courses and how Level 1 e-learning can be used to promote global education and economic development.

First, the features of Level 1 courses appear to create a learning environment conducive to equitable learning outcomes, as their low-context nature introduces the fewest cultural effects: Communication is minimized; interaction is nonexistent; and language is blunt, technical and sparse (Hall, 1981).

Second, learners seem to differentiate between the features of courses generated during the design process (and are thus beyond their control) and those that drive learner interaction with the course, which they prefer to control. This ability to differentiate may be a reflection of a certain level of technical sophistication within these groups of learners; however, knowing this, course developers should expect, at the least, to determine e-learning course goals and objectives, types of learning activities, instructional method(s) and the overall "path" to learning. At the same time, they should expect that learners would prefer facilitation of learning rather than authoritative instruction, control of the pace of learning, learning from experimentation or mistakes and application of learning to their own needs.

Third, since members of both cultures were amenable to trying course features representing contrasting pedagogical paradigms, there is potential to introduce an *eclectic paradigm*—a combination of instructivist/objectivist and constructivist/cognitive, as suggested by Henderson (1996)—to other cultures.

Fourth, certain SMCM dimensions appear to affect e-learning preferences and outcomes. The dimensions of cooperative learning and origin of motivation appear to have strong effects on e-learning preferences and, thus, may be characterized as *critical cultural dimensions*. Three dimensions—teacher role, learner control and possibly value of errors—have indeterminate impact, but are likely to matter and, until further research indicates otherwise, could be treated as critical dimensions. The remaining dimensions—user activity, experiential value and accommodation of individual differences—may be described as *assistive cultural dimensions*.

Finally, there appears to be a dichotomy between the cultural *profiles* of learners and their actual preferences. While several of the large-scale trends that define cultural groups may need to be accommodated in e-learning courses above Level 1, a significant number of these dimensions are best viewed as "possible preferences," rather than as ultimate and final outlooks, and should be explored further. One way in which to do this is to use the cultural adaptation process (CAP) model.

Figure 2. The CAP model, v.2.

	Level 1	Level 2	Level 3	Level 4
Step 1: Evaluate type of content (see examples.)	Simple information, core knowledge, news or updates, such as product knowledge, company procedures	Low-level, cognitive hard skills; simple knowledge and concepts, such as those used in application software; most computer-related skills	Some soft skills; complex knowledge, such as project management, presentation skills, marketing strategy	Mostly soft skills; attitudes and beliefs, such as negotiation skills, motivation, teamwork, conflict resolution
Step 2: Identify media	Lecture, handouts, simple demonstrations (no actual interaction among learners or between instructor and learners)	In this range, several media options are available, but HOW they are used is the important factor. For example, media can provide active or passive access to other learners or to the instructor.		Videoconferencing, Web-based training, streaming media and Web conferencing (real time or simulated interactions among learners or between learners and instructor)
		Visual Media—Satellite broadcasts, audio conferencing, recordings, television, etc. Text-Based Media—Threaded discussions, list servers, online chat, e-mail, etc.		
Step 3: Identify pedagogical paradigm (via instructional methods, etc.)	Instructivist-objectivist, with behavioral objectives and sharply-focused goals; low-context communication; mimetic	More closely related to instructivist-objectivist than constructivist-cognitive paradigm	More closely related to constructivist-cognitive than instructivist-objectivist paradigm	Constructivist-cognitive with cognitive objectives, unfocused goals; high-context communication; transformative

Upon review of targeted learners' cultural dimension (Hofstede, Trompenaars & Hampden-Turner, Hall, etc.), relate learners' cultural profiles to *critical and assistive* characteristics of the course that may support or hinder learners' use or acceptance of course:

Step 3 (a): Identify *critical* cultural characteristics of course	Unsupported ←	Cooperative Learning →	Integral
	Extrinsic ←	Origin of Motivation →	Intrinsic
	Non-existent	← Learner Control →	Unrestricted
	Didactic	← Teacher Role →	Facilitative
	Errorless learning	← Value of Errors →	Learning from experience
Step 3 (b): Identify *assistive* cultural characteristics of course	Mathemagenic ←	User Activity →	Generative
	Abstract ←	Experiential Value →	Concrete
	Non-existent ←	Accommodation of Individual Differences →	Multifaceted

Step 4: Integrate current research findings

Step 5: Adaptation strategies
Such strategies can consist of design changes to the e-learning course itself, or to the e-learning environment.

Step 5 (a): Design strategies	Translation	+ Localization	+ Modularization	Origination

Step 5 (b): Environmental strategies

Step 6: Action planning and testing

The CAP Model: Version 2

The revised version of the original (Edmundson, 2004) CAP model (v. 2) in Figure 2 is proposed as a guideline for offering culturally appropriate e-learning courses (a) by evaluating existing e-learning courses, (b) by creating cultural profiles of targeted learners, and (c) by guiding testing of e-learning courses. This version is based on a synthesis of findings from this study, but it also incorporates findings on cultural dimensions from research in industrial anthropology (Hofstede, Trompenaars, & Hampden-Turner, Hall, etc.) and education (Henderson, Marinetti, & Dunn, etc.), as well as the practical experiences of the researcher (Edmundson, 2005).

The model provides a matrix in which, from left to right, course complexity is considered, and from top to bottom, the steps in adapting an e-learning course for a targeted culture are presented. Users of the model will need to know the cultural dimensions of the targeted learners as they relate to cooperative learning, origin of motivation and, most likely, learner control, teacher role and value of errors. They will need to identify the level of the course they expect to use, adapt or create, and then analyze and evaluate the match of course characteristics to the cultural dimensions and preferences of targeted learners. Quantitative evaluations can be conducted to determine if targeted learners can achieve the intended learning outcomes. In addition, their learning preferences should be assessed, using focus groups, surveys or interviews.

Future research may indicate that other dimensions should be included in the model, that certain assistive dimensions should be rated as critical, or that current dimensions classified as critical are more aptly described as assistive.

The CAP model represents a new, but not complete, perspective on the cultural dimensions of e-learning courses and learners. Feedback from the use of the systematic model and further research would help fashion a reliable tool for consumers of e-learning.

Changes Made to the Model

Based on experiences using the original version of the model (Edmundson, 2004), several changes to the model were implemented (Edmundson, 2006). Summarized, those changes include:

1. Incorporate recent research into the model.
2. Conduct qualitative and quantitative evaluations of the effectiveness of the proposed changes using focus groups and pilot tests, as well as surveys to

Figure 3. The framework for using the CAP model, v.2.

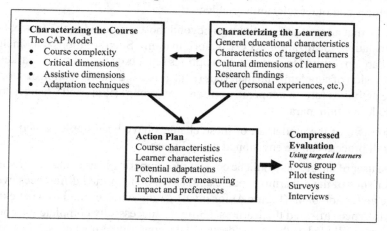

Figure 4. A sampling of potential adaptations to consider (based on a mock example).

Course characteristics	Learner characteristics	Potential adaptations to consider	How to measure or evaluate impact/preferences
Use of American English	Taught in schools with British English	• Change words, idioms, colloquialisms • Provide learners with a glossary • Do nothing	Determine learner familiarity with American English and idioms, and other colloquialisms used in the course.
Use of American icons and brand names, such as Harley Davidson motorcycles	Highly educated, work for Americans and are frequently exposed to American culture through mass media, work, colleagues	• Replace with those known to Indian learners • Explain differences • Do nothing	Determine learner familiarity with American icons, pop culture and other colloquialisms used in the course via focus group
Lacks cooperative activities and group work except through simulations and post-course communications	Prefer cooperative activities and group work	• Create RLOs to replace individualistic activities with more cooperative ones • Create and present a supplemental cooperative activity just for the Indian learners • Do nothing; learners may accept and/or adapt to individualistic activities	Pilot test the course for equitable learning outcomes; survey participants about reaction to activities provided
Embodies cognitive-constructivist educational paradigm	More accustomed to instructivist-didactic approach to teaching	• Create a course based on paradigm to which learners are accustomed • Do nothing; learners accept and/or adapt to different paradigm	Pilot test the course for equitable learning outcomes; survey participants about reaction to activities provided

identify learners' preferences for methods and approaches, their use of course features and other relevant variables.

3.   Show that adaptation solutions go beyond those proposed in the matrix (e.g., translation, localization, RLOs and origination). Such solutions may include, but are not limited to, presentation options (e.g., how the course is marketed); provision of supplemental materials (e.g., glossaries); and creation of support- ive activities (e.g., a cooperative discussion group) (Proposed Changes to the Model section, para. 1).

In version two of the model, all of these changes have been implemented so that the overall process can be envisioned using Figure 3.

Thus, the user of the model would be constantly comparing learner characteristics to characteristics of the e-learning course and, based on identified differences, would generate an 'action plan' (Figure 4) for investigating whether (and to what extent) those differences affected the learners' ability to successfully complete the course. In addition, as alluded to above, the design of the course does not necessarily require adaptation. Instead, as illustrated in Figure 4, the user might identify and consider multiple ways in which to make the e-learning course acceptable to the targeted learn- ers by modifying the environment in which it is presented. Any proposed adaptations would be tested and measured for their effectiveness in a 'compressed evaluation' environment involving representative members of the targeted culture.

Conclusion

Based on findings in this study, the researcher proposed new perspectives on e- learning that could represent the means to effectively adapting or creating e-learning courses for use in other cultures. A revised version of the CAP model was provided as a guideline for culturally adapting e-learning. Such actions could increase access to technology education, improve technological literacy, and introduce new technolo- gies across and between cultures, thereby increasing socioeconomic development across the ever-expanding e-world.

Many factors point the way to success in global e-learning delivery. Learning those factors—both external market and internal capacity—and how the factors work in different countries will be essential to a sound strategy for international growth of [your] programs. (Hezel & Mitchell, 2005, Conclusion section, para. 1)

References

Alberta Online Consortium. (2004). *Flexible e-content (FLEXEC) project overview*. Retrieved January 24, 2006, from www.ataoc.ca/default.asp?V_DOC_ID=867

Campbell, D. T., & Stanley, J. C. (1963). *Experimental and quasi-experimental designs for research*. Boston: Houghton Mifflin Company.

Edmundson, A. L. (2004). *The cross-cultural dimensions of globalized e-learning* (unpublished doctoral dissertation). Minneapolis: Walden University.

Edmundson, A. L. (2005, September 27-30). *Using the cultural adaptation process (CAP) model—Adapting e-learning to the needs of other cultures*. Proceedings of the Advancing the Effectiveness and Sustainability of Open Education Conference, Logan, UT.

Edmundson, A. L. (2006). Using the cultural adaptation process (CAP) model to match e-learning to the needs of other cultures. In A.L. Edmundson (Ed.), *Globalized e-learning cultural challenges*. Hershey, PA: Idea Group.

Gardner, H. (1983). *Frames of mind: The theory of multiple intelligences*. New York: Basic Books.

Gardner, H. (1989). *To open minds: Chinese clues to the dilemma of contemporary American education*. New York: Basic Books.

Hall, E. T. (1981). *Beyond culture: Into the cultural unconscious* (1st ed.). Garden City: Anchor Press.

Henderson, L. (1996). Instructional design of interactive multimedia: A cultural critique. *Educational Technology Research and Development, 44*(4), 85-104.

Hezel, R. T., & Mitchell, J. (2005). *Developing a global e-learning program: From conceptualization to implementation* (white paper). Syracuse: Hezel Associates.

Hofstede, G. H. (1984). *Culture's consequences: International differences in work-related values* (Abridged ed., vol. 5). Newbury Park: SAGE Publications.

Hofstede, G. H. (1997). *Cultures and organizations: Software of the mind* (2nd ed.). London; New York: McGraw-Hill.

Horton, W. (1999, 2003). *Multicultural multimedia: Teaching and reaching the whole wide world*. Retrieved February 14, 2003, from www.horton.com

Jaju, A., Kwak, H., & Zinkhan, G.M. (2002). Learning styles of undergraduate business students: A cross-cultural comparison between the U.S., India, and Korea. *Marketing Education Review, 12*(2).

Jarvis, P. (2002). Globalization, citizenship and the education of adults in contemporary European society. *Compare: A Journal of Comparative Education, 32*(1), 5-19.

Lave, J. (1988). *Cognition in practice: Mind, mathematics, and culture in everyday life.* Cambridge: Cambridge University Press.

Leedy, P.D. & Ormrod, J.E. (2001). *Practical research: Planning and design* (7th ed.). Upper Saddle River: Prentice-Hall.

Marcus, A., & Gould, E.W. (2001). *Cultural dimensions and global Web user-interface design: What? So what? Now what?* Retrieved August 25, 2002, from www.amanda.com

Marinetti, A., & Dunn, P. (2002). *Cultural adaptation: Necessity for global e-learning.* Retrieved September 24, 2005, from www.linezine.com/7.2/articles/pdamca.htm

McLoughlin, C. (1999). Culturally responsive technology use: Developing an online community of learners. *British Journal of Educational Technology, 30*(3), 231-245.

Mosa, A. A. (1999). Culture in education and mass media: Conformation or confrontation. *Educational Media International, 36*(1), 34-41.

Soh, K.-C. (1999). East-West difference in views on creativity: Is Howard Gardner correct? Yes and no. *Journal of Creative Behavior, 33*(2), 112-125.

Thomas, R. M. (Ed.). (1990). *International comparative education: Practices, issues & prospects* (1st ed.). Oxford: Pergamon Press.

Transware, P. (2002, Last update unknown). *What is localization?* Retrieved September 21, 2002, from www.transwareplc.com

Triola, M. F. (2001). *Elementary statistics* (8th ed.). Boston: Addison-Wesley Longman.

Trompenaars, A., & Hampden-Turner, C. (1998). *Riding the waves of culture: Understanding cultural diversity in global business* (2nd ed.). New York, London: McGraw Hill.

Tuckman, B. W. (1978). *Conducting educational research* (2nd ed.). New York: Harcourt Brace Janovich.

UNDP. (2001). *Human development report 2001: Making new technologies work for human development.* New York: United Nations Development Program.

United Nations. (2005). *UN Millennium Development Goals.* Retrieved January 1, 2006, from www.un.org/millenniumgoals/#

Van Dam, N.,, & Rogers, E. (2002). E-learning cultures around the world. *e-Learning, 3*(5), 28-32.

Walker, A., & Dimmock, C. A. J. (Eds.). (2002). *School leadership and administration: Adopting a cultural perspective*. New York: RoutledgeFalmer.

Chapter XII

Project-Based Online Group Collaborative Learning Characteristics

Jianxia Du, Mississippi State University, USA

Byron Havard, University of West Florida, USA

James Adams, Mississippi State University, USA

Gang Ding, East China Normal University, Republic of China

Wei-Chieh Yu, Mississippi State University, USA

Abstract

This chapter illustrates a framework for online group collaborative learning based on Piaget's concepts of assimilation and accommodation and Vygotsky's theory of social interaction. This chapter examined how an online project-based learning approach affected students' cognitive skills development and their motivation, and explored factors leading to successful collaborative projects. The findings indicated that in a project-based online group environment unique characteristics exist for leadership style and individual role, goal setting and project management, accountability and commitment, peer supportive relationships, individual accomplishment and group accomplishments, and mixed gender and race group preference.

Introduction

The value of collaborative learning is widely recognized because of its positive effects on social, cognitive and metacognitive development. One advantage of collaborative learning is that it provides students opportunities for self-reflection and joint construction of knowledge, and this environment frequently leads to higher levels of task-related interaction and behavior (e.g., Johnson, Johnson, & Stanne, 1986). When students are able to participate in active learning activities, they find learning more pleasurable and satisfying than non-participative events.

Small-group dynamics have been studied in educational contexts since the 1970s. Research indicates that small groups facilitate learning as compared to individual learning (e.g., Johnson, Johnson, & Stanne, 1986; Hamm & Adams, 1992; Bruffee, 1999), and that peer group work has significant impacts on varied learning outcomes in both face-to-face and online learning environments (e.g., Harasim, 1990; Scardamalia & Bereiter, 1996; Bruffee, 1999; Uribe, Klein, & Sullivan, 2003). Although much of cooperative learning research initially focused on face-to-face cooperation at the elementary school level, it is now gradually extending into higher education, which is the focus of this study.

Positive interdependence promotes 'group cohesion' and a heightened sense of 'belonging' to a group; and can be achieved through the task, resources, goals, rewards, roles or the environment (Brush, 1998). Individual accountability refers to the extent to which students are individually accountable for jobs, tasks or duties, and was introduced to counter the 'free-rider effect': some students would deliberately not invest any (or little) effort. Both principles, however, relate to group dynamics phenomena 'group cohesion' and 'social loafing' (Du & Havard, 2003), and thus apply to any form of small-group learning. Bosworth and Hamilton (1994) proposed a process-oriented design method for online group-based learning that focused on fostering the envisioned group interaction thought to enhance learning instead of focusing on the formal product of such interaction. This method tends to be the dominant view in most institutions providing higher education and centers on five elements that directly shape group interaction: learning objectives, task type, level of pre-structuring, group size and technological tool used.

The need for systematic design of online learning is amplified by some observations that exhibit conflict regarding coordination during group interaction. These observations suggest conflicts are more likely to occur in asynchronous online settings compared to face-to-face settings (Du & Havard, 2005), since group members are not present at the same time and/or place. Also, the lack of presence concerning immediate feedback and face-to-face setting make asynchronous communication 'unnatural.' Clearly, some support should be designed to help students overcome difficulties in group coordination during asynchronous collaboration.

Group performance effectiveness depends on the groups' use of their alternate opinions and on the handling of increased coordination (Shaw, 1981). Roles, stated functions/duties or responsibilities that guide individual behavior and regulate intra-group interaction (Hare, 1994) can promote group cohesion and responsibility (Boud, Cohen & Sampson, 1999) and, thus, can be used to foster 'positive interdependence' and 'individual accountability' (Hedberg, 2003). In addition, roles can stimulate a group member's awareness of the overall group performance and each member's contribution. Lastly, roles appear to be most relevant when a group pursues a shared goal requiring a certain level of task division, coordination and integration of individual activities.

Despite the potential benefits of collaborative learning, several studies reveal that collaborative learning does not always lead to the desired outcome. For example, free collaboration does not systematically produce learning (Dillenbourg, 2002), and researchers report large variations in the quality of interaction and learning outcomes (Lehtinen, Hakkarainen, Lipponene, Rahikainen, & Muukkonen, 2000). Other variations may include, but are not limited to, the length of studies, technology used, differences in research methodology and the quality of the group processes (Shaw, 1981; Strijbos, Martens, Jochems, & Broers, 2004). Students who have experienced negative online experiences perceived those experiences as weaknesses of online learning. These problems were most often caused by delayed feedback from instructors (Laszlo & Kupritz, 2003), lack of self-regulation and self-motivation, sense of isolation, monotonous instructional methods (Wang, Sierra, & Folger, 2003), and poorly designed assignments (Hedberg, 2003; Thomas, 2000). Problems in collaborative group projects include social loafing and free riding, disorder due to poor leadership and member role identification, low motivation through no common goal and poor management of tasks.

In this chapter, we argue that collaborative learning has moved beyond the question whether it is effective in accelerating knowledge construction, but should focus on the conditions under which these types of learning environments were optimally effective. The aim of this chapter is to describe students' perceptions of online group collaborative learning and examine how an online project-based learning approach affected students' cognitive skills development and motivation. This study will identify specific group dynamics and factors leading to successful collaborative projects.

A Theoretical Framework for Analysis of the Collaborative Learning Process

From a constructivist perspective, knowledge is constructed via interactions between and among the learner and the social world (Crotty, 1998). Accordingly, learning will be enhanced when students are supported by and engage in 'meaning-making' experiences (Jonassen, 1999). Cognitive tools provide the means through which many constructivist learning activities are enacted, enabling a wide array of affor-

Figure 1. Graphical representation of social constructivist principles and concepts derived from the information processing approach to learning

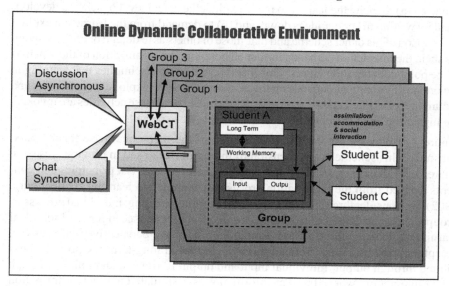

dances with which individuals access, manipulate and otherwise construct knowledge (Jonassen & Reeves, 1996; Lajoie, 2000). Tools play especially important roles in student-centered learning environments (Land & Hannafin, 1996, 1997), where problems are framed in authentic and meaningful contexts, learners engage problems using multiple resources and tools, and knowledge construction is facilitated using technological as well as human scaffolds (Hannafin et al., 1999).

Constructivism is a term used to describe a number of theories. Two dimensions were focused on in this study: the knowledge construction process of individual learners and knowledge construction as a socially situated process (Driscoll, 1994).

The individual learner constructs knowledge by adapting previously constructed schemes. This view is based on Piaget's theory and the concepts of assimilation and accommodation. This process of schema construction and reconstruction implies the selection of stimuli from the project-based environment, continuous storage and retrieval of schemas between long-term memory and working memory in order to organize, elaborate, refine and/or integrate these schemas. This overall process is monitored by metacognitive processes. These processes help the learner to be selective in stimulus selection, storage, retrieval and response organization (Popolov, Callaghan, & Luker, 2002). The online setting influences this complex of cognitive activities in interaction with the nature of the project-based environment.

The knowledge construction process may also be seen as socially situated. This view is based on Vygotsky's theory of social interaction, where the interaction between people plays an important role. This is where the 'social' part of 'social constructivism' becomes evident. The interaction between learners in the online environment is expected (a) to incite the learner to make explicit the actual level of schema development by writing his or her ideas down, and (b) to demand from the learner an explicit comparison of his or her schema and that/those of others as to defend or criticize them. As such, the interaction demands further elaboration and organization of the schemas at the point collaboration enters. This theoretical description implies that learning in the online environment depends on the amount of schema exploitation activities and the amount of explicit comparison and contrast. The more these activities are invoked, the higher the level of knowledge construction to be expected.

Figure 1 provides a graphical representation of the theoretical base for the present study. This scheme is an extension of the framework used in previous research (Hare, 1994; Kitchner, 1983). It integrates social constructivist principles and concepts derived from the information processing approach to learning (Dillenbourg, 2002). We consider three elements or levels regarding learning: individual processes, group member processes and group environment processes (see Figure 1). Individual learning is depicted through an information processing perspective, with sensory receptors providing input, refined through short- and long-term memory, and exhibited through output. Individual input and output is affected and refined through social interaction, where familiar information is assimilated and new information is accommodated. Learning continues at the group environment level, where group input and output is refined through review and critique by other groups.

Framework Application in Online Group Collaboration

The social constructivist notion of interactivity described above was used as a theoretical framework for building an online collaborative learning. The online

Figure 2. Leadership style and peer relationships effect on the nature and outcome of the final product in a project-based learning environment

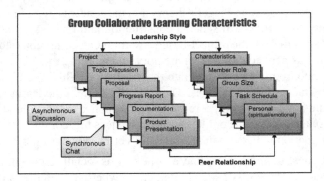

learning environment for this course was created in WebCT. WebCT is a database driven Web-based course management system designed to support online learning environments (Hutchins, 2001). The database elements available in WebCT enable the instructor to record, manage and support the activities and interactions of a large number of students. This multimedia design for instruction course is required of all students enrolled in the Master of Science in Instructional Technology (MSIT) program. Students enrolled in the MSIT program and in this course represent a wide range of diverse backgrounds. They reside throughout the state of Mississippi, Tennessee and Alabama. Each semester, approximately 30 students are enrolled in this course.

In Figure 2, leadership style and peer relationships have a dramatic effect on the nature and outcome of the final product in a project-based learning environment. Both project and group characteristics are impacted by their related characteristics, leadership style and peer relationships (see Figure 2). This project is sequential in nature, with each phase channeling into the next. Peer relationships and leadership style within a group are interrelated, impacting each phase of the project.

Framework Application

We applied the framework during two semesters of a graduate-level multimedia design for instruction course. The purpose of this course was to provide students with an overview of hypermedia/interactive multimedia technology by working with various hypermedia/multimedia tools. Students were introduced to the design and production process of developing multimedia applications and provided the opportunity to learn various tools concentrating on different aspects of the technology: text, graphics, audio, animation and video. By working with these tools, students were expected to develop the skills and understanding required for the creation of instructional tools for application in education and industrial settings. Students were required to apply design principles necessary for the creation of hypermedia/multimedia in developing multimedia-based applications. Several important aspects about this environment regarding skill development, theoretical and technical issues, and the application skills and knowledge towards the successful development of a comprehensive multimedia instructional product (Popolov, Callaghan, & Luker, 2002; Slavin, 1995) were examined. Through online group communication using the asynchronous discussion feature and synchronous chat available through WebCT, students' skills and knowledge regarding multimedia development were enhanced. The social aspect of the learning environment is critical (Vygotsky, 1978). This required focused attention by the instructor, as knowledge is socially constructed and enhanced through peer-to-peer and instructor-to-peer communication (Boud, Cohen, & Sampson, 1999; Kitchner, 1983; Kitchner & King, 1981).

In the multimedia process, students worked in groups and took on different roles. The contexts for learning in this course were primarily interactive, collaborative, multi-disciplinary and student-centered. Students were required to actively participate in weekly discussions regarding specific multimedia development topics. Assignments on learning different tools were given to assess application skills, and students were required to write a research and reflective paper on hypermedia/interactive multimedia instruction. Group projects for the semester both developed and assessed students' ability to comprehensively apply the theoretical and technical requirements for multimedia design for instruction. Students worked together in teams of four or five in developing an instructional Web site as the final course project. The tools used for project development included Macromedia Dreamweaver, Fireworks, Flash, and Hyperstudio. The general target audience for the site included prospective students and teachers. Deliverables beyond the completed Web site included a project proposal, project progress report, project documentation and final presentation of the final product. The project proposal was intended to describe the instructional problem, specific target audience, instructional or training context and objectives to be achieved. The formal project progress report required groups to provide status on their project, including work completed and tasks planned for completion. Project documentation, similar to a detailed design document, revealed details about the product that was developed, justification and use of an instructional design model for product development, audience analysis, formal instructional content, learning objectives, media selection, instructional strategy employed and assessment. Finally, project documentation concluded with a description of the formative evaluation process and findings. Each group presented their final product to the class. Every member of each group was expected to take an active role in the final presentation.

Findings

Accountability and Commitment

By online, we mean that most learners are likely be geographically isolated, studying perhaps from home but with full access to all of the necessary resources via Internet connection. Materials (such as lecture notes) and processes (such as assignment submission) will be electronic, and interaction will be either synchronous (e.g., via chat-rooms or videoconferencing facilities) or asynchronous (e.g., via e-mail or discussion lists). By collaborative, we mean that despite their differing locations, most learners will conduct most of their learning in groups. Such groups are likely to be wholly virtual in the sense that their component members may never meet face to face. They are, however, in all other respects very real, and group members will be highly reliant on each other for the quality of their learning.

Almost all students reported accountability, responsibility, unselfishness, commitment and dedication as major attributes that ensured the success of online collaboration. Students felt that their online collaboration on the project was more successful because students in their group exhibited these characteristics. If a student had to be absent from meetings, legitimate reasons such as a death in the family or in a friend's family, work or having to take care of other family obligations were the norm. Being absent did not prevent the student from being accountable. These students returned to the group concerned about what went on during online discussions in which they were absent and what their assignments were without having to be told by other students in the group. Exhibiting these attributes of accountability and commitment seemed to be contagious within the groups. The more one group member exhibited these traits, the more these traits seemed to become a norm for the behavior of the rest of the group members. There was an "unspoken" appreciation shown by the rest of the group when members participated with this level of commitment, because the rest of the group members seemed to exhibit the same level of behavior when they had to be absent. Complete commitment to the success of the project was exhibited not just by one, but by most of the group members, where leadership with accountability and commitment were practiced.

Leadership Style and Individual Roles

Group dynamics were affected by the leadership style of the online group coordinator. Three groups had female coordinators, two groups had male coordinators. The leadership style exhibited in the group that produced the best results came from a leader who coached his or her team by stepping back and letting team members "shine." The leader quietly led them to meeting deadlines and goals and following the outline of the project, while allowing them to make decisions for the successful completion of the project. The leader allowed the team members to lead, to shine, to be successful, and to feel complete ownership of the finished product, which was not any one individual team member's project, but the project of the committed, concerted efforts of the group. Because group members had ownership in the project and were made to feel the importance of their input, the final project was much more advanced than would have been achieved otherwise. A leadership style that promoted inclusiveness, pride, self-confidence, participation and understanding created a much more productive and self-reliant team that was able to produce beyond the norm. A leader that was more interested in the performance of the team and the quality of the finished product rather than self-recognition produced the more successful product.

One group leader stepped down at mid-semester due to overwhelming outside responsibilities. No one assumed the leadership position and that group was ineffective for 4 weeks, and without instructor directives the group would have failed the project assignment. Two groups had young leaders whom were expected to be at risk, but gained momentum as the semester progressed. Both of the young group leaders initially had difficulty organizing and influencing corporation from the team members, but gradually, with the help of their more experienced team members, the team became focused. One leader, who was a manager by profession, seemed to be the most effective and influenced the team to produce the best project in the class. Another team had high inexperience in Web skills and a leader with a lack of course subject knowledge who was hesitant to lead with firm direction in the beginning. Eventually, this leader pulled the group together to produce a good project.

Individual Accomplishments and Group Accomplishments

By learning, we mean that in group learning environments less emphasis is likely to be placed on memorization, rote learning and cramming for examinations, and more on real-world abilities, such as communication, problem-solving and articulation of solutions. Some groups and some leaders experienced individuals who were more interested in their individual accomplishments than the accomplishments of the team. A few individuals with high Web skills quickly developed the "vehicle" for the final project, but the results were not necessarily compatible with the project goals. Because of existing skills in Web development that some individuals possessed in the group, they may have wanted to take on the design and development of the project without taking into consideration the input of the other team members. Realizing they could produce a product because of their skills did not necessarily mean that their product would excel as well as a product that included the input and talents of all members of the group. The time limitations and the complexity of this project naturally required that it be a group project, thus requiring the talents and input of everyone on the team. Group members questioned and worked through "compatibility of design with team project goals" until the design fit the project idea and theme. Although team members were appreciative of the individual's Web design skills, they wanted their input heard and a finished product that met the guidelines of the project. Team members did not want an individual's accomplishments to overshadow or overrule the accomplishments of the team. Leadership styles definitely affected the group dynamics of each team. These leadership styles included: (1) one that produced the best finished product, (2) lack of leadership when one leader had to step down, (3) inexperienced ones who just needed some practice, and (4) one that required refocusing members who were interested in their accomplishments instead of the team's.

Setting Goals and Managing Team Project

Setting goals and managing the team project assisted the teams in successfully bonding and completing their project (Pate, Du, & Havard, 2004). Students reported that setting a "common goal" and "establishing a bonding" within the group by "dedicated students" was critical in the process of team development and achieving success. Due to the complexity of the project and the amount of time required to complete it, students explained that this kind of dedication and bonding were vital to the success of the team and the assignment. In addition, it was important for a team to plan, manage and meet the timeline, and equally important for the team leader to delegate teamwork to accomplish tasks on time. Missing deadlines and not remaining on schedule also caused a much less polished product at the end of the semester.

Accepting responsibility for group assignments and following through in a timely manner with those assignments affected group productivity. Not only were missed or late assignments an indicator of an individual's dedication to the team, but also indicated the dedication the team member had to the project. A team member without dedication who misses or is late with assignments caused other team members to be late and sometimes miss their assignments, also. Teams that had definite deadlines and frequent communication were able to build more powerful projects than those who had frequent absences and did not honor deadlines. Teams that worked together to demand participation from each member were also more successful. If a team member was not meeting assignment deadlines and goals, improvement would be gained from pressure by the team leader and other members of the group. It appeared that no one in any group wanted to be singled out as the unproductive member. Although there were exceptions, the united strength of the team was much more powerful than just a single individual's leadership role.

Most of the groups referred to their project proposal plans and final project guidelines to evaluate their own development stages and notes. Groups who did not practice referring to their project proposal or the project guidelines, consequently, had project omissions and components that did not relate or fit their design. Often, there were discussions on adding or eliminating parts concerning the project design, and the limitations were not always skill-based. There was a concern that the element did not comply with the project goals or would have to be restructured to fit the project goals. When met with these types of obstacles, the successful groups looked outside the team for advice or help. They either consulted with the instructor, professionals whom they viewed as knowledgeable, online sources or with friends who had experience in a particular area. The successful groups viewed limitations as obstacles to overcome, not as roadblocks for which there was no way around.

Positive Peer Support Spiritually and Emotionally

Peer support served as a positive element in groups and helped to spiritually and emotionally support students through the difficult parts of the project development phases. Several students mentioned "friendship" and "trust" as enjoyable online collaborative learning experiences. This meant "close friends getting along well" and "giving a helping hand to a struggling member." Students seemed to draw an inner strength and purpose when they felt appreciated and were complimented by their fellow group members. This caused the student to be more likely to seek help when needed and to give help where needed. Developing this type of relationship was a gradual process as the group members worked through the obstacles of producing the final project. Gradually, when one member produced a good idea, another member complimented that member and so on. This process of positive team feedback helped make the individual team members more self-confident, thus producing a more self-confident team. This positive peer relationship also enabled the students to "openly discuss problem areas ... and to avoid any potential disagreements." Group members were less likely to engage in disagreements when they had this positive relationship. They could maturely work out any disagreements by openly discussing and agreeing on possible solutions. This positive peer relationship produced group members who were more productive and engaging in timely completion of the final project.

Preference for Mixed Gender and Race Groups

Students preferred mixed gender and race groups for their online discussion groups. In one group, the instructor chose a white male as group leader of a predominately African American female group. Initially, the group leader was apprehensive about his ability to lead this group, as was the group about having him as their leader. When the group of African American women saw that the group leader was not domineering, was inclusive, was open to them taking on leadership roles, and wanted their ideas and participation, they all got together with the leader and produced an outstanding product. Based on observations, African American students perceive group work as a comfortable environment in which to work. When conflicts occurred with group participation, African American students were willing to provide explanations for their conflict and to openly resolve the conflict as soon as possible. When African American students missed an online discussion session, they were quick to seek follow-up information about what they missed. Resistance to group work appeared to be based on lack of some required skills, rather than lack of cooperation to participate in-group. They were only concerned about not being able to assist with certain needs within the group and were not concerned about having to work in a group at all.

Conclusion

Using a socio-cultural view contained in this study as a valuable theoretical framework, individual students in small groups can utilize their own information stored in their working memory and long-term memory interactively with others in their group to organize output that becomes relevant for the other learners, thus providing a meaningful collaborative online learning situation. This active engagement in the learning process when jointly working on a learning task with others becomes meaningful when students are allowed to mutually explain the learning contents, give feedback to the contributions of other group members, and asking and answering questions (Du & Havard, 2005).

Successfully completing a project assigned to an online group was dependent on a number of factors. How successful the project was depended on the leadership style of the group leader, with the most important factor being the success of the group as the main concern. Setting goals and accepting responsibility for the group's project were also major factors in the success of the finished product. These goals and responsibilities were not just the team leaders', but also the entire groups'. Groups also felt that they were more successful with their project when they followed the guidelines and their proposal for the project. Peer support during the development of the group project was a very important part of the success of the project. Students felt that without the spiritual and emotional support of their peers, the project would not have been as successful. If one were looking for a negative factor in online group collaboration, it would not be found in gender or race group preferences. Students worked together regardless of the race or gender of their group members and expressed a preference for having mixed races and genders in their groups. They felt that the variety of contributions from different races and genders was very important to the group work.

The findings of this study can also be used to help identify patterns in which online discussion is conducted effectively in conjunction with course context and individual characteristics for enhancing learning growth. Knowledge of such patterns can facilitate new designs and improvement of online collaborative learning.

References

Bosworth, K., & Hamilton, S. J. (Eds.). (1994). *Collaborative learning: Underlying processes and effective techniques.* San Francisco: Jossey-Bass Publishers.

Boud, D., Cohen, R., & Sampson, J. (1999). Peer learning and assessment. *Assessment and Evaluation in Higher Education, 24*(4), 413-426.

Bruffee, K. (1999). *Collaborative learning: Higher education, interdependence, and the authority of knowledge* (2nd ed.). Baltimore: The Johns Hopkins University Press.

Crotty, M. (1998). *The foundations of social research: meaning and perspective in the research process.* London: Sage.

Dillenbourg, P. (2002). Over-scripting CSCL: The risks of blending collaborative learning with instructional design. In P. A. Kirschner (Ed.), *Three worlds of CSCL: Can we support CSCL?* (pp. 61-91). Heerlen: Open Universiteit Nederland.

Driscoll, M. P. (1994). *Psychology of learning for instruction.* Boston: Allyn and Bacon Erlbaum.

Du, J. X., & Havard, B. (2003). A framework for deep learning in distance education. *Delta Pi Epsilon, 45*(3), 204-214.

Du, J. X., & Havard, B. (2005). Dynamic online discussion: Task-oriented interaction for deep learning. *The Journal of Educational Media, International, 42*(3), 207-218.

Hamm, M., & Adams, D. (1992). *The collaborative dimensions of learning.* Norwood: Ablex Publishing.

Hannafin, M J., Land, S., & Oliver, K. (1999). Student-centered learning environments. In C. M. Reigeluth (Ed.), *Instructional-design theories and models: A new paradigm of instructional theory* (Vol. II, pp. 115-140). Mahwah: Lawrence Erlbaum Associates.

Harasim, L. (1990). Online education: An environment for collaboration and intellectual amplification. In L. Harasim (Ed.), *Online education: Perspectives on a new environment* (pp. 39-64). New York: Praeger.

Hare, A. P. (1994). Types of roles in small groups: A bit of history and a current perspective. *Small Group Reasearch, 25,* 443-448.

Hedberg, J. G. (2003). Ensuring quality e-learning: Creating engaging tasks. *Educational Media International, 40*(3-4), 175-186.

Hutchins, H. M. (2001). Enhancing the business communication course through WebCT. *Business Communication Quarterly, 64*(3), 87-94.

Johnson, D., Johnson, R., & Stanne, M. (1986). Comparison of computer-assisted cooperative, competitive and individualistic learning. *American Educational Research Journal, 23*(3), 382-392.

Jonassen, D. (1999) Designing constructivist learning environments. In C. M. Reigeluth (Ed.), *Instructional-design theories and models: A new paradigm of instructional theory* (Vol. II, pp. 215-239). Mahwah: Lawrence Erlbaum.

Jonassen, D. H., & Reeves, T. C. (1996). Learning with technology: Using computers as cognitive tools. In D.H. Jonassen (Ed.), *Handbook of research on educational communications and technology* (pp. 693-719). New York: Macmillan.

Kitchner, K. S. (1983). Cognition, metacognition, and epistemic cognition: A three-level model of cognitive processing. *Human Development, 26,* 222-232.

Kitchner, K. S., & King, P. M. (1981). Reflective judgment: Concepts of justification and their relationship to age and education. *Journal of Applied Developmental Psychology, 2,* 89-116.

Lajoie, S. P. (2000). *Computers as cognitive tools: No more walls* (vol. 2). Mahwah: Lawrence Erlbaum Associates.

Land, S. M., & Hannafin, M. J. (1996). A conceptual framework for the development of theories-in-action with open-ended learning environments. *Educational Technology Research & Development, 44*(3), 37-53.

Land, S., & Hannafin, M.J. (1997). Patterns of understanding with open-ended learning environments: A qualitative study. *Ed. Tech. Research & Dev., 45*(2), 47-73.

Laszlo, F., & Kupritz, V.W. (2003). The identification of online learning motives in use by undergraduate students. *Delta Pi Epsilon Journal, 45*(1), 63-72.

Lehtinen, E., Hakkarainen, K., Lipponen, L., Rahikainen, M., & Muukkonen, H. (2000). Computer supported collaborative learning: A review. In H. Meijden, R. Simons, & F. De Jong (Eds.), *Computer supported collaborative learning in primary and secondary education. A final report for the European Commission, Project 2017* (pp. 1-46). Nijmegen: University of Nijmegen.

Pate G., Du, J. X., & Havard, B. (2004). Instructional design: Considering cognitive learning needs of older learners. *International Journal of Instructional Technology and Distance Learning, 1*(5), 38.

Popolov, D., Callaghan, M., & Luker, P. (2002). Tying models of learning to design of collaborative learning software tools. *Journal of Computer Assisted Learning, 18*(1), 46-47.

Scardamalia, M., & Bereiter, C. (1996). Computer support for knowledge-building communities. In T. Koschmann (Ed.), *CSCL: Theory and practice of an emerging paradigm* (pp. 249-268). Mahwah: Lawrence Erlbaum Associates.

Shaw, M. E. (1981). *Group dynamics: The psychology of small group behavior* (3rd ed.). New York: McGraw-Hill.

Slavin, R. E. (1995). *Cooperative learning: Theory, research and practice*. Boston: Allyn and Bacon.

Strijbos, J. W., Martens, R. L., Jochems, W. M. G., & Broers, N. J. (2004). The effect of functional roles on group efficiency: Using multilevel modeling and content analysis to investigate computer-supported collaboration in small groups. *Small Group Research, 35*(2), 195-229.

Thomas, J. W. (2000). *A review of research on project-based learning*. Retrieved December 10, 2000, from www.bie.org/tmp/research/researchreviewPBL.pdf

Uribe, D., Klein, J. D., & Sullivan, H. (2003). The effect of computer-mediated collaborative learning on solving ill-defined problems. *Educational Technology Research and Development, 51*(1), 5-19.

Vygotsky, L. S. (1978). *Mind in society*. Cambridge: Harvard University Press.

Wang, M., Sierra, C., & Folger, T. (2003). Building a dynamic online learning community among adult learners. *Edu. Media International, 40*(1-2), 49-61.

Section III

Communications
Technology Education

Chapter XIII

Information Technology Certification:

A Student Perspective

Tanya McGill, Murdoch University, Australia

Michael Dixon, Murdoch University, Australia

Abstract

Certification has become a popular adjunct to traditional means of acquiring information technology (IT) skills, and employers increasingly specify a preference for those holding certifications. This chapter reports on a study designed to investigate student perceptions of both the benefits and risks of certification and its importance in obtaining employment. Certification was perceived as an important factor in achieving employment and students undertaking it anticipate that it will lead to substantial financial benefits. Yet, higher salaries are not seen as the most important benefit of certification. The potential benefits that students believe are most important relate to 'real-world' experience. The respondents were aware of the possible risks of certification but did not appear to be overly concerned about them.

Introduction

Certification has become a popular adjunct to traditional means of acquiring IT skills, and increasing numbers of job advertisements specify a preference for those holding certifications. Certification intends to establish a standard of competency in defined areas. Unlike traditional academic degrees, certifications tend to be specific to narrow fields or even to individual products. They are designed to provide targeted skills that have immediate applicability in the workplace.

Vendors such as Microsoft and Cisco Systems dominate the vendor-specific certification market worldwide, with qualifications such as the Microsoft Certified Systems Engineer (MCSE), Cisco Certified Network Associate (CCNA) and Cisco Certified Internetwork Expert (CCIE). Vendor-neutral certifications, such as those provided by the Institute for Certification of Computing Professionals (ICCP), the Computer Technology Industry Association and the Disaster Recovery Institute, also play a role. It has been reported that there are more than 300 IT certifications available and that approximately 1.6 million people have earned approximately 2.4 million certifications (Nelson & Rice, 2001), and no doubt these figures have already increased dramatically. Gabelhouse (2000) quoted an IDC Inc. report that found that the IT training and testing industries had revenues of $2.5 billion in 1999 and were expected to reach $4.1 billion by 2003.

Vendors create certifications as a way of promoting widespread adoption of their products and technologies, but they have also become important for educational institutions in attracting students and placing graduates (Brookshire, 2000). This chapter explores the perceptions of students who are undertaking courses of study that can lead to certification. It reports on a study designed to investigate student perceptions of both the benefits and risks of certification and its importance in obtaining employment.

Benefits of Certification

Numerous benefits have been proposed to result from IT certification. As Nelson and Rice (2001) note, many of the claims of benefits have originated in the brochures and Web sites of certification agencies; however, there also seems to be a wider recognition of their importance. The major benefits that have been claimed can be categorized as relating to employers, educational institutions and students (i.e., potential employees). The major benefit for employers is believed to be the provision of more capable employees (Ray & McCoy, 2000), and one in eight IT job advertisements have been found to mention certifications (Clyne, 2001; Nelson & Rice, 2001). Some support for the benefit of employee certification to employers is provided in a study by IDC Inc. (1999), which found that 92% of managers surveyed said they realized all or some of the benefits they expected from their certified employees. The major benefits to employers accruing from certified employees were:

- Greater knowledge and increased productivity;
- A certain level of expertise and skill;
- Improved support quality;
- Reduced training costs; and
- Higher morale and commitment.

The major benefit proposed for educational institutions is the opportunity to extend program content and to have an increased assessment capability (Ray & McCoy, 2000). Institutions that successfully offer certifications can become known for their expertise in these areas and attract more students and employers for their graduates (Brookshire, 2000). Student performance on certification exams also provides additional and generalizable measures of student competencies.

The greatest benefits of certification are believed to exist for students (Ray & McCoy, 2000). Marketability is proposed as a major benefit. Students are marketable if their programs of study contain content considered valuable by employers. For example, holders of Cisco certifications should have substantial experience as network administrators, designers and troubleshooters on real networks. Higher salaries are also commonly cited as a benefit, and there is evidence to support this. A survey conducted by *Certification Magazine* (Gabelhouse, 2000) reported that on average certification resulted in a 12% increase in income. This study also reported varying values for different certifications. For example, an MCSE led to an average increase in income of 12.6%, a Cisco CCNA to a 16.7% increase and a Novell CNA to a 13.3% increase. However, Alexander (1999) speculates that increased supply of people with the most popular certifications (such as MCSE) means diminished value in the marketplace. Other proposed benefits associated with increases in marketability and salary include increased self-confidence and credibility (Karr, 2001).

Risks Associated with IT Certification

Despite these benefits, various concerns have been expressed about the current popularity of IT certification. Ray and McCoy (2000) identify the heavy involvement of vendors as an issue for concern, citing the absence of unbiased neutral groups for determining content, creating exams and authorizing examiners. They also recognize that the rapidly changing knowledge base might mean that certification is not of lasting value. Wilde (2000) also highlights the fact that some certifications do not require practical or real-world experience, thus limiting the claims of usefulness.

As IT certifications are increasingly offered by universities and colleges, concerns have been raised that academics might be uncomfortable with the loss of control over content that arises when certification exams determine the content of courses and academic programs (Nelson & Rice, 2001; Ray & McCoy, 2000). Academics might also be uncomfortable with the pressure to maintain their own proficiency levels and certification status.

Given the increasing pervasiveness of certification in the IT profession, more research is needed to verify the benefits of IT certification and to determine the importance of the proposed risks.

The Research Project

The exploratory study reported on in this chapter contributes to the need for further research on the risks and benefits of IT certification by investigating student perceptions of both the benefits and risks of certification, focusing particularly on Cisco certification. This research was conducted by survey. Participants in the study were students enrolled in several electronic commerce, telecommunications management and IT courses at an Australian university. Students who have successfully completed these particular courses can also pursue Cisco certification as the courses make use of the Cisco curriculum. Participants were recruited during class and completed a questionnaire on the spot. It was stressed that the completion of the questionnaire was voluntary and that it formed no part of their assessment in the course.

The questionnaire was designed to be easy to read and understand, and to require no more than 10 minutes to complete. The questionnaire contained four main groups of items. The first section asked about:

- Age;
- Gender;
- Amount of previous work experience (both total and IT experience); and
- Whether the skills provided by their degree are those employers require.

The second group of questions related to the perceptions of the participants about the importance of industry certification for employment. Those participants who were not currently working in the IT industry were first asked to rate the importance of industry certification for obtaining their initial IT employment. This item was measured on a 5-point scale, ranging from (1) 'Not Important' to (5) 'Vital.' They were then asked to indicate how much higher (as a percentage) than the average graduate starting salary they believed their starting salary would be if they obtained various certifications. The list of certifications included those currently available to participants and several other popular certifications (see Table 2 for the list).

Those participants who were currently working in the IT industry were instead asked to rate the importance of industry certification for getting ahead in their current employment. This question also used a 5-point scale, ranging from (1) 'Not Important' to (5) 'Vital.' They were then asked to indicate how much they thought their salary (as a percentage) would increase if they obtained the various IT certifications.

The third group of questions related to participants' perceptions of the importance of various proposed benefits of seeking certification. A list of 11 benefits proposed for IT certification was developed from the literature on IT certification (e.g., Alexander, 1999; IDC Inc., 1999; Karr, 2001; Nelson & Rice, 2001; Otterbourg, 1999). Each potential benefit was rated for importance on a 5point scale, ranging from (1) 'Not Important' to (5) 'Very Important' (see Table 3 for the list).

The fourth group of questions related to participants' perceptions of the importance of various concerns about certification. A list of potential risks of reliance on IT certification was drawn from the literature on certification (e.g., Nelson & Rice, 2001; Ray & McCoy, 2000; Wilde, 2000). Participants rated each potential risk for importance on a 5-point scale, ranging from (1) 'Not Important' to (5) 'Very Important' (see Table 5 for the list).

There were 145 participants in the study, with an average age of 23.4 years (with a range from 18 to 48). Twenty-one (14.5%) were female and 124 (85.5%) were male. The gender proportions in this study are consistent with the low representation of females in IT courses around the world (Downes & Hobbs, 2000; Fitzsimmons, 2000; Klawe & Leveson, 1995). The majority of participants were at the undergraduate level (89.7%), with approximately 10% at post-graduate level. Participants

Table 1. Background information about participants

	Number	Percentage
Gender		
Male	124	85.5
Female	21	14.5
Degree level		
Undergraduate	130	89.7
Postgraduate	15	10.3
Work experience* (mean = 5.8 years)		
No	75	51.7
Yes	70	48.3
* Work experience includes both IT and non-IT experience		
IT work experience (mean = 3.4 years)		
No	97	66.9
Yes	48	33.1

who had previously been employed had on average 5.8 years' work experience, of which 3.4 years were in the IT industry. Table 1 summarizes some of the background information about the participants.

Results and Discussion

Benefits

IT certification was perceived as very important both for obtaining initial IT employment and for getting ahead if currently employed in the IT industry. The average importance rating given to IT certification by those not currently employed in IT was 4.09 (out of 5) and 3.75 (out of 5) for those currently employed in the IT industry (see Table 2 below). These perceptions of students who were not yet certified are consistent with results of a survey of 470 IT contractors described by Alexander (1999). In that study, 83% of the contractors believed that IT certifications were either 'very important' or 'somewhat important' to their prospects for career advancement. Thus, student perceptions of the importance of certification appear to be consistent with industry perceptions. The majority of student participants in the current study also believed that the studies they were undertaking would provide the skills required by employers (yes: 64.5%, not sure: 32.4%, no: 2.8%).

Table 2. Perceived importance of certification

	N	Mean	SD	Min.	Max.
Importance of certification for initial job	119	4.09	1.00	1	5
Importance of certification for current job	24	3.75	1.26	1	5
Anticipated percentage increase in starting salary (if not currently in IT employment)					
CCNA certification	99	18.87	21.46	0	100
CCNP certification	97	25.27	23.85	0	100
Security certification	96	22.88	21.61	0	100
Wireless certification	95	21.27	21.95	0	100
Unix certification	96	21.47	20.55	0	100
MCSE certification	98	19.77	21.26	0	100
Anticipated percentage increase in salary if currently in IT employment					
CCNA certification	19	6.32	4.96	0	15
CCNP certification	20	16.60	14.30	0	50
Security certification	20	19.20	23.31	0	100
Wireless certification	19	10.68	10.19	0	30
Unix certification	18	16.72	23.37	0	100
MCSE certification	18	9.28	14.90	0	60

In general, participants perceived that obtaining IT certification would lead to clear financial benefits. The average increases that students who were not currently working in the IT industry believed they would receive from obtaining certification ranged from a high of 25.27% for CCNP certification down to 18.87% for CCNA certification (see Table 2). The range of increases anticipated by participants was very large, with some suggesting that no increase would result, up to a maximum of 100% for all of the certifications. This wide range of responses suggests that this group of participants did not have a good sense of the value of these certifications in the marketplace. It would be reasonable to expect this result for those certifications not currently available to participants as part of their program of study. But more surprising for the CCNA and CCNP, these certifications are readily available to the participants, and the potential financial benefit resulting from them could be assumed to have influenced their decisions to undertake the courses being surveyed. This lack of knowledge about the financial value of certification is also reflected in the large number of participants who did not provide answers to these items (approximately 20% did not respond to at least one of the questions about salary). Instructors have a major role to play in providing up-to-date information about employers' needs and likely outcomes of obtaining certification. The instructors need to be highly accessible and ensure that their knowledge of the marketplace that graduates will enter remains current so they can help guide students (McGill & Dixon, 2003).

Those participants who were currently working in the IT industry also anticipated financial gains from certification, but the average percentage gains they suggested were lower than those anticipated by students not working in the IT industry. The percentage increases anticipated by those who were currently employed were consistent with the figures available from surveys, such as the one conducted by *Certification Magazine* (Gabelhouse, 2000), suggesting that employed students have realistic expectations. There was also a narrower range of responses provided, suggesting less confusion about likely financial outcomes resulting from certification.

Table 3. Benefits of certification

Rank	Benefits	N	Mean	SD	Min.	Max.
1	Practical experience with real networking tasks	143	4.57	0.60	2	5
2	Experience with real equipment	143	4.55	0.62	2	5
3	Widely recognized qualification	142	4.39	0.71	1	5
4	Greater knowledge/skill	143	4.29	0.64	2	5
5	Able to apply for the increasing number of jobs that require certification	143	4.19	0.75	1	5
6	Obtaining a formal marketable qualification	143	4.11	0.85	1	5
7	Academics that teach certifications must be certified, so you can be confident of their knowledge	143	4.08	0.84	1	5
8	Higher salaries	143	4.00	0.88	1	5
9	Increased credibility	143	3.99	0.77	1	5
10	Increased self-confidence	143	3.89	0.97	1	5
11	Flexibility of study because of online curriculum	142	3.62	0.97	1	5

Presumably, those working in the IT industry would have received better-quality information, as they would have access to IT work colleagues; whereas those without IT work experience might have been receiving information from a pool of people with perhaps limited direct IT industry experience (McGill & Dixon, 2003).

Table 3 presents the average perceived importance of each potential benefit of IT certification. The ratings of benefits are ranked by perceived importance. All benefits were ranked relatively highly, with averages above the midpoint of the scale. The two most highly ranked benefits were practical experience with real networking tasks, and experience with real equipment. Almost 97% of the respondents considered practical experience with real networking tasks to be important or very important. This finding reflects that the participants were primarily undertaking Cisco certifications. Wilde (2000) comments that Cisco Systems has the most 'realistic' certification program, requiring those undertaking certification to perform real tasks, using real equipment. Wilde also raises concerns that some certifications do not emphasize practical skills.

The third-ranked perceived benefit in terms of importance was having a widely recognized qualification. IT certifications are global and enable those who have them great flexibility in terms of obtaining employment around the world. The fourth-ranked benefit was greater knowledge and skill. It appears that the intrinsic value of the knowledge and skill obtained during certification is perceived as important beyond the job-related benefits that can result.

The fifth- and sixth-ranked proposed benefits relate to the role of certification in improving opportunities to obtain jobs. The ability to apply for the increasing number of jobs that require certification was ranked fifth, and obtaining a formal marketable qualification was ranked sixth. Improving employment opportunities is clearly important to those who undertake certification, but the higher rankings of practical experience and improving knowledge and skill suggest that employment is not the sole motivation for undertaking certification. The perceived importance of practical experience obtained goes beyond just improving marketability.

Confidence in the knowledge of those who teach certification programs was ranked as the seventh most important benefit. While having knowledgeable instructors is clearly important (with an average of 4.08 out of 5), the relative ranking perhaps suggests that students perceive those who teach them to be well qualified for the job regardless of whether the unit of study involves a certification and hence requires instructor certification.

Higher salaries were ranked eighth in terms of importance. While potential salaries perhaps receive the most publicity in terms of benefits to holders of certifications, this ranking suggests that salary is not the major driving factor for students. The ninth- and tenth-ranked benefits relate to the importance of certification for how students see themselves. Increased credibility and self-confidence did not appear to be major reasons for undertaking certification. The lowest ranked of the proposed

Table 4. Factor loadings of benefits

	Marketability Benefits	Personal Benefits	Learning Benefits
Experience with real equipment	0.10	0.18	**0.90**
Practical experience with real networking tasks	0.21	0.18	**0.89**
Obtaining a formal marketable qualification	**0.75**	0.13	0.26
Greater knowledge/skill	0.48	0.13	**0.52**
Higher salaries	**0.76**	0.28	0.06
Widely recognized qualification	**0.71**	0.27	0.20
Flexibility of study because of online curriculum	0.12	**0.78**	0.16
Increased credibility	0.34	**0.78**	0.16
Increased self-confidence	0.17	**0.80**	0.19
Able to apply for the increasing number of jobs that require certification	**0.60**	0.46	0.11
Academics that teach the Cisco curriculum must be certified, so you can be confident of their knowledge	0.43	**0.53**	0.06
Percent of variance explained	24.04%	23.20%	18.99%

benefits was the flexibility of study enabled because of online curriculums. While certification providers, such as the Cisco Networking Academies, pioneered delivery of quality e-learning material, online materials are now routinely available to IT students whether or not they are attempting certifications (McCormick, 2000; Peffers & Bloom, 1999), thus reducing the perceived importance of this benefit.

Several themes appear to emerge from the examples of benefits that have been proposed. To determine the number and nature of factors underlying the various benefits identified from the literature, a principal components factor analysis with varimax rotation was performed in SPSS 11.5 using the data from the 145 respondents. Three factors with eigenvalues of greater than one emerged, indicating the existence of three underlying dimensions (see Table 4 for factor loadings).

Examination of the benefits associated with each factor led to naming the factors as follows:

- **Marketability benefits:** Which relate to desirability in the eyes of employers

- **Personal benefits:** Which relate to the impact of the certification on the way in which students perceive themselves and to the ease of their study

- **Learning benefits:** Which relate to intrinsic fulfillment from the type of learning.

These factors summarize the major types of benefits that students anticipate will accrue from certification.

Table 5. Risks of certification

Rank	Risks	N	Mean	SD	Min.	Max.
1	The rapidly changing knowledge base might mean that the certification is not of lasting value	138	3.91	0.82	1	5
2	The absence of an unbiased neutral group for creating exams and approving examiners	139	3.58	0.78	1	5
3	The absence of an unbiased neutral group for determining content	140	3.49	0.81	1	5
4	Heavy involvement of vendors	139	3.47	0.81	1	5
5	Academics might be uncomfortable with the pressure to maintain their own proficiency levels and certification status	138	3.34	0.79	1	5
6	Academics might be uncomfortable with the thought that certification exams determine content of courses and academic programs	138	3.30	0.79	1	5

Risks

Table 5 presents the average perceived importance of each of the potential risks of or concerns about IT certification. The ratings of risks are ranked by perceived importance. The average importance ratings for the risks are mostly well below those of the benefits discussed above. So while the participants were conscious of the potential risks, they did not appear to be overly concerned about them.

The highest-ranked risk was that the rapidly changing knowledge base might mean that certification is not of lasting value. IT has been changing rapidly over a long period, and this rate of change is likely to continue or increase (Benamati & Lederer, 2001; Fordham, 2001). Organizations find it difficult to obtain personnel with the appropriate knowledge and skills to meet the growing demands for IT services (Doke, 1999), and this has contributed to the desirability of certified employees, as they provide a way for employers to obtain a pool of employees with up-to-date skills. However, the rapidly changing knowledge base also means that certification may not be of enduring value, and means that recertification is necessary. Gabelhouse (2000) found that 75% of certification holders shoulder some of the costs of certification, with 45% paying for everything themselves. If regular recertification is required, the costs and investments of time can become prohibitive.

The middle-ranked group of risks relate to the potential for bias in certification. The second-ranked risk was the absence of an unbiased neutral group for creating exams and approving examiners, and the third-ranked risk was the absence of an unbiased neutral group for determining content. The fourth-ranked risk was heavy involvement of vendors. While vendor-neutral certifications do exist, most certifications are linked to vendors, and this has been raised as an issue of concern (Ray & McCoy, 2000). Again, students appear to be aware of the issue, but not overly concerned about it. They appear to accept the central role of vendors in the IT industry.

Concerns have been raised by several authors (Nelson & Rice, 2001; Ray & Mc-Coy, 2000) that academics might not be comfortable with the loss of control over content that occurs because of the role of certification exams. They might also be uncomfortable with the pressure to maintain their own proficiency levels and certification status. Not surprisingly, these are the two lowest-ranked concerns of the students surveyed in this study.

Conclusion

IT certifications are a popular adjunct to traditional means of preparing for a career in IT. Many educational institutions offer a range of IT certifications. This study explored the perceptions of students currently undertaking courses of study that could lead to IT certification. Certification was perceived as an important factor in achieving employment, and students undertaking it anticipate that it will lead to substantial financial benefits. Yet, higher salaries are not seen as the most important benefit of certification. The potential benefits that students believe are most important relate to the 'real-world' experience that is part of some certifications. They also value the potential improvements in knowledge and skill to which certification should lead.

Those respondents who were currently working in the IT industry had realistic perceptions of the likely salary increases available once certification was obtained, but those students with no IT experience appeared to overestimate the potential financial benefits. Instructors should ensure they have current information about salaries and employers' skill requirements so they can help guide students.

The respondents were aware of the possible risks of certification, but did not appear to be overly concerned about them. The issue considered most important was the potential for the rapidly changing knowledge base to mean that certification is not of enduring value.

Obtaining IT certification has become an important consideration for the IT profession. More research is needed to understand the benefits of IT certification and to determine the importance of the proposed risks. The study reported on in this chapter has provided a starting point, but future research should extend it to holders of IT certifications and to employers.

References

Alexander, S. (1999). Sorting out certifications. *Computerworld*, December 13.

Benamati, J. & Lederer, A.L. (2001). Coping with rapid changes in IT. *Communications of the ACM, 44*(8), 83-88.

Brookshire, R.G. (2000). Information technology certification: Is this your mission? *Information Technology, Learning, and Performance Journal, 18*(2), 1-2.

Clyne, M. (2001). Employee recruitment & retention – certification's role. *Professional Certification Magazine*. Retrieved July 9, 2003, from http://www.procertcom.com

Doke, E.R. (1999). Knowledge and skill requirements for information systems professionals: An exploratory study. *Journal of IS Education, 10*(1), 10-18.

Downes, S. & Hobbs, V. (2000, November 9-12). An exploratory study of the representation and performance of females in Information Technology at Murdoch University. *Proceedings of the International Information Systems Education Conference (ISECON)*, Philadelphia.

Fitzsimmons, C. (2000). Doing IT for themselves. *Information Age,* April.

Fordham, D.R. (2001). Forecasting technology trends. *Strategic Finance, 83*(3), 50-54.

Gabelhouse, G. (2000). *CertMag's salary survey*. Retrieved July, 9, 2003, from www.certmag.com/issues/dec00/feature_gabelhouse.cfm

IDC Inc. (1999). *Benefits and productivity gains realized through IT certification*. Retrieved July, 9, 2003, from www.ecertifications.com/idcrep_itcert.html

Karr, S.S. (2001). IT certification pays off. *Financial Executive,* December, 60-61.

Klawe, M. & Leveson, N. (1995). Women in computing where are we now? *Communications of the ACM, 38*(1), 29-35.

McCormick, J. (2000). The new school. *Newsweek, 135*(17), 60-62.

McGill, T. & Dixon, M. (2003). How do IT students stay up to date with employer's skill requirements. In T. McGill (Ed.), *Current issues in IT education* (pp. 144-152). Hershey, PA: IRM Press.

Nelson, M.L. & Rice, D. (2001). Integrating third party-certification with traditional computer education. *The Journal of Computing in Small Colleges, 17*(2), 280-287.

Otterbourg, S.D. (1999). Cisco Systems and Hewlett-Packard prepare the workforce for the future. *Education + Training, 41*(3), 144-145.

Peffers, K., & Bloom, S. (1999). Internet-based innovations for teaching IS courses: The state of adoption, 1998-2000. *Journal of Information Technology Theory and Application, 1*(1), 1-6.

Ray, C.M. & McCoy, R. (2000). Why certification in information systems? *Information Technology, Learning, and Performance Journal, 18*(1), 1-4.

Wilde, C. (2000). Demand for IT pros drives vendor certification growth: But multiple-choice tests aren't always a true measure of skills and experience. *Information Week,* September 25, 214.

Chapter XIV

Management of Telecommunications Services:
A Vital New Content Area and a Course Model for the College of Business

Faye P. Teer, James Madison University, USA

Young B. Choi, James Madison University, USA

Harold B. Teer, James Madison University, USA

Abstract

Telecommunications companies are facing a challenge in satisfying changing customer demands related to telecommunications services. Historically, the industry challenge was managing the changing technology; today, the industry must also focus on the management of telecommunications services. The purpose of this chapter is twofold: (1) to provide an argument for the importance of the management of telecommunications services as a vital new course area at the university level, and (2) to describe one possible model for a new undergraduate course, Management of

Telecommunications Services. The chapter is targeted towards university faculty and administration and corporate representatives responsible for technology education. The ultimate goal of the course is to align university curriculum with the needs of the telecommunications industry and provide the industry with entry-level information technology (IT) employees who have an understanding of the fundamentals of the management of telecommunications services.

Introduction

The deregulatory impact of the 1996 Telecommunications Act resulted in fierce competition for customers by telecommunications firms. This competition has intensified, and in order to increase the size of their customer base, many telecommunications companies are striving to create a competitive advantage through an increased variety of service offerings. These telecommunications companies hope that by adding new types of services to their existing ones they can achieve economies of scope (Grover & Saeed, 2003).

As telecommunications companies face challenges in satisfying customer demands related to telecommunications services, telecommunications providers have been forced to rethink the fundamental way they do business. Historically, the industry was driven by the management of changing technology; today, the industry also has to focus on the management of telecommunications services. Hall (1996, p. 10) summed up the new challenge facing the telecommunications industry regarding the management of telecommunications services: "… services are now being defined in terms of what they provide to users. For suppliers, this requires a radical change of perspective, from being technology providers to becoming service providers, which must also be reflected in the approach to management."

The turmoil in today's telecommunications industry's services sector is a reflection of the state of the service sector in the United States (U.S.). In the U.S. economy, where services account for 73% of the gross domestic product, the entire service sector is in a constant state of change that is causing upheavals in the traditional ways of doing business (Lovelock & Wright, 2002).

Top managers in the telecommunications industry recognize the crucial importance of the effective management of customer services. One industry person noted that, "Several years of good-quality communication service can be shattered in a few minutes if the customer care processes are poor" (Adams & Willets, 1996, p. 1).

In response to the changing critical success factors for telecommunications companies, the field of management of telecommunications services began in the mid 1990s with the initiation of research and applications geared toward providing better management of telecommunications services. Managing the services that telecommunications providers deliver to their customers is defined by Adams and Willetts (1996, p. 29) to mean "the entire customer-service spectrum, including order handling, service quality, problem handling, billing, service development and so on." Adams and Willetts stress that, to satisfy customers' requirements, the effective management of telecommunications services involves the continuous rebalancing of three objectives: (1) reduction of cost; (2) improvement of service quality; and (3) reduction of time-to-market of new services (1996).

Organizations are beginning to realize that adequate attention to the service management function can bridge the gap between the technological functions (element management and network management) and the business management function. Telecommunications industry organizations must effectively manage services to satisfy the level of quality services demanded by customers. In turn, effective service management can generate more revenue and have a positive impact on the successful business management function. The Telemanagement Network (TMN) Framework illustrates the four managerial functions of an organization in the telecommunications industry. A pyramid representing the TMN Framework is composed of four layers, listed here in descending order: Business Management, Service Management, Network and Systems Management, and Element Management (Adams & Willets, 1996, p. 28).

Because service management in the telecommunications industry is not well understood, attention is now being directed to management of telecommunications services. Ward said that for the telecommunications industry, service management remains its least understood area, and that, "The next frontier is service management" (Ward, 1998, p. 157).

This chapter will provide support for the growing importance of the management of telecommunications services as a vital new course area at the university level and describe one possible model for a Management of Telecommunications Services course.

Why Management of Telecommunications Services is a Vital Area of Study

A review of the literature provides ample evidence supporting the significance of the management of telecommunications services as a vital area of study for IT majors. This section will discuss four key factors driving the increasing importance of managing telecommunications services and several important responses by the telecommunications industry. These key factors include: (1) increased competition in the telecommunications industry; (2) unmet service needs of customers;

(3) telecommunications industry recession; and (4) the unique complexities of the telecommunications industry.

Increased Competition in the Telecommunications Industry

The first key factor is the high level of competition in the telecommunications industry. Today's telecommunications industry is described as "a scene of global hyper-competition" (Korhonen & Ainamo, 2003, p. 2). The key to survival in the competitive telecommunications industry is to make certain that an organization's learning outpaces that of their competitors (Johnson & Jakeman, 1997, p. 234). In the telecommunications industry, one critical success factor in outpacing competitors is effective management of customer services. Successful telecommunications organizations will be the ones that effectively manage customer services (Adams & Willetts, 1996).

Unmet Service Needs of Customers

The second key factor is the unmet service needs of customers. In the mid 1990s, many telecommunication providers strived to secure more customers and generate more revenue by introducing a plethora of services. However, the present level of telecommunications services offered by many telecommunications service providers does not fully satisfy the various customers' requirements (Adams & Willetts, 1996; Forouzan & Fegan, 2003; Korhonen & Ainamo, 2003; Rosenbush & Elstrom, 2001). A resulting problem is that the customers' needs may not be met or customers may not adequately understand the services offered.

Telecommunications Industry Recession

A third factor is the worldwide recession that the telecommunications industry has experienced during the last several years (Eyers & Hahn, 2002; Shannon & Schenker, 2003). A recently authored paper by Malcolm Russell, a strategic business manager with Agilent Technologies (Russell, 2003), argued that if the telecommunications industry is to move forward from its current recession, it needs to focus less on technology for its own sake and more on telecommunications services.

Unique Complexities of the Telecommunications Industry

The fourth key factor is the unique complexities of the telecommunications industry and the inherently intangible nature of telecommunications services. For any service-intensive industry, management of customer services is a challenge. In the telecommunications industry, the nature of the product itself makes the management of services especially difficult. Adams and Willets (1996, p. 1) point out that telecommunications "service providers are nearly invisible" and their product "is probably the most intangible product any company might sell." Furthermore, there are unique complexities present in the telecommunications industry that makes service management much more challenging than any other service-based industry. One such complexity is the proprietary nature of many of the existing systems used to manage telecommunications services; these older systems lack the flexibility and quick reaction time necessary in today's dynamic telecommunications industry (Lewis, 1999). Adams and Willets described additional unique complexities of the telecommunications industry that impede effective management of services: (1) Telecommunications involves an extensive service delivery chain that is becoming more complex as the industry changes shape; (2) service providers operate on the leading edge of new technology, while dragging along plants and processes that can date back 100 years; and (3) the communications industry is becoming increasingly distributed as geographical boundaries are stretched (1996).

Industry and Firm Responses

In addition to the response by individual firms to addressing challenges in the management of telecommunications services, the industry as a whole responded by founding the TeleManagement Forum (TM Forum) and the TM Forum's Universities Program. Recognition of the need for better management practices within the telecommunications industry was the impetus that led to the founding of the TM Forum. TM Forum is a "non-profit global organization that provides leadership, strategic guidance and practical solutions to improve the management and operation of information and communications services" (TeleManagement Forum, 2004). Today, TM Forum has a membership of more than 340 companies, most of whom are considered the leading firms in the worldwide telecommunications industry.

Additionally, the TM Forum is in the initial stages of broadening its mission to include partnering with universities and university faculty by developing TM Forum's Universities Program (The Charter, 2003). The TM Forum's Universities Program was established July 31, 2003, to facilitate the formation of much-needed closer working relationships between TM Forum, university faculty and other academic participants. This relationship is designed to assist in promoting teaching and research efforts in the area of the management of telecommunications services and in aligning university curriculum with telecommunications industry needs. Some of the specific goals related to the management of telecommunications services for this new university program are: providing a forum for sharing information pertaining to management of telecommunications services; providing assistance in

Table 1. Member universities of TM Forum's Universities Program

Country	Universities
Croatia	University of Zagreb
Ireland	Trinity College Dublin
Korea	Pohang University of Science and Technology (POSTECH)
Spain	Universitat Politecnica de Catalunya
Russia	St. Petersburg State University of Telecommunications
UK	University College London, University of Glasgow
U.S.	James Madison University; Stevens Institute of Technology; University of Maryland, College Park

the teaching of the management of telecommunications services topics; providing new outlets for faculty publication; and sponsoring faculty research (Members of the TM Forum's Universities Program, 2003).

Currently, a diverse set of universities throughout the world has joined TM Forum's Universities Program. The number of member universities is expanding rapidly and includes those listed in Table 1.

This new focus on service management must be understood and addressed by those responsible for the telecommunications curriculum in universities. To help meet the immediate needs of the telecommunications industry, universities should begin to educate entry-level employees who have a strong foundation in management of telecommunications services. Such employees can more quickly attain leadership roles in customer service, where they can assist in effectively managing customer services. To align the knowledge and skills of entry-level telecommunications employees with the needs of the industry, this chapter proposes a university course, the Management of Telecommunications Services.

A Proposed Model for the Management of Telecommunications Services Course

As a response to the growing importance of the management of telecommunications services, we describe one possible model for a Management of Telecommunications Services course. The proposed course model is based on prior industry experience in research and development in the telecommunications industry, on recommendations by IT professionals, and on experience in teaching the introductory telecommunications course. This model has been proposed and will be used in a course at our university. Since there is an immediate need in the industry for entry-level employees who possess a better understanding of the fundamentals of managing telecommunications services, the course described in the proposed model is intended for the undergraduate level. However, it could be readily adapted to suit the needs of graduate students.

In both the 1997 and 2002 IS Model Curriculum guidelines, developed by a nationwide committee of IT professionals and faculty, it was recommended that universities offer a required introductory telecommunications course (IS, 1997, 2002). An examination of the Web sites of universities and informal conversations with colleagues at professional meetings indicate that a growing number of schools are requiring the introductory telecommunications course as part of the IT degree program (Choi & Teer, 2003). Since many IT programs now have a qualified person to teach the undergraduate telecommunications course, those telecommunications professors should be qualified to teach the Management of Telecommunications Services course.

The proposed Management of Telecommunications Services course is designed to give IT undergraduates an awareness of the issues of service management in the telecommunications industry; an understanding of the core technologies interfacing the management of services; and a survey of current management best practices.

The course model is presented in three parts: (1) course content, (2) teaching resources, and (3) course structure.

Course Content

The rationale for including certain topics in the course content is based on: (1) a careful review of the Model Curriculum Guidelines of IS 1997 and 2002 (IS, 1997, 2002) and, in particular, the material in section IS 2002.6: Networks and Telecommunications (IS, 2002); and (2) recognition of the action items needed to address the key industry factors driving the importance of managing telecommunications services. The following general topics are recommended for the Management of Telecommunications Services course. Under each general topical area are the specific topics to be included.

Fundamental managerial concepts related to services in the telecommunications industry:

1.   Introduction
2.   What is the management of telecommunications services?

The rationale for why effective management of telecommunications services is needed:

3. Service management requirements of providers of telecommunications services

4. Service management perspectives of private network operators

The technical components of the interface of telecommunications core technologies and the management of telecommunications services:

5. Integration of telecommunications services

6. Systems interoperability as it relates to management of telecommunications services

7. Integration architecture as it relates to management of telecommunications services

8. Service management systems framework

The crucial industry leadership role of TM Forum:

9. TM Forum

Technical topics are addressed with real-world, hands-on experience:

10. Business case design for better service management

11. Individual and group research project

Framework, principles and future directions for telecommunications services:

12. Toward an effective service management paradigm

13. Practical implementation principles for successful management and evaluation of services

14. Future directions in the management of telecommunications services.

Teaching Resources

Most of the available reference material for the management of telecommunications services is in the form of (1) industry targeted books, (2) online journals and magazines, (3) magazines and newsletters, (4) journals, and (5) Internet resources.

Since the management of telecommunications services only became an area of major industry concern in the mid-1990s, there are management of telecommunications services books aimed for an industry audience, but there are no textbooks and related ancillary materials for the university market.

Books. Numerous books were reviewed for material relevant to a course in the management of telecommunications services. We found seven books that contained at least one good chapter on the management of telecommunications services. In-

Table 2. Books relevant to Management of Telecommunications Services course

Authors	Title	Year	Publisher	Coverage of Management of Telecommunications Services
Hallows, R.D.	*Service Management in Computing and Telecommunications*	1995	Artech House	Throughout the book; Chapters 1-12
Adams, E.K. Willets, K.J.	*The Lean Communications Provider – Surviving the Shakeout through Service Management Excellence*	1996	McGraw-Hill Inc.	Throughout the book; Chapters 1-23
Hall, J. (Ed.)	*Management of Telecommunication Systems and Services*	1996	Springer-Verlag	Chapter 1 Introduction and Chapter 4 Examples of Service Management
Ward, E.P.	*World-Class Telecommunications Service Development*	1998	Artech House	Chapters 1-22
Strouse, K.G.	*Marketing Telecommunications Services: New Approaches for a Changing Environment*	1999	Artech House	Part V Customer Focus Chapter 14 Customer Care Chapter 15 Customer Profiling and Data Management Chapter 16 Customer Loyalty and Managing Churn
Odon, A. Ward, K. Savolaine, C. Daneshmand, M. Hoath, P.	*Telecommunications Quality of Service Management: From Legacy to Emerging Services*	2002	Inspec	This book surveys the key issues related to the delivery and management of customer quality of service. This book covers especially topics of consumer and user groups and comparisons of performance.
Carr, H.H. Snyder, C.A.	*Management of Telecommunications – Business Solutions to Business Problems Enabled by Voice and Data Communications*	2003 2nd Ed.	McGraw-Hill/Irwin Inc.	Chapters 12 and 13 (Part 4 Managing Telecommunications)
Korhonen, T.O. Ainamo, A. (Eds.)	*Handbook of Product and Service Development in Communication and Information Technology*	2003	Kluwer Academic Publishers	Chapter 3 User Centered Design of Telecommunications Services

formation on these seven books, including the depth of coverage of management of telecommunications services topics, is given in Table 2.

We believe *The Lean Communications Provider* (Adams & Willets, 1996) to be the seminal work for the management of telecommunications services. Even though it is presently out of print, it can still be purchased and is available in many libraries. The topics included and depth of coverage of those topics makes this an excellent resource book for the teaching of the management of telecommunications services. This four-part book is based on technical contributions from the members of TM Forum and includes a balance of technical components and managerial issues.

The book's first part, "When Service is Your Business," introduces: (1) the emergence, definition and importance of the management of telecommunications services; (2) service management requirements; and (3) the perspectives of service providers and private enterprise network operators.

The second part, "It's All about Integration," covers: (1) service integration and the architecture for service management; (2) the interoperability between different service management systems; and (3) barriers to excellent service management.

The third part, "It's Best Not to Go It Alone," emphasizes the importance of cooperation with other organizations in the global telecommunications environment.

The fourth part of the book, "Getting to Excellence," covers: (1) the purpose of TM Forum and the importance of a common model for effective communication among participating members; (2) the service management business process model; (3) major service areas in telecommunications, such as order handling, problem handling, performance reporting, billing and the transition of business process agreements to technical specifications; and (4) a systematic approach on the issues of software platform modeling, interoperability, legacy systems and conformance requirements.

Online Journals and Magazines. Online journals and magazines provide current material on the issues involved in the management of telecommunications services. Some of the more noteworthy publications are:

1. *Institute of Electrical and Electronic Engineers (IEEE) Communications Surveys and Tutorials (www.comsoc.org/livepubs/surveys/index.html)*

    IEEE Communications Surveys and Tutorials is the free IEEE ComSoc (Communications Society) online magazine for generalist throughout the field of communications and communications networking. Readers are the people involved in research and development, deployment, or instruction in fields related to communications.

2.   *Telephony Online (www.internettelephony.com/)*

Telephony is the leading publication for all communications service providers: new and incumbent, wired and wireless. It delivers insightful and thoughtful coverage of the news, technologies and business strategies driving the industry for more than 70,000 providers. Major topics are access technology, finance, back office, optical, broadband services, regulatory, enterprise and wireless.

Magazines and Newsletters

1.   *Telecommunications Magazine (www.telecoms-mag.com)*

Telecommunications Magazine is aimed at satisfying the information needs of service providers, and is targeted mainly to professionals at the decision-making level. A version for the 'Americas' and one for the 'International' markets are published, and provide the latest news on broadband access, optical networking, service provisioning, monitoring analysis, and wireless and service providers.

2.   *IEEE Communications Magazine (www.comsoc.org/pubs/commag/)*

IEEE Communications Magazine provides timely information on all aspects of communications: technology, systems, services, market trends, development methods, regulatory and policy issues, and significant global events. It is also available online and is a publication of the IEEE Communications Society. This magazine features issues in March each year on Telecommunications Management.

3.   *Service Management Europe Magazine (www.servicemanagement.co.uk/pages/index.cfm?pageID=872)*

Published by **Penton Media Europe,** this is the UK's premier high-tech field service publication. It features a wide range of articles offering in-depth analysis and insights into the spectrum of existing and emerging service challenges that decision makers face today.

4.   *Service Management Europe Newsletter (www.servicemanagement.co.uk/newsletters/index.cfm)*

This newsletter complements the *Service Management Europe Magazine* by providing regular issue-driven, electronic newsletters (*SM News*), so that subscribers remain in constant touch with what is happening.

Journals

1.   *International Journal of Services and Standards (IJSS) (www.inderscience.com/catalogue/s/ijss/indexijss.html).*

IJSS presents current practice, models and theory in services and standards development, design, management, implementation and applications. The objectives are to develop, promote, and coordinate the development and practice of services and standards. *IJSS* aims to help professionals working in the field of service and standards, academic educators, and policy makers to contribute, disseminate knowledge and learn from each others' work in the area.

2. *Journal of Service Research* (*www.rhsmith.umd.edu/ces/Journal of Service Research.html#board*)

This multi-disciplinary journal has an international service research scope. The journal's mission is to be the leading outlet for the most advanced research in service marketing, e-service, service operations, service human resources and organizational design, service information systems, customer satisfaction and service quality, and the economics of service.

3. *International Journal of Network Management* (*www3.interscience.wiley.com/cgi-bin/jhome/5703*)

This journal provides practical information for more effective management, operation and maintenance of communications networks. Articles facilitate the readers' evaluation of equipment and systems, provide a detailed description of performance issues, and discuss the advantages and disadvantages of a variety of networking approaches. Target readers are telecommunications managers, engineers, researchers and students of communications technology.

4. *Journal of Network and Systems Management* (*www.cstp.umkc.edu/jnsm/*)

This journal covers a wide range of telecommunications topics, including: architecture; analysis; design; software; standards and migration issues related to the operation, management and control of distributed systems; and communication networks for voice, data, image and networked computing.

Internet Resources. While one has to be cautious about the credibility of Internet resources, there are some excellent sources for the management of telecommunications services. Some of the best are:

1. Telecommunications services management guide (*www.digitalfuel.com/TelecomServices.asp*)

2. Telecom service management software directory (*www.capterra.com/telecom-service-management-software*)

3. Telecommunications management – comprehensive directory of useful resources (*http://homepage.tinet.ie/~slevin/tm/tm-info1.htm*)

4. Telecom management information – resource for better telecom cost and information management (*www.telecominfo.com/*)

5.   Tech library – white papers, case studies and product information on hot tele-communications technologies (*http://techlibrary.commweb.com/*)

Course Structure. Delivery methods for the course material and the associated learning activities should be tailored to each professor's preferred teaching style. The suggested course structure outlined here is one that fits our preferences and is deemed to be a generalized model adaptable to most teaching styles.

Lectures utilizing material obtained through books, journals, the Internet, and trade publications should be used throughout the course to assist in building a framework of understanding that will enhance the students' understanding of assigned readings and projects. The order, frequency and depth of lectures will depend on the professor's preferences and the previously assigned reading material.

As part of the Management of Telecommunications Services course model, three specific course activities are recommended: (1) an individual research project; (2) a group research project; and (3) a hands-on project using service management software.

The syllabus distributed at the beginning of the semester should include the detailed assignment guidelines for the individual research project and the group research project, a description of the deliverables and the evaluation criteria. It is recommended that the performance of each individual project and each group project be monitored, by requiring students to turn in two or three intermediate progress reports at predefined points in the individual and group research projects. The deliverables from the individual and group research projects should be evaluated on content, format, style, and other predefined criteria.

Individual research project. The instructor should provide students with a list of possible research topics from which they can choose. These topics should coincide with current course content or current issues in the management of telecommunications services. To aid undergraduate students in the literary search necessary for their research, it is suggested that a professional business librarian from the university library be invited to class to provide a tutorial on performing a literary search.

Group research project. After completing an individual research project, group research projects should be assigned to groups of three or four students. The group research project will be useful in stimulating students' learning of new and interdisciplinary concepts in the more flexible and comfortable learning environment of the peer education process. This will also provide students with experience in working in teams, a skill that they need to further develop and practice before entering the workplace.

It is recommended that the group research topic be based on a real-world business and an existing service in that business. Using real-world cases in the group research projects will afford students the opportunity to experience things firsthand, such as realistic content, real-world business objectives, organizational impacts, social values, and ethical issues (Hackney, McMaster & Harris, 2003; Gendron & Jarmoszko, 2003). The research topic can be selected by brainstorming among group members, or the professor can assign them. The students are asked to complete their group research project as follows:

1. Select a target telecommunications service provider (e.g., a particular mobile phone service provider) and one service delivered by that provider (e.g., family calling plan).

2. Survey existing literature regarding the specific service provider and service selected to fully understand what is happening in today's marketplace.

3. Propose new, improved features to the existing service by using available management of telecommunications services techniques learned as part of the course.

4. Suggest new ideas to improve legacy services currently offered to customers.

At the completion of the projects, each group will present the results to the entire class. In addition to a class presentation, utilizing presentation software such as Microsoft PowerPoint, the students should provide the professor with a presentation file, a written project report and a few test questions the group feels the class could answer after listening to the formal presentation. The questions collected from all the groups may be used on the final exam to test the level of understanding of all students on all research project presentations. Such a procedure can be very useful in garnering student attentiveness during all group presentations. The instructor and all class members will evaluate each of the group research projects based on prearranged guidelines.

Hands-on practice using service management software. To enhance the students' understanding of technology and its application in the real world, it is important to give students hands-on experience with technology in a telecommunications lab in the class room (Greca, Cook, & Harris, 2004). Hands-on practice opportunities in which the students actually use service management software will be beneficial in enhancing their understanding of the course's technical components. Depending on the learning environment desired by the professor, the hands-on practice opportunities can be offered as lab sessions or as individual take-home assignments.

Students' hands-on work with software should follow a process designed to foster the incremental building of students' software skills, from basic to advanced.

Therefore, it is recommended that students begin with data service management software, then migrate to network monitoring and analysis software; then utilize network management software; and finally try hands-on practice with management of telecommunications services software.

Unfortunately, due to the high cost of software, there is minimal management of telecommunications services software available for the hands-on training of university students. With limited university budgets, the use of downloadable public-domain software meets the needs of universities' telecom labs (Choi, 2003). Although public-domain software specifically for the management of telecommunications services does not appear to be presently available, public-domain data communications network software can be substituted, since data communication network software closely matches the features of management of telecommunications services software. Through the relationship with the industry fostered through the TM Forum's University Program, telecommunications faculty should be able to eventually secure full-fledged management of telecommunications services software for their universities' telecommunications lab facilities.

Conclusion

Since the effective management of telecommunications services is critical in the telecommunications industry, a new Management of Telecommunications Services course is needed to prepare students for the demands made by employers.

An awareness of the importance of the management of telecommunications services and the developed course model will be of interest to three groups. First, researchers in academic communities should be aware of the important role of management of telecommunications services in the industry and the resulting implications for needed IT research. Second, IT curriculum planners will find this information helpful as they strive to design curricula that will meet employee training needs of the IT industry. And third, telecommunications professors need to know the importance of management of telecommunications services and need to have a working course model from which they can begin structuring a course.

The proposed course model is meant to serve as a call to action and to be an initial step toward the development of a needed telecommunications course. Future research on empirical evidence gleaned from students who have participated in this course and feedback from their employers will provide information needed for adjustments and enhancements to the course content and delivery methods.

References

Adams, E. K., & Willets, K. J. (1996). *The lean communications provider: Surviving the shakeout through service management excellence*. New York: McGraw-Hill.

Carr, H. H., & Snyder, C. A. (2003). *Management of telecommunications: Business solutions to business problems enabled by voice and data communications* (2nd ed.). New York: McGraw-Hill/Irwin.

Choi, Y. B. (2003, August 8-10). A Web-based network analysis framework based on the public domain software. *The US-Korea Conference on Science, Technology, and Entrepreneurship*, Pasadena, CA.

Choi, Y. B., & Teer, F. P. (2003, October). A telecommunications service management course model for the college of business. In *Proceedings of the 2003 International Association for Computer Information Systems (IACIS) Conference*, Las Vegas, NV (pp. 1-4).

Eyers, D., & Hahn, W.L. (2002). IT telecom forecast scenarios, 2001-2004. *Dataquest*, December 2.

Forouzan, B. A., & Fegan, S. C. (2003). *Business data communications*. New York: McGraw-Hill Higher Education.

Gendron, M., & Jarmoszko, A. T. (2003). The integration of technology theory and business analysis: A pedagogical framework for the undergraduate MIS course in data communications and networking. *Journal of Information Systems Education, 14*(4), 361-371.

Greca, A. N., Cook, R. P., & Harris, J. K. (2004). Enhancing learning in a data communication and networking course with laboratory experiments. *The Journal of Computing in Small Colleges, 19*(3), 79-88.

Grover, V., & Saeed, K. (2003). The telecommunication industry revisited – The changing pattern of partnerships. *Communications of the ACM, 46*(7), 119-125.

Hackney, R., McMaster, T., & Harris, A.J. (2003). Using cases as a teaching tool in IS education. *Journal of Information Systems Education, 14*(3), 229-234.

Hall, J. (Ed.). (1996). *Management of telecommunication systems and services*. Berlin: Springer.

Hallows, R. D. (1995). *Service management in computing and telecommunications*. Norwood: Artech House.

IS '97. (1997). *Model curriculum guidelines for undergraduate degree programs in IS*. Retrieved December 6, 2004, from www.is2000.org/is97/rev/review1.html

IS 2002. (2002). *Model curriculum guidelines for undergraduate degree programs in IS*. Retrieved December 6, 2004, from http://192.245.222.212:8009/IS-2002Doc/Main_Frame.htm

Johnson, T., & Jakeman, M. (1997). *The customer challenge*. London: Pitman.

Korhonen, T. O., & Ainamo, A. (Eds.). (2003). *Handbook of product and service development in communication and information technology*. Boston: Kluwer Academic Publishers.

Lewis, D. E. (1999). A developmental framework for open service management systems. *Journal of Interoperable Communication Networks*, *2*(1), 11-30.

Lovelock, C., & Wright, L. (2002). *Principles of service marketing and management* (2nd ed.). Upper Saddle River: Prentice Hall.

Members of the TM Forum's Universities Program. (2003, July 31). *Charter of Tele-Management Forum's Universities Program* (White paper). Pasadena, CA.

Odon, A., Ward, K., Savolaine, C., Daneshmand, M., & Hoath, P. (2002). *Tele-communications quality of service management: From legacy to emerging services*. London: Inspec.

Rosenbush, S., & Elstrom, P. (2001, August). Eight lessons from the telecom mess. *Business Week, 13*, 60-67.

Russell, M. (2003). *Beyond the gloom horizon: The way forward for telecoms*. Agilent Technologies white paper, July 1.

Shannon, V., & Schenker, J. L. (2003, October 10). Chastened mood at telecom trade show. *International Herald Tribune*, 1.

Strouse, K. G. (1999). *Marketing telecommunications services*. Norwood: Artech House.

TeleManagement Forum. (2004). *About the TM forum*. Retrieved December 6, 2004, from www.tmforum.org

Ward, E. P. (1998). *World-class telecommunications service development*. Norwood: Artech House.

Section IV

Teaching and Learning with Technology

Chapter XV

Mind the Gap!:
New 'Literacies'
Create New Divides

Andrew D. Madden, University of Sheffield, UK

J. Miguel Baptista Nunes, University of Sheffield, UK

M. A. McPherson, University of Leeds, UK

Nigel Ford, University of Sheffield, UK

Dave Miller, University of Sheffield, UK

Abstract

The rapid incursion of information and communication technologies (ICT) into the classroom has meant that, within the space of a few years, computers have moved from being peripheral to being an integral part of the learning environment. However, our perceptions of a technology are affected by the age at which we encounter it. This chapter draws on the findings of a number of research projects at the University of Sheffield. These findings are used to explore some of the 'generation gaps' that arise from differing perceptions of learning technologies. The data discussed provide insights into the ICT-based generation gaps that currently exist between and within groups of students, teachers and parents. It is argued that a fundamental gap may exist between students differing in age by as little as 5 years. Results from a related project exploring Networked Information and Communication Literacy Skills (NICLS) are used to introduce a discussion on the nature of any skills gap that must be addressed in light of these generation gaps.

Introduction

The Sudden Rise of Computers in the Classroom

Computing technologies have been criticized by educationalists and educational philosophers, many of whom feel that they promote shallow learning, mindless copying and pasting, and the decontextualized acquisition of definitions and facts. In short, they are dismissed as being a tool for:

"jogging the memory, not for remembering ... *[providing students] with the appearance of intelligence, not real intelligence ... they will seem to [have] wide knowledge, when they will usually be ignorant."*

The quotation above however, is not from a modern educationalist, mistrustful of new technology, but is adapted from Plato's 'Phaedrus' (p. 69), in which the author recalls Socrates' criticisms of writing.

It is easy to forget that reading and writing are ICT and, like all technological innovations, would have been subject to reactions ranging from unquestioning enthusiasm to reactionary scepticism. Reading and writing, however, permeated society over hundreds of years, so systems could adapt gradually. ICT has had a much more sudden impact.

Douglas Adams (1999) observed that our attitude to technology is determined by the age at which we first encounter it:

1.   Everything that's already in the world when you're born is just normal;

2.   Anything that gets invented between then and before you turn 30 is incredibly exciting and creative, and with any luck you can make a career out of it;

3.   Anything that gets invented after you're 30 is against the natural order of things and the beginning of the end of civilization as we know it, until it's been around for about 10 years, when it gradually turns out to be alright, really.

Madden, Nunes, Ford, McPherson, and Miller (2003b) looked at the development of various computer technologies in light of this analysis. Adams, somewhat arbitrarily, selected 30 as the age above which technological developments cease to be readily acceptable. Madden et al. considered developments in computing in the 30 years prior to their report. It provided a useful reminder of the speed with which computers have impacted on society.

30 years: 1973 saw the first appearance in print of the term 'microcomputer'; Wang unveiled its 'word-processing' system; and IBM introduced the Winchester hard disk (Professional Software Systems, 2004). Computers were expensive and delicate machines, to which only highly trained personnel had access.

20 years: In 1983, Time magazine nominated the IBM PC (released in 1981) as its "man of the year"; Microsoft released Word 1.0; and the first IBM PC-based graphics program, PC-Draw, was introduced (Professional Software Systems, 2004). Ten million computers were in use in the United States (US): They were beginning to appear on desktops in the workplace. Few people would have had access to them, however, until they began work or entered higher education. The youngest of teachers in 2003 were 3 years old.

10 years: By the end of January 1993, there were 50 World Wide Web servers known to exist. Later in the year, Mosaic, the first graphic browser (on which Netscape came to be based) was introduced; and the Pentium processor was released (Professional Software Systems, 2004). Encarta 1993 made no mention of the Internet, and dedicated just 62 words to ARPANET. PCs had become familiar sights in universities and offices around the country, and were beginning to become commonplace in schools (although access was restricted). In 1993-'94, the average secondary school in England had one microcomputer per 10 students: Only 30% of these were capable of supporting a Graphic User Interface (GUI) (Department for Education, 1995). Use of computers in schools was limited to specific lessons in subjects, such as science and math. Although the National Curriculum (which required the incorporation of ICT) had been in place for 5 years, limitations in ICT usability and availability severely restricted the use to which computers could be put across the curriculum (Opie & Katsu, 2000). For most lessons, therefore, the educational technologies used to teach students in 1993 were the same as those that had been used for teaching their parents.

Since 1993: In the intervening years, the learning landscape has changed markedly. GUIs, such as Windows, have become standard; so computer technology has become more intuitive, making it easier for schools to adopt ICT across the curriculum; a factor that presumably has contributed to the rapid growth in computer numbers, as shown in Table 1 (Department for Education and Skills (DfES), 2002a, 2004). These figures are somewhat misleading, since many of the computers in the early 1990s could not have supported GUIs; but this proviso makes the growth in primary schools all the more noteworthy. Even more remarkable, though, has been the rate at which schools have been gaining access to the Internet.

Table 1. Statistics relating to primary and secondary schools in England (DFES, 2002a, 2004)

	Mean no. of students per computer		Percentage of schools connected to the Internet	
	Primary	Secondary	Primary	Secondary
1994	23.0	10.0		
1996	19.0	9.0	5	47
1998	17.6	8.7	17	83
1999	13.4	8.4	62	93
2000	12.6	7.9	86	98
2001	11.8	7.1	96	99
2002	10.1	6.5	99	99
2003	7.9	5.4	-	-

A Practical Educational Technology

The brief history above provides a reminder that, for most teachers, the idea of using ICT in their teaching would have been impractical until very recently. Furthermore, they could not have used their own childhood experience of school as a model to guide them.

Teachers in secondary schools and in Further Education[1] have had a little longer than their primary school colleagues to become accustomed to the incursion of computers into the classroom. In 1999, Selwyn (p. 163) predicted that:

Smaller schools catering for younger learners ... are probably going to attract less ... funding per learner.

Statistics from the DfES (2002b) (Table 2) confirm the accuracy of this prediction. On average, secondary schools in England have 4.2 times as many full-time students as primary schools. In 1998, shortly before Selwyn published his prediction,

Table 2. ICT expenditure in English schools (DfES: Survey of Information and Communications Technology in Schools, 2002)

	Average expenditure/school (£)					Increase in computing power between 1998 and 2002 (by Moore's Law)
	1998	1999	2000	2001	2002	
Primary	3600	7000	8300	10300	15400	68.444
Secondary	40100	45400	50100	60300	76900	30.683
Ratio	11.139	6.486	6.036	5.854	4.994	

average expenditure on ICT in secondary schools was more than 11 times greater than expenditure in primary schools. Since then, however, ICT spending in primary schools has risen far faster than in secondary schools. The gap has now closed; and in 2002, secondary schools spent five times as much on ICT as primary schools.

More Powerful Computers

The impact of increased expenditure is even more remarkable when Moore's Law is taken into consideration. In 1965, G.E. Moore, co-founder of Intel, observed that:

The complexity for minimum component costs has increased at a rate of roughly a factor of two per year... (p. 115)

In practical terms, this means that a computer designed in 2006 will have twice the processing power of a computer designed in 2005; four times the power of those designed in 2004 and so forth. Assuming that the cost of a new computer remains constant, then, if a school has as much to spend on ICT this year as it did last year, that same sum of money can buy approximately twice as much computing power. In other words, according to the data in Table 2, secondary schools in 2002 could afford 31 times as much computing power as they could in 1998, and primary schools could afford 68 times as much.

This rise in processing power has played a large part in making the PC a practical tool in the classroom. It has allowed GUIs to become universal, making PCs easier to use; it has accelerated performance, thereby decreasing user frustration and reducing the risk of students repeatedly pressing buttons on the grounds that "it didn't work last time"; and it has allowed drawing packages to become ubiquitous.

This last point is significant because many primary school students are still coming to terms with reading and writing; so any text-based activity on the PC will have difficulties associated with it that have nothing to do with the technology. It is not surprising, therefore, that drawing is the preferred activity on computers among primary school students (Selwyn & Bullon, 2000; BECTa, 2001a).

Younger Users

Because of the rise in expenditure on ICT in education, the age at which students have routinely come into contact with ICT has dropped rapidly over the last 10 years. Ten years ago, students were unlikely to make regular use of ICT until they went to work or college. One of the much publicized aims of the United Kingdom (UK) Labour Party when it entered government in 1997 was the promotion of ICT in schools. On coming into office, it announced that it was going to make available £700 million to upgrade ICT resources in schools and to connect schools in a National Grid for Learning (NGfL). A further £230 million (New Opportunities Fund) was provided to train teachers to use the new technology.

The figures in Table 2 show that secondary schools were the first to benefit from this initiative. Where ICT was used in primary schools, it often served the function of a 'pacifier,' used to provide an activity for students who finished a task before their peers (Selwyn & Bullon, 2000). Students arrived from primary school to find substantially better ICT resources than they had previously encountered and, in most cases, teachers could confidently treat them as ICT beginners. Increasingly, however, this is changing, and students arrive at secondary school with ever greater ICT skills (Madden, Bates, White, & Apthorpe, 2004), resulting in teachers feeling more and more left behind.

The Skills Gap Between Teachers and Students

A recent project, funded by the UK's Arts and Humanities Research Board, looked at aspects of the impact of the Internet on education in English schools, and revealed clear differences between the abilities of teachers and students to work with the new technologies. Eighteen semi-structured interviews were carried out in January and February 2002 with staff at The City School in Sheffield (Madden, Ford et al., 2003). The City School was selected for the project because of the excellence of its ICT facilities and the experience of its staff in using ICT in their teaching. Nevertheless, many interviewees commented that their ICT skills were more limited than those of their students. One head of department confessed to having supervised classes of students using the Internet, despite never having used it himself. Others recognized its value, but were conscious of being less competent users than their students. Examples of the type of comments made by interviewees are as follows:

The kids are ahead of me [in using ICT] ... I wish I was better at using it.

I haven't experienced [problems with students lacking technical skills] ... I think it's the opposite; I think it's the staff sometimes that don't have the technical skills ...

I have learnt a lot from kids in the past about what to do [on the computer] ...

I always say at the beginning 'Look—I'm an old teacher—I don't know as much

Figure 1. Teacher's responses to questionnaire statements

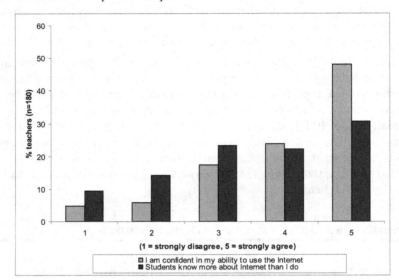

about computers as you—I know how they can be used, I know how they're useful,
I know how important they are.

These interviews were used to generate a questionnaire that was sent to the heads of
departments in all the state-funded secondary schools in Sheffield (Madden, Ford,
Miller, & Levy, 2005). The questionnaire comprised a series of statements with
Likert scales of 1-5. Two of the statements were as follows:

1.   I am confident in my ability to use the Internet.
2.   Students know more than I do about the Internet.

A Spearman's Rank Correlation showed responses to these two variables to be
significantly negatively correlated (p=0.01), suggesting that the more confidence
teachers have in their ability to use the Internet, the less likely they are to feel that
students know more about the Internet than they do. This finding is much as would
have been expected. Despite the correlation, however, most teachers (52.9%) still
feel that students know more about the Internet than they do (Figure 1), including
a large minority (29.6%) who feel confident in their own abilities (Table 3).

Table 3. Percentages of teachers agreeing with both statements

I am confident in my ability to use the Internet.		Students know more than I do about the Internet.		
		(Likert score)		
		4	5	**Total**
(Likert score)	4	8.5	6.9	15.3
	5	9.0	5.3	14.3
	Total	17.5	12.2	29.6

The Skills Gap Between Parents and Children

Evidence for a skills gap between parents and children arose from a project carried out by Sheffield University and The City School (Project 2). In September 2002, a questionnaire was circulated among parents of students newly arrived from primary school. Among other things, parents were asked to assess their own ICT skills and those of their children on a five-point Likert scale. Shortly afterwards, students were given an online test designed by a member of the school's ICT department to assess their ICT skills. Two measures of student ICT ability, therefore, were available:

1.   Based on parents' observations and their understanding of ICT skills
2.   Based on results of a test developed by the school's ICT department.

The school's ICT test correlates significantly with measures of performance in math, English and science taken at the students' primary schools (Table 4); and with parents' assessment of their own ICT skills. Parental assessment of their children's

Table 4. Factors significantly correlated with assessments of students' ICT skills

Student skills (as assessed by parent) correlate with:	
Student sex (boys' skills rated higher than girls').	1% significance, n=65
Perceived standard of primary school resources.	1% significance, n=65
Perceived standard of primary school teaching.	1% significance, n=63
English Key Stage 2.	1% significance, n=57

Student skills (as assessed by school's ICT test) correlate with:	
Parents' perception of their own ICT skills.	1% significance, n=65
Level of ICT concern.	(Negative correlation) 1% significance, n=65
English Key Stage 2.	0.1% significance, n=57
Maths Key Stage 2.	0.1% significance, n=58
Science Key Stage 2.	0.1% significance, n=57

ICT ability is unrelated to the schools' measures, but is significantly correlated to the child's sex ($p<0.05$: boys are considered more skilled) and with the perceived standard of school resources ($p<0.001$) and teaching ($p<0.01$) in a child's primary school. It seems reasonable to assume, therefore, that the parents surveyed were not in a position to assess the ICT skills of their children.

The Skills Gap Among ICT-Literate Adults

Evidence of another skills gap emerged during the development of a part-time Continuing Professional Distance Education course designed to lead to a master's degree in IT Management (MA in ITM) (McPherson & Nunes, 2004). This MA is delivered via a combination of face-to-face and online learning materials.

In the process of developing the MA, it became apparent that technical skills on their own are not sufficient for a student to make successful use of ICT in learning: A range of social and information skills is also required.

The MA ITM course is designed for professionals in the Information Technology (IT) sector. Initially, it was assumed that, because of the students' technological background, no particular training was required to use the online facilities provided for those on the course (Nunes, McPherson et al., 2000a). However, studies of the usage of these facilities revealed a number of problems. Early intakes of students did not make full use of the available resources; and where use was made, it was often inappropriate. Many students, for example, showed behaviors incompatible with the purpose for which the system was designed (e.g., flaming and lurking).

By contrast, according to teachers at The City School, their students are enthusiastic users of online communication:

I can go into a room and see youngsters who are supposedly getting information from the Internet—you find them on the chat line.

This is despite the fact that they have received no formal training:

... we've never taught chat in school. We've never taught them to log into chat rooms, or anything else, but ultimately, if you gave them 5 minutes, then you find them on Music Channel Chat room ...

It is also in opposition to the wishes of teachers:

I don't like them going in there, so I keep them out of there, but that's another way of communication which gets them on to a computer and once they see that, that excites them.

Discussion

The three projects referred to above provide evidence of gaps, both in technical skills and in perceptions of technology, between different interested parties in education. These gaps occur not only in the obvious areas—between adults/children and teacher/student—but also between students with differing experiences of ICT in education. The consequences of these gaps are discussed in further detail below.

The Impact of ICT on Learning

In the survey of Sheffield teachers mentioned above, department heads were asked to respond to the following statement:

I am under no pressure to use the Internet in my teaching

Fifty-two percent (n=169) did not agree with the statement. The majority of teachers, therefore, either disagreed (25%) or were ambivalent (27%). Clearly, therefore, many teachers not only feel that that they may be under pressure to use the Internet, but they also believe that their students know more about it than they do. Such a combination of circumstances could result in educationalists failing to recognize the potential of ICT within the learning environment, leading to under usage and inappropriate usage.

Old Teaching and New Technology

Teachers often use new technologies as though they were something old and familiar. That way, they can satisfy any requirement to use the technology without needing to amend their teaching methods. An example of such use is the numerous computer assisted learning (CAL) programs that are little more than electronic books.

Such superficiality in the use of ICT has long been criticized. In 1971, a 2-day symposium was organized by the Science Research Council and the Social Science Research Council. At the symposium, CAL was criticized on the grounds that:

*using computers for pre-stored material, that is, computerized programmed learn-
ing, combined inordinate expense with a very superficial philosophy of learning.*
(Annett, 1976)

Similar concerns were voiced 25 years later, in the report on the evaluation of the
Teaching and Learning Technology Programme (Coopers & Lybrand, 1996), where
it was felt that the projects would have benefited from:

*... a more serious and helpful attempt to encourage projects to engage with peda-
gogic issues* (para 283)

More recently, in a report on the use of interactive whiteboards (IW) in teaching,
students are reported as expressing:

*... disappointment and frustration with some approaches to using the IW, particularly
when they consider that its capabilities are being under-exploited. For example: 'If
teachers are going to use them [as a traditional whiteboard], then I wouldn't bother
wasting all that money'.* (Levy, 2002, p. 17)

Students, therefore, are clearly better able to appreciate the opportunities afforded
by ICT than their teachers (Madden, Ford, Miller, & Levy, 2006).

Networked Literacy

Such usage of ICT in teaching neglects not only the 'added value' that new educational technologies can bring, but it also ignores the fact that, to obtain that value,
students need to acquire new skills.

As was learned from the experience with the MA ITM, technical knowledge, though
necessary, is not sufficient. Many other skills are required by students learning online using computer-mediated technologies. Nunes, McPherson and Rico (2000a)
have described such skills as NICLS.

Networked literacy complements traditional basic skills with a new set of information and communication literacy skills. Information literacy requires students
to recognize their information needs; to identify ways of addressing gaps in their
knowledge; to construct strategies for locating information; to locate and access
information; to compare and evaluate information; and to organize, apply and synthesize information (Webber & Johnston, 2000).

In addition, if successful communication is to take place online, learners must change their behavior. The skills required when communicating online form what can be considered communication literacy. NICLS (Nunes et al., 2000b) include information literacy skills (as described above), and online collaboration and cooperation skills. These latter comprise:

- **Technical aspects**, including the skills needed to use computer-mediated communications (CMC) in an online learning situation
- **Social aspects**, needed to compensate for the unavailability of social cues traditionally delivered by auditory and visual channels.

The technical aspects of NICLS are relatively easy to address, but the social aspects have often been overlooked (Nunes, McPherson & Rice, 2000b; Hara, 2000; McDowell & Pickard, 2000). As a result, experiences such as those in the MA ITM course are common: Communications are misinterpreted, causing unintended offence and provoking inappropriate hostility. Students, therefore, need to be aware of crucial social issues involved in using CMC technologies (Webber & Johnston, 2000).

NICLS at School

Another relevant statement in the AHRB survey of school teachers is as follows:

My Internet skills were acquired informally (e.g., self-taught, learned from friends/colleagues, etc.), rather than on a taught course.

Eighty-five percent of respondents (n=188) agreed with this statement; 67% agreed strongly. As can be seen in Figure 2, for teachers younger than 55 years, age seems to make little difference. The youngest respondent was 24 years old; she agreed with the statement.

As stated above, the technical aspects of NICLS are relatively easy to address. However, of the teachers who responded to the survey, more than 95% never used chat rooms: The importance of the social aspects of NICLS, therefore, is likely to be unrecognized among them. E-mail was used, at least occasionally, by 70% of responding teachers; but as is the case with interactive whiteboards, e-mail can be related to an existing technology (mail) with which the teachers are already familiar. Two interesting questions, therefore, emerge:

1.   What, if any, online social skills are evolving among school children who appear to be enthusiastic users of chat rooms? Are there misunderstandings similar to those encountered on the MA ITM and, if so, how are they dealt with?

Figure 2. Percentage of teachers of differing ages agreeing with the statement: 'My Internet skills were acquired informally (e.g., self-taught, learned from friends/colleagues etc.), rather than on a taught course.'

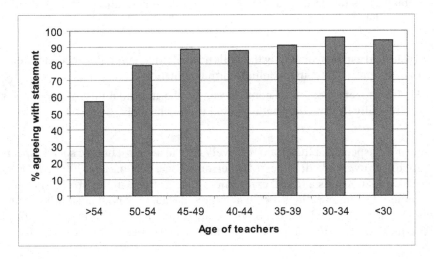

2.   Does the age at which e-mail skills are acquired affect the nature of e-mails? In particular, do students who learned to write letters before they learned to write e-mails produce more formal and more carefully worded e-mails?

NICLS Post-1997

The statistics cited in Tables 1 and 2 show how recently ICT resources became widely available in schools. It could reasonably be argued, therefore, that, prior to 1997, it was not practical to teach many of the NICLS identified by Nunes et al. (2000a) until students moved to further or higher education. As a result, the nature and range of information sources to which today's students have access is markedly different from those used by students finishing school prior to 1997.

Another significant development took place in the 2003-'04 academic year. DfES (2003) introduced amendments to the teaching of ICT in English schools. The new ICT course is designed to emphasize the relevance of ICT to all national curriculum subjects. If successful, many more students will leave school with NICLS. In all probability, however, for reasons discussed above, they will have been taught the technical aspects of NICLS, but will have evolved the social aspects by experimentation with their peers.

ICT Generations and the Resulting Gaps

The title of this chapter refers to a new generation gap: In fact, there may be several generation gaps, arising not only from the introduction of technology, but also from the successful incorporation of NICLS. The rapidly changing ICT environment within the class will lead to different generations of students having very different experiences at school, as follows:

- **Pre-1997:** ICT resources, where available, are just used for the teaching of subjects relating to math, science and technology. Teaching and learning are largely unaffected, otherwise. Some students acquire technical skills, but there is little opportunity to use computers as a tool for communication. Most students only become familiar with the Internet after leaving school.

- **1997-2003:** ICT resources become widely available. Pockets of expertise in the application of ICT to teaching begin to develop, but most teachers apply the technology cautiously, if at all. Students increasingly make use of ICT (particularly the Internet) as a learning resource. Many teachers (and parents) regard such usage with suspicion. NICLS are acquired rather than taught.

- **2003-2008:** ICT is increasingly embedded within the national curriculum. Teachers need to demonstrate their usage of it, but often it is employed as though it was an extension of existing technologies (e.g., electronic book) and it is under used. Students begin to learn ICT in primary school, along with reading and writing. More systematic teaching of NICLS begins.

- **Post-2008:** Schools begin to employ newly qualified teachers who grew up with ICT. It was a natural part of their learning environment, so they have no qualms about their students using it. Formalized instruction in the social aspects of NICLS begins.

Consequences of the ICT Generation Gap

The versatility of ICT and its potential value as an educational technology make it probable that, in the future, it will be ubiquitous at all levels of education. Adult learners, therefore, must acquire NICLS if they are successfully to complete any course of which online learning forms a significant component. Failure to do so will result in much frustration for the students, and eventually to lower levels of success (Hara & Kling, 1999).

Such frustrations are unlikely to be experienced, or even understood, by students who became familiar with online learning environments during their formative years.

Zafeirou, Nunes and Ford (2001) provide an example of a divide based on varying levels of NICLS, when they describe the problems some students encountered due to lack of typing skills. When using a Virtual Learning Environment (VLE), they experienced what amounted to a virtual speech defect, which severely hampered their efforts to communicate with fellow students.

Further inequities could arise where teachers fail to appreciate the potential of a technology. When home computers first became affordable, teachers were often impressed by well-presented, word-processed assignments. They quickly came to recognize the signs of 'cut-and-paste' essays; but before they did so, many students received high marks for work that owed more to their ICT skills than their understanding of the subject material.

Social Impact

The consequences referred to above are fairly obvious. Other, more subtle and more profound consequences may also arise, which may be as great as the impact of literacy on education in ancient Greece. It is hard to appreciate exactly what this might have been, because records of educational methods among pre-literate ancient Greeks are textual and, therefore, were made by practitioners of the new technology. Nevertheless, in "Preface to Plato," Havelock (1963) identifies numerous profound changes arising from the development of writing. According to Havelock, the orally based educational regime of pre-literate Greece was based on rote learning of rhythmically structured patterns that were recited and repeated without analysis (which is somewhat ironic, given Socrates' criticism of writing). Their role was, arguably, to stamp on learners the world view of their community. But then:

> ... at some time towards the end of the fifth century before Christ, it became possible for a few Greeks to talk about their 'souls' as though they had selves or personalities which were autonomous and not fragments of the atmosphere nor of a cosmic life force, but what we might call entities or real substances. (p. 197)

The change is attributed to the spread of writing. In due course, this made it possible for learning to transcend the immediate community. Groups of people, making "... parallel use of texts, both to structure the internal behavior of the groups' members and to provide solidarity against the outside world" are described as 'textual communities' (Stock, 1983).

The spread of reading and writing, therefore, affected individuals, communities and, indeed, the evolution of world culture (Madden, 2004) in ways that would probably have been inconceivable to Socrates and his contemporaries.

Conclusion

It took hundreds of years for literacy to become commonplace. Its effects, therefore, took many generations to permeate through communities and cultures. By contrast, ICT has the potential to change education radically in a fraction of a generation.

Some issues arising from the use of ICT in learning and teaching may be subtle and far-reaching. If writing made it possible for ancient Greeks to begin thinking of themselves as individuals, what could be the impact of increasingly sophisticated virtual learning zones?

Questions such as this are impossible to answer without greater experience and additional research, but the kind of meta-analysis of related projects that has been presented in this chapter has allowed a better understanding of the ICT generation gap.

As the 'new' literacies discussed earlier cease to be new but become incorporated in the educational system, the generation that has already passed through that system may be excluded from an increasingly important sector of the education market. Planning, therefore, is necessary to ensure that their needs can be addressed by life-long learning and Continuing Professional Development programs.

In the UK, perhaps one of the most significant developments in the use of computers as an educational technology has been adoption of the acronym ICT in place of IT. The emphasis on communication as well as information is an indication of the growing awareness of the new technology's role in facilitating exchanges and discussions, thereby addressing the shortcomings that Socrates noted arising from use of the (then) new technology of writing. Properly used, ICT allows students to move from being "hearers of many things" to being active processors of their readings and discussers of many things. In other words, ICT has the potential to enrich the learning process, facilitating an education based on interaction and social negotiation of meanings. Had Socrates been able to use ICT, he could still have subjected students to his methods.

References

Adams, D. (1999). How to stop worrying and learn to love the Internet. *Sunday Times, News Review,* August 29. Retrieved February 10, 2003, from www.douglasadams.com/dna/19990901-00-a.html

Annett, J. (1976). Computer-assisted learning 1969-1975: A report prepared for SSRC (Social Science Research Council).

Becta. (2001). Primary schools – ICT and standards. A report to the DfES on Becta's analysis of national data from OFSTED and QCA.

Coopers & Lybrand, Institute of Education, & Tavistock Institute. (1996). Evaluation of the teaching and learning technology programme (HEFCE).

Department of Education. (1995). Statistical bulletin: Survey of information technology in schools (issue no 3/95). Government Statistical Service.

DfES. (2002a). *Survey of information and communications technology in schools.* Retrieved February 10, 2003, from www.dfes.gov.uk/statistics/DB/SBU/b0360/index.html

DfES. (2002b). *Statistics of education: Schools in England.* Retrieved February 10, 2003, from www.dfes.gov.uk/statistics/DB/VOL/v0359/dfes_schools_final.pdf

DfES. (2003). *Key stage 3: National strategy key messages from the ICT launch.* Retrieved February 24, 2004, from www.standards.dfes.gov.uk/midbins/keystage3/launch_key_messages.PDF

DfES. (2004). *Survey of information and communications technology in schools.* Retrieved October 20, 2005, from www.dfes.gov.uk/rsgateway/DB/SFR/s000480/SFR27-2004v6.pdf

Hara, N. (2000). Students' distress with a Web-based distance education course. *Information, Communication & Society, 3,* 557-579.

Hara, N., & Kling, R. (1999). Students' frustrations with a Web-based distance education course. *First Monday, 4*(12), December. Retrieved February 24, 2004, from http: //firstmonday.org/issues/issue4_12/hara/index.html

Havelock, E. A. (n.d.). *Preface to Plato.* Cambridge: The Belknap Press of Harvard University Press.

Levy, P. (2002). *Interactive whiteboards in teaching and learning.* Report published by the Sheffield Excellence in Cities Partnership.

Madden, A. D. (2004). Evolution and information. *Journal of Documentation, 60*(1), 9-23.

Madden, A. D., Bates, L, White D., & Apthorpe, C. (2004). *Bridging the gap: ICT in the transition year. A report on the ICT Research Bursaries 2002-03.* ICT in Schools Research and Evaluation Series, No. 16.

Madden, A.D., Ford, N.J., Miller, D., & Levy, P. (2003). Schoolchildren searching the Internet – Teachers' perceptions. In A. Martin & H. Rader (Eds.), *Information and IT literacy: Enabling learning in the 21st century.* London: Facet.

Madden, A.D., Ford, N.J., Miller, D., & Levy, P. (2005). Using the Internet in teaching: The views of practitioners. A survey of the views of secondary school teachers in Sheffield, UK. *British Journal of Educational Technology, 36,* 255-280.

Madden, A. D., Ford, N. J., Miller, D., & Levy, P. (2006). Children's use of the Internet for information-seeking: What strategies do they use, and what factors affect their performance? *Journal of Documentation, 62*(6).

Madden, A. D., Nunes, M. B., Ford, N J., McPherson, M., & Miller, D. (2003b, December). A new generation gap: The consequences of increasingly early ICT first contact. *Proceedings of the 2nd International Conference on Multimedia ICT's in Education* (Vol. 1, pp. 6-16).

McDowell, L., & Pickard, A. (2000, April 17-19). Let's be careful out there: Learning in the world of electronic information. *Proceedings of the 2nd International Conference of Networked Learning.* Retrieved July 8, 2003, from http://collaborate.shef.ac.uk/nlpapers/McDowell%20Pickard-p%20Web.htm

McPherson, M. A., & Nunes, J. M. (2004). *Developing innovation in online learning, An action research framework.* London: Routledge-Falmer.

Moore, G. E. (1965). Cramming more components onto integrated circuits. *Electronics, 38*, 114-117

Nunes, J. M., McPherson, M. A., & Rico, M. (2000a, June 5-6). Instructional design of a networked learning skills module for Web-based collaborative distance learning. *Proceedings of the European Conference on Web-Based Learning Environments (WBLE 2000)* (pp. 95-103).

Nunes, J. M., McPherson, M., & Rico, M. (2000b). Design and development of a networked learning skills module for Web-based collaborative distance learning. *Proceedings of the 1st ODL International Workshop 2000* (pp. 117-131).

Opie, C., & Katsu, F. (2000). A tale of two national curriculums: Issues in implementing the national curriculum for information and communications technology in initial teacher training. *Journal of Information Technology for Teacher Education, 9*, 79-94.

Plato. (2002). *Phaedrus.* Robin Waterfield (trans.). Oxford: OUP.

Professional Software Systems. (2004). Retrieved February 24, 2005, from www.prof-soft.com/CompHistory.htm

Selwyn, N. (1999). Schooling the information society? The place of the information superhighway in education.. *Information Communication & Society, 2*, 156-173.

Selwyn, N., & Bullon, K. (2000). Primary school children's use of ICT. *British Journal of Educational Technology, 33*, 321-332

Stock, B. (1983). *The implications of literacy.* Princeton: Princeton University Press.

Webber, S., & Johnston, B. (2000). Conceptions of information literacy: New perspectives and implications. *Journal of Information Science, 26*, 381-397.

Zafeiriou, G., Nunes, J.M.B., & Ford, N. (2001). Using students' perceptions of participation in collaborative learning activities in the design of online learning environments. *Education for Information, 19*, 83-106.

Endnote

[1]   Teaching children aged 16-18 years

Chapter XVI

An Interactive Tool for Teaching and Learning LAN Design

Nurul I. Sarkar, Auckland University of Technology, New Zealand

Abstract

It is often difficult to motivate students to learn local area network (LAN) design, because many students appear to find the subject rather dry, technical and boring. To overcome this problem, the author has developed a software tool (named LAN-Designer) that gives students an interactive learning experience in LAN design concepts. The LAN-Designer is suitable for classroom use in introductory computer networking courses. This chapter describes LAN-Designer and its effectiveness in teaching and learning LAN design. The effectiveness of LAN-Designer has been evaluated both formally by students and informally in discussion within the teaching team. The feedback from students indicates that the development and implementation of LAN-Designer were successful. It also discusses the impact of LAN-Designer on student learning and comprehension.

Introduction

LANs are often included as a topic in computer science, information technology (IT), engineering and business courses, as LANs are a fundamental component of IT systems today. Unfortunately, motivating students to learn about LAN design is often difficult, because they find the subject rather technical, dry and boring. However, the view is frequently supported in educational literature (Anderson, Reder, & Simon, 1996; Young, 1993) that incorporating practical demonstrations into these courses, thereby illustrating theoretical concepts and providing opportunities for interactive learning experiences, significantly enhances student learning about LAN design. Yet, despite the Chinese adage attributed to Confucius (551-479 BC), 'I hear, I know. I see, I remember. I do, I understand,' only a limited amount of material designed to supplement the teaching of LAN design is publicly available, as searches of the Computer Science Teaching Center (Grissom, Knox, Fox, & Heller, 2005) and SIGCSE Education Links (Anonymous, 2005) sites reveal.

The author strongly believes, as do many others (Belding-Royer, 2004; Casado & McKeown, 2005; Hacker & Sitte, 2004; Lopez-Martin, 2004; Midkiff, 2005; Moallem, 2004), that students learn more effectively from courses that provide for active involvement in interactive learning experiences. To that end, the author has developed LAN-Designer (using Authorware 6 under MS Windows), which facilitates an interactive teaching and learning of LAN design concepts.

LAN-Designer can be used either in the classroom or at home. Both teacher and students can benefit from the use of LAN-Designer in different teaching and learning contexts. For example, a teacher is able to use LAN-Designer in the classroom as a demonstration, to liven up the traditional lecture environment; students, on the other hand, can use server-based networking tutorials and verify the results of in-class tasks and exercises on LAN design.

LAN design concepts are described in many textbooks (Forouzan, 2003, 2004; Kurose & Ross, 2005; Palmer & Sinclair, 2003; Stamper, 2001), and commercial LAN design is described extensively in the literature (Fitzgerald & Dennis, 2002).

The main contribution and strength of this chapter is the emphasis that an interactive learning experience using a software tool is crucial in motivating students to learn LAN design concepts. Perhaps the innovative aspect of this work is the development and evaluation of such a tool so as to be effective in complementing the lecture content of LAN design. The chapter is organized as follows. First is a review of some existing network simulation and modeling tools, followed by a description of LAN-Designer and highlights of its educational benefits. Test results are presented to verify the successful implementation of LAN-Designer. The effectiveness of LAN-Designer is evaluated, and a brief conclusion ends the chapter.

Existing Simulation and Modeling Tools

Many network researchers have developed network simulation and modeling tools suitable for classroom demonstration of various aspects of computer and data communication networks. The motivation for designing such tools is to create a substitute environment for a live network (Tymann, 1991) so students can experiment with various network topologies without any risks of damaging the networks (Davis, Ransbottom, & Hamilton, 1998). Many network simulators provide animation and visualization to develop a better understanding of the real-world systems.

A number of both open-source and commercial simulation and modeling tools are available for developing a variety of LAN models (Chang, 1999; Zheng & Ni, 2003). White (2001) categorized network simulation tools into four classes: 1) network loads and topology display; 2) network topology design; 3) Web traffic analysis and display; and 4) multimedia-based pedagogy. LAN-Designer, further introduced later, is a class of tool for network physical topology simulation and display diagrams. In this chapter, for brevity, we refer only to a selected set of literature indicative of the approaches used in the first two categories mentioned above.

- **ns-2** (Fall & Varadhan, 2003): ns-2 (network simulator) is a powerful text-based simulation software package suitable for modeling and performance analysis of computer and communication networks. It is a discrete event simulator originally developed at Lawrence Berkeley Laboratory at the University of California – Berkeley as part of the Virtual InterNetwork Testbed (VINT) project. The Monarch project at Carnegie Mellon University has extended the ns-2 by adding support for IEEE 802.11 wireless LANs (Monarch, 2004).

- **OPNET Modeler** (OPNET, 2005): Opnet is a popular commercial software package commonly used by researchers and practitioners for modeling and simulation of computer networks. It is menu driven, with an easy-to-use graphical user interface for rapid model construction, data collection and other simulation tasks. It might be suitable for advanced networking classes in which students can develop new network models for experimentation.

- *cnet* (McDonald, 2005): The *cnet* network simulator allows students to experiment with various protocols at the data link, routing and transport layers in networks consisting of any combination of LANs and wireless LAN links. Although *cnet* is being used worldwide, the need to prepare a network topology file as the basis of network topology display might be a challenging task for beginners.

- **DlpSim** (King, 2004): DlpSim (data link protocol simulator) may be suitable for classroom use as an aid to enhance teaching and learning network protocols by simulation. However, DlpSim emphasizes data link layer protocols.

- **JASPER** (Turner & Robin, 2001): JASPER (JAva Simulation of Protocols for Education and Research) is a protocol simulator that can be used as an aid to enhance teaching and learning communication protocols. It is an extensible tool in which students can readily add new protocols.

- **WebTrafMon** (Hong, Kwon, & Kim, 1999): WebTrafMon is a Web-based system for network analysis and traffic monitoring, including traffic loads, types, sources and destinations. However, the system focuses exclusively on network analysis and traffic monitoring.

- **NetMod** (Bachmann, Segal, Srinivasan, & Teorey, 1991): NetMod is a network modeling tool that uses some simple analytical models, providing designers of large interconnected LANs with an in-depth analysis of the potential performance of such systems. The tool can be used in university, industrial or governmental campus networking environments, and might serve as a useful tool for classroom demonstration.

- **WLAN-Designer** (Sarkar, 2004): WLAN-Designer is a Web-based software tool (prototype) for modeling wireless LANs. The software is easy to use and can be accessed through the Internet. It is suitable for classroom use to enhance teaching and learning various aspects of wireless LAN design. However, the current version of WLAN-Designer requires an improvement.

- **iNetwork** (Sandrasegaran & Trieu, 2005): iNetwork is an interactive software tool for teaching and learning data communication networks. It allows students to assemble and build customized networks using networking devices, such as workstations, switches, routers, domain name system (DNS) and dynamic host configuration protocol (DHCP) servers. Through experimenting with key parameters, students gain insights into the key concepts of communication network design and analysis.

- **Network Intelligence** (Nieuwelaar & Hunt, 2004): Network Intelligence (NI) provides an easy way to view complex traffic patterns in a wide-area networking environment. NI can perform simulations of network topologies using actual gathered data, as opposed to arbitrary data.

In conclusion, the proposed LAN-Designer seems to be almost alone in its goals and capabilities.

Description of LAN-Designer

Figure 1 shows a structured diagram of the system. LAN-Designer is an easy-to-use, user-friendly tool and can be used as an aid to enhance teaching and learning LAN design concepts. The main features of LAN-Designer are described below:

Figure 1. Structure diagram of the LAN-Designer

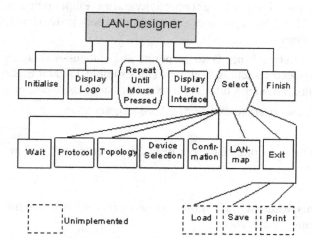

- **Channel access protocol:** This is an important parameter that needs to be considered when designing LANs. The channel access protocol efficiently controls the transmission when multiple users shared a common channel (i.e., a transmission medium). LAN-Designer allows users to select either Ethernet carrier sense multiple access with collision detection (CSMA/CD) or token passing network access protocols.

- **Physical topology:** A topology represents the physical layout (i.e., architecture) of the network. It is another of the important parameters in server-based LAN design. In the case of Ethernet CSMA/CD networks, either bus or star physical topology can be chosen. For token passing networks, either physical ring or bus topology can be chosen.

- **Network component selection:** This feature allows users to enter LAN components, such as the number of workstations and the number of printers for the proposed LAN design. A file server will be selected by default.

- **Confirmation:** This feature allows users to verify LAN components that have been selected for LAN design and make changes if necessary before proceeding to the final step of LAN modeling.

- **LAN-map:** Based on the user selection of an access protocol, physical topology and LAN components, the LAN-map displays the proposed LAN diagram on the screen. With this, students can verify the solution of LAN design exercises.

- **Mesh topology:** The mesh physical topology is not very common for a LAN design because of large wiring connectivity and more input/output ports required per node. This feature provides a short tutorial (both textual and graphical) on mesh topology.

- **Advanced networking:** Both corporate and campus-wide LANs are based on a high-speed switching backbone (for example, Gigabit Ethernet switch). This feature provides a tutorial on switched-based LAN design.

- **Exit:** It allows users to exit from LAN-Designer at any time.

The following three features have not been implemented yet, and are considered as future work:

- **Load:** This feature will allow users to view existing LAN modeling for further analysis and modifications.

- **Save:** It will allow users to save LAN modeling on disk for later use.

- **Print:** This feature will allow users to produce a hard copy of LAN diagrams.

Additional information about channel access protocol, physical topology, cabling, hubs and switches is presented at the bottom part of relevant pages (see Figure 2).

To extend the functionality of LAN-Designer, we have recently developed a Web-based tool called WebLan-Designer for interactive teaching and learning both wired

Figure 2. A sample screenshot of the interface of LAN-Designer

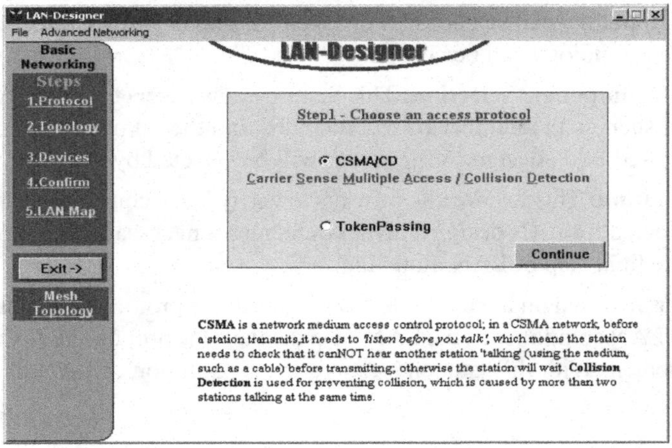

Figure 3. A sample screenshot of the LAN modeling page of WebLan-Designer

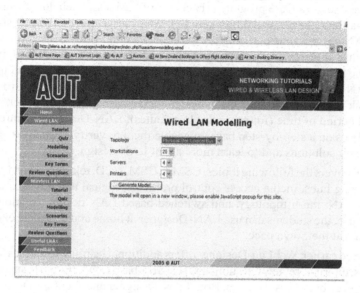

and wireless LAN design (Sarkar & Petrova, 2005). Figure 3 shows the wired LAN modeling page of WebLan-Designer. Let us briefly highlight some of the important features of WebLan-Designer. Using the 'modeling' page, students can experiment with a variety of LAN topologies and channel access protocols. Students can also test their knowledge about various aspects of LAN design by using two interactive quizzes. Each quiz consists of a set of 25 multiple-choice questions, and each question has four possible answers. At the end of each quiz session, the system displays the total score, which allows students to assess their prior knowledge about LAN design. The system provides a friendly environment for interactive quiz management. This is particularly useful for the teacher to update quizzes on a regular basis. Although WebLan-Designer has more functionalities than LAN-Designer, both tools can be used independently.

LAN-Designer in Practice

For simplicity and ease of use, LAN-Designer has been implemented with a graphical user interface (GUI). The point-and-click GUI interface is easy to use and self-explanatory, which makes LAN-Designer well suited to both students and teachers.

Now let us briefly highlight the value of LAN-Designer and how we use this tool in the teaching and learning context. At the Auckland University of Technology

(AUT), we teach various aspects of LAN design, including wireless networking across three undergraduate programs (bachelor of business, bachelor of computer and information sciences, and diploma in IT). We observe that motivating students to learn LAN design concepts using the traditional lecture-only method is very difficult, because students find the subject rather technical and dry and, thus, boring. To make the lesson more interesting and to encourage students' class participation, we use LAN-Designer as an integral part of a 2-hour session. In the classroom, an in-class task is given to the students to design server-based LANs on paper. After a prescribed period of time (for example, 15 minutes), LAN-Designer is introduced to the students on a step-by-step basis to enable them to verify (visually and interactively) their solutions and to learn more about LAN design.

The tutorial covers the following topics: CSMA, CSMA/CD, token passing, Ethernet and token ring hubs, media access control protocols, logical and physical topologies for a LAN, mesh topology, and switched-based LAN design. In addition to classroom use, the students can use LAN-Designer at home and complete exercises and tutorials at their own pace.

As mentioned earlier, WebLan-Designer offers additional learning resources, including quizzes, tutorials, review questions and scenario-based LAN design to supplement teaching server-based LAN design. Both LAN-Designer and WebLan-Designer are available at no cost for educational use (more information about these tools can be found by contacting the author). The suggested study guideline using LAN-Designer and WebLan-Designer are shown in Figures 4(a) and 4(b), respectively.

Figure 4. A suggested sequence of study using LAN-Designer and WebLan-Designer

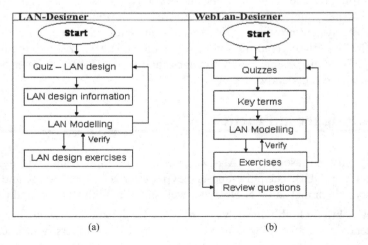

(a)   (b)

Benefits of LAN-Designer

LAN-Designer provides the following main benefits:

- **Hands-on:** LAN-Designer facilitates an interactive learning experience in LAN design.

- **Modeling:** It provides a simple and easy way to develop a variety of LAN models. With this, students can experiment with a variety of LAN topologies and channel access protocols to enhance their knowledge and understanding of LAN design concepts.

- **Ease of use:** LAN-Designer is an easy-to-use, user-friendly tool and can easily be installed on PCs operating under MS Windows.

- **Usefulness:** It enhances face-to-face teaching with online learning and can be used either in the classroom or at home.

- **Challenging:** It provides a challenging yet friendly environment where students can test their knowledge about LAN design concepts.

Test Results

To evaluate its performance and robustness, LAN-Designer has been installed and tested on various PCs in computer laboratories across campuses. Figures 5 and 6

Figure 5. 10Base T. A server-based Ethernet LAN with five PCs and two printers (physical star topology)

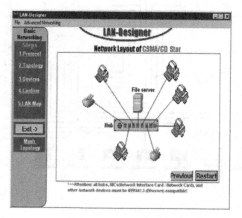

Figure 6. 10 Base 2. A server-based Ethernet LAN with five PCs and one printer (physical bus topology)

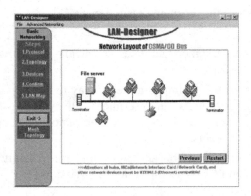

Figure 7. A model of an Ethernet LAN with 12 workstations, two servers and one printer (physical and logical star topology)

Summary

Topology: Physical & Logical Star

Workstations: 12

Servers: 2

Printers: 1

There are many ways of connecting up a network. To see a different way of
connecting this network up, press the "F5" button or click *Refresh*.
Once you have finished viewing the model, click *Close*.

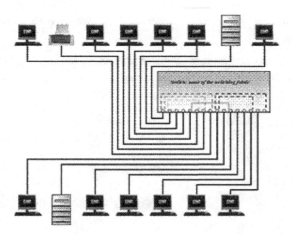

Figure 8. Wireless LAN modeling with 10 mobile workstations, eight PDAs and one printer using infrastructure network

Summary

Topology:	Infrastructure
Mobile Workstations:	10
PDAs:	8
Printers:	1

There are many ways of connecting up a network. To see a different way of connecting this network up, press the "F5" button or click *Refresh*. Once you have finished viewing the model, click *Close*.

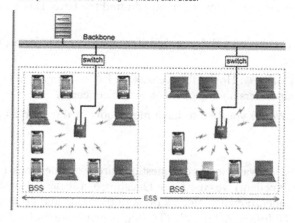

show screenshots of LAN-Designer test results. For 10Base T network, the following components have been selected and LAN-Designer has produced the valid LAN diagram (see Figure 5): Access protocol: Ethernet CSMA/CD; Physical topology: Star; Number of PCs: 5 (excluding a server); Number of printers: 2.

For 10Base 2 network, the following components have been selected and the LAN-Designer has produced the valid LAN diagram (see Figure 6): Access protocol: Ethernet CSMA/CD; Physical topology: Bus;

number of PCs: 5 (excluding a server); number of printers: 1.

The screenshots of WebLan-Designer test results for wired LAN and wireless LAN modeling are shown in Figures 7 and 8, respectively.

Evaluation by Student Feedback

To assess the educational value of LAN-Designer, it has been evaluated extensively both formally by students (in survey form) and informally by discussion within the teaching team. The evaluation of LAN-Designer was conducted in the classroom by a member of the teaching team, and anonymity of the respondents was protected. As part of the formal evaluation process, students were asked to complete a questionnaire, and were asked the following six questions:

1. **User interface:** How useful did you find the user interface of the LAN-Designer to use?

2. **LAN design information:** How useful did you find the information about LAN design to be?

3. **Easy to use:** How easy (overall) did you find the LAN-Designer to use and follow?

4. **Robustness:** How easy did you find it to start and exit from the LAN-Designer?

5. **Measure of success:** How effective was the LAN-Designer in helping you to improve your understanding of LAN design concepts?

6. **Hands-on:** Would you like to have more tools of this kind as part of your course?

A 5-point Likert scale was used in the questionnaire. For Questions 1 to 5, a scale of 1 (Poor) to 5 (Excellent) was used. For Question 6, a scale of 1 (no) and 5 (Yes) was used. Fifty undergraduate students (about 60% male and 40% female) from both E-business IT Infrastructure (EBITI) and Networking and Telecommunications (N&T) courses completed the questionnaire, and their responses are plotted in Figure 9. The responses were interpreted as follows:

1. The GUI of the LAN-Designer is found to be easy to use. Forty-eight students indicated they were quite satisfied with the LAN-Designer interface, whereas the other two students were neutral (see Figure 9a).

2. Forty-six students have indicated that the LAN design information presented at the bottom part of each page is very useful. One student was not very satisfied about LAN design information, whereas the rest (three) were neutral (see Figure 9b).

3. LAN-Designer was found to be a user-friendly tool. Forty-seven students indicated they were happy with the current version of the LAN-Designer, and the other three were neutral (see Figure 9c).

4. LAN-Designer is easy to install and run, and can be exited from at any time. All 50 students indicated they found LAN-Designer to be robust (see Figure 9d).

Figure 9. Student-response graphs illustrating the number of respondents in each category for each of the six questions in the questionnaire

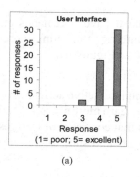

(a)

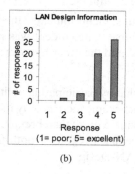

(b)

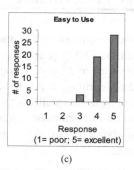

(c)

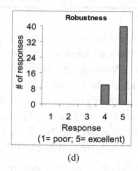

(d)

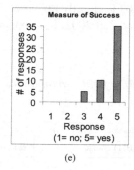

(e)

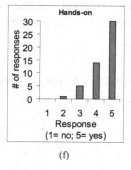

(f)

5.   Forty-five students indicated that LAN-Designer had clearly assisted them in developing a better understanding of the concepts of LAN design; the other five were neutral (see Figure 9e).

6.   Forty-four students indicated they would like to have more hands-on activities in the course. One student was not very interested in trying more hands-on activities, and the other five were neutral (see Figure 9f).

We observed that by participating in the hands-on interactive activities in the classroom, students became increasingly motivated to learn more about LAN design and enjoyed this course more than previous courses that consisted of lectures only. We are seeking feedback regularly both from students and staff for further improvement of the LAN-Designer.

Impact of LAN-Designer on Students' Performance

We have run LAN-Designer in our two undergraduate courses, EBITI and N&T, in Semester 1 of 2004 and Semester 2 of 2003. Both the EBITI (Petrova, 2000) and N&T (Sarkar & Petrova, 2001) courses are at level 6, or first-year degree level, and constitute 15 credit points (150 hours of student learning) at AUT. Most of the EBITI students are studying toward their bachelor of business qualification and have a very limited background in the IT and computer and information sciences (CIS) fields. On the other hand, the N&T students are studying toward the bachelor of IT and have a good background in the IT and CIS fields.

LAN-Designer has had quite a positive impact on students' learning about LAN design. As seen in Table 1, the overall student pass rate in the final examinations in both Semester 1 of 2004 and Semester 2 of 2003 is slightly higher compared to students in Semester 1 of 2003 and Semesters 1 and 2 of 2002. It is considered that

Table 1. Comparison of student performance in the final examinations with and without LAN-Designer experience

			Student pass rate (%)	
			EBITI course	N&T course
With LAN-Designer	1	2004	100	96
	2	2003	100	95
Without LAN-Designer	1	2003	95	92
	2	2002	93	91
	1	2002	95	92
Pass-rate improvement (with LAN-Designer)			up to 7%	up to 5%

Figure 10. Assignment grade comparison of student performance in the N&T assignment with and without LAN-Designer experience

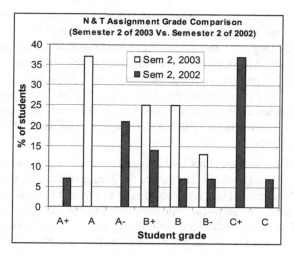

much of this difference can be accounted for by the fact that students in both Semester 1 of 2004 and Semester 2 of 2003 used LAN-Designer, whereas the students in Semester 1 of 2003 and Semesters 1 and 2 of 2002 did not get an opportunity to use LAN-Designer. We also observed that EBITI students benefited even more from LAN-Designer (7% pass-rate improvement) than the N&T students (5% improvement) did. This is probably due to EBITI students' limited background in the IT and CIS fields compared to N&T students.

In Figure 10, we plot student grade in assignment of the N&T course vs. the percentage of students in Semester 2 of 2003 and Semester 2 of 2002. The grading scheme used for assessing assignment (according to the B.InfoTech program) was as follows: A+ (90-100), A (85-89), A- (80-84), B+ (75-79), B (70-74), B- (65-69), C+ (60-64), C (55-59), C- (50-54) and D (0-49). Note that A+ to C- is pass grade and D is the fail grade.

We found that students in Semester 2 of 2003 have done better in the assignment than students in Semester 2 of 2002. It is believed that much of the improvement in students' grade in the assignment is due to the LAN-Designer experience students had in Semester 2 of 2003.

Conclusion

A software tool (LAN-Designer) has been developed that can be used either in the classroom or at home to enhance the teaching and learning of various aspects of LAN design. LAN-Designer was evaluated by students, and their responses to the questionnaire about LAN-Designer were mostly favorable. Students indicated that they found LAN-Designer easy to use and robust, and that it helped them gain an understanding of LAN design concepts. LAN-Designer has had a positive impact on students' performance. Results show that both EBITI and N&T students scored better in the final examinations with LAN-Designer experience students without LAN-designer experience.

Currently, LAN-Designer displays LAN diagrams involving components of up to eight (including a server), which is adequate for demonstration purposes. The software can be easily upgraded to accommodate any number of LAN devices. Features such as access protocol, physical topology, component selection, confirmation, LAN-map, mesh topology, advanced networking and exit have been implemented. More features (e.g., load, save and print) are still under development.

We have developed a Web-based tool called WebLan-Designer to extend LAN-Designer by including wireless LAN components. Both LAN-Designer and WebLan-Designer can be used independently either in the classroom or at home. The incorporation of Gigabit Ethernet and TCP/IP networking is suggested for future work. More information about LAN-Designer and WebLan-Designer can be obtained by contacting the author.

Acknowledgment

I would like to thank Jason Lian for programming LAN-Designer. An earlier version of the chapter appears as: Sarkar, N.I. (2005). LAN-Designer: A software tool to enhance learning and teaching server-based LAN design. *International Journal of Information and Communication Technology Education, 1*(2), 74-86.

References

Anderson, J. R., Reder, L. M., & Simon, H. A. (1996). Situated learning and education. *Educational Researcher, 25*(4), 5-11.

Anonymous. (2005). *SIGCSE education links.* Retrieved October 10, from *http:// sigcse.org/topics/*

Bachmann, D. W., Segal, M. E., Srinivasan, M. M., & Teorey, T. J. (1991). NetMod: A design tool for large-scale heterogeneous campus networks. *IEEE Journal of Selected Areas in Communications, 9*(1), 15-24.

Belding-Royer, E. M. (2004, March 14-17). *Escape from the computer lab: Education in mobile wireless networks.* Proceedings of the IEEE 2nd Annual Conference on Pervasive Computing and Communications Workshops.

Casado, M., & McKeown, N. (2005, February 23-27). The virtual network system. *Proceedings of the 36th SIGCSE Technical Symposium on Computer Science Education,* St. Louis, MO.

Chang, X. (1999, December). *Network simulations with Opnet.* Proceedings of the 1999 Winter Simulation Conference: Simulation – A bridge to the future, Piscataway, NJ.

Davis, N., Ransbottom, S., & Hamilton, D. (1998). Teaching computer networks through modeling. *ACM SigAda Ada Letters, 18*(5), 104-110.

Fall, K., & Varadhan, K. (2003). *The ns manual.* Retrieved from www.isi.edu/ns-nam/ns/

Fitzgerald, J. & Dennis, A. (2002). *Business data communications and networking* (7th ed.). New York: John Wiley & Sons.

Forouzan, B.A. (2003). *Local area networks* (1st ed.). New York: McGraw Hill.

Forouzan, B.A. (2004). *Data communications and networking* (3rd ed.). New York: McGraw Hill.

Grissom, S., Knox, D., Fox, E., & Heller, R. (2005). *Computer Science Teaching Center (CSTC).* Retrieved October 30, 2005, from www.cstc.org/

Hacker, C., & Sitte, R. (2004). Interactive teaching of elementary digital logic design with WinLogiLab. *IEEE Transactions on Education, 47*(2), 196-203.

Hong, J. W.-K., Kwon, S.-S., & Kim, J.-Y. (1999). WebTrafMon: Web-based Internet/Intranet network traffic monitoring and analysis system. *Computer Communications, 22*(14), 1333-1342.

King, P.J.B. (2004). *Data link protocol simulator.* Retrieved from www.cee.hw.ac.uk/~pjbk/dlpsim/index.html

Kurose, J. F., & Ross, K. W. (2005). *Computer networking: A top-down approach featuring the Internet* (3rd ed.). New York: Addison Wesley.

Lopez-Martin, A. J. (2004). Teaching random signals and noise: An experimental approach. *IEEE Transactions on Education, 47*(2), 174-179.

McDonald, C. (2005). *The cnet network simulator (v2.0.9).* Retrieved January 10, 2005, from www.csse.uwa.edu.au/cnet/

Midkiff, S.F. (2005). An experiential course in wireless networks and mobile systems. *Pervasive Computing, IEEE, 4*(1), 9-13.

Moallem, M. (2004). A laboratory testbed for embedded computer control. *IEEE Transactions on Education, 47*(3), 340-347.

Monarch. (2004). *CMU Monarch project.* Retrieved October 10, 2005, from www.monarch.cs.cmu.edu

Nieuwelaar, M. V. D., & Hunt, R. (2004). Real-time carrier network traffic measurement, visualisation and topology modelling. *Computer Communications, 27*, 128-140.

OPNET. (2005). *OPNET Technologies – Commercial simulation software.* Retrieved September 20, 2005, from www.opnet.com

Palmer, M. & Sinclair, R.B. (2003). *Guide to designing and implementing local and wide area networks* (2nd ed.). Canada: Course Technology.

Petrova, K. (2000). Teaching electronic commerce: An information technology infrastructure design & management approach. *New Zealand Journal of Applied Computing & Information Technology, 4*(1), 70-77.

Sandrasegaran, K., & Trieu, M. (2005). INetwork: An interactive learning tool for communication networks. In N.I. Sarkar (Ed.), *Tools for teaching computer networking and hardware concepts.* Hershey, PA: Idea Group Publishing.

Sarkar, N. I. (2004, August 30-September 1). *WLAN-designer: A Web-based software tool to enhance learning and teaching wireless LAN design.* Proceedings of the 4th IEEE International Conference on Advanced Learning Technologies, Joensuu, Finland.

Sarkar, N. I., & Petrova, K. (2001, July 2-5). *Teaching computer networking & telecommunications: A network analysis and software development Approach.* Proceedings of the 14th annual conference of the NACCQ, Napier, New Zealand.

Sarkar, N. I., & Petrova, K. (2005). *The WebLan-Designer.* Retrieved October 15, 2005, from http://elena.aut.ac.nz/homepages/weblandesigner/

Stamper, D. (2001). *Local area networks* (3rd ed.). New Jersey, NJ: Prentice Hall.

Turner, K. J., & Robin, I. A. (2001). An interactive visual protocol simulator. *Computer Standards & Interfaces, 23*, 279-310.

Tymann, P. (1991, March). *VNET: A tool for teaching computer networking to undergraduates.* Proceedings of the 22nd SIGCSE Technical Symposium on Computer Science Education, San Antonio, TX.

White, C. (2001). Visualization tools to support data communications and computer network courses. *Journal of Computing in Small Colleges, 17*(1), 81-88.

Young, M. F. (1993). Instructional design for situated learning. *Educational Technology, 41*(1), 43-58.

Zheng, P., & Ni, L. M. (2003, March 30-April 3). *EMPOWER: A network emulator for Wireline and wireless networks.* Proceedings of the 22nd annual joint Conference of the IEEE Computer and Communication Societies, San Francisco.

Chapter XVII

Diffusion of Educational Technology and Education Reform:
Examining Perceptual Barriers to Technology Integration

LeAnne K. Robinson, Western Washington University, USA

Abstract

This study examines educators' perceived barriers to technology integration and the relationship to education reform. Educators and administrators from four elementary schools in Washington state were interviewed in their classrooms during a 3-month period. The schools differed in size, location and social economic status, and reported variances in their Washington Assessment of Student Learning (WASL) scores. While all of the schools reported similar barriers to the use of educational technology, distinct differences appeared between those schools that had done long-range planning during the reform process and those that had not. Specifically, staff in the two schools that coordinated curricula, performance standards and a variety of assessment tools while simultaneously allowing teachers the flexibility to alter the curricula were more likely to state personal responsibility for student learning, and they were also more likely to have overcome barriers to the use of technology.

Background

In a recent campaign commercial, a candidate spoke of the need to improve education and to create quality schools. Lined up along a white wall behind him were rows of computers with elementary students quietly absorbed in the computer screens. The message to the public was clear: Computers and computing technology are not only necessary for quality schools, but are indicative of good teaching and student learning. If the state was to have youth who would eventually be competitive in a global economy, technology would need to be at the forefront of funding and government support.

Computing technology has been marketed as the current solution to education's problems (Rockman, 2000), and the quest for technologically equipped schools has grown dramatically. In 2000, the number of computers in schools numbered more than 10 million (Becker, 2000). By 2003, nearly 100% of all public schools had Internet access, and more than 93% of all instructional classrooms were wired for access. The mean average of computers per school was nearly 136 (NCES, 2004). The estimated cost of technology per pupil in the United States (US) was $103 per pupil in 2005 alone (Education Week, 2005).

Purpose

Research in the integration and institutionalization of educational technology was limited in scope in 1994 (Seels & Richey, 1994), and although educational technology is now available, it is not integrated into classrooms today (Becker, 2000; NCES, 2000). Only 43% of elementary classrooms surveyed used computers on more than 20 occasions during the school year (Becker, 2000). Nationwide, school districts are grappling with education reform and accountability while simultaneously attempting to financially support computing technology and encourage integration by classroom teachers. Currently, there is no clear rationale that explains the apparent difficulty with incorporating the use of educational technology and whether or not there is a relationship between the level of technology integration and the pressure teachers experience as a result of education reform efforts. The purpose of this study was to examine how educators in several schools in a Northwestern state were responding to the pressure to integrate technology while simultaneously being accountable for student achievement.

Review of the Literature

In January 2002, President Bush reauthorized the Elementary and Secondary Education Act. This bill contained an even larger allotment of money and support for technology from the federal government than previous education bills (Fletcher, 2002). Currently, 48 states have adopted or are developing assessments that align with standards-based reform efforts (Stecher & Chun, 2001). Reform and standards have impacted classroom practice, and schools and teachers have responded in multiple ways (Adcock & Patton, 2001). Often, technology reform and education reform have paralleled each other as opposed to being incorporated (Peters, 2000), meaning that in many instances the purchasing of computing tools and related technology, as well as a plan for staff development, were not coordinated with a building's reorganization and examination of the curriculum and instructional processes. When both education reform and technology integration have been fully combined with curriculum reform, which includes examining pedagogy, positive results have been found for students (Bain & Smith, 2000).

Barriers to Technology Use

In spite of significant pressure to integrate the use of technology into the curriculum, the presence and accessibility of computers in the schools has not shown that the technology is being used by educators or that students actually can or do use it (Cuban, Kirkpatrick, & Peck, 2002; Kalkowski, 2001). Although they are accessible, computers have not transformed the practices of a majority of teachers (Becker, 2000; Labbo & Reinking, 1999) and Willis, Thompson, and Sadera (1999) have pointed out that integration of computers into the classroom actually has been a slow process.

Defining Barriers

In initial efforts to understand why teachers have failed to integrate technology, barriers have been defined as being 'primary' and 'secondary' (Judson & Sawada, 2000; Prater, 2001; Ertmer, Addison, Lane, Ross, & Woods, 1999). Both primary and secondary barriers are explained as being intrinsic and extrinsic (Ertmer, Addison, Lane, Ross, & Woods, 1999). Primary barriers include: lack of access to computers and software, insufficient time to plan instruction, and inadequate technical and administrative support. Secondary barriers include: beliefs about teaching, beliefs about computers, established classroom practices and unwillingness to change.

Diffusion of Innovations and Educational Technology

In addition to defining barriers, researchers have sought to understand why some specific technologies are adopted. The diffusion of innovations is the study of the process by which the use of a perceived new idea, practice or object is adopted within a given social system (Rogers, 1995). The study of the diffusion of innovations is present in many research traditions, including anthropology, marketing, geography, communication and education. Within the overall research arena, fewer than 10% of the studies of innovations have been conducted in education (Rogers, 1995). While Rogers (1995) provides a generic model of the process of the adoption of an innovation, case studies are showing that alternative models may be more applicable to school systems. These models specifically identify educational technology as the innovation being studied, thus the phrase 'diffusion of educational technology' is often used in place of 'diffusion of innovations.'

The diffusion of educational technology models that have been recently presented are non-linear, implying that many factors are involved in the adoption (or lack of adoption) of educational technology (Dooley, 1999; James, Lamb, Bailey, & Householder, 2000; Rogers, 2000; Sherry, Billig, Tavalin, & Gibson, 2000). These models vary from the commonly cited model posed by Everett Rogers (1995), as they focus solely on educational technology and attempt to identify more specifically those factors that will lead to the adoption of an innovation in a school setting. All of the models have been developed using a limited number of schools, and none of the models clearly indicate why technology integration has been a slow process.

Pilot Study on Media Selection

In spring 2001, the researcher conducted a pilot study at a K-6 elementary school to determine how teachers in this particular setting made decisions regarding media selection. While the majority of staff verbally supported the use of computing tools, few used educational technology and instead tended to blame others or cite circumstances they felt were out of their control for a lack of use. The common theme that emerged from the interviews was that regardless of the reason for failing to integrate technology, the teachers in the building were making the majority of decisions based on a highly structured reading program that had been adopted during a school reform process. All related the lack of technology use to some aspect of the school's focus on educational reform and to their concerns related to teacher accountability and a state-required assessment. The results of the pilot study provided an additional foundation for further examination of the relationship between education reform, educational technology and educators' perceived barriers to technology integration.

Methodology

Theoretical Underpinnings

Authentic technologies (Clark & Estes, 1999) are "educational solutions resulting from systematic analysis that identifies the problem being solved, selects and translates appropriate, well-designed research and applies it to design culturally appropriate educational solutions" (p. 243). A four-stage model proposed by Clark and Estes (1999) for conducting research in the development of authentic technologies provided the theoretical underpinnings for this study. Authentic technologies can include teaching strategies and processes, not merely computing tools. This research is based in the first, or Descriptive Scientific Research Stage, where the defining of constructs and hypotheses generation are the key goals.

Two research questions guided the study:

1.   What are teachers' perceptions of barriers to the use of educational technology/technology integration, and how do the barriers connect to education reform?

2.   What are the connections between perceived barriers to the responsibility for computing technology?

Site Selection

Four separate sites from the same Educational Service District in a Northwestern state were purposely selected. A stratified sample was used (Patton, 1990), meaning that the four sites represented four different subgroups for comparison. Two of the schools were located in rural settings and reported variances between their WASL scores (demographics are reported in Table 1 and Table 2). Access was granted through a key individual at each site, and snowball sampling (Patton, 1990) was used. Semi-structured questions were asked and observations were made of the classroom setup and equipment available.

Table 1. Demographics of selected sites, 2001

School	Location	Enrollment	% of Free and Reduced Lunch
Wrangle	Urban	370 K-6	56.8
Sandal Creek	Suburb	444 K-4	10.3
East Lake	Rural	263 K-6	34.4
Woodland	Rural	304 K-6	44.4

Table 2. WASL scores for selected sites, 2001

School	% Passing Reading WASL (66.1 state)	% Passing Math WASL (43.9 state)	% Passing Writing WASL (43.5 state)	% Passing Listening WASL (72.4 state)
Wrangle	48.8	23.3	27.9	58.1
Sandal Creek	52.7	28	43	71
East Lake	55.8	30.2	23.3	72.1
Woodland	73.2	39	43.9	80.5

Data Collection

Twenty individuals were interviewed between March and May, 2002. Interviewees included: three administrators, one administrative intern, three reading specialists, 13 classroom teachers, a counselor and a physical education (PE) teacher. Each interview lasted between 45 and 90 minutes. All of the interviews occurred within the individual teacher's classroom or the administrator's office. Following the transcriptions of the interviews and during the analysis, the initial contact person at each school remained available to answer specific questions via phone and e-mail.

The International Society for Technology in Education (ISTE) has developed frameworks that provide progressive descriptions, ranging from teachers who do not integrate technology to teachers that fully integrate technology (ISTE Homepage, 1999). These frameworks were converted into a survey and each teacher was asked to identify his or her current level of technology integration. Notes were taken during the interviews, and observations and comparisons were made between the information gathered during the interview and the teacher's reported level of integration.

Data Analysis

Each interview was read multiple times and the researcher looked for themes within each broad category. A list of themes was generated and selective sections of the interviews that corresponded to the potential themes were labeled. For the teachers, the following themes were identified: primary barriers, secondary barriers, school climate, favorite parts of teaching, frustration/needs, teaching practices, accountability and technology-specific responses.

Interviews were coded and sorted in several ways. The responses of those who had high integration scores on the technology integration survey and those that scored lower were separated for comparison. In addition, responses to both primary and secondary barriers were separated into two groups: those who saw an identified barrier as an obstacle that they could not or would not overcome; and those that were attempting to, or had overcome, the identified barrier. Patterns within and between schools were identified, including those who rated themselves high on the integration survey and those who rated themselves lower. Individual profiles for each school were developed and used to confirm the researcher's initial findings from the organizational charts.

Interpretation

After reviewing the analysis, several distinct differences and similarities appeared between the schools. Remarkably similar were the hindrances to technology integration. All barriers cited in the literature were mentioned at every school. These included: inappropriate training or in-service (Kay, 1996; Maor, 1999); collegial jealousy or pre-defined roles (Sherry & Billig, 2002; Reinking & Watkins, 2000; Wood, 2000); lack of appropriate or relevant software instruction (Becker, 2000; Rockman, 2000; Rogers, 2000; Ruberg, 1993; Sia, 1992); teachers failing to find the relevance of technology use or applications to classroom practices (Maor, 1999; Sherry, Billig, Tavalin, & Gibson, 2000; Rogers, 2000); as well as teachers having a lack of space and time within the curriculum (Cuban, Kirkpatrick, & Peck, 2001; James, Lamb, Bailey, & Householder, 2000).

What differed were the role of curricula within the school reform process, the types and uses of assessments and teachers' statements of personal responsibility for both the use of technology and for student learning. Although all of the schools had participated in school reform efforts, the connection between curricula, assessment and instruction varied. These connections and teacher statements of responsibility at the four elementary schools will be highlighted in the following section.

Curriculum, Assessment, Instruction and Teacher Responsibility for Student Learning: Looking at a Disconnect: Sandal Creek and Wrangle

A disconnect between curriculum, assessment and instruction existed in two of the four schools: Sandal Creek and Wrangle. At Wrangle, teachers were using the structured curriculum as the primary means of addressing problems with student achievement in reading. Teachers were not the decision makers when it came to reading instruction. Instead, representatives from the adopted reading program and a reading coordinator reviewed scores on a regular basis and directed adjustments. The adjustments were not generally instructional, but related to group placement. Teachers felt that they had little say in what and how to teach and were frustrated. In addition, this highly structured curriculum impacted all other school decisions.

I wish I had more time in the day to teach what we are being expected to teach, for one thing. I wish I could veer from the hard and fast philosophy we are living with now. ... I would like to branch out and be a little more creative. It is the way I used to teach. Now we have to stay with the party line. It is boring for me and it is boring for the kids. (Sixth grade teacher, Wrangle, March 28, 2002)

At the other end of the spectrum was Sandal Creek, where very little structured curricula existed. Like Wrangle, teachers at Sandal Creek were also frustrated, but because of a lack of structure.

Actually, I am sitting on a committee right now that is trying to purchase a curriculum. We are all frustrated with the hodgepodge. (Third grade teacher, Sandal Creek, May 8, 2002)

For new teachers [the reading program] is really hard. The program itself is really hard to follow, because the way it is set up, and there are two different books. It is just hard logistically because the materials that come with it, well, there aren't any ... philosophically [the teachers] like it, but it is not helpful as far as providing resources. (Reading teacher and administrative intern, Sandal Creek, May 8, 2002)

Sandal Creek had virtually no structure or connection between curriculum, assessment and classroom instruction. No curriculum existed, just frameworks. Wrangle teachers were not the decision makers, but were directed by adopted curriculum. Neither of these two schools had teachers who commented on being responsible for the actual learning of the students.

"I know there needs to be some sort of accountability ... but I wish they were less centered on the teachers ... and that the politicians who actually came up with this stuff would point their finger where the real issue is, which is in the home. (Sixth grade teacher, Wrangle, March 28, 2002)

Making a Connection: East Lake and Woodland

At the two other elementary schools, East Lake and Woodland, teachers discussed multiple types of assessments and multiple purposes for assessment. WASL scores were reviewed, but the results from this assessment were not the only measure of student success. District and classroom assessments were used to adjust instruction and determine individual student needs. Both formal and informal assessments were combined to assist in curricular decisions and teachers were expected to make decisions based on their own professional judgment.

Like I said, in major areas [the District does] have priorities where you can teach. Now the way you get there, obviously, is up to the teacher and up to your classroom. There are other teachers in our district, in our school, that don't stick closely to the adopted reading curriculum, but they do hit the major component parts of it. (Sixth grade teacher, East Lake, May 6, 2002)

... and if all [the curriculum process] has been done, the curriculum is critical; how it's adjusted and adapted and delivered to the students is totally a professional obligation and responsibility of that classroom teacher, but they need to be able to know the curriculum well enough to [know] how to adapt it. I would encourage all teachers the first year to use the curriculum closely ... They are going to have to do some adapting and they'll probably have to work with the special education teachers. We check every day on how they are doing. (Principal, Woodland, May 10, 2002)

I don't feel really badly if we don't make the [state test] because it is a different cohort. There are other conditions that apply. Certainly it is a goal for us to look at, and it certainly is one measurement, but I am more interested in looking at individual students over time. If I see that kids aren't making adequate progress in our classroom assessment, then we have to do something different, and that's going to adjust our school plan, which ultimately should result in the [state test] improvement. (Principal, East Lake, March 28, 2002)

Table 3. The role of curricula between Wrangle, Woodland, East Lake and Sandal Creek; comparison of assessments, curricula, instruction and responsibility

	Schools			
	Wrangle	East Lake	Sandal Creek	Woodland
Primary Assessments				
Classroom		X	X	X
School	X		X	X
District			X	X
State	X	X	X	X
Role of Curricula				
Highly Structured	X		X	X
Adopted Curricula and District Frameworks with Flexibility to Adjust			X	X
No Adopted Curricula and District Frameworks		X		
Teachers State Responsibility for Student Learning			X	X
Teachers State Responsibility for Technology Integration	X*		X	X
Teachers State Plans for Overcoming Barriers	X*		X	X
* Indicates a single teacher				

Assertion 1. Comparing the four schools, it appeared that when education reform efforts included the integration of curriculum, assessment and classroom instruction, such as at Woodland and East Lake, teachers were more likely to take personal responsibility for student learning. At East Lake and Woodland, curriculum, assessment and classroom instruction seemed closely connected. There was a clear understanding of both formal and informal assessments. It was only at these two schools that teachers commented on being responsible for student learning, being accountable to themselves. As one teacher stated, "It's the teacher's responsibility."

Integrating Technology with Reform and Teacher Responsibility

At Sandal Creek and Wrangle, technology remained separate from the rest of the school happenings. For example, a technology plan was being developed for Sandal Creek at the district level, as opposed to the school staff formulating the plan. Staff at both schools rarely cited efforts to overcome barriers. They blamed others for the existing barriers and individuals, and made no problem solving references to how to personally overcome an obstacle or influence policy and practice related to technology integration.

... because people aren't telling us what the research base is, so I'm just finding whatever's there and that's what I will use, but I'm not using it to teach kids with. I'm using it as like a reward for having completed whatever things they've done in the classroom, so I'm not thinking of it in terms of curriculum. It is more like ... it is not part of our curriculum, it is something extra for kids who are finished and need an extension of whatever. (Second grade teacher, Wrangle, May 7, 2002)

At both Woodland and East Lake, teachers were more likely to have mentioned having overcome obstacles to technology use. Technology use was seen as part of the total overall piece of instruction, not as something that was separate from or in addition to the existing curriculum. There had been both long-range planning and the integration of assessment with instruction. Technology had been used as a part of the process; both districts had adopted software that committees felt had supported the curriculum and classroom instruction.

I think [technology]'s supportive of the curriculum, it just depends on what you're going to use it for. (Fifth grade teacher, Woodland, May 10, 2002)

Technology is a tool. It is not to be, I mean it is not the goal, the technology is not the goal, it is the means to the end and the is ... we model this for kids ... we don't have time in the day to do those free-standing things that aren't tied directly to goals we have for student learning. (Principal, Woodland, May 10, 2002)

Assertion 2. Teachers took more responsibility for technology use when technology integration was not separate from curricula and/or reform efforts. Even if a teacher had not fully integrated technology, teachers at East Lake and Woodland made statements of personal responsibility for technology use:

It is definitely not what we have now; you know, last year I could have said we don't have great computers. But I think it is just a comfort level for me and I think I need to get in and experiment to how to use it myself and then be able to expect my kids do that, so I think it is something that will happen, maybe next year. (Third grade teacher, Woodland, May 10, 2002)

Access to Technology

The concept of homophily (Rogers, 1995) suggests that the adoption of a new technology is more likely to occur if someone similar, such as an equal colleague, introduces it or is successful at using the new technology. It was interesting to note that Wrangle was one of the schools with a disconnect between curriculum, assessment and instruction, yet had more computers per student than any of the other schools. Three of the teachers had received a total of four large grants and every teacher had at least one computer in his or her classroom. Of all of those interviewed, Wrangle also had a teacher that scored higher than any other on the integration survey. However, Wrangle had less technology use as measured by the Technology Integration Scale. The large grants received by one specific teacher seemed to have isolated her. The technology provided by the grant stayed within the individual classrooms, although the grant recipients did collaborate with each other. On the other hand, Woodland had received a large grant where the technology moved with the students. Following the initial grant year, the student took the technology, in this case portable word processors, with them to the next grade. The new teachers then began utilizing the technology because the students were accustomed to it and it was still available to them.

Wood (2000) found that teachers who were next to one grant recipient often were jealous and those with the technology were often discouraged from sharing, isolating them from their peers. This was seen at Wrangle. Teachers were often angered by the technology grant recipients who, every year, collaborated in the creation of a play. Two classrooms were involved in the development of the play and the integration of technology throughout was apparent; brochures, advertising, film editing, lights and music were all developed. One of the teachers who was interviewed and had observed the play asked the researcher to figure out, "How, exactly, does that fit with curriculum?"

Assertion 3. For technology to be used in a school, access to technology needs to be made for all. It should be noted that the literature suggests that access to technology does not guarantee that teachers will utilize it (Cuban, Kirkpatrick & Peck, 2001). At Woodland, where the lab provided ample access, some teachers still hadn't used the lab. However, even though the teachers were hesitant, they were not unwilling to try or had future plans to increase use. Once access is provided, addressing individual perceptual barriers and actual needs may be the next step. In schools where there is no access or access is restricted to specific classrooms, it seems unlikely that other teachers will seek to integrate technology.

Discussion

Schools cannot be centered solely on technology, or just assessment or curricula. Schools that become too focused on one area can neglect the others. To better understand how technology use can be supported, the school processes need to be viewed from the perspective of student learning first. What are the factors that directly influence and impact student learning? Such things as the relationship of curricula, assessment, accountability, leadership style, resources and the individual needs of the teacher need to be examined in a global context. Technology integration fits into many of the categories, but technology alone will not guarantee student learning. It is simply one factor that may contribute towards meeting student learning goals.

Two models of the diffusion of educational technology have identified that the point of rejection of a new technology occurred when teachers failed to see relevance for the learner (Sherry, Bilig, Tavalin & Gibson, 2000; Rogers, 2000). On completion of this study, it seems necessary to further define the diffusion of educational technology models so that they encompass more than one technology and provide direction related to the overall process of technology integration. Technology integration within schools must exceed the adoption or use of a single technological device or application. Most of the models of adoption take a technology-centered view. Even a holistic model presented by Dooley (2000), where internal and external factors of integration are viewed in the context of the school along with types of change facilitators, presents technology as the central focus.

Conclusion

Re-Conceptualizing the Role of Technology

The integration of technology into today's classroom needs to be viewed as an integral component of a more comprehensive package of education reform. Although the literature often uses the phrase "integrate technology" to imply that technology is to be part of multiple areas of education, including curriculum, assessment and instruction, it is often presented as the focal point or treated as a separate component. Student learning is truly at the center of education. Perhaps a more appropriate phrase would be to, "Enhance teaching and learning through the effective use of technology." Performance standards or frameworks are in place in almost every state. Curriculum and assessment should be used to inform instruction. Technology and best practices need to be examined within the context of each area of the educational system, and technology integration needs to be re-conceptualized and presented within the context of an entire school system (Figure 1).

Figure 1. Conceptualization of the role of technology

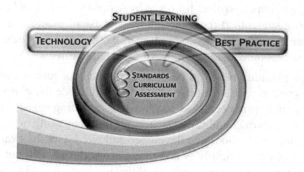

For teachers to overcome barriers to technology integration, teachers need to feel in control both of the classroom and the available technology, be able to take responsibility and have a sense of accomplishment. These three areas can be applied to the use of a single technological innovation, but can and should be applied to the broader context of a school system. Too many schools are taking away the ability for teachers to be responsible. Teachers are being given scripted curricula and are told what to teach and which assessments must be given, as opposed to being given the freedom to make appropriate choices about instruction and appropriate assessment.

Recommendations for School Improvement

Several recommendations can be made for school improvement and restructuring.

First, combine technology with other reform efforts. Make the connection between the uses of certain technologies or best practice with continued student achievement. This can take many forms; projects for increasing student learning, specific software applications for student use, appropriate assessment and continued classroom management. Isolating technology, or any other component of reform, such as curricula, creates frustrations and limits vision.

Second, schools need to have the ability to overcome multiple primary barriers. Focusing on one barrier, such as access, neglects the others. Teachers are unique, have differing skills, and need different opportunities for growth. Meeting one need does not guarantee integration; other barriers will arise and the ability to address them needs to be available for all. This includes not limiting materials and resources provided by a grant to a single classroom. This can isolate a teacher from his or her peers and create potential school climate issues. If a teacher does receive a grant, plans for future growth for other teachers within the building need to be thought through. This is the same for the students. What about those students who spend a year in a technology-rich classroom, followed by several years in a technology-poor classroom, or those students at the same grade, because of placement in a certain classroom are then denied access to computing tools? Solutions to the one technology classroom may include team teaching, or cross-age projects.

Third, long-range planning needs to be done for all school restructuring. School goals need to be created within a holistic context that include the close scrutiny of curriculum, assessment practices, how teachers are matching classroom practices with established frameworks and how teachers are implementing best practices in instruction. Building goals should be developed followed with the examination of individual teacher needs. It simply is not enough to set goals without taking into consideration different barriers that individual teachers may face. Teachers need to be active participants in the decision-making process. Student needs are more likely to be met when teachers are able to make active decisions regarding curriculum, assessment, instruction and the use of technology.

References

Adcock, S. G., & Patton, M. M. (2001). Views of effective early childhood educators regarding systemic constraints that affect their teaching. *Journal of Research in Childhood Education, 15*(2), 194-208.

Bain, A., & Smith, D. (2000). Technology enabling school reform. *Technological Horizons in Education Journal, 28*(3), 90-97.

Becker, H. J. (2000). Findings from the teaching, learning, and computing survey: Is Larry Cuban right? *Education Policy Analysis Archives, 8*(51).

Clark, R. E., & Estes, F. (1999). New directions: How to develop "authentic technologies." In R.E. Clark (Ed.), *Learning from media: Arguments, analysis, and evidence* (pp. 241-262). Greenwich: Information Age Publishing.

Cuban, L., Kirkpatrick, H., & Peck, C. (2001). High access and low use of technologies in high school classrooms: Explaining an apparent paradox. *American Educational Research Journal, 38*(4), 813-834.

Dooley, K. E. (1999). Towards a holistic model for the diffusion of educational technologies: An integrative review of educational innovation studies. *Educational Technology and Society, 2*(4). Retrieved October 17, 2001, from http://ifets.ieee.org/periodical/vol_4_99/kim_dooley.html

Education Week. (2005). *Technology counts 2005, 8th annual report.* Retrieved January 6, 2006, from http://edweek.org

Ertmer, R. A., Addison, P., Lane, M., Ross, E., & Woods, D. (1999). Examining teachers' beliefs about the role of technology in the elementary classroom. *Journal of Research on Computing in Education, 32*(1), 54-62.

Fletcher, G. (2002). Education act sets stage for technology reform. *Technological Horizons in Education Journal, 29*(7), 56.

ISTE (2000). *National educational technology standards for teachers.* United States and Canada. Eugene, OR: International Society for Technology in Education.

ISTE Home Page. (1999). Online supplement: Levels of technology implementation framework. *Learning and Leading with Technology, 26*(8). Retrieved April 16, 2002, from www.iste.org/L&L/archive/vol26/no8/supplements/moersch/table2.html

James, R. K., Lamb, C. E., Bailey, M. A., & Householder, D. L. (2000). Integrating science, mathematics, and technology in middle school technology-rich environments: A study of implementation and change. *School Science and Mathematics, 100*(1), 27-35.

Judson, E., & Sawada, D. (2000). Examining the effects of a reformed junior high school science class on students' math achievement. *School Science and Mathematics, 100*(8), 419-425.

Kalkowski, M. A. (2001). Focus on learning and technology. *Communication: Journalism Education Today, 34*(4), 19-22, 25, 27.

Kay, A. (1996). Revealing the elephant: The use and misuse of computers in education. *Educom Review, 31*(4). Retrieved November 5, 2001, from www.educause.edu/pub/er/reviewArticles/31422.htm

Labbo, L. D., & Reinking, D. (1999). Negotiating the multiple realities of technology in literacy research and instruction. *Reading Research Quarterly, 34*(4), 478-492.

Maor, D. (1999). Teachers-as-learners: The role of multimedia professional development program in changing classroom practice. *Australian Science Teachers Journal, 45*(3), 45-50.

NCES (2000). *The condition of education 2000. Quality elementary and secondary educational environments.* Retrieved October 17, 2001, from http://nces.ed.gov/pubs2000/coe2000/section4/indicators45.html

NCES (2004). Libraries and educational technology. *Digest of Educational Statistics.* Retrieved January 6, 2006, from http://nces.ed.gov/programs/digest/d04/ch_7.asp

Patton, M. Q. (1990). *Qualitative evaluation and research methods* (2nd ed.). Newbury Park: Sage Publications.

Peters, L. (2000). Joining forces: A third millennial challenge: Harness the power of educational technology to advance the standards movement. *Technology Horizons in Education Journal, 28*(2), 94-102.

Reinking, D., & Watkins, J. (2000). A formative experiment investigating the use of multimedia book reviews to increase elementary students' independent reading. *Reading Research Quarterly, 35*(3), 384-419.

Rogers, E. (1995). *Diffusion of innovations* (4th ed.). New York: The Free Press.

Rogers, P. L. (2000). Barriers to adopting emerging technologies in education. *Journal of Educational Computing Research, 22*(4), 455-472.

Ruberg, L. (1993). The impact of digital technologies on the elementary school classroom. In *Virtual literacy in the digital age: Selected readings from the Annual Conference of the International Visual Literacy Association* (ERIC Document Reproduction Services No. ED370566).

Schneiderman, B. (1998). *Designing the user interface* (3rd ed.). Reading: Addison Wesley Longman.

Sia, A. (1992, February). *Enhancing instruction through software infusion.* Paper presented at the American Technology Education Conference, Orlando, FL.

Seels, B. B., & Richey, R. C. (1994) *Instructional technology: The definition and domains of the field.* Washington, D.C.: Association for Educational Communications and Technology.

Sherry, L., & Billig, S. H. (2002). Redefining a "virtual community of learners." *Tech Trends, 46*(1), 48-51.

Sherry, L., Billig, S., Tavalin, F., & Gibson, D. (2000). *New insights on technology adoption in communities of learners.* Proceedings of the Society for Information Technology & Teacher Education International Conference, San Diego, CA (ERIC Document Reproduction Services No. ED 444 565).

Stecher, B., & Chun, L. (2001). *School and classroom practices during two years of education reform in Washington state.* Los Angeles: University of California.

Willis, J., Thompson, A., & Sadera, W. (1999). Research on technology and teacher education: Current status and future directions. *Educational Technology Research and Development, 47*(4), 29-45.

Wood, J. M. (2000). *Innovative teachers hindered by the green-eyed monster.* Retrieved March 3, 2002, from www.edletter.org/past/issues/2000-ja/innovative.html

Chapter XVIII

Perspectives on 21st Century E-Learning in Higher Education

Lalita Rajasingham, Victoria University of Wellington, New Zealand

Abstract

This chapter explores a new higher education paradigm given the changing environment that will come with the advance of globalization and the rapid development of the Internet. As economies evolve around a global network and the value of knowledge, societies rely on universities to help shape future education in an emerging knowledge society. As teachers and learners already find that they need to adapt to the presence of the Internet, university managers and administrators will need to adapt their structures, strategies, procedures and programs to deal with the processes of globalization. Based on international research, this chapter presents a vision, and a paradigm from which higher education might be constructed. The Sloan-C Five Pillars of Quality Online Education and new applications, HyperReality and Croquet, are examined as potential platforms to reframe future developments.

Introduction

In describing the concept of paradigms, Thomas Kuhn (1962), in his text, *The Structure of Scientific Revolutions,* meant "what members of a scientific community, and they alone, share" (Kuhn, 1977, p. 294) and went on further to suggest that "when paradigms change, the world itself changes with them" (1962, p.110).

Another equally important related concept as we examine changes in society is worldview—*zeitgeist*—which Michel Foucault calls an episteme, by which he means an all-encompassing body of unconscious knowledge peculiar to a particular time and place, and concludes that it is not possible for people in one episteme to comprehend the way people in another episteme think (Foucault, 1970).

Historically, higher education has seen many global paradigm shifts, with varying degrees of turmoil. The medieval university taught the word of God and began in monasteries in Europe and in temples, madrassas and churches in other parts of the world. Essentially elitist and male, it served princes and priests.

The emergence of communications technologies, especially the printing press and the railways, gave birth to industrialization and nation states. Universities moved from explaining the world in terms of God's word to become part of the structure of the industrial age, explaining reality in terms of scientific rationalism, catering for a nation's managerial and professional elite, gradually including women. This is the paradigm of national higher education that we know today. However, with the developments of the Internet, the World Wide Web, broadband, digitalization, wireless, satellite, mobile phones and new applications of virtual reality, HyperReality and artificial intelligence to build collaborative, immersive simulated environments, our children and grandchildren will face very different educational environments. Higher education is once again undergoing a paradigm shift, as technologies add new global perspectives, and universities worldwide face new challenges at a time of unprecedented demand for higher education.

Current Scan

John Daniel (1996) suggests that given the demand for higher education and the inability of conventional universities as we know them to cope, even sustaining the current level of participation in higher education and particularly the growing demand in India and China, one new major institution would need to be created somewhere in the world each week for the next 30 years. Clearly, a solution is needed that moves universities from being based on building and transport technologies, which are becoming increasingly costly, to also operate with computers and telecommunications. Students, particularly adults, seek life-long learning opportunities anytime and anywhere more convenient for their dual roles of juggling personal and professional needs.

Donald Hanna (2002) argues the need to develop greater understanding of how teaching and learning, knowledge generation and preservation, organizational design and evaluation, and leadership can all function together within a changing and increasingly competitive external environment and create new ways to respond to diversity within higher education. He approaches the challenge of access and suggests that traditional campus-based universities are opening access points through technology enhanced e-learning, and the large 'mega-universities' described by Daniel (1996) are beginning to build more robust mechanisms, including interactions among students and faculty that are both face to face and supported by advanced information and communications technologies (ICT), such as the Internet. Providing access to higher education for increasing demand, both in the developed and developing societies, remains one of the main challenges facing governments. In his paper, Poley examines this issue from the perspective of gender, poverty and race (2000).

In the United States (U.S.), for-profit universities are being established to serve working adults, and new online, virtual universities and strategic consortia are also emerging; Hanna (2002) and Poley (2000) stress the importance of leadership with vision as universities become competitive and commercialized in the age of

Table 1. Mega-universities: Basic data (Potashnik & Capper, 1998)

	Name of institution	Established	Students in degree programs [1]	Graduates per year	Budget (million dollars)	Percentage of budget from Student fees	Percentage of budget from Government grants	Unit cost [2]
China	China TV University System	1979	530,000	101,000	1.2 [3]	0	75	40
France	Centre national d'enseignement à distance	1939	184,614	28,000	56	60	30	50
India	Indira Gandhi National Open University	1985	242,000	9,250	10	42	58	35
Indonesia	Universitas Terbuka	1984	353,000	28,000	21	70	30	15
Iran	Payame Noor University	1987	117,000	7,563	13.3	87	13	25
Korea	Korea National Open University	1982	210,578	11,000	79	64	36	5
South Africa	University of South Africa	1873	130,000	10,000	128	39	60	50
Spain	Universidad Nacional de Educación a Distancia	1972	110,000	2,753	129	60	40	40
Thailand	Sukhothai Thammathirat Open University	1978	216,800	12,583	46	73.5	26.5	30
Turkey	Anadolu University	1982	577,804	26,321	30 [4]	76	6	10
United Kingdom	Open University	1969	157,450	18,359	300	31	60	50

[1] Enrollment figures vary by year between 1994 and 1996
[2] Unit cost per student as an approximate percentage of avg. cost per student for other universities in the country
[3] Central unit only
[4] Open Education Faculty only

knowledge (Poley, 2000). According to Potashnik and Capper (1998), there are 11 mega-universities, each of which enrolls more than 100,000 students per year, with a combined enrollment of some 2.8 million.

E-learning and increasing fiscal constraints faced by modern universities are introducing some new pedagogical frameworks, learning environments and stakeholder demographics. University fees turn students into customers that demand life-long education. Rectors and vice chancellors are employed as chief executives rather than distinguished scholars. Research becomes that which is funded and formulaic instead of a search for knowledge and truth. These are the early symptoms of the coming paradigm shift. A play on Harold Lasswell's Communications dictum, the question is who will teach what to whom in what channel, with what effect in the knowledge society?

It is possible that the new paradigm of higher education will be located in cyberspace, as the changes we are likely to see over the next 20 to 30 years assumes that computing technology will continue to converge with telecommunications, that cellular and digital environments will become ubiquitous, that the trend to wear information technology will continue, that we will access distributed virtual realities as we do mobile phones now and that artificial intelligence will have a growing role (Tiffin, 2004). Such developments make it possible to rethink every aspect of higher education, from curricula assessment, instructional methodology, student entry, satisfactory academic status, fees, terms and timetables within the framework of the Sloan-C Five Pillars of Quality Online Education.

Sloan-C Five Pillars of Quality Online Education

The Sloan Consortium Report to the Nation (2002), by George Lorenzo and Janet Moore, established the Five Pillars of Quality Online Education-- learning effectiveness, student satisfaction, faculty satisfaction, cost effectiveness and access-- as the values, principles and goals of asynchronous learning networks. Asynchronous learning networks (ALN) today commonly refer to 'online learning,' 'flexible learning,' 'e-learning,' 'virtual classes' and 'virtual universities,' reflecting the use of computer and Internet technologies to facilitate interactive communications between teachers and learners in an online learning environment. The Five Pillars are interrelated, and conventional universities have a long and successful history of established procedures and structures for the interaction between the Pillars (Lorenzo & Moore, 2002). However, the rapid advances in speed and power of new clusters of digital technology enable fully immersive learning environments to replicate in different locations the communications functions of the multimediated, conventional face-to-face classroom. This will impact on the interrelation between Sloan-C Five Pillars, changing how teaching, learning, and knowledge creation and dissemination—the universals of universities—will be conducted in the future.

A Universal of Higher Education: The Teaching/Learning Function

There are some critical factors that constitute higher education, the universals of a university that will not change whatever the episteme, the place, the language, the culture or the medium used. From a neo-Vygotskyian (Vygotsky, 1978) perspective, higher education is interactive communication where teachers who have graduated help learners who have not yet graduated to apply knowledge to solve real-life problems. The main difference that distinguishes e-learning from on-campus learning is that instead of bringing students and teachers together physically by means of local transport systems and buildings for face-to-face interaction, it uses computers and telecommunications to bring them together as tele-presences on the global Internet.

The Internet is still evolving and will continue to do so. Curricula designed for use in a particular institution within a particular nation and context and posted on the Internet are now open to scrutiny from a global perspective, as the professional application of knowledge increasingly takes place in a global and a local context. The conventional university system is designed and localized for the nation in which it operates, teaching people how to be doctors, lawyers, teachers and pilots in the paradigm of one particular country, and operate according to the rules, regulations, laws and language of that country.

However, with advances in the Internet, professionals need to know about international practice as they compete in the global economy. Pilots fly internationally as well as nationally. AIDS, SARS and Avian Flu know no frontiers, and doctors need to be able to collaborate internationally to deal with these pandemics. Students now compare and evaluate what is taught in other countries by using the World Wide Web, and linking in chat rooms with students from around the world. The inevitable march of higher education into a global tempo will only increase and will need curricula to match.

Globalizing Curricula

In his 1902 collection of essays on the Idea of a University, John Newman said:

A university, I should lay down, by its very name professes to teach universal knowledge. (Newman, 1996, p. 25)

Georgette Wang (personal communication with J. Tiffin & L. Rajasingham on "The Purpose of a University", November 23, 1999) suggests that the purpose of a university is to address the great issues of its time. Today, in any media in any country we are informed about tsunamis (2004), hurricanes (2005), new viruses and pandemics, genetic engineering, free trade, terrorism and the impact of technology in all human communications. These issues echo the way world problems are listed and taxonomically mapped in the Encyclopedia Plus of World Problems and Human Potential (1996). These are the great issues of our time, and they are problems of global dimensions. Global problems need cadres of professionals equipped with skills to offer global solutions.

It follows that to be effective in e-learning, higher education needs to globalize its curricula. The World Trade Organization's (WTO) General Agreement on Trade and Services (GATS) regards higher education as an information service that can be traded globally. A global trade in teaching has begun, as evidenced by the increasing number of online, virtual and e-learning courses on the Internet. However, as companies and institutions that market globally have discovered, there is more to globalizing a product than putting what works well in one country, in one paradigm and one episteme up for sale in another on the Internet.

The timely and useful book, Partnering in the Learning Marketspace (2001), foreshadows issues as education becomes global and competitive using innovative technologies. There is a growing smorgasbord of educational courses and degrees on the Internet, giving birth to a new marketspace where all our transactions—learning, business, shopping and working—are moving from place to cyberspace. "Marketspace" is a term coined by Rayport and Sviokla (1994) to distinguish the new virtual world of bits of information from the atomic physical world, and Kevin Kelly (1998) notes, "people will inhabit places, but increasingly, the economy inhabits space" (p. 94).

While the idea of a market where teachers and learners can trade is not new, the medium in which it takes place is new. As the Internet grows in power and robustness, a global trade in teaching is enabled as learners become customers and buyers, and teachers and universities become sellers of products and services in competition in the global marketspace (Tiffin & Rajasingham, 2001).

To respond to an increasingly sophisticated and market-driven learner satisfaction, academic departments in universities need to rethink, reformat and redesign their programs and structures as e-learning moves from being teacher-controlled to learner-centered, and becomes more connected with personal and professional experiences. Furthermore, learning and teaching will need to become increasingly interdisciplinary to mirror and respond to real-life problems and issues from multicultural perspectives. According to Drucker (1999, 2000) the trend is amplified by learners' desire for a 'holistic' constructivist approach to knowledge, not just from their own specialized discipline.

The tendency today is to take an existing course designed for one country and adapt it to another, with serious consequences, especially for developing countries. Often, issues of cultural relevance, language, learning styles and protocols seem intractable because of copyright and institutional intellectual ownership issues, resulting in programs and courses being mothballed, wasting scarce financial resources. What is needed is curricula design for the global market to allow societies to act global and then localize in consonance with local thinking. This has the potential to upgrade relevance of what is taught. According to Tiffin and Rajasingham (2003), with instructional design principles for Internet-based learning, basic courses that are the currency of higher education-- whatever the country-- can be readdressed from the multiple perspectives of different countries, cultures and languages to develop new curricula to match global concerns.

The process of designing, accrediting, validating and assessing global curricula is critical in the higher education paradigm. The Chronicle of Higher Education and the Times Higher Education increasingly report academics worldwide deploring declining standards as universities become businesses for profit, reducing staffing, increasing on-seat student numbers and cutting staff and student support systems. The Oxford and Cambridge one-to-one tutorials as well as the five-to-eight student tutorials that existed in many universities in the Western world have now succumbed to planned obsolescence. As staff/student ratios rise, inevitably, standards fall.

Universities historically are places where students learn how to learn and develop critical thinking skills to apply what they learn to real-life problems. If universities continue their traditional ways of measuring learning via lecture mode and in abstract, passive, relatively unconnected assessment processes such as class examinations, multiple-choice tests and other forms of memorization and recall, they will increasingly be at a competitive disadvantage (Hanna, 2002). In the knowledge society, collaboration and new construction of knowledge in culturally diverse learning environments will be the valued skills for competitive advantage.

Traditionally, it was the teacher who decided what goes into a conventional curriculum and how it will be assessed by setting and grading exams and summative measures if learning has taken place. This process has inherent flaws, because we still do not know what learning is and as yet there are no global standards by which to measure a degree, a diploma or a credit. There is no way of knowing if a degree from Peking is better or worse than one from Harvard, Heidelberg or Madras. Many countries have some kind of ranking for institutions of higher education that indicate a pecking order of prestige. Also, there are global listings that rank universities, but they do so on the basis of research, not teaching and effective learning outcomes. The report Academic Ranking of World Universities – 2005 outlines the complex issues involved in ranking universities (Liu & Cheng, 2005). In a situation where there are no standards, how can universities compete in the new business world while maintaining their universals: the creation and dissemination of knowledge for the public good?

Adam Smith wrote, "When a man has learned his lesson very well, it surely can be of little importance where or from whom he learned it" (Peacock, 2001, p. 6). The proliferation of click for a 'degree.com' tends to devalue well-designed virtual courses, such as the digital content of the Massachusetts Institute of Technology (MIT) now available on the Web.

To be successful in the new technological environment, e-learning in higher education will need to adopt a rigor in course design, accreditation and assessment, and introduce new processes and strategies beyond that which now operate in conventional institutions. This includes separating summative assessment from teaching and developing curricula in conjunction with national and international associations in the subject field, and so setting new global standards (Tiffin, 2004).

Access, Quality, and Costs: Non-Zero Sum Variables

In his thought-provoking paper, Daniel (2004) argues that sustainability as a route to development is a critical factor if open-distance education is to build on the respectability it has earned. Open and distance learning allows education to break out of the iron triangle that has constrained its impact throughout history, which Daniel describes as the vectors of access, quality and cost, where the assumption by educators and the public is that education is a zero-sum game between these variables. On this assumption, increasing access to education will lower quality and raise overall cost. Similarly, raising quality will increase costs and therefore reduce access. Daniel challenges universities to break this iron triangle and the link between quality and exclusivity in education.

While to change or not to change is no longer an option for institutions of higher learning, there are a variety of routes to making those changes, some producing greater success than others. Many of the strategies for change referenced in the current higher education literature that involve restructuring and quality management are framed around barriers to change and re-engineering processes that are not working, and begin from the perspective of cost deficit. Cost factors associated with going online are increasingly open to critical analysis, and there is a growing body of literature that addresses the issue of costing e-learning. Theoretically, cost is related to volume, and the more units produced, the lower the unit costs, thus introducing competitive trade in teaching.

Rumble (1997, 1999, 2001) suggests that any attempt to do comparative cost analysis between online education and conventional face-to face or traditional print-based distance education is fraught with complexity because it is difficult to agree on the critical variables in each educational approach, and the different interpretations of what is meant by online education. Some take it to mean asynchronous Web-based learning, and others include synchronous interactivity, and what should be included in the costs (Rumble, 2001)? In costing e-learning, Rumble includes the costs of:

1. Developing e-materials
2. Teaching students online
3. Administering students online
4. Providing the infrastructure and support within which e-education can operate
5. Planning and managing e-education.

Rumble notes that cost studies in these areas are few; in the area of e-administration within education, he found none. Furthermore, he notes that none of the studies comprehensively identify overhead costs (Rumble, 1997).

Ling, Inglis and Webster (1999) discuss costing flexible learning, providing useful comparative costing analysis between on-campus and off-campus learning and teaching environments. Further studies on the subject of costing online learning and considering the cost benefits by Daniel (1996, 2003), Mason (1998), Bacsich (1999), Jewett, Finkelstein, Frances, and Scholz (2000), and Bates (1995) posit a major economic argument in favor of distance learning that produces graduates cheaper than from a conventional institution.

E-learning based on advances in innovative technologies has the inherent capability to cope with the future escalation of global higher education, and implies the adoption of a new educational paradigm where students are empowered with teachers as advisors. There is no longer one answer, but the construction of collaborative and culturally appropriate understanding of meanings and knowledge. Universities in transition to a new paradigm need to think beyond their current norms, structures and processes, and cannot afford to withstand too many stories of institutional failures.

Changing Teacher Roles

It is the teaching profession that faces some of the greatest challenges in future higher education as teacher roles change. In 1982, Dede made a prognosis for education, suggesting a new model of teaching and learning with new teacher roles, new teacher skills, new pay scales that will be fundamentally different from the last 100 years, and it will almost be a completely new profession. He has proved to be significantly prophetic.

In a world where communications and information technologies impact on all our endeavors, universities intent on meeting the challenges of innovative technology will need to invest in staff who have the skills of designing student-centered learning in new technological environments. Many of these technologies are already emerging, providing alternate loci of learning, not to replace the conventional classroom, but as its complement.

Emerging Applications on the Wings

Virtual classes use mobile phones and laptops to link with students from anywhere at anytime and in different time zones, everyone viewing the same power points and audio and video clips during the synchronous interaction, making it possible for communication between teachers and students independent of place. Eliminating building maintenance, transportation systems and the support infrastructures that bring people to them can mean that costs go down.

3G mobiles are used as accessories in handbags, around the neck, waist or wrist watches, where students send each other pictures of where they are and what they are doing, often with far greater familiarity and sophistication than their teachers in the new cellular, digital environment. In the real world, learners are going to have to use this technology as they apply the knowledge gained from teachers to the problems they will encounter in the real world.

Information technology continues to shrink and become part of the environment. The race is on to develop the first nanofactories to introduce nanodevices in diagnostic and clinical medicine in the next 10 years. MIT has a research institute for applying nanotechnology to military purposes. It is argued that nanotechnology in higher education could introduce a future where students and teachers wear the kind of nanodatasuits that Drexler (1990) describes, where billions of interlinked nanocomputers and nanotransceivers are embedded in the fabric of people's clothes. Dressed in such smart clothing, students could step into a virtual class as they would a conventional class, only it would be a fully immersive and sensually realistic experience that improves on the conventional classrooms that students have known for the last 4,000 years. Rather than the classroom being a staid four-walled room, it could be the subject of the class--a volcano, the eye of a hurricane, a diseased heart, a Parisian catwalk or a performance of Hamlet in the Globe Theatre.

HyperReality

Some technological applications are emerging that would allow wraparound, immersive, collaborative and distributed learning, replicating the communications functions of a conventional classroom where teachers help learners to apply knowledge to problems in culturally appropriate ways.

Smart suits would give entry to HyperReality. HyperReality is the brainchild of Nobuyoshi Terashima, at Waseda University Japan. Between 1986 and 1996, Terashima led a team that developed a form of distributed virtual reality for teleconferencing he called Telesensation (Terashima, 1993). The technology allowed people who were physically present in different places to meet as telepresences to work together on a common task. Something similar was developed in the U.S. by Jaron Lanier, who calls it Tele-immersion (Lanier, 2001). Revising the concept in 1996, Terashima began working on the idea of a spatio-temporal field of communication that makes connection not only between the real and the virtual, but also between artificial intelligence and human intelligence. He called this HyperReality (HR) (Terashima, 2001).

HR is the technological capability to intermix virtual reality (VR) with physical reality (PR) and artificial intelligence (AI) with human intelligence (HI) in a way that appears seamless and allows interactive communication. Two-dimensional (2D) images from one place can be reproduced in three-dimensional (3D) VR at another place. The 3D images can then be part of a physically real setting in such a way that physically real things can interact synchronously with virtually real things. It allows people not present at an actual activity to observe and engage in the activity as though they were present. The technology will offer the experience of being in a place without having to physically go there. Real and unreal objects will be placed in the same 'space' to create an environment called a HyperWorld (HW). Here, imaginary, real and artificial life forms and imaginary, real and artificial objects and settings can come together from different locations via information superhighways, in a common plane of activity called a coaction field (CF), where real and virtual life forms can work and interact together ... What holds a CF together is the domain knowledge (DK) that is available to participants to carry out a common task in the field (Terashima, 2001).

The HyperClass

The domain of knowledge in a CF could be the curriculum of a course in higher education that could be conducted in a HyperClass. A HyperClass is a space where a conventional class is intertwined with a virtual class in such a way that virtual components can interact with physically real components. The components are people, objects and settings and the mode of interaction face to face (Tiffin & Rajasingham, 2003). The first experiments took place between Victoria University of Wellington in New Zealand and Waseda University in Japan in 1998. To the Japanese, the New Zealanders (as avatars) were virtual and to the New Zealanders, the Japanese (as avatars) were virtual. In other words, whether the participants were virtual or real depended on where they were in relation to each other. It was a form of teleconferencing where the avatars, the setting and the objects of study were 3D and virtual objects could be handled by, modified collaboratively and passed between the virtual and real people, allowing learning to take place in consonance with the learners' own cultural milieu. Although HR has still some way to go, the rate of development, particularly the increasing computer processing power and speed, suggests that in the future there will be no technological limitations to the number of centers and countries that can be linked together in a HyperClass.

Terashima's concept of HR, unlike Lanier's concept of Tele-immersion, has a further dimension. It is also a place where AI can interact with HI and enables artificial life developed in VR to cross into the physical world. So far, AI has developed logical-numerical intelligence that can be applied in clearly defined domains. This is why it is so readily adaptable to the HR device of a CF and to the paradigmatic nature of university subjects. Wherever knowledge can be expressed as a closed system with clearly defined rules and procedures, AI can be applied.

Just-in-Time Artificially Intelligent Teachers (JITAITs)

Vygotsky (1978) postulates that when a learner finds he or she cannot solve a problem by themselves, a Zone of Proximal Development (ZPD) opens. It is the role of the teacher to close that ZPD as quickly and effectively as possible, and hence the critical need to have interactive communication between student and teacher. However, today human teachers can only respond immediately to a learner during working hours and if there is only one student seeking help. In large classes, student questions have to wait until a teacher is available. In higher education, much learning is done asynchronously and students get feedback on an assignment a week or more after doing it. This is hardly an efficient way to close a ZPD. Most students have forgotten the things they found difficult. It is time for the JITAIT. As the name implies, this is an AI teacher that can be available whenever and wherever a student needs help (Tiffin & Rajasingham, 2003).

JITAITs are expert systems, effective where the domain of knowledge they address is restricted, paradigmatic and orientated toward problem solving. A JITAIT can, therefore, be an expert teacher on a subject that formed the domain knowledge of a CF in HR. JITAITs would always be ready to help any learner in the CF and would improve from each encounter with a learner, provided it received feedback from a human teacher. JITAITs could take over low-level repetitive student-teacher interactions, such as spelling and grammar checks that today are a standard component of computers, and frequently asked questions (FAQs).

JITAITs could also act as personal teachers to individual students. They could search for information, keep track of a student's individual program of study and help organize learning activities. Interlinked intelligent agents that manage schedules, meetings, e-mail and workflow are already used in office systems. The Web-based organization of programs of study taking place in universities around the world provides a framework for such a development. JITAITs could have avatar form and a personality and act as a guide and mentor in the manner of the servant-tutor pedagogues of ancient Greece, or the paper clip wizard that today pops up when not needed (or when it is needed, it is less than useful and more of an irritating distracter). But it does not mean that in the future, these agents will not become more intuitive and intelligent.

JITAITS in the Levels of Teaching

Teaching has three hierarchical levels. Lower-level activities consist of marking those parts of tests, exams and assignments that have set answers, collating marks, registering attendance and managing class schedules. Such automatic activities could be computerized to leave teachers to teach.

The middle level is that of tutoring. It is where teachers interact with students to guide their learning. It involves listening to students, comprehending the difficulties they have in mastering a subject and its application, eliciting performance, explaining and demonstrating, monitoring student practice, marking assignments, tests and exams where answers are open ended, providing detailed feedback and answering student questions. This takes up teaching time and keeps student-teacher ratios down, because it involves one-on-one or small group communications, as much of the work at this level needs human understanding, although much is very repetitive. Each intake of students asks the same questions and has the same problems, and wherever this is the case, a JITAIT can be used. So the second level could be shared between human and AI tutors. As time went by and JITAITs handled more and more FAQs, their role would increase and the student-teacher ratio could be progressively increased without lowering standards.

The upper level of the hierarchy is that of the subject specialist, the professors and professionals who have achieved academic stature through research, publications and experience and can arbitrate on content. Their primary purpose is to communicate a synthesis of the subject matter in a way that brings it up to date, places it in context and encourages students to question. They do this by lecturing. In the U.S., it is common in large universities to have such a person supported by a team of teaching assistants who do the tutoring, leaving the professor to lecture to very large classes. With e-learning, the professors could stream their lectures to the whole world, and there need be no limits to the numbers who could attend. Instead of being salaried employees, professors who could attract such numbers would be valuable property. They could relate to their universities in the way authors relate to their publishers (Katz, 1999), receiving royalties for each student taking their program.

Croquet

This is another potentially useful application. The need for designing a more responsive, collaborative, online, global, virtual university environment led Julian Lombardi and his team in the division of information technology, University of Wisconsin – Madison to develop Croquet. A multi-user 3D environment, it is a multi-institutional initiative under development at the Universities of Wisconsin – Madison, Minnesota, Kyoto and the Hewlett Packard Research Labs. Croquet is an 'overlapping windows' computer interface and represents the next step beyond today's desktop computer interface; and unlike HR, which today is dependent on proprietary software, Croquet capitalizes on open-source programming language and advanced networking capabilities available in university campuses.

According to Lombardi, the aim is a learning environment for spontaneous interaction between cross-disciplinary and cross-institutional communities of practice. Within the Croquet environment, faculty, staff and students of the participating institutions will be visible to one another (as digital avatars) and able to move quickly and seamlessly among multimedia learning resources, including 3D models, whiteboards, Web pages, video footage, flash animation, simulations, streaming video, television broadcasts and PowerPoint presentations. As in a traditional face-to-face classroom, learners will see one another 'handling' learning objects and resources, and support each other with real-time feedback. Croquet is scheduled to be commercially available in 2007 (Lombardi, 2004).

The Research Function

Another universal of higher education—the creation, dissemination and application of knowledge—is its research function that defines the nature of higher education, whatever the medium used. This is an important function of universities, to grow the economy, lift the level of innovation and help understand social needs.

Learners enter higher education from a basic educational system in which the knowledge they learn to apply is approved and sanctioned by society. However, when learners leave higher education systems and apply the knowledge they have learned to real-life problems, they discover the difference between practice and theory. A universal of higher education is learning to question received knowledge and endlessly re-address it in search of a better way. According to Tiffin and Rajasingham (2003) without this process, knowledge becomes dogma and formulaic, and education becomes training.

The essence of teaching in higher education is to encourage questioning of the knowledge paradigm. It is why higher education should be linked to research and why a JITAIT could never replace a human teacher or professor. A JITAIT can respond to

FAQs and assess assignments that already have answers, but it does so from within the logic of the paradigm. A JITAIT would not be able to deal with the contradictions that arise from problems that do not fit the knowledge paradigm. It requires a human with an open, critical mind to cope with the paradox in knowledge.

Will an institute of higher education in an e-learning environment that grows increasingly dependent on JITAITs be able to cope with the questing nature of knowledge? If a JITAIT encounters a new question from a student that it cannot answer, it passes it on to a human teacher who, in effect, programs the JITAIT to answer such a question in the future. If, however, the human teacher cannot answer the question, then he or she passes it to the content specialist; and if the specialist cannot answer, there is a basis for research. Such a system would allow interesting questions of our times to emerge, and generates the need for further ongoing research.

Conclusion

Higher education takes place in a communication system where mature learners and teachers interact so learners can apply knowledge to problems and question what they are doing. The technology that makes this communications possible is changing, and will continue to change. What will not change is the interactive communication process of higher education, where we will continue to explain, demonstrate, question and set problems, and we will do this by talking and writing, as we have been doing since the days of Pythagoras, Socrates, Confucius and Buddha.

However, within the framework of the Sloan-C Five Pillars for Quality Online Education, it is argued that e-learning in higher education has the capability to make higher education more efficient, more cost effective and more accessible, and increase student and staff satisfaction, offering a paradigm shift beyond current norms and processes. But will it improve the way we learn and teach? Just as doctors seek to understand what causes disease, educators have yet to understand what causes learning. Until we have such knowledge, we need to continue the old way of doing things face to face that has worked since classes were held in caves. E-learning in higher education will need to find an optimum mix of the old and new.

No matter how sophisticated and multimediated the virtual class, learners still strive for the soft touch of the tangibly real. Both HR and Croquet, and other technological applications yet to emerge, have the potential to signal a new paradigm of education that resonates with the Sloan-C Five Pillars for Quality Online Education for effective e-learning appropriate for the multicultural, networked global knowledge society of the 21st century.

This chapter is predicated on continued technological advances, particularly broadband infrastructures that, in many countries, are still some way into the future. But as Robert Austin and Stephen Bradley argue in their article in the Harvard Business Review, The Broadband Explosion: Thinking about a Truly Interactive World (2005), when true broadband arrives, everything will change – work, play and society. Education will not be an exception. The higher education paradigm has already begun to shift.

References

Austin, R., & Bradley, S. (2005). The broadband explosion: Thinking about a truly interactive world. *Harvard Business School Working Knowledge,* September 12.

Bacsich, P. (1999, October 25-27). Planning and costing virtual universities. Proceedings of the Euro-Med Conference on Technology in Learning Environments, Tel Aviv.

Bates, A. (1995). *Technology, open learning and distance education.* London: Routledge.

Daniel, J. (1996). *Mega-universities and knowledge media: Technology strategies for Higher education.* London: Kogan Page.

Daniel, J. (2003, November 7-9). *Mega-universities: Mega-impact on access, cost and quality.* First Summit of Mega-Universities, Shanghai, China. Retrieved September 11, 2005, from http://portal.unesco.org/education/en/ev.php-URL_ID=26277&URL_DO=DO_TOPIC&URL_SECTION=201.html

Daniel, J. (2004, June 9). *The sustainable development of open and distance learning for sustainable development.* Proceedings of the Commonwealth of Learning Institute Strategies for Sustainable Open and Distance Learning, Canada. Retrieved September 9, 2005, from www.col.org

Drexler, E. (1990). *Engines of creation.* London: Fourth Estate.

Drucker, P. (1999). The shape of things to come. In F. Hesselbein & P. Cohen (Eds.), *Leader to leader: Enduring insights on leadership from the Drucker Foundation's award winning journal.* San Francisco: Josey-Bass.

Drucker, P. (2000, May 15). Putting more into knowledge. *Forbes Magazine, 165,* 84-88.

Encyclopedia Plus of World Problems and Human Potential (4th ed.) [CD ROM]. (1996). Union of International Associations. Munchen; New Providence; London; Paris: K.G. Saur.

Foucault, M. (1970). *The order of things.* New York: Pantheon House.

Hanna, D. (2002). Building a vision for the future: Choices, challenges and leadership for universities. *Oxford Roundtable.* Oxford: Oxford University.

Jewett, F., Finkelstein, M., Frances, C., & Scholz, B. (2000). *Estimating the cost of courses, interpreting the results, drawing conclusions.* American Council on Education: Oryx Press.

Katz, R. N. (1999).Competitive strategies for higher education in the information age. In R.N. Katz & Associates (Ed.), *Dancing with the devil: Information technology and the new competition in higher education.* San Francisco: Josey Bass.

Kelly, K. (1998). *New rules for the new economy: 10 radical strategies for a connected world.* New York: Penguin.

Kuhn, T. S. (1962). *The structure of scientific revolutions.* Chicago: University of Chicago Press.

Kuhn, T. S. (1977). Second thoughts on paradigms. In *The essential tension: Selected studies in scientific tradition and change.* Chicago: University of Chicago Press.

Lanier, J. (2001). Virtually there. *Scientific American,* April 1.

Ling, P., Inglis, A., & Webster, L. (1999). *Costing flexible learning.* Retrieved September 15, 2005, from www.celts.monash.edu.au/assets/ other/costing-flexible-learning.pdf

Liu, N.C. & Cheng, Y. (2005). *Academic ranking of world universities – Methodologies and problems.* Institute of Higher Education, Shanghai Jiao Tong University. Retrieved September 12, 2005, from http://ed.sjtu.edu.cn/rank/file/ARWU-M&P.pdf

Lombardi, J. (2004, November 18). Croquet. Interview with author. Madison: University of Wisconsin, Information Technology Division. Retrieved December 1, 2004, from www.opencroquet.org

Lorenzo, G., & Moore, J. (2002). *Five pillars of quality online education.* The Sloan Consortium Report to the Nation. Retrieved September 8, 2005, from www.sloan-c.org/effective/pillarreport1.pdf

Mason, R. (1998). *Globalising education: Trends and applications.* London: Routledge.

Newman, J. (G. Sampson, Ed.). (1902). *Newman's university sketches.* London: The Walter Scott Publishing Co. Ltd.

Newman, J. (1996). *The idea of a university.* New Haven: Yale University Press.

Peacock, A. (2001). How necessary are universities? In F. M. Turner (Ed.), *Journal of the Institute of Economic Affairs, 21*(3), 6-11.

Poley, J. (2000). Global access to learning: Gender, poverty, and race. In D. Hanna (Ed.), *Higher education in an era of digital competition: Choices and dhallenges* (pp. 239-255). Madison: Atwood Publications.

Poley, J. (2000). Leadership in the age of knowledge. In D. Hanna (Ed.), *Higher education in an era of digital competition: Choices and challenges* (pp. 165-181). Madison: Atwood Publications.

Potashnik, M., & Capper, J. (1998). *Distance education: Growth and diversity.* Washington: World Bank. Retrieved June 12, 2004, from www.worldbank. org/fandd/english/0398/articles/0110398.htm

Rayport, J., & Sviokla, J. (1994). Managing in the marketspace. *Harvard Business Review*, November-December, 141-150.

Rumble, G. (1997). *The costs and economics of open and distance education.* London: Kogan Page. Retrieved September 15, 2005, from www.iec.ac.uk/resources/e_education_costs.pdf

Terashima, N. (1993, December 10). *Telesensation – A new concept for telecommunications.* Proceedings of the TAO First International Conference on 3D Images and Communications Technologies, Tokyo.

Terashima, N. (2001). Definition of HyperReality. In J. Tiffin & N. Terashima (Eds.), *HyperReality; Paradigm for the third millenium.* London: Routledge.

Tiffin, J. (2004, November 17). *E-learning in higher education: Toward realizing the vision.* Keynote address to the National Institute of Multimedia Education (NIME), Tokyo.

Tiffin, J., & Rajasingham, L. (2003). *The global virtual university.* London; New York: Routledge.

Vygotsky, L. S. (1978). *Mind in society: The development of higher psychological processes.* Cambridge: Harvard University Press.

Chapter XIX

Guiding Our Way:
Needs and Motivations of Teachers in Online Learning Modeling Responsive Course Design

Kathleen P. King, Fordham University, USA

Frank J. Melia, Fordham University, USA

Marlene D. Dunham, Howard Everson & Associates, USA

Abstract

Increased accountability for student outcomes among teachers led to an examination of the needs and motivations of 324 K-12 educators who participated in 6-week on-line professional development (PD) modules of study. This research was conducted through focus groups and an online survey. The most telling findings indicate four themes regarding teacher online PD: learner expectations, learner support and access, incentives and content. This project illuminates issues that arise in formal education online learning environments as we continue to discover how to best serve educators' learning needs. This two-step study uses surveys and focus groups to empirically identify critical factors in instructional design and implementation. It benefits from large samples and the application of knowledge derived from Group A experiences to Group B. Follow-up research of 944 participants at year four of the project provides additional insight into technology use and motivation.

Introduction

Accountability means teachers must implement standards-based instruction and raise student achievement. The Anytime Anywhere Learning PD School (AALPDS) partnership developed a distance learning PD model to address this problem as it was emerging on the United States (U.S.) national educational horizon in the year 2000. Today, in 2006, it is clear how this need extends to the classroom, as teachers and schools, faculty and educational institutions face increased and incessant demands to integrate technology into teaching and learning, raise student test scores, and meet or exceed academic and content-area standards. This robust distance learning development, training and research project spans the years 2000-2005 and explores how online PD can offer a valuable vehicle for convenient, 24 hours-a-day/7-days-a-week access to a PD community and content that can address these challenges. Timing for the field of education to learn how online learning and hybrid learning can help advance these needs is at a critical stage.

AALPDS is an extensive online course delivery system of multiple 6-week courses. Each course passes through stages of development, implementation, evaluation and revision in a cycle of continual improvement. This distance learning project was funded by a U.S. Department of Education Fund for the Improvement of Postsecondary Education (FIPSE) Learning Anytime Anywhere Partnership (LAAP) grant.

The project set out to (1) design a system of PD that applies current national standards of PD, (2) adapt PD courses to local standards of learning, and (3) increase the capacity of local educators to implement and evaluate their own school-based PD programs. The strategy was to use emerging distance learning technologies to scale up the PD efforts required by standards-based accountability demands. By using Web-enabled technologies, the AALPDS project sought to relieve participating school districts from the burden of creating the PD courses, managing the technology—the networks and systems—needed to deliver the instruction. The earliest phase was directed at organizational alignment and restructuring, and was followed by a more extended period of course development and online implementation. The project created AALPDS, which served educators in 32 states even as the project evolved.

This project is distinctive because of its focus on the needs of teachers as adult learners, the development of local and distant learning communities, and unique content in the areas of standards-based teaching, online learning, adult learning and high-performance classrooms. The online courses consist of instructor-guided, interactive, asynchronous formats that present in-depth material, promote the application of technology-based learning in teachers' classrooms and facilitate teachers' critical reflection and collaboration in online threaded discussions and group projects. The project sought to assist experienced as well as new teachers in the implementation of high-quality, standards-based instructional programs in a climate of increased national, state and local demands for improvement and accountability.

Since the project's inception in 2000, and going live with its first class in March 2001, we have experienced many changes in partnerships and a significant formative reorientation of our direction and implementation.

While the primary goals of the PD school have remained the same, the path of implementation has shifted based on formative evaluation data collected through online surveys and focus groups. For example, the survey data showed that the 8-week duration of the first series of online modules was too long to sustain learner participation. Online learners stated a preference for shorter modules as evidenced by the higher completion rates with the 6-week format. With the collaboration of the entire project team, all of the modules were revised into 6 weeks, leading in turn to subsequent revisions in plans for additional courses and content. It is from this perspective that this chapter offers a discussion of two especially important research questions: What characterizes the strength of this distinctive online learning format? and What needs do teacher education and PD face within online learning environments?

Literature Review

In considering the needs of educators in online PD, two areas of the literature in particular inform our discussion: PD from an adult learning perspective and distance education. The project built on a unique framework and depth of understanding that adult learners would respond to; a system that recognized PD is a valuable opportunity for building reflective perspectives and practice.

PD

In considering the needs of educators in their ongoing PD, one salient perspective is to recognize them as adult learners (Cranton, 1996; King, 2002a, 2005; Lawler & King, 2000). The growing literature in this area brings to the forefront characteristics of adult learners that are especially meaningful in cultivating a climate of respect, building on prior experience, learning for application, encouraging active participation, using collaborative learning and empowering participants (Lawler & King, 2000). These broad principles are then interpreted for and applied to the PD context more specifically.

Rather than focusing on "skills" and "methods," the approach envisioned learning opportunities that evaluates the past, looks at new possibilities and carefully develops approaches to teaching and learning that incorporate new learning and perspectives. Online learning formats were designed with this perspective and incorporated Web-based bulletin boards and online journals as tools for in-depth individual contemplation and group dialog about teaching, learning, philosophy and practice (Beyerbach & Walsh, 2001; Hawkes, 2001; King, 2001, 2002c; Paloff & Pratt, 2001; Twigg, 2001).

The climate in which educators work is critical in forming perspectives of teaching and learning. When educators work within an environment in which they are highly valued and in which they are addressed as professionals, they can develop responsibility for and invest time in their PD. Intrinsic motivation is a stronger determinant of success than extrinsic rewards, and can be communicated through the organization, individual relationships and the manner in which PD is planned and delivered.

Similarly, building on prior experience enables educators to scaffold their learning and advance in thought and practice while validating their expertise (Lawler & King, 2000). This approach emphasizes transfer of learning and immediate application while also encouraging reflective practice.

Such learning is well received when educators interact with the content and one another through multiple instructional strategies (King, 2002b). Collaborative learning offers one way to cultivate this interaction with experience, content and application and build opportunities for reflection, application and dialog, which can becoming increasingly "transformative learning opportunities" (King, 2005). Online learning is increasingly used to foster collaborative discussions and can be used to explore and develop ideas and application (Simonson, Smaldino, Albright, & Zvacek, 2003).

Ultimately, these adult learning strategies can move PD initiatives towards empowerment of educators. Rather than PD stopping when an in-service program ends, educators have the opportunity to continue learning both individually and together when their organization supports and validates their learning, experience and collaboration.

Several authors build on this view of educators as adult learners to recognize that PD is a valuable opportunity for building reflective perspectives and practice (Brookfield, 1995; Cranton, 1996; King 2002a). Rather than focusing on "skills" and "methods," the approach envisioned learning opportunities that evaluate the past, look at new possibilities and carefully develop approaches to teaching and learning that incorporate new learning and perspectives.

Online learning formats were designed that incorporated this perspective and included Web-based bulletin boards and online journals as tools for in-depth individual contemplation and group dialog about teaching, learning and philosophy, and practice (Beyerbach & Walsh, 2001; Hawkes, 2001; King, 2001, 2002c; Paloff & Pratt, 2001; Twigg, 2001).

Distance Education

With the advent of online learning via Internet, and specifically the World Wide Web in the early 1990s, a new wave of possibilities emerged for distance education (Eastmond, 1995; Palloff & Pratt, 2001; Simonson et al., 2003). Instructional design concerns took new capabilities of user-friendliness, and interactivity emerged. The Web's graphical interface, increased options for Internet connections and decreased costs of Internet-ready computers played important parts in building a base of users who could engage in online learning.

Building on the view of educators as adult learners, critical issues that emerge in this literature are climate, expectation, experience and interactivity. The widespread adoption of the Web as a major source of information, news and entertainment has brought the use of the Internet into the mainstream. This culture and climate of online dependency is critical in introducing and sustaining the viability of online learning. In the corporate sector, a large portion of PD is being moved to distance modalities and, more specifically, online (Berge, 1998). Online learning platforms are likely to foster such collaborative discussion and can be used readily to facilitate further exploration and development of ideas and application (Hawkes, 2001; King 2002c, Simonson et al., 2003). The emerging instructional technology of online platforms held out the promise of fostering positive climates for learning, raising teachers' expectations of themselves and their students, and providing an environment for richer interactive learning experiences (Alexander & Boud, 2001).

These dynamics create expectations within organizations and among individuals that need to be addressed in online learning programs. The literature has shown that online learning usually takes considerably more time than learners expect and, despite their experience with using online resources for other purposes, until they engage in online learning, learners do not fully comprehend the dynamics, possibilities and responsibilities (Palloff & Pratt, 2001).

Additionally, experience and interactivity can be incorporated successfully in online learning. These issues necessitate careful planning that considers a variety of online instructional strategies, pedagogical issues, learner needs and program/course objectives (Palloff & Pratt, 2001). Online learning offers opportunities to draw out learner experience in not only instructor-learner dialog, but also peer-to-peer dialog (King, 2002b). Indeed, these limits and interactivity can be extended so far that educators and learners alike may need to set boundaries for their own participation (Palloff & Pratt, 2001).

All of these dynamic possibilities have continued to develop a challenging pathway for online learning and workplace training as the possibilities and limitations of this multifaceted, still evolving delivery mode is experienced, pressed to new limits and tested under new changing educational, economic, technological, sociological and political conditions. This discussion serves as a brief representation of the wide base of support for this research as it approaches online learning from adult learning principles, online technology, distance learning and PD.

Methodology

This research integrates two modes of data collection—focus groups and online surveys—within a mixed, quantitative and qualitative design (Creswell, 2003). This mixed design allows researchers to include a broad base of participants, as in the online survey (N=324), and also to explore a greater depth of experience through qualitative methods, such as questioning techniques in focus groups (N= 13, 8). Findings that are particularly relevant to faculty teaching, evaluation and development are presented here. This research and development project consisted of two phases over its first 2 years, according to the method and type of information collected.

During Phase One, the first 8 months, findings were discussed informally and frequently, and adapted as appropriate into project design. Phase Two began in the 9th month, as data collection became more routine and project management shifted from a development phase to a schedule of project coordination and monitoring. In Phase One, focus group findings were based on participant experience with one course offered at the earliest part of the project. During Phase Two, data were gathered through focus group findings and the online survey.

Online Survey. The more quantitative study consisted of an online survey. The 128-item online survey was voluntarily completed by learners within the 4th-6th weeks of their online course. Learners were notified when and how to access the survey by course facilitators. Respondent identity is kept confidential through passwords devised by each participant through a set formula that utilizes their user name. Then, one program administrator who does not have access to the responses of participants forwards those passwords to the evaluator, who accesses the responses without knowing who the participants are. The survey is a combination of multiple choice, Likert items, and free responses that cover nine broad topics: demographics (7), satisfaction (4), motivation (23), course and course impact (45), online learning (23), technology experience (2), access (12), barriers (5) and contacts (7). This chapter focuses on the data collected from 34 items concerning demographics, satisfaction and motivation.

We instituted a Web-based survey that enabled us to utilize learner feedback to modify and adjust the program of courses to better meet the needs of teacher learners. The survey was developed by the external evaluation team, with a review and revision process that included input from program directors and course content specialists. Pilot testing of survey questions were distributed to the first focus group in person and via e-mail. A survey response rate of 33% (N=324) was achieved from among those who completed the courses.

Participants. All participants were enrolled in the project courses. Contact with the largest group of participants was primarily through the Web-based online survey, because courses are available to any educators in participating districts or who are members of Classroom Connect's total learner community (80,000 Web visitors annually). All courses were delivered exclusively online.

Survey. Among the 324 participants, 287 were female and 35 male. Regarding background, 279 were self-identified as White, 13 as African American, 8 as Hispanic and 5 multiethnic. Teaching experience of the participants ranged from 0 to 16 years and more: 100 had 16 or more years, 149 had 6 to 15 years, 65 had 1 to 5 years; and 2 had no teaching experience. For 102 (31.5%) respondents, this was their first online course.

Based on responses to descriptors in the survey, participants identified themselves as follows: 158 (48.8%) early adopters—first to try something new; 152 (46.9%) like to try technology after it's been tried by others; 7 (2.1%) resist using technology; and 7 (2.1%) no response. Additional findings includes 207 (63.9%) who describe themselves as advanced technology users; 85 (26.2%) with some experience; and 25 (7.7%) as beginners. Furthermore, 32 (9.9%) were enrolled in a degree program and 11 (3.4%) indicated that the course was part of the requirements for that program.

The majority of survey respondents were female (88.6%) and non-minority (86.1%). The majority also lived in suburban communities 168 (52%); 65 (20.1%) had more than 21 years of professional educational experience, and nearly two-thirds, 201 (62%), held a master's degree. Less than one-fourth of the respondents, 77 (23.8%), lived in rural areas and less than one-fourth lived in an urban location 71 (21.9%). Studies indicate that there is a large economic and racial gap between users and non-users of the Internet, and our respondent demographics appear to confirm this gap for our online learners (Burdenski, 2001).

Focus Groups. Two focus groups were conducted by the project evaluation team at two critical points in the project: (1) at the initial implementation phase, and 2) when the project had been underway for 9 months. These on-site focus groups were conducted in the learners' school communities and included refreshments. Major differences between the two sessions were evident at these different points in time: first, the format of the session; and second, the availability of course offerings (as a result of maturation/development of project). The first focus group of 13 teachers occurred when they had been exposed to the first online course available (1 month after the project began in March, 2001). The 2-hour afternoon session consisted of a presentation by the project director, followed by an open question-and-answer session. The project evaluator was present and distributed written surveys at the close of the session. Data were gathered through observation and notes by evaluator and journal notes of the project director. The session was held at a local community college, in a major urban area.

The second focus group of eight learners occurred in the evening at the district office in a large suburban district. Over 3 hours, discussion revolved around 15 questions developed by the district coordinators of the program. Discussion was audiotaped. The project evaluator recorded the discussion by question and tabulated responses.

Focus Group One. Thirteen participants (all female) attended the first focus group, among which 10 were African American, 1 Hispanic and 2 white. Eleven had taught for 16 or more years. Although they were all "technology" teachers, all had far less technology experience than teaching experience. Most had less than 5 years' experience in technology and rated themselves as "no experience," beginners and limited experience. This course was their first online course. All the teachers had been required by their school or district to participate in the PD activities. All were required, by the district administrator, to come to the focus group.

Focus Group Two. Ten participants, 9 females and 1 male, attended the second focus group. They were invited to the focus group by the district administration, but not required to attend. Ethic identification was 2 African American and 8 White. The group represented various positions in five district schools and the district office: one was a high school computer teacher; one worked in the high school guidance office, three were elementary teachers, three were experienced media or resource specialists working in two elementary schools, two were district technology coordinators. Their range of technical expertise extended from "needing help with e-mail," resisting using technology to experienced. For half of the group (5), this was their first online course, as they had been selected by their district to participate and were characterized by intrinsic motivation, curiosity and determination.

Analysis. Objective survey responses were tabulated and coded for frequencies, percentages and correlations. Focus groups and discussion board transcripts and survey free responses were coded by constant comparison, as themes were determined from the data and then the data tabulated and grouped within those themes (Creswell, 2003). Gathering data from several sources provided a broad view of the online experience among these educators.

As commonly used in mixed design research, the multiple sources of data provide support for the validity of the data (Creswell, 2003). Survey items consisted of attitude scales and open-ended free-response answers. The focus groups and discussion boards served to validate the survey responses, as these participants had participated in both modes and the responses could be compared to one another. Construct validity of the survey instrument was a priority for the survey designers, as each section had multiple items relating to the construct being used to ensure fit with the purposes of the survey and the population being surveyed. Hypothesized relationships among different sections of the survey instrument were tested with empirical observations in focus groups. Items covered both negative and positive responses; for example, the items about assistance in accessing the computer was balanced by items about barriers to access. Both items had write-in responses, also.

The internal consistent reliability of the rating scales were tested using coefficient alpha, showing reliability of .8581. Both validity and reliability were priorities for the instrument designers, and several items were written and some items were not used after pilot results were evaluated. The online survey system prevented redundancy of respondents because individual, unique, single-use passwords had to be developed for each participant each time they took a course, thereby preventing any individual learner "stacking" the responses with multiple entries.

Procedures. All teacher responses in the data collection process are coded and remain anonymous, and responses regarding individual teacher demographics, teaching experience and teacher opinion are kept confidential. Prior to completing the online survey, participants are informed that the project courses are being studied to assist in course development and to learn more about online learning. Learners may decline to participate without negative consequences.

Findings and Discussion

Four major themes emerged as the data from the focus groups, online surveys and hybrid classes were analyzed. The subjects and topics that occurred repeatedly in each method of data collection were: (1) learner expectations, (2) learner support and access, (3) incentives, and (4) content. Each theme will be discussed within the context that they were gathered.

The focus groups provide the best indication of the effects on the adult learner of district-mandated implementation of online PD programs. The first focus group discussions centered on obstacles to participation and effective implementation in District A, shedding light as to the practicability, usability and efficacy of a district-required, online PD program The second focus group, District B in the suburbs of a large metropolitan area, provided information after 9 months of implementation. District B's district technology coordinator facilitated teacher participation, assuring familiarity with school organization and procedures. This embedded familiarity was critical to the pre-implementation stage to correct assumptions about teacher motivation and usage, and was influenced by changes made as a result of District A's feedback.

Two tables summarize findings from the focus groups. Table 1 captures the differences in both the individual characteristics of focus group participants and the differences in district implementation and support of the online learning courses. Two contrasting district styles as well as two dissimilar groups of learners emerge in Table 2. Although the focus groups are not comparable, the findings help describe characteristics of successful implementation for both the adult learner and the dis-

Table 1. The learner in the district

Implementation in Two Districts: Comparison of Focus Group Learner Characteristics and Support Provided by District		
Learner Background	**District A**	**District B**
Previous online learning experience	None	50% had previous experience
Learner attitude and motivation	Felt imposed, not enough time, already too busy	Privileged, honored, curious, personal growth motivation
Technology experience/Proficiency	All were inexperienced	Moderate and advanced experience (50%)
Computer access	50% had computers a home. All had computers at work.	All had computers at home. All had computers at work.
Web-based learning style	Not comfortable reading screens; download and print all information	Comfortable reading screens; sets priorities/identifies materials to download
District/School Support Provided		
Online learning policy implementation strategy	A district mandate: Teachers required but not enforced	Invited. Level of implementation varied by school
Introduction of system, initial and continuing communication to teachers	Severely limited. District level only.	Better at district level; varied by school
District support team providing ongoing support to teachers at implementing sites	Inactive and inexperienced	Active and experienced
Training to use system	None	None
Goals and follow-through	Unclear	Goals and follow-through set by district.

Table 2. Summary of themes that emerged in the focus groups

Needs for Successful Implementation of Online Instruction for Adult Learners in the Public School Setting		
Learner Expectations	**District A**	**District B**
Materials and content: relevance to professional work	Perceived as interesting, but not relevant	Perceived as relevant and interesting
Perception of time required	Took more time than expected	Courses varied; some took more time than others
Reason for not completing course	Time, lack of meaningful incentives, did not know how to use, not relevant	Courses more work than expected; would be easier fit into schedule; too much reading; too much intensity
INCENTIVES		
Incentive/Reward for participation	None felt by participants	Identified by participants
SUPPORT		
Communication, training and support	Severely limited; teachers on their own	Better, but teachers still on their own
Use of support provided: Web, e-mail, toll-free telephone	None used; some deleted pertinent e-mails, not knowing they were about the class	Used support

trict/school. We need to remember that these are results for two unique districts and we need to exercise caution in generalizing these themes.

Learner Expectations

Learner expectations prior to and during the courses surfaced repeatedly in the focus groups and were directly influenced by district/school/administrator communication about the program, the learner's level of technical proficiency and lack of experience with online courses. The context raised issues of technology placement and use; the social networks that developed between and among teachers and school leaders; and the timeframes, budgets and incentives governing use of the PD programs in the schools.

In District A, sometimes information was mis-communicated or not communicated, leading to unrealistic expectations for learners. For example, the purpose and expectations of participating in the courses was incorrectly conveyed to the teachers by district administration. Communicating accurate information to learners was difficult for the Web-based course deliverers, whether by the technical team or the course guide/facilitator. Many of the learners were novice technology users whose lack of understanding led them to repeatedly delete e-mails without reading them.

In District B, participating teachers included resource coordinators and teachers from different schools in the district. Communication was handled better and learners felt "honored and privileged" that they were asked to participate. The level of basic technology skills and lack of understanding about online learning was not an issue for most of these teachers. However, sometimes teachers (even those who had taken previous online courses) found the workload to be greater than expected. This mismatch of expectations may be seen in District B, where learners, although highly motivated, sometimes found they could not continue a course.

Learner Support and Online Access

The need for learner support is multifaceted and far-reaching in online PD. The focus groups indicated the need for ongoing district support for adult learners in mandated PD programs, especially when the users are novices in technology and online course-taking. The focus groups revealed the lack of district support in these areas: (1) a clearly articulated initial introduction with explanatory materials, and (2) a continuous PD program that follows up with teachers, troubleshoots and resolves problems. If such a support system had been in place in District A, teachers may not have been deleting e-mail due to lack of training. During focus group, it was the research team (not the district) that was able to determine (from participants) that greater technical expertise was needed among the learners. This valuable information focused our recruitment for participants and further support efforts, but it was too late to prevent the frustration in District A. In District B, training in how to submit online projects might have prevented the loss of a learner's paper and subsequent frustration.

In an online learning system that is not district based, learner support is primarily provided by the technical online course team. A district's support of an online learning program should include initial communication, training and follow-up with participating learners. Even though these courses included online, e-mail and toll-free telephone support, the novice learners still struggled greatly, including problems with the course registration process.

Discussion with teachers from District A revealed that teachers were unaware of the extent of the Web site and the course offerings, even though they are using the system. District A teachers demonstrate the need for ongoing structured and formalized support and training in the basics of how to use the system. When these novice learners were further oriented to the online course environment and Web site, they expressed greater interest in continuing and learning more.

Incentives

The role of incentives emerged as one of the most important needs among educators in this environment. Intrinsic incentives as well as extrinsic incentives need to be included, based on learners' comments. Online learning takes such great a time commitment amidst such overburdened teacher schedules that there has to be great motivation to pursue such efforts.

The most favored extrinsic incentive mentioned in the focus groups was financial, followed by academic credit incentives, such as graduate credit, continuing education units (CEUs) or certification that would result in financial rewards, and public or professional authority recognition for work accomplished. Teachers expressed that they are motivated by a combination of incentives, including personal and professional incentives, such as the desire to use technology and apply learning to their classrooms, and developing the content standards knowledge that would result from course participation.

District A is an example of how incentives affected the direction of the initiative, as the teachers would not gain financially (salary increments). The primary incentives were personal knowledge gain and CEUs. The learners made it very clear that personal knowledge was not sufficient. In District B, all the learners were interested in implementing new technology and saw enrolling and completing the course as a personal goal. The focus groups provide evidence that teachers lacking intrinsic and extrinsic motivation withdrew from participation.

For some teachers, personal satisfaction and learning are enough, but for others, incentives ought to include a combination of indirect or direct financial rewards. In other situations, the learner is a source of his or her own support and motivation. Without district mandates, incentives and support, teacher perseverance to complete the course was dependent on personality style, time management and learning style. District B's focus group tended to be interested in implementing new technology and they set enrollment and completion as personal goals. District A teachers felt the program was imposed on them as a district goal – not an individual goal-- and combined with their lack of technology skill, they were not able to get as much out of the courses. Personality style and learning style vary, as learners appear to be very individualistic and idiosyncratic. We have more to learn about how variation in learning style impacts course completion.

Content

In online learning, the role of course content is critical, particularly that it is perceived by the learner as interesting and, even more importantly, relevant to the learner's professional work. Content surfaces as a priority because the learning experience relies so heavily on the course itself rather than spontaneous discussion, explanations or sample examples and applications. Both focus groups clearly illustrate that the curriculum content must satisfy the needs of learners or it will lose them.

District A was eager to begin, and enrolled the technology teachers in the first available course, Introduction to Online Learning. However, the learners were not interested enough in the content area, seriously hampering their continued involvement. Consistent with characteristics of other adult learners, these teachers wanted a course that could directly apply and immediately relate to their teaching in the classroom.

In contrast, District B began to participate when the project was almost a year underway and knew the entire scope of courses available. Several teachers in the District B focus group had participated in two or three courses, and were planning to participate in more, as they were quite enthusiastic about the courses with standards content. As they expressed, it was the first time they were able to see standards information presented in an organized and helpful manner.

Teacher needs and content need to match in a district implementation, as the choice of who is offered participation must match the courses being offered. District A used novice technology teachers instead of teachers who would be directly involved with implementing standards in the classroom. District B selected technology and resource teachers and teachers involved with implementing standards in the classroom. As additional districts have participated, they were informed of the recommendations below as ways to encourage greater participation and course completion.

Teachers and administrators face many demands in our high-stakes assessment climate. Even as many stakeholders remain critical of public education, this model of PD offers opportunities for new and veteran teachers to improve their effectiveness and meet some of these demands. For example, the threaded Web boards of each course enable teacher/learners to share their insights and expertise across the nation as they develop and increase their own knowledge and skills.

Summary

We learned much about personal online experiences and district support systems for online learning from the participants in the focus groups. These adult learners were located in specific district PD implementation projects. Next, we look at the respondents to the Web-based survey, who are adult learners primarily from the larger Connected University (CU) community. They are not connected to a specific district and the primary way of contacting them is via the web.

Online Survey

From the 324 survey respondents, we compiled a profile of the successful learner in these courses. Though respondents comprise a non-diverse group, we are presented with the opportunity to increase the diversity of learners online. Online educators and learning providers should consider addressing the needs that surface in the emerging profile of the potentially successful learner: (1) diverse learner expectations, (2) learner support and online access availability, (3) incentives, and (4) rigorous content. Each of these areas is discussed in depth below.

Learner Expectations

Many potential and participating online learners have false preconceptions of online experiences. The reality is that quality online learning takes a substantial investment of time: Learners spent 140 minutes every time they logged in. Most respondents allocated minutes: 20 minutes reviewing assignments; 10 downloading information; 30 searching the Internet; 30 reading the forum; 15 posting on the forum; 30 working on course project and reading e-mail; and 5 reading public postings. Learners logged onto the course every week and 42.9% (139) said they logged in "once every few days." Just more than 100 (105, 32.4%) said they logged in every day, and 114 (35.2%) respondents thought the course took more time than they expected. Very few, 13 (4.0%), thought it took less time than they anticipated. As

Table 3. Professional experience of respondents to AALPDS online surveys

Years of Professional Education Experience	% Total Respondents
One to five	19%
Six to ten	26%
11 to 15	20%
16 to 20	14%
21 or more	18%

shown in Table 3, survey respondents came to the online format from a wide range of professional experience.

Learner Support and Online Access Availability

We find that the potentially successful online teacher-learner needs to be a self-directed learner, self-disciplined and have minimum technology proficiency of Internet searching, e-mail skills and Internet usage. In our initial survey of 324 teacher-learner participants, almost three-quarters, 237 (73.2%), reported they had had 3 or more years' experience with computers, and almost half of the respondents, 149 (46.0), had 6 or more years' experience. About half of the learners, 158 (48.8%), described themselves as "early adopters who are one of the first to try new programs or software." Only a small percentage, 7 (2.2%), said, "they resist using technology," and when they rated their technology expertise, two-thirds, 207 (63.9%), said they were "intermediate" and just more than one-fourth, 85 (26.2%), rated themselves as "advanced." Less than 10%, 25 (7.7%) said they were "beginners." When self-direction, self-discipline and comfort with technology are not present, numerous problems arise that may become insurmountable and learners may drop out of their course.

In a follow-up survey taken about 1 year later, the base of teacher learner participants expanded to 944. This larger group responded to the same question about classroom-based usage of computers, and the results are shown in Table 2. It is

Table 4. Experience using computers in the classroom

Years Using Computers in Classroom	% Total Respondents N=944
0-2	10%
3-5 years	26%
6 plus years	62%

Table 5. Motivating factors (N=944)

Motivating Factor	% of Total number of respondents
Topics are of interest to me.	88%
More convenient (time-wise) than attending a college or university. Convenience was a motivating factor, as many of the respondents said they had families and were looking for time-saving learning options.	83%
Thought it would be intellectually challenging.	83%
Thought it would be rewarding to communicate with other professionals across the country.	71%
Thought the course would be fun.	72%
Wanted to meet interesting people in my class.	38%
Required as part of my program/school.	19%
Live in a location where access to PD is difficult.	22%

interesting to see that with the passage of time and the increased experience level of those responding, it appears that the more experienced the teachers, the greater the use of computers in the classroom. This also may reflect the increased market penetration of computer technology in schools.

In that same follow-up study of 944 teacher learners, we asked teachers what motivated them to enroll in an online PD course; the responses are summarized in Table 5. Though convenience appeared to play an important role, interest in the topics and the intellectual challenge appear to be almost as important factors. School or program requirements did not motivate more than one-quarter of respondents. It is also interesting to note that the potential remoteness from PD did not draw much more than one-fifth of the learners.

The focus groups indicated that lack of very basic technology proficiency made simple instructions and Web interface daunting. What the developers had defined as "basic skills" was considered intermediate-advanced skills to most of these teachers in 2000-2002. Of course, these definitions are dictated somewhat socio-historically, culturally and geographically and are changing rapidly, so in 2005 our definition of a novice user is different still. The lesson learned is to enumerate the skills needed.

While we do not know the economic status of our learners, we do know that 212 (96.3%) had computers at home, 299 (92.3%) had classroom access and 275 (84.9%) had access to a school computer lab. The most frequent responses regarding barriers that prevented them from accessing the course were: "personal time issues" (241, 74.4%) and "slow computer connections" (119, 36.7%).

Finally, regarding support and access, home computers appear to be the almost universal commonality of all the learners. We suggest it is essential for the successful online learner (Palloff & Pratt, 2001). When we combine these findings with the demographic profiles of our learners, it raises questions about equity and access, including attention to the economic issues of hardware, software and Web connection fees.

Incentives

We learned much about intrinsic incentives from the survey. The third most-frequent response regarding motivation was convenience (269, 83.0%). The most frequent write-in responses were convenience (112/227, 40.4%), freedom (54, 19.5%) and flexibility (46, 16.6%). The most frequent reward for posting in the Web-based asynchronous forum was that online peers were interesting and engaging (306, 94.4%); secondly, it was rewarding to communicate with peers across the country (290, 89.5%); and thirdly, they enjoyed positive feedback (286, 88.3%).

Content

Fourth, substantial and relevant content is needed in developing online courses. Educators and other Internet users look for courses that have new information, perspectives and application. The AALPDS courses are in several areas, including content areas of reading, writing and mathematics at three levels: K-2, grades 3-5 and grades 6-8. Another area is courses about creating high-performance classrooms, and courses were added in science, grades 3-5; social studies grades 6-8; educational technology; and online learning.

Tying back to motivation, educators, like other adult learners (Brookfield, 1995, King, 2002a), look to learn what they can use in their work, their classroom. Most of the respondents (291, 89.9%) were motivated to enroll in the course by intellectual challenge (277, 85.4%) as a secondary motivating factor. Two hundred twelve (65.5%) believe an online course is more current and 175 (54.0%) believe an online course is more interesting compared to other types of PD. About one-third, 109 (33.6%), believe these courses are more rigorous than other types of PD.

These findings demonstrate how online teacher PD confirms the centrality of felt needs and relevance. Focusing online course content can guide online PD efforts and resources. Courses will draw teacher learners if they hold promise for providing rich, interesting and relevant content, as well as offering means of learning that are more easily personalized, flexible and adaptable to learner needs. The findings demonstrate how online teacher PD courses—developed around clear content and taught with rigor—can strengthen the centrality and relevance of PD efforts and investments.

Recommendations

Online PD programs can benefit from building on the strengths of this program. Seven major recommendations are offered here.

1. **Clarity of expectations:** Online developers need to be familiar with district school procedures and expectations to prevent communication issues that may hinder effective implementation.

2. **Intrinsic motivation:** District and teacher motivation are often two separate issues, and mutually agreed-upon goals must be reached for teacher-ownership. For some teachers, personal satisfaction and learning are enough; but for others, this must be combined with either an indirect or direct financial reward. This is especially the case in highly formalized settings in which any activity out of the "contract" may be tied to a demonstrable incentive.

3. **Supports are needed to enhance technology skills:** District initiatives should provide both initial and ongoing opportunities to extend and support teachers with fewer technology skills. An introduction to the use of computer technology may be an appropriate enhancement for novices interested in adapting technology for their learning. Even teachers in the position of "technology teacher" may need more technology expertise.

4. **Using content as a powerful motivator:** Addressing felt needs of teachers in content supports intrinsic motivation by offering a variety of courses, especially courses that directly apply to the classroom.

5. **Exploring collaborative learning further:** To maximize online PD efforts, local support and collaborative groups would be beneficial. Hybrid models support teachers as learners by incorporating face-to-face sessions in support of online components.

6. **Building on the momentum of Leave No Child Behind (NCLB) legislation and initiatives:** This project stands as an example of the benefits of the scalability of delivering high-quality, instructor-led, online courses on the subject of standards-based curriculum and focused on teaching practice.

7. **Teaching, learning, technology and research:** Each decade brings new discoveries, curricular innovations, technological breakthroughs and philosophical favorites; this project, and others like it, demonstrate how teaching, learning, technology and research can be used to assist educators in the future.

References

Alexander, S., & Boud, D. (2001) Learners still learn from experience when online. In J. Stephenson (Ed.), *Teaching and learning online* (pp. 3-15). Sterling: Kogan Page.

Berge, Z. (1998). *Distance training.* San Francisco: Jossey-Bass.

Beyerbach, B., & Walsh, C. (2001). From teaching technology to using technology to enhance student learning. *Journal of Technology and Teacher Education, 9*(1), 105-127.

Brookfield, S. D. (1995). *Becoming a critically reflective teacher.* San Francisco: Jossey-Bass.

Burdenski, T. K. (2001). Web-based data collection. *The APAGS Newsletter, 13*(2), 19.

Coomey, M., & Stephenson, J. (2001). Online learning: It is all about dialogue, involvement, support and control – According to the research. In J. Stephenson (Ed.), *Teaching and learning online* (pp. 37-52). Sterling: Kogan Page.

Cranton, P. (1996). *Professional development as perspective transformation.* San Francisco: Jossey-Bass.

Creswell, J. W. (2003). *Research design* (2nd ed.). Thousand Oaks: Sage.

Eastmond, D. (1995). *Alone, but together: Adult distance study through computer conferencing.* Cresskill: Hampton.

Hawkes, M. (2001). Variables of interest in exploring the reflective outcomes of network-based communication. *Journal of Research on Computing in Education, 33*(3), 299-315.

King, K. P. (2001). Professors' transforming perspectives of teaching and learning while learning technology. *Journal of Faculty Development, 18*(1), 25-32.

King, K. P. (2002a). *Keeping pace with technology, Vol. 1: The promise and potential for K-12 educators.* Cresskill: Hampton Press.

King, K. P. (2002b). Identifying success in online teacher education and PD. *The Internet and Higher Education, 5*(3), 231-246.

King, K. P. (2005). *Bringing transformative learning to life.* Malabar: Krieger.

Lawler, P. A., & King, K. P. (2000). *Planning for effective faculty development; using adult learning strategies.* Malabar: Krieger.

Murphy, D., Walker, R., & Webb, G. (Eds.). (2001). *Online learning and teaching with technology.* Sterling: Kogan Page.

Palloff, R., & Pratt, K. (2001). *Lessons from the cyberspace classroom.* San Francisco: Jossey-Bass.

Passig, D. (2001). Future online teachers' scaffolding. *Journal of Technology and Teacher Education, 9*(4), 599-606.

Simonson, M., Smaldino, S., Albright, M., & Zvacek, S. (2003). *Teaching and learning at a distance: Foundations of distance education* (2nd ed.). New York: Pearson.

Stephenson, J. (Ed.). (2001). *Teaching and learning online: Pedagogies for new technologies.* Sterling: Kogan Page.

Sujo de Montes, L. E. (2000). Been there, done that: Reaching teachers through distance education. *Journal of Technology and Teacher Education, 8*(4), 351-371.

Twigg, C. A. (2001). *Innovations in online learning: Moving beyond a significant difference.* Troy: Center for Academic Transformation.

Endnote

The project has continued to mature after this study was completed. More learners have completed the courses, and additional programmatic results were realized. Revisions to the text reflect these facts with insights regarding (1) needed PD incentives, (2) changes in content, (3) recommendations that link to current trends in education, and (4) recommendations regarding research and technology innovation.

This research and development project was a partnership funded by a U.S. Department of Education FIPSE/Learning Anytime Anywhere Partnership (LAAAP) grant to develop and extend innovative capacity for online teacher PD. It began in 2000 and has served more than 2,000 educators across the U.S. as of December 2005. Additional information may be found through Fordham University's Regional Educational Technology Center, www.retc.fordham.edu.

Chapter XX

Quality of Online Learning Applications:
Impact on Student Enjoyment, Motivation, and Anxiety

Leping Liu, University of Nevada, Reno, USA

Abstract

The purpose of this study was to explore the influence of the design-quality of current online K-12 learning applications on student learning via three learning-related variables (student enjoyment, motivation and anxiety level when using those online applications). Nine hundred online K-12 applications (WebQuests, online drills, games, tests and other applications) were evaluated in terms of four design factors (quality of information, design of information, quality of technology use and design of technology use) in relation to the three learning-related variables. Three prediction models were generated and tested in this study. An intermediate effect was found between the design of online application and student learning, which may provide some insights for teachers when they integrate online applications into teaching and learning. The target audience of this chapter may be school teachers, designers or professionals who use online applications for educational purposes.

Introduction

The Internet has been used in many ways to promote teaching and learning (Aviv & Golan, 1998; Barnard, 1997; Berge, 1997; Coombs & Rodd, 2001; Lengel & Lengel, 2006; Thorsen, 2006), from the use of Web-based resource to the employment of Web-based instruction (Berge, Collins, & Dougherty, 2000; Bonk, Cummings, Hara, Fischler, & Lee, 2000; Cunningham & Billingsley, 2006; Fishman, 1997; Miller & Miller, 2000; Riel, 1992; Trentin, 2001). In the literature, one common use of the Web in K-12 teaching and learning appeared to be the utilization of existing online learning applications, such as tutorials, drills, games or video products developed and posted onto the Web by other educators or designers (Clark & Jorde, 2004; Glazer, 2004; Hillman & Moore, 2004; Liu, 2001; Lombard, 2004; Murphy, 2004; Perkins & McKnight, 2005; Shelly, Cashman, Gunter, & Gunter, 2003; Stvan, 2005). It is hard to imagine and estimate the number of learning applications available on the Web today: A Google search on "math game" resulted in 691,735 items; and a random exploration on 10 links found that on average, 25 to 35 online math games were under each link.

Unfortunately, the effectiveness of using those online learning applications on student learning achievement was ambiguous (Maddux, Ewing-Taylor, & Johnson, 2002). In a study that consisted of 102 technology integration cases, Johnson and Liu (2000) found that the use of existing Web activity did not significantly contribute to either the success of the technology integration or student learning outcome. The issue is that if the use of those online applications could not effectively improve learning, such tremendous amount of resources would be a huge waste, and sometimes may cause confusion.

Many studies have explored the possible causes of such unsatisfied use of the Web, and suggested that a lack of design was one common weakness in educational applications, such as online communication, online course and online instructional content or activity (Liu & Maddux, 2003; Liu, 2003; Schweizer, Whipp, & Hayslett, 2002; Boer & Collis, 2001). The purpose of this study is to explore the influence of the design quality of current K-12 online learning applications on student learning.

In this chapter, first, the definitions and major types of K-12 online learning applications are introduced. Next, variables examined in this study are identified, including four design-related variables that are derived from a technology integration model (Liu & Velasques-Bryant, 2003; Liu & Johnson, 2003a, 2003b), and three learning-related variables that have been found to have direct impact on learning achievement (Liu & Johnson, 1998; Liu, Maddux, & Johnson, 2004). The four design-related variables are then used to evaluate the quality of 900 online K-12 learning applications in relation to the three learning-related variables. At the end, a set of quality-related models that illustrate the relationships are generated and tested.

Literature Review

Online Learning Applications

In the context of current study, the term *online learning application* can be defined as *any entity of instructional contents or activities delivered through the Web* that has the following features:

1. It intends to teach a focused concept
2. It meets specific learning objectives
3. It provides a learner-centered context
4. It is an individual piece that can be used and reused.

The concept of *learning application* in this chapter is very much similar to that of a widely discussed term—*learning object*, besides that a learning object is an object-oriented application (Barker, Winterstein & Wright, 2004; Murphy, 2004; Dodero, Aedo, & Diaz, 2002). The author carefully chose not to use the term *learning object,* because some learning applications examined in this study were not object-oriented, and could not concisely fit the definition of a learning object.

Types of Online Learning Applications

A learning application can present learning content, provide learning activity, contain simulation or allow for student assessment. Generally, types of online learning applications can be sorted by format and function.

Two major formats of online learning application are: (a) hypertext-format, and (b) hypermedia-format. Hypertext-format learning applications are developed with HyperText Markup Language (HTML) or other hypertext editors. Examples include WebQuests, online lecture notes, reading materials or other text-based instructional materials. There are two types of hypermedia-format learning applications: One type includes applications developed directly with scripting language, such as HTML, DHTML, XHTML or JAVA; incorporating with multimedia products, such as graphics, animations, video or audio clips. The other type includes those initially developed with multimedia authoring software, such as Flash, Director, Authorware, ToolBook or HyperStudio. They are converted to a Web run-version, and then published onto the Internet. Examples can be online games, drills, tests or video products.

Two major functions of current online learning applications are: (1) providing information, and (2) providing interactions. Some applications are developed to provide content information or guidelines to learning activities, most of which are hypertext format. Some dynamic Web activities or those pre-designed multimedia instructional programs are developed to carry out interactions, which enable users to interact with the learning application directly from the Web. Currently, more and more online learning applications tend to have both functions.

To select an appropriate online learning application for students, teachers may want to consider whether its format and function fit the learning objectives, content structures, the nature of activities or the grade level of the students. The selection is usually based on the design-related quality of the application.

Design of the Study

Design-Related Variables

According to a design model Liu and Velasques-Bryant (2003) summarized from a review of 20 years' research and practice in the field of technology integration, successful design of a technology-based instructional application should reflect the *merging* of three components: information, technology and instructional design. Based on this model, four variables are identified to measure the design-related quality of an online learning application:

1. **Quality of information:** Evaluates the quality of content information (e.g., the accuracy, clarity, currency or verifiability of the contents).

2. **Design of information:** Measures the extent to which instructional design components are integrated into the content (e.g., audience analysis, content analysis, assignment design and delivery, assessment implementation, or the match between the required thinking skill and the developmental stage of the targeted audience).

3. **Quality of technology-use:** Measures the quality of technology applied in the learning application (e.g., screen design, orientation, navigation or interactions).

4. **Design of technology-use:** Examines the extent to which instructional design principles are integrated into the use of technology (e.g., the match between content information and the media use or delivery methods, or the match between required technology skill and the grade level of targeted audience).

All online learning applications in this study were evaluated with these four design-related variables in relation to three learning-related variables.

Learning-Related Variables

Research findings suggest that student learning achievement is influenced by three variables: enjoyment, motivation and anxiety (Liu, Maddux & Johnson, 2004; Liu, 1999; Liu & Johnson, 1998). Students tend to have better performances and higher achievement scores when they enjoy learning (Temple & Lips, 1989; King & Bond, 1996), are motivated to learn (Kellenberfer, 1996; Clariana, 1993; Keller, 1983) or feel less anxious to learn (Liu, 1997; Ayersman, 1996). This study examined these three learning-related variables in terms of how students feel about using an online learning application:

1. **Enjoyment:** Measures the degree to which a student enjoys learning with an online application

2. **Motivation:** Measures the extent to which a student is motivated to learn with an online application

3. **Freedom from anxiety:** Measures the anxiety level of a student when he or she learns with an online application.

According to the purpose of this study, the three learning-related variables were examined to determine an *intermediate effect,* as described in the following logic procedures.

Underlying Logic of the Study

This study was designed to explore the relationships among: A) the design-quality of an online learning application, B) learning-related variables, and C) student learning achievement. The underlying logic of current study follows the three steps:

1. We have known that B influences on C (from literature)
2. If we can determine that A influences B (to be determined), then
3. We can conclude that A can influence C via B (conclusion).

Based on this conclusion, we say that B is the intermediate *variable* between A and C; and the influence "transferred" via B between A and C is the *intermediate effect.* In other words, knowing that learning-related variables influence learning achievement, if the quality of learning applications influences the learning-related variables, we can conclude that the quality of the learning applications influence learning achievement indirectly, and therefore, an *intermediate effect* exists. This is a method known as *detecting intermediate variable or effect* in educational research (Liu, Maddux & Johnson, 2004). In this study, only the second step was examined.

Research Questions

The research questions for this study were:

1.   Can *enjoyment* (the degree to which a student enjoys learning with an online application) be predicted by any of the four design variables?
2.   Can *motivation* (the extent to which a student is motivated to learn with an online application) be predicted by any of the four design variables?
3.   Can *freedom from anxiety* (the anxiety level of a student when he or she learns with an online application) be predicted by any of the four design variables?

Methodology

Samples

The sample of this study was 900 online K-12 learning applications on the subject areas of arithmetic, algebra, geometry, reading, writing, science, Spanish, history, geography and social science. They were WebQuests, instructional materials, drills, games, tests and instructional video clips. More than 92% of the WebQuests and instructional materials were hypertext information; and more than 86% of the drills, games and tests were hypermedia applications with online interactions.

Of the 900 online learning applications, 375 (see Table 1) were selected by 75 graduate teacher education students, from six classes of an introductory technology course in a western state university from 2002 to 2004. The other 525 applications (see Table 2) were selected by 105 graduate teacher education students, from four classes of an introductory technology course and four classes of a design course in an eastern state university from 1999 to 2002. The distribution of the subject areas and the types of applications are shown in Tables 1 and 2.

Table 1. Online learning applications evaluated at the Western site

		Types of Learning Application							
		WebQuests	Instructional Materials	Drills	Games	Tests	Videos	Other Activities	Total
Subject Areas	Arithmetic	12		14	16	10			52
	Algebra	10		12	13	3			38
	Geometry	8	1	6	12	2		1	30
	Reading	14	8	5	5	9	1	1	43
	Writing	5	2	15	15	5	4	1	47
	Science	6	3	11	18	6	4		48
	Spanish	10	2	15	3	8	1		39
	History	5	5	12	4	2	4		32
	Geography	4		5	8	3	1		21
	Social Study	5	5	7	6	2			25
	Total	79	26	102	100	50	15	3	375

Table 2. Online learning applications evaluated at the Eastern site

		Types of Learning Applications							
		WebQuests	Instructional Materials	Drills	Games	Tests	Videos	Other Activities	Total
Subject Areas	Arithmetic	24	5	8	18	10		1	66
	Algebra	10	2	8	8	7			35
	Geometry	8	1	16	10	5			40
	Reading	21	4	18	11	8	2	1	65
	Writing	19	3	16	12	10	2		62
	Science	10	4	15	16	12	1		58
	Spanish	20	5	11	10	8	2	1	57
	History	12	3	12	9	10	1	1	48
	Geography	9	6	11	10	8			44
	Social Study	23	5	7	9	6			50
	Total	156	38	122	113	84	8	4	525

Procedures

The author was the instructor of all three courses in the two universities. In the introductory information technology course, students learned basic computing skills and the strategies of technology integration. In the design course, students learned theory and design of computer-based instruction, and created multimedia instructional segments using authoring tools such as Director or ToolBook.

Data were obtained from a technology integration project required for all three courses. In completing this project, each student (referred to as a *mentor*) first located a K-12 student at any grade level (referred to as a *protégé*). Together, they then determined five learning objectives in one to two subject areas.

After the objectives were determined, the mentor needed to select five online learning applications. He or she was required to do a thorough search on the Web, evaluate seven or more K-12 online learning applications using the design-quality instrument (Appendix A), and determine five applications consistent with the learning objectives.

The mentor then developed five lesson plans. He or she was required to create five learner-centered activities with the use of the five online applications. The instructor provided an instructional worksheet for the mentor to design those learning procedures and activities, which ensured that the major components and procedures of instructional design were included.

The protégé followed the lesson plans, interacted with the five online applications, performed the five activities and completed the assigned learning tasks. Simultaneously, the mentor observed the learning process, and scored the performances in terms of the protégé's enjoyment, motivation and anxiety level toward each online application (using the instrument in Appendix B).

By the time the technology integration project was completed, each mentor had evaluated five online applications and observed the protégé's performances on five learning activities. Therefore, he or she had collected 10 sets of data: five sets of quality evaluation scores on the online learning applications, and five sets of observation scores on the three learning-related variables.

The same procedures were repeated in all classes involved in this study from the two universities. All data were coded and saved for data analysis.

Instruments, Measurements and Scoring

As described above, two instruments were used in this study: The four design-related variables (*quality of information, design of information, quality of technology-use* and *design of technology-use*) were measured by a Likert-Style instrument (Appendix A) consisting of 32 positive statements sorted into four categories, with eight statements in each category. The eight statements in each category measured one design-related variable. Each statement was scored from 1 (strongly disagree) to 5 (strongly agree). The score for each variable was the sum of eight statements, and the highest possible score was 40. Higher scores represented better qualities of a learning application. The reliability coefficient alpha for this instrument was 0.826 from current study.

The three learning-related variables (*enjoyment, motivation and freedom from anxiety*) were measured by another Likert-Style instrument (Appendix B) consisting of 18 statements sorted into three categories, with three positive statements and three negative statements in each category. The six statements in each category measured one variable. The answer for each statement must be chosen from: strongly disagree (SD), disagree (D), undecided (U), agree (A) or strongly agree (SA). For the positive statements, the score for answer SA was the highest (5 points) and for SD was the lowest (1 point); for negative statements, reversely, the score for answer SD was the highest (5 points) and for SA was the lowest (1 point). The score for each variable was the sum of the six statements, and the highest possible score was 30. Higher scores indicate a more positive approach toward the use of an online learning application. The reliability coefficient alpha for this instrument was 0.832 from current study.

The seven variables were qualitative variables. In this study, they were measured quantitatively with the scoring method described above. The Likert scaling implied that each of the items had the same "level of difficulty." That is, respondents found them equally easy or difficult to endorse. The reliability coefficient alpha values (0.825 and 0.832) indicated that each instrument did reliably measure each variable, and the scores were "reasonably reliable for respondents like those in this study" (Green & Salkind, 2003, p. 315).

Data Analysis and Results

Data analysis was performed in two phases. In the first phase, the *western-data* (data from the western state university, N = 375) were used to perform multiple regression analyses in developing the prediction models. In the second phase, the *eastern-data* (data from the eastern state university, N = 525) were used to test the prediction models with paired *t* tests.

Data exploration plots showed that the assumptions of normality and equal variance were not violated, and no extreme outliers were found in the two sets of data.

Phase One: Model Development and Results

The western-data (N = 375) was used in three multiple regression analyses to develop the prediction models in correspondence with the three research questions. The four design-related variables were treated as predictor variables, and regressed to each of the three learning-related variables.

Results from the First Regression Analysis. In the first regression analysis, the predictor variables were the four design variables: *quality of information* (QI), *design of information* (DI), *quality of technology use* (QT) and *design of technology use* (DT); and the response variable was *Enjoyment* (E).

In the first run that included the four predictor variables, linear model was found significant ($F_{(4, 374)}$ = 96.373, $p < 0.0001$), but one predictor variable—QI—was found not significant to the model ($t = 0.664$, $p < 0.507$). Therefore, the next run only included the other three variables: DI, QT and DT. The results showed as the following

The linear regression trend was significant ($F_{(3, 374)}$ = 128.546, $p < 0.0001$). The F ratio indicated that the linear model was the desired model that represented the data better than other regression models. The t statistic for each predictor variable was significant: DI ($t = 2.296$, $p < 0.022$), QT ($t = 5.491$, $p < 0.001$) and DT ($t = 5.339$, $p < 0.0001$), indicating that all three variables significantly contributed to the variation of the response variable E. R-Square of the model ($R^2 = 0.510$) indicated that around 51% of the variation of the response variable E could be explained by this model, or by the variation in the three design-related variables.

The regression analysis generated a set of coefficients that were used to formulate the *Regression Equation 1*:

E = -3.088 + 0.335(DI) + 0.105 (QT) + 0.342(DT)

According to this equation, a one-unit increase in DI, for example, would increase 0.335 units on the E score.

Results from the Second Regression Analysis. In the second regression analysis, the predictor variables were the same three design variables: DI, QT and DT, because QI was, again, found not significant to the model ($t = 0.222$, $p < 0.825$). The response variable was *Motivation (M)*. The results showed as the following:

The linear model was significant ($F_{(3, 374)}$ = 128.546, $p < 0.0001$), and the three predicator variables significantly influenced the response variable M, because the t statistics for all three variables were significant: DI ($t = 6.241$, $p < 0.010$), QT ($t = 2.259$, $p < 0.010$) and DT ($t = 5.179$, $p < 0.0001$). R-Square of the model ($R^2 = 0.539$) indicated that around 54% of the variation of the response variable M could be explained by this model, or by the variation in the three design-related variables. The regression analysis generated a set of coefficients that were used to formulate the *Regression Equation 2*:

M = -4.098 + 0.398(DI) + 0.123 (QT) + 0.324(DT)

According to this equation, a one-unit increase in QT, for example, would increase 0.123 units on the M score.

Results from the Third Regression Analysis. In the third regression analysis, only two predictor variables were included: DI and DT, because QI ($t = 1.413$, $p < 0.153$)

and QT ($t = 0.071$, $p < 0.944$) were found not significant to the model. The response variable was *Freedom from Anxiety (FA)*. The results showed as the following.

The linear model was significant ($F_{(2, 374)} = 174.435$, $p < 0.0001$), and the two predicator variables significantly influenced the response variable *FA*, because the t statistics for both variables were significant: DI ($t = 3.689$, $p < 0.010$) and DT ($t = 8.056$, $p < 0.0001$). Around 48% ($R^2 = 0.483$) of the variation of the response variable *FA* could be explained by this model, or by the variation in the three design-related variables. The regression analysis generated a set of coefficients that were used to formulate the *Regression Equation 3*:

$$FA = -3.299 + 0.259(DI) + 0.531(DT)$$

According to this equation, a one-unit increase in DT, for example, would increase 0.531 units on the score of *FA*.

The data analyses generated three prediction models, illustrated by equations 1, 2 and 3. The three models were then tested in the next phase.

Phase Two: Model Testing and Results

The *eastern-data* (N = 525) were used to test the three prediction models; that is, to examine whether the three models and the relationships developed from *western-data* (N=375) could be used to predict the relationships in the *eastern-data*.

To test the first model (Enojyment), for example, first we calculated the predicted values of *E* using *Regression Equation 1* (generated from the *western-data*) with the raw data in the *eastern-data*, through four steps:

1. Opening the *eastern-data* file from Excel

2. Creating a new column named "predicted enjoyment scores" next to the column that coded the original raw scores of *E*

3. Adding a calculation function on to this new column according to *Regression Equation 1*: $E = -3.088 + 0.335(DI) + 0.105 (QT) + 0.342(DT)$. In the calculation function, exact column names for the three predictor variables (DI, QT and DT) were used correspondingly. For example, in the datasheet, if the three variables were in columns C, D and E, then the function added into the first cell of the new column should be "$=-3.088 + 0.335*C1 + 0.105*D1 + 0.342*E1$"

4. Copying this function onto all the cells in the new column. All the calculated values then appeared in this new column, which were the predicted *E* scores.

Second, we tested the enjoyment model (expressed in *Regression Equation 1*) by examining whether there was any difference between the *predicted* values and the original *observed* values of the variable *Et*. If there was no difference, this model developed from the *western-data* had successfully predicted the relationships in the *eastern-data*.

Using this model testing method, we calculated the predicted values of the three response variables: *E, M* and *FA*. In addition, three paired *t* tests were conducted to compare the predicted values and observed values of each variable. Results showed that there was no difference between the predicted values and the observed values for each of the three variables: E ($t_{(524)} = 0.108, p<0.914$), M ($t_{(524)} = 0.403, p<0.687$) and FA ($t_{(524)} = 0.011, p<0.991$). The results indicated that these models could reliably predict the relationships between the quality of online application design and how students feel about using the applications.

The three prediction models have been tested and confirmed, and they can be summarized into the three model functions:

E = f **[DI, QT, DT]**	-----------------------------------	(1)
M = f **[DI, QT, DT]**	-----------------------------------	(2)
FA = f **[DI, DI]**	-----------------------------------	(3)

f [   ] indicates a significant linear relationship ("a linear function of …")

Function 1 reads "The extent to which students enjoy using the online learning applications is a linear function of the three design-related variables-- *design of information, quality of technology-use* and *design of technology-use*." Functions 2 and 3 can have the similar interpretation.

Conclusion and Discussions

In summary, the three research questions have been answered, and three prediction models have been generated, tested and summarized into three model functions. Following the underlying logic of the research design, we may conclude that an *intermediate effect* has been found: the design-quality of online learning applications may have impact on student learning via its influence on students' enjoyment, motivation and anxiety.

Specifically, when the content materials of the applications were accurate, easy to understand, consistent with the grade level, designed in a learner-centered approach to engage critical thinking and closely related to the learning tasks; and when the application provided a clear layout, interesting interface, easy navigation, convenient assistance information, active interaction and bug-free running time, the learners would feel more delighted, inspired and less nervous to learn with the online applications. Therefore, they could have better performance and higher learning achievement.

According to the three prediction models, a learner's *enjoyment* and *motivation* were influenced by the *design of information, quality of technology-use* and *design of technology-use*; and his or her *anxiety* level was influenced by the *design of information* and *design of technology-use*. The variable *quality of information* was not significant to any of the three learning-related variables. This does not mean that the variable *quality of information* is not important. One possible cause to the insignificance of this variable may be that all the mentors may have chosen applications with high quality of information presentation and, hence, the variation within this variable was not large enough to make any difference among the scores of the response variable.

The author believed that the sampling of the online applications and the methods of model development had strengthened the study. The 900 learning applications were on the Web over the past 5 years and covered a variety of subject areas, formats and functions. They were evaluated and selected by mentors from two geographical areas in the United States. They should reflect the current trends of online applications. The model development involved two sets of data. The models were generated from one set of data and then tested in the other, which demonstrated the reliability of the models.

Limitations of the Study

The author also realized some limitations of the study. First, this study aimed at the overall quality of online learning application design. The author did not conduct in-depth analyses to compare the quality of specific types of learning applications, analyze the quality of specific items under each design-related variable or examine the quality of the applications by different designers. All the information had been collected, and further analyses will be conducted to explore those details.

Second, the first step in detecting the intermediate effect was based on the literature. In this study, the author did not analyze learning outcomes of the protégés in relation to the three learning-related variables (enjoyment, motivation and anxiety level). To provide a complete picture of the intermediate effect, the impact of the learning-related variables on student learning achievement will be examined with first-hand data in further studies.

Third, the mentors were students from the classes that the author taught over the past 5 years, and the protégés were chosen by the mentors. Although a total of 180 mentors and 180 protégés were not a small sample, they were not randomly selected from the two states. This may influence the generalization of the findings. Therefore, a careful statement may be made that the results and findings best explained the situation within the context of this study, and they may be used as references by other educators and researchers.

Fourth, the measurements for motivation, enjoyment and anxiety were based on the mentor's observations and interactions with the protégé, not responses directly from the protégé him or herself, which may raise a potential issue whether these scores accurately reflected the protégé's feelings. The study was designed to have the mentor score the three variables because, most of the time, teachers were the ones who selected learning applications for their students. They should see how their students interacted with the applications and what kind of applications was appropriate for the students. Analyses based on the teachers' observation would be a meaningful reference for other educators' teaching practice.

This chapter has taken an initial step in developing those models. The author hopes that other educators and researchers could apply or test these models in their practice, and conduct further studies to revise the models with their new findings.

References

Aviv, R., & Golan, G. (1998). Pedagogic communication patterns in collaborative telelearning. *Journal of Education Technology Systems, 26*(3), 201-201.

Ayersman, D.J. (1996). Effects of computer instruction, learning style, gender, and experience on computer anxiety. *Computers in the Schools, 12*(4), 15-30.

Barker, S., Winterstein, A. P., & Wright, K.E. (2004). Tools for creating e-learning: Learning objects. *Athletic Therapy Today, 9*(1), 10-15.

Barnard, J. (1997). The World Wide Web and higher education: The promise of virtual universities and online libraries. *Educational Technology, 37*(3), 30-35.

Berge, Z. (1997). Computer conferencing and the online classroom. *International Journal of Educational Telecommunications, 3*(1), 3-21.

Berge, Z.L., Collins, M., & Dougherty, K. (2000). Design guidelines for Web-based courses. In A. Beverly (Ed.), *Instructional and cognitive impacts of Web-based education* (pp. 32-40). Hershey, PA: Idea Group Publishing.

Boer, W. D., & Collis, B. (2001). Implementation and adaptation experiences with a WWW-based course management system. *Computer in the Schools, 17*(3/4), 127-146.

Bonk, C. J., Cummings, J. A., Hara, N., Fischler, R. B., & Lee, S. M. (2000). A ten-level Web integration continuum for higher education. In A. Beverly (Ed.), *Instructional and cognitive impacts of Web-based education* (pp. 56-77). Hershey: Idea Group Publishing.

Clariana, T. B. (1993). The motivational effect of advisement on attendance and achievement in computer-based instruction. *Journal of Research on Computing in Education, 20*(2), 47-51.

Clark, D., & Jorde, D. (2004). Helping students revise disruptive experientially-supported ideas about thermodynamics: Computer visualizations and tactile models. *Journal of Research in Science Teaching, 41*(1), 1-23.

Coombs, S.J., & Rodd, J. (2001). Using the Internet to deliver higher education: A cautionary tale about achieving good practice. *Computers in the Schools, 17*(3/4), 67-90.

Cunningham, C. A., & Billingsley, M. (2006). *Curriculum Webs: Weaving the Web into teaching and learning* (2nd ed.). Boston: Allyn and Bacon.

Dodero, J. M., Aedo, I., & Diaz, P. (2002). Participative knowledge production of learning objects for e-books. *The Electronic Library, 20*(4), 296-305.

Fishman, B. J. (1997, March). *Student traits and the use of computer-mediated communication tools: What matters and why?* Proceedings of the Annual Meeting of the American Educational Research Association, Chicago.

Glazer, E. (2004). K-12 mathematics and the Web. *Computers in the Schools, 21*(3/4), 37-44.

Green, S.B., & Salkind, N.J. (2003, 3rd Ed.). *Using SPSS for Windows and Macintosh: Analyzing and understanding data.* Upper Saddle River: Prentice Hall.

Hillman, M., & Moore, T.J. (2004). The Web and early literacy. *Computers in the Schools, 21*(3/4), 15-22.

Johnson, D. L., & Liu, L. (2000). First steps toward a statistically generated information technology integration model. *Computers in the Schools, 16*(2), 3-12.

Kellenberger, D. W. (1996). Preservice teachers' perceived computer self-efficacy based on achievement and value beliefs within a motivational framework. *Journal of Research on Computing in Education, 29*(2), 124-140.

Keller, J. M. (1983). Motivational design of instruction. In C.M. Reigeluth (Ed.), *Instructional design theories and models: An overview of their current status* (pp. 384-434). Hillsdale: Lawrence Erlbaum Associates.

King, J., & Bond, T. (1996). A rash analysis of a measure of computer anxiety. *Journal of Educational Computing Research, 14*(1), 49-65.

Lengel, J. G., & Lengel, K. M. (2006). *Integrating technology: A practical guide.* Boston: Allyn and Bacon.

Liu, L. (1997, October 22-24). *Repeated measures analysis on preservice teachers' attitudes towards the subjects taught in school.* Proceedings of the Western Users of SAS Software Conference, Los Angeles, CA.

Liu, L. (1999). The influence of different teaching methods on student attitudes toward technology. *Technology and Teacher Education Annual 1999* (pp. 1400-1405). Charlottesville: AACE.

Liu, L. (2001). Online delivery of multimedia courseware: Issues and effects. In J.D. Price, D.A. Willis, N. Davis, & J. Willis (Eds.), *Technology & teacher education annual 2001* (pp. 1126-1131). Charlottesville: AACE.

Liu, L. (2003). Communication design for online courses: Effects of a multi-layer approach. In G. Marks & A. Rodssett (Eds.), *E-learn in corporate, government, healthcare and higher education annual 2003* (pp. 1699-1702). Charlottesville: AACE.

Liu, L., & Johnson, D. L. (2002). Assessing student learning in instructional technology courses within the dimensions of learning model: Static vs. dynamic assessment. *Computers in the Schools, 18*(2/3), 79-95.

Liu, L., & Johnson, L. (1998). A computer achievement model: Computer attitude and computer achievement. *Computers in the Schools, 14*(3-4), 33-54.

Liu, L., & Johnson, L. (2003a). A new approach of design: Technology integration as information system development. In C. Crawford, N. Davis, J. Price, R. Weber, & D.A. Willis (Eds.), *Technology & teacher education annual 2000* (pp. 1010-1016). Charlottesville: AACE.

Liu, L., & Johnson, L. (2003b). A technology integration model and weak areas. In W. Pearman, M. Mallott, E. Oshiro, R. Stiller, E. Flower, T. Gregson, & D. Yang (Eds.), *Hawaii International Conference on Education: Conference Proceedings* (p. 5) Honolulu: HICE.

Liu, L., & Maddux, C. (2003). Online course design and research. In G. Marks & A. Rodssett (Eds.), *E-learn in corporate, government, healthcare and higher education annual 2003* (pp. 1078-1081). Charlottesville: AACE.

Liu, L., Maddux, C., & Johnson, L. (2004). Computer attitude and achievement: Is time an intermediate variable? *Journal of Technology and Teacher Education, 12*(4), 593-607.

Liu, L., & Velasques-Bryant, N.J. (2003). An information technology integration system and its life cycle: What is missing? *Computers in the Schools, 20*(1/2), p. 93-106.

Lombard, R.H. (2004). Social studies and the Web today. *Computers in the Schools, 21*(3/4), 45-52.

Maddux, C.D., Ewing-Taylor, J., & Johnson, D.L. (2002). The light and dark sides of distance education. *Computers in the Schools, 19*(3/4), 1-7.

Miller, S.M., & Miller, K.L. (2000). Theoretical and practical considerations in the design of Web-based instruction. In A. Beverly (Ed.), *Instructional and cognitive impacts of Web-based education* (pp. 156-177). Hershey, PA: Idea Group Publishing.

Murphy, E. (2004). Moving from theory to practice in the design of Web-based learning using a learning object approach. *E-Journal of Instructional Science and Technology, 7*(1). Retrieved March 10, 2004, from www.usq.edu/elect-pub/e-jist/

Orme, M. P., & Monroe, E. E. (2005). The nature of discourse as students collaborate on a mathematics WebQuest. *Computers in the Schools, 22*(1/2), 135-146.

Perkins, R., & McKnight M. L. (2005). Teachers' attitudes toward WebQuest as a method of teaching. *Computers in the Schools, 22*(1/2), 123-134.

Riel, M. (1992). A functional analysis of education telecomputing: A case study of learning circles. *Interactive Learning Environments, 2*(1), 15-29.

Schweizer, H., Whipp, J., & Hayslett, C. (2002). Quality control in online courses: Using a social constructivist framework. *Computers in the Schools, 19*(3/4), 143-158.

Shelly, G.B., Cashman, T. J., Gunter, R. E., & Gunter, G. A. (2003*). Teacher discovering computers: Integrating technology in the classroom* (3rd ed.). Boston: Course Technology.

Stvan, L. S. (2005). Inferring new vocabulary using online text. *Computers in the Schools, 22*(1/2), 85-96.

Temple, L., & Lips, H. M. (1989). Reliability and generalizability of the Collis attitudes toward computers survey. *Educational Research Quarterly, 13*(4), 6-9.

Thorsen, C. (2006). *TechTacTics: Technology for teachers* (2nd ed.). Boston: Allyn and Bacon.

Trentin, G. (2001). Designing online education courses. *Computers in the Schools, 17*(3/4), 47-66.

Appendix A: Evaluation Criteria for Online Learning Applications Design

Information:

1. Language is accurate.
2. Language is easy to understand.

3.   Language is error free.
4.   Language and materials are at the identified grade level.
5.   Resources are sufficient.
6.   Resources are updated.
7.   Materials and resources are verifiable.
8.   Designer's information is included.

Design of Information:

9.   Activity goals/objectives are clearly presented.
10. Task and processes are designed to achieve the goals/objectives.
11. Task and processes are designed for learners at the identified grade level.
12. Higher-level thinking is engaged.
13. Processes are designed in a learner-oriented approach.
14. Resources are closely related to the task/activities.
15. Assignments/exercise requirements reflect the knowledge/skills that match objectives.
16. Evaluation criteria match the activity processes and objectives.

Technology:

17. Screen layout is balanced, and graphics are positioned appropriately.
18. It is easy to find where you are in the program.
19. It is easy to find where you want to go within program.
20. Users can stop and find a way to exit when they need.
21. All resource links work well.
22. Help or assistance instructions are provided and easy to access.
23. Instruction materials can be downloaded or printed out in a clear layout.
24. Interactions between user and the program are user-friendly.

Design of Technology-Use:

25. Web is appropriate for performing this activity.
26. Technology skills needed for the activity match learners' developmental level.

27. Interface design is appropriate to the grade level and the topic/subject area.
28. Organization of resource links matches the activity processes.
29. Use of (multi-)media matches the objectives of the activity.
30. Design approach (linear or non-linear) matches task processes and objectives.
31. The interactions are designed to meet the learning objectives.
32. Mapping of the contents and activities is available.

Appendix B: Measurements of Enjoyment, Motivation, and Anxiety

Enjoyment:

1. This program is not very interesting to my students.
2. My students enjoy learning about this concept with this program.
3. My students do not like learning about this concept with this program.
4. Learning about and working with this program is enjoyable and stimulating to my students.
5. This program is dull and boring.
6. My students like trying to solve new problems with this program.

Motivation:

7. My students want to develop their knowledge and skills and study more with this program.
8. My students do not want to work any more on this program than they have to.
9. My students are interested in acquiring further knowledge with this kind of program and activities.
10. My students are not willing to work more on this kind of activities.
11. My students like to work on as many activities like this as they can during their studies.
12. My students are motivated to work very hard on this kind of program or activities.

Freedom from Anxiety:

13. Working on this kind of program or activities make my students feel nervous and uncomfortable.

14. My students are very calm when learning with these activities.

15. This kind of activities and content make my students feel uneasy and confused.

16. Trying to understand this concept with this program does not make my students anxious.

17. Working on online activities is one of the most dreaded subjects for my students.

18. My students did not get upset when studying with this program.

About the Authors

Lawrence A. Tomei, EdD, is associate vice president of academic affairs and associate professor of education at Robert Morris University. Born in Akron, Ohio, he earned a BSBA from the University of Akron (1972) and entered the U.S. Air Force, serving until his retirement as a Lieutenant Colonel in 1994. Dr. Tomei completed his MPA and MEd at the University of Oklahoma (1975, 1978) and EdD from USC (1983). His articles and books on instructional technology include: *Professional Portfolios for Teachers* (1999); *Teaching Digitally: Integrating Technology Into the Classroom* (2001); *Technology Facade* (2002); *Challenges of Teaching with Technology Across the Curriculum* (2003); and *Taxonomy for the Technology Domain* (2005).

* * *

James Adams has been assistant professor in the Department of Instructional Systems, Leadership, and Workforce Development at Mississippi State University for the past 5 years. He earned a BA from Mississippi State University, a Masters in Adult Education from Georgia Southern University, and a doctorate in occupational and adult education from Oklahoma State University. He has 10 years' teaching experiences in public education and numerous years in adult and GED education. His research interests include hegemony and culture, welfare-to-work, GED pedagogy and issues of diversity. His professional accomplishments include more than 20 articles and professional presentations.

J. Miguel Baptista Nunes (j.m.nunes@sheffield.ac.uk) received a License in Applied Mathematics from the Universidade Autónoma of Lisbon, Portugal (1992), a Masters in Information Management from the University of Sheffield (1993), and a PhD in information studies from the same university in 2000. He is currently a lecturer in information management and program coordinator for the Masters of Science in Information Management with the Department of Information Studies at the University of Sheffield, UK. He is also a visiting associate professor with the ISEGI at the New University of Lisbon. He has more than 60 publications as conference proceedings, has refereed publications and published a recent book on online learning. He has consulted widely for companies in South Yorkshire, UK, in his research areas of educational informatics and information systems.

Samantha Bax is an associate lecturer in the School of Information Technology at Murdoch University, Western Australia. Her research interests include end-user development and information systems success, as well as online learning environments.

Jon Beedle (Jon.Beedle@usm.edu) is an assistant professor of technology education in the College of Education and Psychology, University of Southern Mississippi (USM) in Gulfport. He teaches technical and occupational education and instructional technology courses at USMs campuses on the Mississippi Gulf Coast. Beedle's research interests include career and technical education, legal concerns with technology and education, and issues related to multiplayer computer gaming.

Anol Bhattacherjee received his PhD in information systems from the University of Houston and is currently an associate professor at the University of Southern Florida. He holds undergraduate and graduate degrees from the Indian Institute of Technology and has previously worked for Citicorp. His primary areas of research include information technology adoption and implementation, knowledge creation/transfer in social networks and medical informatics. Bhattacherjee's prior research has been published in *Management Information Systems (MIS) Quarterly*, *Information Systems Research*, the *Journal of MIS*, *Decision Sciences*, *Decisions Support Systems*, *IEEE Transactions*, *Data Base*, and *Information & Management*. He serves on the current editorial board of *MIS Quarterly*.

Sherry Y. Chen (Sherry.Chen@brunel.ac.uk) is a lecturer in the Department of Information Systems and Computing at Brunel University, UK. Her major research interests focus on Web-based learning and human-computer interaction. Current research projects, funded by the Engineering and Physical Science Research Council (EPSRC) and the Arts and Humanities Research Board (AHRB), investigate human factors in the design of personalized Web-based applications. For further information, visit www.brunel.ac.uk/~csstsyc.

Young B. Choi is an assistant professor with the Computer Information Systems and Management Science Department at James Madison University (USA). Choi has been teaching telecommunications and computer information systems courses since 2002. Before joining James Madison University, Choi worked for SERI and ETRI in the Daedeok Valley of Korea as a senior member of the engineering staff and as a research team leader; at COMPAQ Computer, Birlasoft; and CREATIVE Technology in Silicon Valley, CA as a principal engineer. His major research interests are telecommunications network, service, and business management; telemedicine; and Internet geographic information systems (GIS).

Gang Ding has been a professor and dean in the College of Education at East China Normal University, ROC. He earned a BA from Heilongjiang University, and a Masters in Literature and PhD in eeducation from East China Normal University. His research areas are culture of education, Chinese culture and education, teacher education and teacher professional development, and curriculum and instruction. He is chief editor of *China's Education: Research & Review* journal, and advisory editor for numerous book series. He has published numerous books and articles in the U.S. and China.

Michael Dixon is a senior lecturer in information technology at Murdoch University, Western Australia. He holds a PhD from Murdoch University and an MBA in telecommunications management from Golden Gate University. He is also a certified Cisco Certified Network Professional (CCNP), Cisco Certified Design Professional (CCDP) and Cisco Certified Academy Instructor (CCAI). His major research interests include information technology education, data communications and neural networks.

Jianxia Du earned her BA from Southwest Normal University in China, where she later served as assistant professor. After coming to the U.S., she received an MA in educational policy and a PhD in educational technology from the University of Illinois at Urbana-Champaign. She has enjoyed her role as assistant professor at Mississippi State University for the past several years in the Department of Instructional Systems, Leadership and Workforce Development. Her research interests include online education, online discussion, collaborative learning and the social-cultural dimensions of technology. Du's professional accomplishments include more than 30 articles and professional presentations.

Marlene D. Dunham is the author of studies regarding the impact of adult learning on student achievement within school/district-wide programs. Her 18 years in educational policy include experience as a researcher, evaluator, program director, production developer, and teacher. At Arizona State University, she manager pre-college programs which emphasized rigorous instruction for all students. For the past 12 years, at the College Board in New York City, she has studied urban and rural schools, with a focus on the interconnectivity of cognition, policy, equity, access, and resources. Currently, as director of implementation for a nationwide program that combines classroom instructional strategies with online diagnostic tools, she works with school and district administrators and middle and high school teachers across the U.S.

Andrea L. Edmundson (PhD, educational technology) is the director of eWorld Learning (www.eWorldLearning.com), providing presentations and educational consulting services for corporations, online universities and other educational organizations that are expanding their e-learning investments beyond local markets. She has been faculty, corporate trainer, business owner and consultant for 20 years, working in more than 15 countries throughout Africa, Eastern Europe, Asia, the Pacific and the Caribbean. Edmundson was also the professional development manager of a multinational medical software company, responsible for training and educating 1,200+ employees in five countries, extensively using educational information and communication technology. Her research and hands-on experiences led her to publish the book, *Globalized E-Learning Cultural Challenges* (2007). Her expertise in educational technology, adult learning, training and international development make her uniquely qualified to creating culturally accessible e-learning.

Stephanie J. Etter (setter@mtaloy.edu) is an assistant professor of IT and director of the Title III Project at Mount Aloysius College in Cresson, Pa. She holds a DSc from Robert Morris University and a Master of Science in Management and Technology from Carlow University. Her current research interests focus on online consumer behavior; pedagogical issues, such as distance education, incorporating technology across the curriculum and academic dishonesty; and computer and information security.

Nigel Ford received a BA in French from the University of Leeds, and an MA in librarianship from Sheffield University, UK. He lectures in the Department of Information Studies at Sheffield University, and has published in many areas of information studies, including information storage and retrieval; artificial intelligence and expert systems; the psychology of human information processing; computer-assisted learning; libraries and learning; and academic librarianship.

Taralynn Hartsell (taralynn.hartsell@usm.edu) is an assistant professor of instructional technology at The University of Southern Mississippi within the College of Education and Psychology. Hartsell lectures on topics pertaining to the field of instructional technology that includes educational applications of computers, foundations, instructional design, distance learning systems, professional development and sociological perspectives in technology. She received her bachelor's and master's degrees in media arts, and her PhD in language, reading and culture from The University of Arizona. Her primary research interests lie within gender studies, online learning, instructional design and faculty development.

Byron Havard earned a BS from Auburn University, an MS in instructional design and development from the University of South Alabama, and a PhD in instructional technology from Georgia State University. Harvard has roughly 9 years of corporate experience in instructional design, needs assessment and evaluation. Several years ago, Havard began serving as assistant professor in instructional systems at Mississippi State University and currently serves as an assistant professor in instructional and performance technology at the University of West Florida. His research interests include collaborative learning, online discussion, social-cultural dimensions in instructional technology, and instructional strategies. Havard's professional accomplishments include more than 30 articles and professional presentations.

Kathleen P. King is a professor of education and director of the Regional Educational Technology Center at Fordham University in New York City. She coordinates several grants and programs that provide professional development of educators and other adult learners in educational technology and non-technology content areas. She has written numerous books and articles; her research areas and publications include professional development, educational technology, adult learning, distance learning, transformative learning and emerging technologies. In her work, King seeks to find innovative ways to extend teaching and learning that will reach more learners.

Paul Lajbcyier (paul.lajbcyier@infotech.monash.edu.au) received his BSc from Melbourne University (1991), a Masters of Finance from RMIT University (1994) and his PhD from Monash University (2000). He is currently a senior lecturer in the School of Business Systems, Faculty of Information Technology. Lajbcyier was a visiting scholar at the London Business School in 1996-1997 and at New York University, Stern School of Business in 2000. He has more than 40 publications in journals, conference proceedings and book chapters. He has consulted widely for funds managers, banks and commodity trading advisors domestically and internationally in his research area of computational finance.

Leping Liu is an associate professor in the Department of Counseling and Educational Psychology, University of Nevada, Reno. She teaches courses on information technology in education, and has authored or co-authored many academic articles and published nine books. She is also the editor-in-chief of an online journal, *International Journal of Technology in Teaching and Learning*.

Andrew D. Madden (a.d.madden@sheffield.ac.uk) began research life as a plant ecologist. In 1995, he became involved in a project to develop computer-assisted learning materials for teaching undergraduates about land use and environmental sciences. As a result of this experience, he became interested in the use of computers in education and has worked, both as a practitioner and a researcher, at schools, colleges and universities in England and Scotland.

Tayna McGill is a senior lecturer in the School of Information Technology at Murdoch University, Western Australia. She has a PhD from Murdoch University. Her major research interests include end-user computing and information technology education. Her work has appeared in various journals, including the *Journal of Research on Computing in Education*, *European Journal of Psychology of Education*, *Journal of the American Society for Information Science*, and *Journal of Organizational and End User Computing*.

M.A. McPherson is a senior lecturer of information and communication technology in education within the School of Education at the University of Leeds. Prior to this position, she served as a lecturer in information studies at the University of Sheffield. McPherson is a member of the Council for the Institute of Management of Information Systems (IMIS) and has been involved in e-learning research over the last 12 years. Notable among McPherson's extensive publications is a co-authored book entitled, *Developing Innovation in Online Learning: An Action Research Framework*.

Frank J. Melia was associate director of the Regional Educational Technology Center (RETC) at Fordham University at the time this research was conducted. He is now president of a consulting firm that specializes in leadership development and school change. Previously, Melia was a principal and superintendent and was president of the New York City High School Principals Association. Currently, he is a candidate for the EdD at Fordham University.

Jeffrey W. Merhout (merhoujw@muohio.edu) is an assistant professor of managing information systems at Miami University in Oxford. He holds a PhD and MBA from Virginia Commonwealth University, and is a CPA. He has 2 years' auditing experience in public accounting and another year as an operational internal auditor. Merhout has information systems consulting experience in several industries, including financial services, manufacturing and retail. His current research interests focus on qualitative methodological issues, particularly in positivist case studies; pedagogical issues, such as adult training and development; and information risk management, information technology security and information systems auditing. He has presented and published his research at several MIS conferences and in the *International Journal of Information and Communication Technology Education* and *Technology In Society*.

Dave Miller recently retired as computing manager for the University of Sheffield's Department of Information Studies, a post he held from 1991 to 2005. Before coming to Sheffield, he carried out research in psychology at Sussex and Leeds Universities. Miller maintained an active interest in research while at Sheffield, and helped to establish several projects in the area of community informatics (i.e., the use of information and communication technology in local communities). In particular, he played a key role in a number of projects aimed at supporting economic regeneration in South Yorkshire.

Anthony Olinzock is a professor and department head in the Department of Instructional Systems, Leadership and Workforce Development at Mississippi State University. He earned his doctorate from the University of Pittsburgh. Olinzock has taught at both the secondary and university levels; his initial teaching experience was at Uniontown Area Senior High School, Uniontown, Pa. He has also taught at The Ohio State University, the University of Wisconsin and the University of Pittsburgh. Olinzock's professional accomplishments include more than 20 published textbooks and more than 100 articles and professional presentations.

Lalita Rajasingham (BA, Melbourne; MA, Cambridge; PhD, Victoria University of Wellington) is associate professor of communications studies, School of Information Management, Victoria University of Wellington, New Zealand. Her long and varied career in communications includes radio and television broadcasting experience in Malaysia, Australia, Britain and New Zealand. Widely published, Rajasingham has acquired an international reputation for her research into the implications of new information technology for education, and her concern for their cultural implications with a focus on enabling anyone to access culturally appropriate quality education from anywhere at any time. With John Tiffin, she has been involved in a long-term action research project to develop a virtual class, the HyperClass and the global virtual university. This pioneer research led to two co-authored books that introduced the concept of the virtual class on the Internet: *The Virtual Class: Education in an Information Society* (1995) and the sequel, *Global Virtual Univer-*

sity (2003). Both are published by Routledge. Rajasingham is a consultant with the Asia Institute of Broadcasting Development, the Commonwealth of Learning, The World Bank and the Commonwealth Secretariat. She is also a member of several editorial boards of international journals and is an information and communication technology specialist in education boards in New Zealand.

LeAnne K. Robinson is currently an assistant professor of instructional technology and special education at Western Washington University. She teaches courses in instructional technology, instructional design and special education. Her current research interests include integrating technology throughout the phases of the teaching and learning cycle and the use of curriculum-based measurement in teachers' instructional decision-making processes. Robinson received her PhD in education from Washington State University.

Clive Sanford (sanford.cc@gmail.com) received his PhD in MIS from the University of South Carolina and is currently an associate professor of information systems. He previously worked at Honeywell as a subcontracted engineer on the space shuttle. Recently, he has served as a Fulbright scholar and as a Peace Corps volunteer. He has published books and articles in journals such as *MIS Quarterly, Journal of Global Information Management, Information & Management,* where he is now on the editorial board, the *International Journal of Information and Communication Technology Education,* and *Journal of Database Management.* His current research is e-participation, e-government, and IT adoption and implementation.

Nurul I. Sarkar (nurul.sarkar@aut.ac.nz) is a senior lecturer in the School of Computer and Information Sciences at the Auckland University of Technology, New Zealand. He has more than 10 years of teaching experience in universities at both undergraduate and post-graduate levels. Sarkar has taught a range of subjects, including computer networking, data communications, computer hardware and e-commerce. He has authored the book *Tools for Teaching Computer Networking and Hardware Concepts*, and has published in international journals and conferences, and contributed chapters to several edited research compilations. Sarkar's research interests include wireless communication networks and tools to enhance methods for teaching; and learning computer networking and hardware concepts. He is currently serving as chair of the IEEE NZ Communications Society and is a member of IEEE.

Christine Spratt (Christine.Spratt@utas.edu.au) has a PhD in education from Deakin University and varied experience in distance education and educational design. Spratt is currently responsible for the quality assurance portfolio in the School of

Nursing and Midwifery at the University of Tasmania. Previously, she managed a major academic staff development initiative at Monash University in relation to the implementation of a new online learning management system. Spratt's PhD thesis explored the relationships between "flexibility" and "corporatization" in the higher education sector and the way in which critical teachers as technology innovators have adapted to the changing demands on their lives as academics.

Ronnie Stanford (rstanfor@bamaed.ua.edu) is an associate professor in secondary curriculum, teaching and learning at The University of Alabama and also serves as director of the College of Education's International Programs. His research interests include international education, teacher education curriculum and school accreditation.

Andrew Targowski is a professor of computer information systems at Western Michigan University (U.S.) and former chairman of the advisory council of the Information Resource Management Association. He published 20 books and 250 papers on informatics, politics and history. He is a pioneer of the information superhighway concept (INFOSTRADA, Poland 1972) and he developed the award-winning digital city Web site (www.telecity.org) for Kalamazoo, Mich. in 1997.

Faye P. Teer is professor of information systems in the Computer Information Systems and Management Science Department at James Madison University. She teaches statistics and a technology-enhanced decision-making course in the College of Business. In addition to her past administrative service as assistant dean of the College of Business, she has served as the faculty member in residence for James Madison University's programs in three other countries. She has published numerous journal articles primarily in the area of information systems curriculum development.

Harold B. Teer is professor *emeritus* of marketing at James Madison University. His primary areas of expertise are marketing management, marketing research and direct marketing. He has published numerous articles in U.S. and international journals and specializes in research in higher education issues. He has taught for leading graduate and undergraduate schools in their overseas business programs. In addition to his past experience working full time for a leading medical products manufacturer, he has current business consulting experience with both large and small for-profit and not-for profit organizations in the U.S. and abroad.

Lorna Uden (L.uden@staffs.ac.uk) is a senior lecturer in the Faculty of Computer, Engineering and Technology. She has published more than 100 papers in conference, journals, books and workshops. She is editor of *International Journal of Web Engineering and Technology* (IJWET) and *International Journal of Learning Technology* (IJLT), published by Inderscience, UK. She is also an editorial board member to many international journals, and program committee member for many conferences. Uden was keynote speaker at international conferences and has co-authored the book, *Technology and Problem Based Learning,* from Ideal publishers. She heads the Knowledge Management in Organization (KMO) Group.

Vivian H. Wright (vwright@bamaed.ua.edu) is an assistant professor of instructional technology in the College of Education at The University of Alabama in Tuscaloosa. In addition to teaching in the graduate program, she works with teacher educators on innovative ways to infuse technology in the curriculum to enhance teaching and learning, and has helped initiate and develop projects such as electronic portfolios for the preservice teacher, master technology teacher, and technology on wheels. Her research interests include K-12 technology integration and asynchronous education.

Linda Wojnar (lwojnar@western-school.com) designed the distance learning strand of courses in the Instructional Technology program at Duquesne University and has achieved local, regional and international recognition (i.e., Northern Ireland) for her work with e-learning. She currently teaches both graduate and doctoral students in the instructional technology program. In addition to higher education experience, Wojnar has background in the corporate, medical and military professions. She was an invited opening keynote speaker at the National Association for Advisors in Computer Education (NAACE) Conference (2003) in Torquay, UK. Wojnar's main areas of interest are training teachers proactively how to be successful online teachers, teaching effective teaching and learning strategies, conducting and evaluating asynchronous and synchronous discussions, raising thinking to higher levels through oral questioning techniques, instructional design, pedagogical aspects of online teaching, globalization of online learning, and building communities of learners in any environment. Her maxim is "Setting everyone up for success."

Wei-Chieh Yu is presently a doctoral student at Mississippi State University, USA. He received a BSBA from Ohio State University in finance, and a Master of Science in Teaching English to Students of Other Languages from the University of Pennsylvania. His research interests include instructional technology, education research, multicultural/global education, socialinguistics and computer assisted language learning.

Index

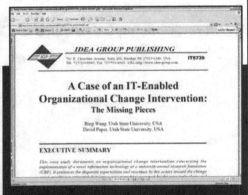